Public Religions in the Modern World

José Casanova

Public Religions in the Modern World

The University of Chicago Press
Chicago and London

José Casanova is associate professor of sociology at the New School for Social Research, New York.

The University of Chicago Press, Chicago 60637
The University of Chicago Press, Ltd., London
© 1994 by The University of Chicago
All rights reserved. Published 1994
Printed in the United States of America
03 02 01 00 99 98 97 96 95 94   1 2 3 4 5
ISBN: 0-226-09534-7   (cloth)
        0-226-09535-5   (paper)

Library of Congress Cataloging-in-Publication Data

Casanova, José
    Public religions in the modern world / José Casanova.
        p.   cm.
    Includes bibliographical references and index.
    1. Religion and sociology.   I. Title.
    BL60.C375   1994
    306.6—dc20
    [322.43'3'0882]   93-37485
                                                                         CIP

♾ The paper used in this publication meets the minimum requirements of the American National Standard for Information Sciences—Permanence of Paper for Printed Library Materials, ANSI Z39.48-1984.

For Ika and Olexa

Contents

Acknowledgments

A study on the relevance of traditions to the vitality of the modern public sphere can hardly skirt the tradition of acknowledging its many debts, even though I feel for this tradition the same ambivalence I feel for all religious traditions. My deepest debts are private, and here I would like to respect sacredly those boundaries between the private and the public spheres which are so crucial to sustaining and protecting both of them.

Through the years I've learned from many teachers. Two in particular formed my thinking on religion. A theologian at the University of Innsbruck, Franz Schupp, one of the first victims of the post–Vatican II purges, taught me that critical theory can be a form of religious practice. A comparative historical sociologist, Benjamin Nelson, taught me the limits which "the sociological reality principle" sets to critical theory. Two others, Arthur Vidich and Stanford Lyman, aided in my sociological education and offered support at critical junctures.

The project for this book first originated in the "public sphere" of *Telos*. My intellectual development owes much to this experience, particularly to the friendship of and conversation with Paul Piccone, Juan Corradi, and, above all, Andrew Arato, Seyla Benhabib, Jean Cohen, and Joel Whitebook, who took seriously Habermas's claim that discourse ethics were relevant both for critical theory and for the public sphere.

In the same way as churches and religious institutions can concentrate on their primary task of caring for the welfare of individual souls, universities and academic institutions can concentrate on their primary task of attaining and transmitting knowledge. When they neglect their duties as public institutions, however, the resulting void affects the life of the spirit, the quality of the knowledge they impart, and the vitality of the public sphere. I was fortunate to find an alma mater and an academic home, the New School for Social Research, which has resisted the trend of academic privatization.

Many friends and colleagues have read drafts of the manuscript. Those whose critical reading, comments, and ongoing conversation helped improve the text were my brother Julián Casanova, Jeffrey Alexander, Said Arjomand, Talal Assad, Josetxo Beriain, Richard Bernstein, Ralph Della Cava, Mustafa Emirbayer, Robert Fishman, Carlos Forment, Vittorio Hösle, Ira Katznelson, János Kis, Juan Linz, Otto Maduro, José María Mardones, Martin Marty, Elzbieta Matynia, Martin Riesebrodt, Catalina Romero, Roman Szporluk, Jadwiga Staniszkis, Frank Sysyn, Charles Tilly, Louise Tilly, Edward Tiryakian, Arthur Vidich, Francisco Weffort, Jeff Weintraub, and Alan Wolfe. I am particularly indebted to Andrew Arato for his ideas, his support, and his critical skill through the years. The encouragement and support of Jeffrey Goldfarb also deserve special mention.

Parts of the book were first presented at various conferences, lectures, and seminars at Columbia University, the Center for European Studies at Harvard University, UCLA, the University of Michigan, and the New School for Social Research. I thank those who invited me. Above all, my argument was developed in conversation with numerous students from the Graduate Faculty and Eugene Lang College. Perry Chang, Harry Dahms, Randal Hepner, Susan Pearce, and Amy Siskind have been the longest and most effective conversants. Alas, my dialogue with Carmen Espaillat was interrupted tragically, all too soon.

Finally, I must acknowledge that the task of publishing this book was made much easier, even enjoyable, thanks to the care, guidance, and editorial expertise of Doug Mitchell and Jennie Lightner at the University of Chicago Press.

I

Introduction

Pre-text: Religion in the 1980s

Religion in the 1980s "went public" in a dual sense. It entered the "public sphere" and gained, thereby, "publicity." Various "publics"—the mass media, social scientists, professional politicians, and the "public at large"—suddenly began to pay attention to religion. The unexpected public interest derived from the fact that religion, leaving its assigned place in the private sphere, had thrust itself into the public arena of moral and political contestation. Above all, four seemingly unrelated yet almost simultaneously unfolding developments gave religion the kind of global publicity which forced a reassessment of its place and role in the modern world. These four developments were the Islamic revolution in Iran; the rise of the Solidarity movement in Poland; the role of Catholicism in the Sandinista revolution and in other political conflicts throughout Latin America; and the public reemergence of Protestant fundamentalism as a force in American politics.

During the entire decade of the 1980s it was hard to find any serious political conflict anywhere in the world that did not show behind it the not-so-hidden hand of religion. In the Middle East, all the religions and fundamentalisms of the region—Jewish, Christian, and Muslim—fed by old power struggles, were meeting each other in civil and uncivil wars. Old feuds between the various world religions and between branches of the same religions were flaring up again from Northern Ireland to Yugoslavia, from India to the Soviet Union. Simultaneously, religious activists and churches were becoming deeply involved in struggles for liberation, justice, and democracy throughout the world. Liberation theologies were spreading beyond Latin America, acquiring new forms and names, African and Asian, Protestant and Jewish, black and feminist. With the collapse of socialism, liberation theology seemed the only "International" that was left.

The decade, which began in 1979 with the Iranian and Nicaraguan revolutions, the visit of the Polish pope to Poland, and the establishment of the "Moral Majority," ended as dramatically and as ambiguously as it had begun, with the Salman Rushdie "affair," the death of Ayatollah

3

Khomeini, the final triumph of Solidarity reverberating throughout Eastern Europe, and Gorbachev's visit to the pope. It was symbolically fitting that even the Romanian Revolution was sparked by a Hungarian Reformed pastor. No less telling was the fact that in El Salvador the decade which had opened with the assassination of Archbishop Romero closed with the murder of yet six more Jesuits by state terror.

Throughout the decade religion showed its Janus face, as the carrier not only of exclusive, particularist, and primordial identities but also of inclusive, universalist, and transcending ones. The religious revival signaled simultaneously the rise of fundamentalism and of its role in the resistance of the oppressed and the rise of the "powerless." Ali Shariati, the intellectual father of the Islamic revolution, in translating Franz Fanon's *Les Damnés de la Terre,* chose the resonant Koranic term *mostaz'afin* (the disinherited). The term "the disinherited of the earth" was to occupy a central place in the rhetoric of the Islamic revolution.[1] Gustavo Gutiérrez, the father of liberation theology, effected a similar transvaluation from secular back to religious categories when he turned the proletariat into the biblical *los pobres.* "The eruption of the poor in history" became one of the central categories of Gutiérrez's eschatological theology.[2] A similar term, "the power of the powerless," was coined by Vaclav Havel, the father of the "velvet" revolution.[3] It all looked like modernization in reverse, from rational collective action back to primitive rebellion.

It is unlikely that these are mere historical coincidences. They can be seen rather as examples of biblical prophetic politics linking the Middle East, Latin America, and Eastern Europe. The transvaluation of values which, according to Nietzsche, biblical slave morality had introduced into the dynamics of classical aristocratic civilization was apparently still at work. The archetypal dream of a liberating Exodus from enslavement had not yet lost its utopian, eschatological force.[4]

I have selectively left out of my account of religion in the 1980s many other religious phenomena which also gained wide publicity throughout the decade and certainly had public and political significance, but which were not in themselves varieties of what I call "public" religion. I have in mind such phenomena as "New Age" spirituality; the growth of cults and the ensuing controversies surrounding them; televangelism with all its peccadillos; the collective suicide of the residents of the People's Temple in Jonestown; the spread of evangelical Protestantism in Latin America; the rapid growth of Islam in the United States; the seriousness with which so many people in modern secular societies—including Nancy Reagan while at the White House—took astrology; the fact that

Manuel Noriega may have practiced voodoo; or the fact that most people everywhere continued to practice, or not to practice, religion in the 1980s in the same way they had in the 1970s.

Those were significant religious phenomena, and any comprehensive history of religion in the 1980s would have to include them. It is likely that quantitative surveys would select precisely those phenomena as being the typical, normal, and relevant ones. Nevertheless, one could still argue that they were not particularly relevant either for the social sciences or for the self-understanding of modernity, at least insofar as they do not present major problems of interpretation. They fit within expectations and can be interpreted within the framework of established theories of secularization. As bizarre and as new as they may be, they can nonetheless be taken for granted as typical or normal phenomena in the modern world. They can be classified as instances of "private" or of what Thomas Luckmann called "invisible" religion. Such religious phenomena per se do not challenge either the dominant structures or the dominant paradigms.

What was new and unexpected in the 1980s was not the emergence of "new religious movements," "religious experimentation" and "new religious consciousness"—all phenomena which caught the imagination of social scientists and the public in the 1960s and 1970s[5]—but rather the revitalization and the assumption of public roles by precisely those religious traditions which both theories of secularization and cyclical theories of religious revival had assumed were becoming ever more marginal and irrelevant in the modern world. Indeed, as Mary Douglas has rightly pointed out, "No one credited the traditional religions with enough vitality to inspire large-scale political revolt."[6]

The central thesis of the present study is that we are witnessing the "deprivatization" of religion in the modern world. By deprivatization I mean the fact that religious traditions throughout the world are refusing to accept the marginal and privatized role which theories of modernity as well as theories of secularization had reserved for them. Social movements have appeared which either are religious in nature or are challenging in the name of religion the legitimacy and autonomy of the primary secular spheres, the state and the market economy. Similarly, religious institutions and organizations refuse to restrict themselves to the pastoral care of individual souls and continue to raise questions about the interconnections of private and public morality and to challenge the claims of the subsystems, particularly states and markets, to be exempt from extraneous normative considerations. One of the results of this ongoing contestation is a dual, interrelated process of repoliticization of the private religious and moral spheres and renormativization of the public economic and political spheres. This is what I call, for lack of a better term, the "deprivatization" of religion.

I do not mean to imply that the deprivatization of religion is something altogether new. Most religious traditions have resisted all along the process of secularization as well as the privatization and marginalization which tend to accompany this process. If at the end they accepted the process and accommodated themselves to the differentiated structures of the modern world, they often did so only grudgingly. What was new and became "news" in the 1980s was the widespread and simultaneous character of the refusal to be restricted to the private sphere of religious traditions as different as Judaism and Islam, Catholicism and Protestantism, Hinduism and Buddhism, in all "three worlds of development."

The inelegant neologism "deprivatization" has a dual purpose, polemical and descriptive. It is meant, first, to call into question those theories of secularization which have tended not only to assume but also to prescribe the privatization of religion in the modern world. Yet, while I agree with many of the criticisms that have been raised lately against the dominant theories of secularization, I do not share the view that secularization was, or is, a myth. The core of the theory of secularization, the thesis of the differentiation and emancipation of the secular spheres from religious institutions and norms, remains valid. But the term "deprivatization" is also meant to signify the emergence of new historical developments which, at least qualitatively, amount to a certain reversal of what appeared to be secular trends. Religions throughout the world are entering the public sphere and the arena of political contestation not only to defend their traditional turf, as they have done in the past, but also to participate in the very struggles to define and set the modern boundaries between the private and public spheres, between system and life-world, between legality and morality, between individual and society, between family, civil society, and state, between nations, states, civilizations, and the world system.

Basically, one can draw two lessons from religion in the 1980s. The first is that religions are here to stay, thus putting to rest one of the cherished dreams of the Enlightenment. The second and more important lesson is that religions are likely to continue playing important public roles in the ongoing construction of the modern world. This second lesson in particular compels us to rethink systematically the relationship of religion and modernity and, more important, the possible roles religions may play in the public sphere of modern societies. In this respect, the story of religion in the 1980s serves literally only as a *pre-text* for the book.

The Text: The Structure of the Book

The book itself is a study, both theoretical and empirical, of public religions in the modern world. The first two chapters address this task theoretically, trying to answer a question which, at least implicitly, would seem to be a contradiction in terms for theories of secularization as well as for most theories of modernity, namely, what are the conditions of possibility for modern public religions?

Chapter 1, "Secularization, Enlightenment, and Modern Religion," offers a critical review of the concept and the theory of secularization, embedded in a historical account of the development of Western modernity. It argues that the deprivatization of religion forces us to rethink and reformulate, but not necessarily to abandon uncritically, existing theories of secularization. The analysis shows that what passes for a single theory of secularization is actually made up of three different propositions: secularization as religious decline, secularization as differentiation, and secularization as privatization. It stresses the need to differentiate analytically and to evaluate differently the three main premises of the classical paradigm. The assumption that religion will tend to disappear with progressive modernization, a notion which has proven patently false as a general empirical proposition, is traced genealogically back to the Enlightenment critique of religion. The analysis affirms that the thesis of the differentiation of the religious and secular spheres is the still defensible core of the theory of secularization. But it holds the related proposition that modern differentiation *necessarily* entails the marginalization and privatization of religion, or its logical counterpart that public religions *necessarily* endanger the differentiated structures of modernity, to be no longer defensible.

What we need are better theories of the intermeshing of public and private spheres. In particular, we need to rethink the issue of the changing boundaries between differentiated spheres and the possible structural roles religion may have within those differentiated spheres as well as the role it may have in challenging the boundaries themselves. Chapter 2, "Private and Public Religions," begins to address some of these issues. It does not try to develop either a general theory or a comprehensive and exhaustive typology of public religions. It is a partly theoretical, partly typological exercise which draws on two different traditions, the comparative sociology of religions and theories of the public sphere and civil society, in order to examine those forms of modern public religion which may be both viable and desirable from a modern normative perspective. By "viable," I mean those forms of public religion which are not intrinsically incompatible with differentiated modern structures. By "desirable," I mean those forms of public religion which may actually contribute to strengthening the public sphere of modern civil societies.

The core of the book, chapters 3 through 7, offers empirical studies of what could be called varieties of public religion in the modern world. It presents five cases of transformation of contemporary religion, chosen from two religious traditions—Catholicism and Protestantism—in four different countries: Spain, Poland, Brazil, and the United States. Each of the case studies tells a different and independent story of transformation. In the case of Spanish Catholicism, the problem at hand is the change from an established authoritarian state church to the disestablished church of a pluralist civil society. In the case of Poland, the analysis traces the more subtle change from a disestablished church that protects the nation against foreign rule to a national church that promotes the emergence of civil society against a Polish authoritarian state. The chapter on Brazilian Catholicism analyzes the radical transformation of the Brazilian church from a state-oriented oligarchic and elitist institution to a civil society–oriented populist one. Moving on to the United States, chapter 6 analyzes the transformation of Evangelical Protestantism in America from its public hegemonic status as a civil religion during the nineteenth century to its sectarian withdrawal into a fundamentalist subculture in the late 1920s to its public reemergence and mobilization in the 1980s. The last case study analyzes the transformation of American Catholicism from an insecure sect to a defensive private denomination to an assertive public one.

Since the criteria for choosing these particular case studies may not be self-evident, let me offer a rationale for the choice. From a hermeneutic point of view each story is intrinsically justifiable. Moreover, each of the five stories not only is interesting in itself but also serves to illustrate empirical instances of various types of public religion. Therefore, I have tried as much as possible to let the different stories speak for themselves without forcing an external analytical framework upon them. Placing all of them together, however, in a comparative-historical framework within a single sociological study brings out some asymmetries.

First, the comparison involves one Protestant and four Catholic cases. Such an asymmetry could be problematic if one were setting out to compare Catholicism and Protestantism as "private" religions of individual salvation. Viewed as salvation religions, Spanish, Polish, Brazilian, and American Catholicism are, despite some striking differences, fundamentally alike. In terms of religious beliefs and practices, the international differences within transnational Catholicism probably are not greater than those which may exist between the various sectors of the Catholic population within each country. In any case, the four Catholic churches share the same basic doctrines, rituals, and ecclesiastical structure. As "public" religions, however, the various national Catholic churches have exhibited historically clear and fundamental differences. Indeed, the comparison of Spanish, Polish, Brazilian, and American Catholicism seems to indicate that, at least since the emergence of the modern state, the public character of any religion is primarily determined by the particular structural location of that religion between state and society. Therefore, in studying possible varieties of public religion, a comparative group made up of four Catholic and one Protestant religions may be justified fully if it is instrumental in helping to develop an internally consistent typology of public religions.

Furthermore, the overconcentration on Catholicism can also be justified on theoretical grounds. Catholicism served as the central focus of the Enlightenment critique of religion. It offered for centuries the most spirited, principled, fundamentalist, and apparently futile resistance to modern processes of secularization and modernization in all spheres. It fought capitalism, liberalism, the modern secular state, the democratic revolutions, socialism, the sexual revolution. In brief, it has been the paradigmatic form of antimodern public religion. In the mid-1960s, however, the Catholic church inaugurated a tortuous process of official *aggiornamento* to secular modernity and accepted the legitimacy of the modern age. Yet it refuses to become a private religion. It wants to be both modern and public. Indeed, since the Second Universal Council (Vatican II) it has kept a highly public profile throughout the world.[7]

A second obvious asymmetry results from the fact that the group under consideration appears to be composed of three integral units and two fractions of a much larger unit, that is, by three national churches with quasi-monopolistic control over the religious market in their respective countries and two structurally very different denominations within a single, free, and highly pluralistic religious market. Again, the apparent imbalance may actually be theoretically helpful. Since freedom of religion and pluralism may be assumed to be structural conditions of modernity, the inclusion of two different denominations, U.S. Catholicism and Protestant fundamentalism, which illustrate different structural locations as well as different types of public religion within the same free and pluralistic religious system, may turn out to be an advantage in a comparative study which sets out to examine the conditions of possibility for public religions in the modern world.

Finally, either from the temporal-developmental perspective of modernization theory or from the spatial-developmental perspective of world system theory, questions could be raised about a study which includes countries at such different stages of modernization—that is, secularization—and which occupy such hierarchically asymmetrical positions within the world system. But the inclusion from the (no longer extant) "three worlds" of development, or from the three world-systemic spaces—center, semiperiphery, and periphery—also turns out to be an advantage. If the study is able to show that public religions exist or have reemerged recently in all worlds of development, it will serve to support the assertion that the deprivatization of religion is indeed a global phenomenon.[8]

The final chapter, "The Deprivatization of Modern Religion," recapitulates the main theoretical arguments developed in the first two chapters, now substantiated by the historical evidence presented in the five case studies, draws out some comparisons and general conclusions from those studies, and reformulates more systematically the thesis of deprivatization, placing it in a more general and global perspective.

I acknowledge, however, a real imbalance. The present study is clearly a Western-centered study, both in terms of the particular cases chosen for investigation and in terms of the normative perspective guiding the investigation. Certainly, it would have been highly desirable to include the Iranian revolution as an additional case study. After all, the public resurgence of Islam has been one of the main developments thrusting religion back into public view. Studies of the deprivatization of Judaism in Israel, or of the deprivatization of Hinduism in India, or of the deprivatization of Buddhism in Burma would have been equally appropriate and desirable. Of course, such an immense task would have required a modification and expansion of my typology of public religions, of the theory of religious and political differentiation, and of the general analytical framework employed in this study. While difficult, such a task would not have been impossible.

Unfortunately, I have to plead limited time, knowledge, and resources, as well as a postmodern enhanced awareness of the dangers of excessive homogenization. I do not think, however, that non-Western cultures are "the other." All human languages are translatable, and all discourses are ultimately comprehensible. The room for misunderstanding and misinterpretation is certainly much greater in intercultural communications, but not necessarily different in principle from the dangers inherent in everyday communication, where we also frequently fail to get each other's messages. Moreover, anybody can be converted to any "faith." After all, it is the enduring revelation which humanity owes to *all* the universalistic salvation religions that any human person—irrespective of gender, race, class, clan, caste, tribe, ethnos, etc.—may be "born again" into a new "self." We are all—we have become whether we like it or not—citizens of one single human civil society. It is up to all of us either to find or to make the rules which will govern our unavoidable communicative discourse.

1   Secularization, Enlightenment, and Modern Religion

Who still believes in the *myth* of secularization? Recent debates within the sociology of religion would indicate this to be the appropriate question with which to start any current discussion of the theory of secularization. There are still a few "old believers," such as Bryan Wilson and Karel Dobbelaere, who insist, rightly, that the theory of secularization still has much explanatory value in attempting to account for modern historical processes.[1] But the majority of sociologists of religion will not listen, for they have abandoned the paradigm with the same uncritical haste with which they previously embraced it. Indeed, some are mocking the rationalists, who made so many false prophecies about the future of religion, in the same way the philosophes before them mocked religious visionaries and obscurantist priests. Armed with "scientific" evidence, sociologists of religion now feel confident to predict bright futures for religion. The reversal is astounding when one thinks that only some twenty years ago practically nobody was ready to listen when, in the first "secularization debate," the first voices were raised by David Martin and Andrew Greeley questioning the concept and the empirical evidence, or lack thereof, behind the theory of secularization. But how could anybody listen attentively then, when even the theologians were proclaiming the death of God and celebrating the coming of the secular city?[2]

How can one explain this reversal? How could there have been so much myth before and so much light now? It is true that much empirical counterevidence has been accumulated against the theory since the 1960s, but similar counterevidence had existed all along and yet the evidence remained unseen or was explained away as irrelevant. The answer has to be that it is not reality itself which has changed, as much as our perception of it, and that we must be witnessing a typical Kuhnian revolution in scientific paradigms. Some may object to the use of the word "scientific" in this particular context. But there can be no doubt that we are dealing with a radical change in intellectual climate and in the background worldviews which normally sustain much of our social-scientific consensus.

At the entrance to the field of secularization, there should always hang the sign "proceed at your own risk." Well aware of the traps, let me nonetheless proceed in the hope of introducing some analytical distinctions which, should they prove useful, may convince some of the unbelievers to take a second look before discarding a theory, some aspects of which may be not only salvable but necessary if we are to make sense of some important aspects of our past, of our present, and, I would say, even more, of our global future. Let me begin by introducing a distinction between the concept and the theory of secularization. Then I shall make a further distinction between three different moments of the theory which *must* be kept clearly apart.[3]

Secularization as a Concept

The distinction between the concept "secular," or its derivation "secularization," and the sociological theory of secularization proper is important because the concept itself is so multidimensional, so ironically reversible in its contradictory connotations, and so loaded with the wide range of meanings it has accumulated through its history. Perhaps it would even be reasonable to abandon the concept, were it not for the fact that to do so would pose even greater problems for sociology.[4] The concept's very range of meanings and contradictions makes it practically nonoperational for the dominant modes of empirical scientific analysis.[5] Consequently, ahistorical positivist sociology has to reduce it to clear and testable hypotheses, easily verifiable through longitudinal surveys which try to count the heads, hearts, and minds of religious people. But to drop the concept altogether would lead to even greater conceptual impoverishment, for in such a case one would also lose the memory of the complex history accumulated within the concept, and we would be left without appropriate categories to chart and to understand this history. A sociology of religion self-engrossed in the present of American secular society could perhaps afford to eliminate the concept, but comparative-historical sociology cannot do so.[6]

Let me recall only three historical moments of the concept to illustrate the way in which they are enmeshed with real historical processes of secularization. Looking at the concept's etymology, we learn that the medieval Latin word *saeculum* had three undifferentiated semantic connotations. The equivalent nouns in the Romance languages (*secolo, siglo, siècle*) have preserved those three meanings. The entry *siglo* in Cassell's Spanish dictionary reads "century; age; world." Yet, in the contemporary secular "age" and in the contemporary secular "world," only the first of the three connotations, "century," has preserved its usage in everyday life, since the differentiation of time and space into two different realities, a sacred one and a profane one, became truly meaningless long ago, even in Catholic Spain.

A related but different semantic moment comes from Canon Law, where secularization refers to what could be called a "legal action" with real legal consequences for the individual. Secularization refers to the legal (canonical) process whereby a "religious" person left the cloister to return to the "world" and its temptations, becoming thereby a "secular" person. Canonically, priests could be both "religious" and "secular." Those priests who had decided to withdraw from the world (*saeculum*) to dedicate themselves to a life of perfection formed the religious clergy. Those priests who lived in the world formed the secular clergy. When Max Weber designates as secularization the process whereby the concept of "calling" moves or is relocated from the religious to the secular sphere to signify, now for the first time, the exercise of secular activities in the world, he is using as analogy the canonical meaning of the concept.

Finally, in reference to an actual historical process, the term "secularization" was first used to signify the massive expropriation and appropriation, usually by the state, of monasteries, landholdings, and the mortmain wealth of the church after the Protestant Reformation and the ensuing religious wars. Since then, secularization has come to designate the "passage," transfer, or relocation of persons, things, functions, meanings, and so forth, from their traditional location in the religious sphere to the secular spheres. Thus, it has become customary to designate as secularization the appropriation, whether forcible or by default, by secular institutions of functions that traditionally had been in the hands of ecclesiastical institutions.[7]

These historically sedimented semantic moments of the term "secularization" only make sense if we accept the fact that, "once upon a time," much of reality in medieval Europe was actually structured through a system of classification which divided "this world" into two heterogeneous realms or spheres, "the religious" and "the secular." The separation between the two realms in this particular, and historically rather unusual, variant of the sacred-profane division was certainly not as heterogeneously absolute as Durkheim always thought it was. There was ample ambiguity, flexibility, permeability, and often outright confusion between the boundaries, military orders being a case in point. What is important to realize is that the dualism was institutionalized throughout society so that the social realm itself was dualistically structured.[8]

The existence of "two swords," the spiritual and the temporal, both of them claiming to possess their own autonomous source of charisma—a kind of institutionalized dual sovereignty—necessarily had to be the source of much tension and open conflict, as well as of attempts to put an end to the dualism by subsuming one of the spheres under the other. The repeated "investiture" conflicts were the manifest expression of this ever-present tension. The theocratic claims of the church and spiritual rulers to possess primacy over the temporal rulers and, thus, ultimate supremacy and the right to rule over temporal affairs as well, were met with the caesaropapist claims of kings to embody sacred sovereignty by divine right and by the attempts of temporal rulers to incorporate the spiritual sphere into their temporal patrimony and vassalage.

A similar dualist structure, with the same room and propensity for intellectual tension and conflict, became institutionalized in the emerging medieval universities, where faith and reason became separate but parallel epistemological foundations, supposedly leading to the one single Truth: God. Here also the absolutist claims of theology set in motion the counterclaims first of self-assertive rational philosophy, which rejected its ancillary relationship to theology, and then of early modern science, which asserted its claims that the Book of Nature should rank along with the Book of Revelation as separate but equal epistemological ways to God.

This structured division of "this world" into two separate spheres, "the religious" and "the secular," has to be distinguished and kept separate from another division: that between "this world" and "the other world." To a large extent, it is the failure to keep these two distinctions separate that is the source of misunderstandings in discussions of secularization. One may say that, properly speaking, there were not two "worlds" but actually three. Spatially, there was "the other world" (heaven) and "this world" (earth). But "this world" was itself divided into the religious world (the church) and the secular world proper (*saeculum*). Temporally, we find the same tripartite division between the eternal age of God and the temporal-historical age, which is itself divided into the sacred-spiritual time of salvation, represented by the church's calendar, and the secular age proper (*saeculum*). Ecclesiologically, this tripartite division was expressed in the distinction between the eschatological "Invisible Church" (the *Communio Sanctorum*), the "Visible Church" (the *Una, Sancta, Catholica, Apostolica* Roman church), and secular societies. Politically, there was the transcendental City of God (Heavenly Kingdom), its sacramental representation here on earth by the Church (the Papal Kingdom), and the City of Man proper (the Holy Roman Empire and all Christian Kingdoms). In modern secular categories, we would say that there was natural reality and supernatural reality. But the supernatural realm itself was divided between nonempirical supernatural reality proper and its symbolic, sacramental representation in empirical reality.

We may say, therefore, that premodern Western European Christendom was structured through a double dualist system of classification. There was, on the one hand, the dualism between "this world" and "the other world." There was, on the other hand, the dualism within "this world" between a "religious" and a "secular" sphere. Both dualisms were mediated, moreover, by the "sacramental" nature of the church, situated in the middle, simultaneously belonging to the two worlds, and, therefore, able to mediate sacramentally between the two. Such a system of classification, of course, rested solely on the claims of the church and was able to structure reality accordingly only as long as people took those claims for granted. Indeed, only the acceptance, for whatever reasons, of the claim of superiority of the religious realm over the secular realm could have maintained within bounds the conflicts inherent in such a dualist system.

Secularization as a concept refers to the actual historical process whereby this dualist system within "this world" and the sacramental structures of mediation between this world and the other world progressively break down until the entire medieval system of classification disappears, to be replaced by new systems of spatial structuration of the spheres. Max Weber's expressive image of the breaking of the monastery walls remains perhaps the best graphic expression of this radical spatial restructuration. The wall separating the religious and the secular realms within "this world" breaks down. The separation between "this world" and "the other world," for the time being at least, remains. But from now on, there will be only one single "this world," the secular one, within which religion will have to find its own place. If before, it was the religious realm which appeared to be the all-encompassing reality within which the secular realm found its proper place, now the secular sphere will be the all-encompassing reality, to which the religious sphere will have to adapt. To study what new systems of classification and differentiation emerge within this one secular world and what new place religion will have, if any, within the new differentiated system is precisely the analytical task of the theory of secularization.

So far, our analysis of religion has been solely spatial-structural, in terms of the location of religion within the system of classification that served to structure the social reality of medieval Christendom. Nothing has been said about the individuals living in this social space, about their religious beliefs, their religious practices, their religious experiences, that is, about the private dimensions of individual religiosity. We may speak with some confidence about two of the public dimensions of individual religiosity. Membership in the church was practically one hundred percent. With some exceptions, such as among the Jews and some Muslims who were permitted to live in their special enclaves within Christendom, membership in the church was compulsory and, therefore, in itself tells us little about individual religiosity. Everybody was a Christian. Even dissent and heresy, which encountered the same inhuman treatment they suffer in modern authoritarian states, were expressed regularly as a reformation of Christendom or as a sectarian return to the purity of origin, not as its rejection.[9] Concerning the so-called religious factor or consequential dimension of religion—that is, the extent to which behavior in the secular realm was influenced by religion—we may also say that since life in the *saeculum* itself was regulated, at least officially, according to supposedly Christian principles, by definition Christians within Christendom led Christian lives.

Naturally, like every society, Christendom had its share of offenders. In fact, the official doctrine was that everybody was a sinner. There were the venial sinners, the capital sinners, those who lived in permanent sin, and those who lived beyond the pale and were excommunicated. There was, to be sure, differentiation and tension between Canon Law, Roman Law, and Common or Germanic Law. But the differentiation between religious sin, moral offense, and legal crime was not yet clear. In any case, about the statistical distribution of the various categories of sinners, or about the extension and intensity of their religious beliefs, practices, and experiences, we have scant reliable or generalizable data. Even when historians are able to determine with relative certainty the proportion of priests and religious persons within society, this statistic in itself tells us little about their actual religiosity. We have sufficient information about widespread corruption in the papal court, about rampant hedonism in the monasteries, and about simoniacal priests. If the religious virtuosi led such lives, there is no reason to believe that ordinary Christians led more virtuous lives. Indeed, precisely because the official Christian structure of society guaranteed that everybody was leading Christian lives, it was not so necessary to stress personal devotion. It was the structure itself that was religious, that is, Christian, not necessarily the personal lives that people lived within it. Within this structure, there was much room for fusion as well as fission between Christian and pagan, official and popular forms of religiosity. It is from the records of the conflicts between orthodoxy and heresy and the tensions between official and popular religion that ethnologists and social historians are extracting new revisionist perspectives on medieval and early modern religion.[10]

Assuming that the ideal-typical characterization presented so far, as oversimplified as it may be, is nevertheless a fair one, we may say with certainty that the assumption that premodern Europeans were more religious than modern ones reveals itself precisely as that, as an assumption in need of confirmation.[11] Those versions of the theory of secularization which begin precisely with such an unfounded assumption and conceive the process of secularization as the progressive decline of religious beliefs and practices in the modern world are indeed reproducing a myth that sees history as the progressive evolution of humanity from superstition to reason, from belief to unbelief, from religion to science. This mythical account of the process of secularization is indeed in need of "desacralization." But this does not mean that we ought to abandon altogether the theory of secularization. What the sociology of religion needs to do is to substitute for the mythical account of a universal process of secularization comparative sociological analyses of historical processes of secularization, if and when they take place.

The Theory of Secularization

Any discussion of the theory of secularization, particularly any attempt to trace its genealogy and its history once it was incorporated into the social sciences, especially into sociology, where the theory eventually found its home, has to begin with the statement of a striking paradox. The theory of secularization may be the only theory which was able to attain a truly paradigmatic status within the modern social sciences. In one form or another, with the possible exception of Alexis de Tocqueville, Vilfredo Pareto, and William James, the thesis of secularization was shared by all the founding fathers: from Karl Marx to John Stuart Mill, from Auguste Comte to Herbert Spencer, from E. B. Tylor to James Frazer, from Ferdinand Toennies to Georg Simmel, from Émile Durkheim to Max Weber, from Wilhelm Wundt to Sigmund Freud, from Lester Ward to William G. Sumner, from Robert Park to George H. Mead.[12] Indeed, the consensus was such that not only did the theory remained uncontested but apparently it was not even necessary to test it, since everybody took it for granted. This means that although the theory or, rather, the thesis of secularization often served as the unstated premise of many of the founding fathers' theories, it itself was never either rigorously examined or even formulated explicitly and systematically.

The foundations for the more systematic formulations of the theory of secularization are to be found in the work of Émile Durkheim and Max Weber. By freeing themselves from the positivist and the Enlightenment critiques of religion—even though Durkheim remained an avowed positivist and Weber always saw himself as a disenchanted product of the Enlightenment, duty bound to carry out without illusions and to its outer limits the task of scientific enlightenment—they established the foundations for the social-scientific study of religion.[13] By separating the

question of the truth of religion from that of its symbolic structure and
social function, Durkheim's sociology served as the foundation for later
structural-functionalist analysis in anthropology as well as in sociology.
Weber, on his part, by abandoning the obsession of reducing religion to
its essence and concentrating on the task of studying its most diverse
meanings as well as its social-historical conditions and effects, established the foundations for a comparative, historical, and phenomenological sociology of religion.

For Durkheim as well as for Weber, it may be said that the sociology
of religion stands at the center of their sociological work; that the theory
of differentiation, though markedly different in both cases, forms the
core of their sociological theories; and that the thesis of secularization
forms the core of their theories of differentiation, serving both as the
premise and as the end result of processes of differentiation.[14] Strictly
speaking, the theory of secularization is nothing more than a subtheory
of general theories of differentiation, either of the evolutionary and universal kind proposed by Durkheim or of the more historically specific
kind of Western modernization theory developed by Weber. Indeed, the
theory of secularization is so intrinsically interwoven with all the theories
of the modern world and with the self-understanding of modernity that
one cannot simply discard the theory of secularization without putting
into question the entire web, including much of the self-understanding
of the social sciences.[15]

Even Durkheim and Weber, however, while laying the foundation for
later theories of secularization, themselves offer scant empirical analysis
of modern processes of secularization, particularly of the way in which
those processes affect the place, nature, and role of religion in the modern
world. Even after freeing themselves from some of the rationalist and
positivist prejudices about religion, they still share the major intellectual
assumptions of the age about the future of religion. Their prognoses may
be different, but their diagnoses of the present share the view that the
old historical religions cannot survive the onslaught of the modern
world. Both take for granted that, in Durkheim's words, "the old gods
are growing old or already dead"[16] and that, in any case, they will not
be able to compete either with the new gods, which Durkheim believed
modern societies would create for themselves, or with the modern polytheism of values and its unceasing and irreconcilable struggle which,
according to Weber, has resulted from the process of differentiation of
the various secular spheres as they press to realize their own "internal
and lawful autonomy." The old churches, for Weber, remain only as a
refuge for those "who cannot bear the fate of the times like a man" and
are willing to make the inevitable "intellectual sacrifice."[17]

Notwithstanding the widespread consensus within sociology over the secularization thesis, it was not until the 1960s that one finds attempts to develop more systematic and empirically grounded formulations of the theory of secularization. It was then that the first flaws in the theory became noticeable and the first critics were heard.[18] For the first time it became possible to separate the theory of secularization from its ideological origins in the Enlightenment critique of religion and to distinguish the theory of secularization, as a theory of the modern autonomous differentiation of the secular and the religious spheres, from the thesis that the end result of the process of modern differentiation would be the progressive erosion, decline, and eventual disappearance of religion. The new functionalist theory of secularization, formulated most systematically in Thomas Luckmann's *The Invisible Religion,* did not postulate the inevitable decline of religion in modern societies, only the loss by religion of its traditional societal and public functions, and the privatization and marginalization of religion within its own differentiated sphere. Since many of the "new" religions and religious movements of the 1960s and 1970s could be interpreted as instances of Luckmann's "invisible religion," few people used them as evidence against the theory of secularization. Only in the 1980s, after the sudden eruption of religion into the public sphere, did it become obvious that differentiation and the loss of societal functions do not necessarily entail "privatization."

In any case, the old theory of secularization can no longer be maintained. There are only two options left: either, as seems the present inclination of most sociologists of religion, to discard the theory altogether once it is revealed to be an unscientific, mythological account of the modern world, or to revise the theory in such a way that it can answer both its critics and the questions which reality itself has posed.

Three Separate Moments of the Theory of Secularization

The main fallacy in the theory of secularization, a fallacy reproduced by apologists and critics alike that has made the theory nearly unserviceable for social-scientific purposes, is the confusion of historical processes of secularization proper with the alleged and anticipated consequences which those processes were supposed to have upon religion. As already mentioned, the core and the central thesis of the theory of secularization is the conceptualization of the process of societal modernization[19] as a process of functional differentiation and emancipation of the secular spheres—primarily the state, the economy, and science—from the religious sphere and the concomitant differentiation and specialization of religion within its own newly found religious sphere. To this central thesis, which may be called the differentiation thesis, two other subtheses have often been attached which allegedly explain what will happen to religion as a result of this process of secularization. One subthesis, the decline-of-religion thesis, postulated that the process of secularization would bring in its wake the progressive shrinkage and decline of religion until, some extreme versions added, it eventually disappeared. The other subthesis, the privatization thesis, postulated that the process of secularization would bring in its wake the privatization and, some added, the marginalization of religion in the modern world. Only if we separate these three theses analytically can we fully make sense of the complexity of modern historical reality.

The Differentiation and Secularization of Society

To view modern historical transformations from the perspective of secularization means, to a large extent, to view reality from the perspective of religion, since the secular, as a concept, only makes sense in relation to its counterpart, the religious. The advantage of such a perspective derives from its ability to show the radical extent to which Western societies have changed precisely in this respect. The medieval dichotomous classification of reality into religious and secular realms was to a large extent dictated by the church. In this sense, the official perspective from which medieval societies saw themselves was a religious one. If the main category of thought was that dividing the religious from the secular, then everything within the *saeculum* remained an undifferentiated whole as long as it was viewed from the outside, from the perspective of the religious. Only the end of this dichotomous way of thinking permitted the secular realm to establish new perspectives from which it could view itself differentiatedly.[20] The fall of the religious walls opened up a whole new space for processes of internal differentiation of the various secular spheres. Now, for the first time, the various secular spheres could come fully into their own, become differentiated from each other, and follow what Weber called their "internal and lawful autonomy." Weber's theory of differentiation, as developed in his masterpiece "Religious Rejections of the World and Their Directions," is a theory of secularization precisely because it views this differentiation from the perspective of the radical clash of each of the spheres, as they follow their "internal and lawful autonomy," with the charismatic religious ethic of brotherliness or with the organic social ethics of the church.[21]

The analysis of the same process of differentiation from the perspective of the differentiation of each of the spheres not from religion but from one another would necessarily look different. Such a perspective would show that, in the particular case of the transition to modernity, some of the secular spheres, particularly the emerging modern absolutist state and the emerging capitalist economy, were more lawful and more autonomous than the others. It would probably show as well that it was their differentiation from one another, their mutual dependence and their clashes, that more than anything else dictated the dynamics of the whole process.[22] Actually, these two secular spheres, states and markets, now tended to dictate the very principles of classification which served to structure the new modern system. In spatial-structural terms we may say that if reality before was structured around one main axis, now a multiaxial space was created with two main axes structuring the whole. In the language of functionalist systems theory, each subsystem became the environment for the others but two subsystems became the primary environment for all. In the new spatial structure, therefore, the religious sphere became just another sphere, structured around its own autonomous internal axis but falling under the gravitational force of the two main axes. Irrespective of which perspective we choose, however, it will show that the religious sphere now became a less central and spatially diminished sphere within the new secular system. Moreover, from the new hegemonic perspective of modern differentiation one may add that, now for the first time, the religious sphere came fully into its own, specializing in "its own religious" function and either dropping or losing many other "nonreligious" functions it had accumulated and could no longer meet efficiently.[23] The theory of secularization does not need to enter into the controversial search for the first cause which set the modern process of differentiation into motion. From its particular perspective, it may be sufficient to stress the role which four related and simultaneously unfolding developments played in undermining the medieval religious system of classification: the Protestant Reformation; the formation of modern states; the growth of modern capitalism; and the early modern scientific revolution. Each of the four developments contributed its own dynamic to modern processes of secularization, that is, each of them was one of the carriers of the process of secularization. The four of them together were certainly more than sufficient to carry the process through.[24]

The role of the Protestant Reformation can be analyzed at three different levels. At the very least, most observers will agree that the Protestant Reformation played a destructive role. By undermining the very claims to unity, sanctity, catholicity, and apostolicity of *the* church, which from now on will require the qualifiers Roman Catholic to distinguish it from other competing Christian churches, it destroyed the system of Western Christendom and thus opened up the possibility for the emergence of something new.[25] By destroying the old organic system, it helped to liberate, perhaps unwittingly, the secular spheres from religious control.[26] At a higher level, Protestantism may be viewed not only as the corrosive solvent which made room for the new but also as the religious superstructure of the new order, as the religion of bourgeois modernity, as a religious ideology which, at a time when ideological and class struggles were still fought in religious garb, served to legitimate the rise of bourgeois man and of the new entrepreneurial classes, the rise of the modern sovereign state against the universal Christian monarchy, and the triumph of the new science against Catholic scholasticism.[27] There is finally the view that Protestantism, particularly what Weber calls "ascetic Protestantism," not only helped to offer religious legitimation to processes already under way but itself through the introduction of new religious principles and new secular ethics served to impel and shape these processes in a particular direction. Protestantism would be from such a perspective not only a secularizing force but a form of religious internal secularization, the vehicle through which religious contents would take institutionalized secular form, thereby erasing altogether the religious/secular divide.[28]

If the universalist claims of the church as a salvation organization were undermined by the religious pluralism introduced by the Reformation, its monopolist compulsory character was undermined by the rise of a modern secular state which progressively was able to concentrate and monopolize the means of violence and coercion within its territory. In the early absolutist phase the alliance of throne and altar became even more accentuated or, properly speaking, it came actually into its own. New secular *raison d'état* principles of legitimation were mixed with old sacro-magical ones, and absolutist rulers claimed divine right along with thaumaturgic powers.[29] The churches attempted to reproduce the model of Christendom at the national level, but all the territorial national churches, Anglican as well as Lutheran, Catholic as well as Orthodox, fell under the caesaropapist control of the absolutist state. The political costs of enforcing conformity became too high once religious nonconformism turned into political dissent. The principle *cuius regio eius religio* soon turned into the principle of religious tolerance and state neutrality toward privatized religion, the liberal state's preferred form of religion. Officially, church establishment may have lasted much longer, in some cases until today, but in the process the established churches have only become weaker and no longer able to emancipate themselves from the state. Of all religions, the "established" churches of secular states, caught as they are between a secular state which no longer needs them and people who prefer to go elsewhere if and when they want to satisfy their individual religious needs, are the least able to weather the winds of secularization.[30]

Before it became a self-reproducing system governed by impersonal laws, capitalism, that revolutionizing force in history which "melts all that is solid into air and profanes all that is holy,"[31] had already sprouted within the womb of the old Christian society in the medieval towns. The church's attempt to regulate the new economic relations in accordance with traditional Christian principles was bound to fail. No amount of economic casuistry could hide the distance between just price theory and capitalist profit or the irreconcilable conflict between the new capitalist relations and the traditional "moral economies," that is, the communitarian brotherly ethics or the organic social ethics. Nor could the church's ever more desperate official condemnations of usury stem the growth of financial and merchant capitalism, a growth to which the church's own avid search for larger revenues contributed in no small part. No other sphere of the *saeculum* would prove more secular and more unsusceptible to moral regulation than the capitalist market. No other media of exchange and social interaction would prove as impersonal and as generalizable as "money." Nowhere is the transvaluation of values which takes place from medieval to Puritan Christianity as radical and as evident as in the change of attitude toward "charity"— that most Christian of virtues—and toward poverty. The evangelical injunction "blessed be the poor," which had led to the elevation of begging into a religious "profession" by the mendicant orders, turned into the condemnation of almsgiving and the view of poverty as a divine punishment for sin. Following Weber, one could distinguish three phases and meanings of capitalist secularization: in the Puritan phase, "asceticism was carried out of monastic cells into everyday life" and secular economic activities acquired the meaning and compulsion of a religious calling; in the utilitarian phase, as the religious roots dried out, the irrational compulsion turned into "sober economic virtue" and "utilitarian worldliness"; finally, once capitalism "rests on mechanical foundations," it no longer needs religious or moral support and begins to penetrate and colonize the religious sphere itself, subjecting it to the logic of commodification.[32]

The tension between faith and reason was intrinsic to medieval intellectual life. It was the great achievement of medieval scholasticism, particularly of the Aristotelian-Thomist synthesis, to have institutionalized the tension into an all-encompassing metaphysical system. Late medieval nominalism introduced such cracks into the system that it became necessary to search for new foundations, for new certainties and certitudes in the sphere of faith as well as in that of reason. Hence the similarities and parallelisms between the early modern revolutions in scientific, philosophical, and theological thought.[33] Only now could the three become clearly differentiated as they embarked on their separate modern journeys. It is well known that the conflict between the church and the new science, symbolized by the trial of Galileo, was not about the substantive truth or falsity of the new Copernican theories of the universe as much as it was about the validity of the claims of the new science to have discovered a new autonomous method of obtaining and verifying truth. The conflict was not, strictly speaking, one between the contents of religion and a particular scientific paradigm, but one between the church and the new method's claim to differentiated autonomy. Thus, the attempts of all the pioneers—Galileo, Kepler, and Newton—to enthrone the Book of Nature as a legitimate, separate but equal, epistemological way to God, along with the Book of Revelation.[34]

The attempt was successful in Puritan England but failed in Lutheran and, miserably so, in Catholic countries. The Puritans would become pioneers in the differentiated institutionalization of the modern scientific enterprise.[35] The Newtonian Enlightenment established a new synthesis between faith and reason, which in Anglo-Saxon countries was to last until the Darwinian crisis of the second half of the nineteenth century. As the Newtonian Enlightenment crossed the Channel, however, it became patently radicalized and militantly antireligious.[36] Science was transformed into a scientific and scientistic worldview which claimed to have replaced religion the way a new scientific paradigm replaces an outmoded one. The process of secularization now found new historical carriers, the various militant secularist movements, ready to do battle with ignorance and religious superstition wherever they found it. Some of those, such as the British secularist movements, turned out to be rather innocuous and petered out, in part because society itself became largely secular.[37] Others emerged in unexpected places, like the adoption in the second half of the nineteenth century by many Latin American states of "positivism" (Comtian or Spencerian) as official state ideology.[38] Others, however, turned nefarious, and not only for religion, as they gained state power. Parallel to its plans of forced industrialization from above and its war on the peasantry, the Soviet state undertook campaigns of forced secularization from above and its war on religion. The only official place left for religion in the Communist state would be the museums of atheism, where the antireligious tirades of the philosophes became enshrined in a petit bourgeois philosophy of history documenting the "ascent of man" from religious superstition to the zenith of scientific enlightenment, Marxism-Leninism in its Stalinist version.[39]

If one views secularization as a modern historical process and accepts the view that, above all, these four simultaneous developments—the Protestant Reformation, the rise of the modern state, the rise of modern capitalism, and the rise of modern science—set in motion the dynamics of the process by undermining the medieval system and themselves became at the same time the carriers of the processes of differentiation, of which secularization is one aspect, then it follows that one should expect different historical patterns of secularization. As each of these carriers developed different dynamics in different places and at different times, the patterns and the outcomes of the historical processes of secularization should vary accordingly. Intuitively, even a superficial knowledge of the various histories tells one that this is the case, yet it is striking how few comparative historical studies of secularization there are.[40]

If Protestantism, for reasons much more complex than the ones adduced here, is itself one of the carriers of secularization, then one should expect to find different patterns of secularization in Protestant and Catholic countries.[41] If the modern state in its own right is also a carrier of processes of secularization, then one should expect that different patterns of state formation, let us say in France, England, and the United States, should also have some effect on different patterns of secularization. If science and even more so scientific worldviews are also autonomous carriers of processes of secularization, then one should expect that the different character of the Enlightenment in the Continent, England, and the United States, as well as the presence or absence of a militant critique of religion, would in itself also be an important factor affecting patterns of secularization. Only when it comes to capitalism has it been nearly universally recognized that economic development affects the "rates of secularization." This positive insight, however, turns into a blinder when it is made into the sole main variable accounting for different rates of secularization. As a result, those cases in which no positive correlation is found, as expected, between rates of secularization and rates of industrialization, urbanization, proletarianization, and education, in short, with indicators of economic development, are termed "exceptions" which deviate from the "norm."[42]

Only if secularization is conceived as a universal teleological process whose eventual final outcome one already knows, is it understandable that social scientists may not be particularly interested in studying the different paths different societies may take getting there. Moreover, if, as it has been proclaimed so often, the outcome is going to be "the death of god," then it has to be possible to find simple measurable and generalizable indicators to determine how far along in the process the various societies are. Only the conviction that religion was going to disappear may explain the fact that the overwhelming evidence showing that different modern societies evince significantly different patterns of secularization could have been ignored or found irrelevant for so long.

The Decline of Religion Thesis

The assumption, often stated but mostly unstated, that religion in the modern world was declining and would likely continue to decline until its eventual disappearance was so widespread and dominant among social scientists that only in the 1960s do we find the first theories of "modern" religion, namely, theories that ask themselves which specifically modern forms religion may take in the modern world. By "modern" I mean religions that are not only traditional survivals or residues from a premodern past but rather specifically products of modernity.[43] But what empirical evidence is or was there for the assumption that religion is likely to decline in the modern world? Since, unlike those who believe that this assumption is only a myth, I believe that there is some empirical evidence behind the assumption, let us first examine the evidence, before looking at the mythical components of the assumption.

One should begin with some caveats. First, from a global perspective, sufficient empirical evidence is not available and that which does exist is very uneven and not conducive to comparison. But the evidence available may be sufficient and adequate if one only wants to make some empirically informed statements which could serve as the point of departure for further discussion. Second, one should keep in mind the well-known difficulties, apparently inherent in the field of religion, when it comes to evaluating the existing evidence. There is no consensus, perhaps there will never be, as to what counts as religion. Furthermore, even when there is agreement on the object of study, there is likely to be disagreement on what it is that one ought to be counting, that is to say, on which of the dimensions of religiosity (membership affiliation, beliefs, ritual and nonritual practices, experiences, doctrinal knowledge, and their behavioral and ethical effects) one should measure and how various dimensions should be ranked and compared. Finally, one should be very careful when applying to non-Western religions categories and measures derived from the study of Western religion.[44]

Nevertheless, on the basis of the tentative evidence gathered in Frank Whaling's (ed.) *Religion in Today's World*,[45] one can begin with the following factual statements:

—From a global perspective, since World War II most religious traditions in most parts of the world have either experienced some growth or maintained their vitality. This has been the case despite the fact that throughout the world since World War II, there have been rapid increases in industrialization, urbanization, education, and so forth.

—The main exceptions to this apparently global trend are the rapid decline of primal religions, the sudden and dramatic decline of religion in communist countries following the establishment of communist states, and the continuous decline of religion throughout much of Western Europe (and, one could add, some of its colonial outposts such as Argentina, Uruguay, and New Zealand).

How should one evaluate this tentative evidence? We may safely disregard the evidence concerning the decline of primal religions, since it appears that people leave them often "under duress" and mostly for other religions (Muslim, Christian, etc.).[46] We may also disregard the evidence concerning the decline of religion in communist countries, since it is a clear case of state-imposed decline, which appears to reverse itself dramatically the moment state coercion either disappears or lessens. The contemporary religious revival in China and the dramatic revival of religion along with nationalism in the former communist countries of Eastern Europe seem to confirm the reversibility of the process.[47]

What remains, therefore, as significant and overwhelming evidence is the progressive and apparently still continuing decline of religion in Western Europe. It is this evidence which has always served as the empirical basis for most theories of secularization, and one should not discard it lightly. Indeed, Western European societies are among the most modern, differentiated, industrialized, and educated societies in the world. Were it not for the fact that religion shows no uniform sign of decline in Japan or the United States, two equally modern societies, one could still perhaps maintain the "modernizing" developmentalist assumption that it is only a matter of time before the more "backward" societies catch up with the more "modern" ones. But such an assumption is no longer tenable. Leaving aside the evidence from Japan, a case which should be crucial, however, for any attempt to develop a "general" theory of secularization, we are left with the need to explain the obviously contrasting religious trends in Western Europe (meaning here all countries and regions of Europe which were part of Western Christendom, i.e., Catholic and Protestant Europe) and the United States.[48]

At least since the beginning of the nineteenth century, European visitors have been struck by the vitality of American religion and by the fact that Americans seem to be such a religious people when compared with Europeans. This impression was shared by Beaumont and Tocqueville, as well as by Thomas Hamilton, in the 1830s. Marx uses this evidence in his essay "On the Jewish Question" against Bruno Bauer to argue that since America is both the example of "perfect disestablishment" and "the land of religiosity par excellence," it follows that Bauer's proposal of political emancipation of the state from religion cannot be the solution to full human emancipation.[49] The same argument could be used to demonstrate that industrialization, urbanization, scientific education, and so forth does not necessarily bring religious decline.

We have, moreover, not only anecdotal evidence from European visitors. Historians have begun to show that the story of religion in America from 1700 to the present is one of ascension rather than declension, of growth rather than decline.[50] Longitudinal survey research also shows that there has been no discernible decline of religion in America in this century.[51] Since the evidence of decline in European religion, however, appears to be equally overwhelming, how do we explain these contrasting trends?[52]

Until very recently, most of the comparative observations as well as attempts at explanation came from the European side. Looking at those explanations, what is most striking at the outset is the fact that Europeans never seemed to feel compelled to put into question the thesis of secularization in view of the American counterevidence. Actually, the assumption that European developments are the modern norm is so unquestioned that, what from a global perspective is truly striking, namely, the dramatic decline of religion in Europe, does not seem to demand an explanation. What requires an explanation, though, is what they assume to be the American "deviation" from the European norm. Basically, the explanations tend to fall into two groups, both of which reveal a clear strategy to avoid having to question the paradigm of secularization.

The first strategy, a casuistic one, is to rule out the American evidence as irrelevant. "Closer scrutiny," so Weber's argument goes, reveals that American religion itself has become so "secular" that it should no longer count as religion, because the functions it fulfills are purely secular ones.[53] Luckmann, in the first systematic attempt to explain "the differences in the character of church religion in Europe and America," uses a similar strategy to reach the similar conclusion that "traditional church religion was pushed to the periphery of 'modern' life in Europe while it became more 'modern' in America by undergoing a process of internal secularization."[54] The second typical strategy, used more informally, is to resort to the "last resort," "American exceptionalism," and imply that America is the exception that confirms the European rule, the corollary being that the European rule does not need to be questioned.

Turning the European explanation on its feet, what truly demands explanation are two things: namely, the striking European pattern of secularization, that is, the dramatic decline of religion there; and the fact that Europeans, and most social scientists, have refused for so long to face or to take seriously the American counterevidence. In other words, we need to explain the lasting convincing power of the secularization paradigm in the face of overwhelming contrary evidence. Here we can only hint at possible explanations to the two questions. A plausible answer to the first question requires a search for independent variables, for those independent carriers of secularization present in Europe but absent in the United States. Looking at the four historical carriers mentioned above, it is clear that neither Protestantism nor capitalism can serve as a plausible candidate. All the major American Protestant denominations

(Episcopalian, Congregationalist, Presbyterian, Baptist, Methodist) are basically transplants from British Protestantism.[55] Prima facie, capitalist developments in both places were also not as strikingly different as to warrant their consideration as a plausible independent carrier. The state and scientific culture, however, could serve as plausible independent variables, since church-state relations and the scientific worldviews carried by the Enlightenment were significantly different in Europe and America.

What America never had was an absolutist state and its ecclesiastical counterpart, a caesaropapist state church. This is what truly distinguishes American and European Protestantism. Even the multiple Protestant establishments of the colonies were never strictly speaking caesaropapist churches. The denominational logic of American Protestantism was already at work well before the constitutional separation of church and state. In the absence of state churches, the *raison d'être* of nonconformist sects disappears as well, and all religious bodies, churches as well as sects, turn into denominations.[56]

It was the caesaropapist embrace of throne and altar under absolutism that perhaps more than anything else determined the decline of church religion in Europe. The thesis is not new. It was put forth by Tocqueville and restated differently, because of his different normative perspective, by Marx.[57] It becomes evident to American observers the moment they look at European trends.[58] It should have been evident to Europeans as well, had they looked at the striking differences within Europe itself between, on one hand, Catholic Ireland and Catholic Poland, which never had a caesaropapist state church, and, on the other, Catholic France and Catholic Spain. Besides, consistently throughout Europe, nonestablished churches and sects in most countries have been able to survive the secularizing trends better than has the established church.[59] It is not so much the minority versus majority status that explains the difference but the presence or absence of establishment. One may say that it was the very attempt to preserve and prolong Christendom in every nation-state and thus to resist modern functional differentiation that nearly destroyed the churches in Europe.

If church establishment explains to a large extent the decline of church religion, what explains the fact that the available evidence remained ignored and invisible for so long? Plausibly, one could answer, the same factor which maintains and sustains the taken for granted nature of every paradigm. Namely, as long as there is consensus within the community of practitioners that they already possess a coherent, consistent, and convincing explanation of the phenomena in question, there is no reason why one should look for alternative explanations when the available ones seem to work. The Enlightenment critique of religion provided the social sciences with such an explanation, and this explanation apparently remained plausible as long as the basic assumptions inherited from the Enlightenment persisted. Surely, religious changes and overwhelming counterevidence eventually contributed to undermining the paradigm, but much of this evidence itself became visible only when new questions were asked as a result of a crisis, one could almost say, of a sudden collapse of the underlying assumptions.[60]

The Enlightenment critique of religion. To a certain extent, the Enlightenment critique of religion became in many places a self-fulfilling prophecy. The Enlightenment and its critique of religion became themselves independent carriers of processes of secularization wherever the established churches became obstacles to the modern process of functional differentiation. By contrast, wherever religion itself accepted, perhaps even furthered, the functional differentiation of the secular spheres from the religious sphere, the radical Enlightenment and its critique of religion became superfluous. Ideas from the Newtonian Enlightenment, which in England were the respectable and established currency among scientific circles, educated publics, and even in the royal court, became seditious and sacrilegious in France and in continental absolutist Europe once Montesquieu, Voltaire, and others imported them. Forced underground into Masonic lodges and conspiratorial societies, these ideas re-emerged only more radicalized and spread wherever ecclesiastical institutions tried to maintain intellectual, political, or moral control over individuals or groups striving for emancipation from the absolutist state, from hierarchically stratified social relations, from the church, or from any "self-incurred tutelage."[61]

The Enlightenment critique of religion had three clearly distinguishable dimensions: a cognitive one directed against metaphysical and supernatural religious worldviews; a practical-political one directed against ecclesiastical institutions; and a subjective expressive-aesthetic-moral one directed against the idea of God itself. In its first cognitive phase, the Enlightenment critique was directed against those religious worldviews which stood in the way of the legitimation and institutionalization of modern scientific methods. As the natural sciences first and the social and cultural sciences later had to establish their autonomy and legitimacy against traditional religious-metaphysical explanations of nature, culture, and society, those sciences began to inflate their own absolute claims to superiority over prescientific worldviews and their ability to provide total and exclusive explanations of reality. Reduced to a prescientific and prelogical primitive form of thought and knowledge, religion necessarily had to disappear with the ever-progressive advancement of knowledge, education, and scientific worldviews. The "darkness" of religious ignorance and superstition would fade away when exposed to the "lights" of reason. Naturally, such a critique of religion was particularly effective wherever the church was still committed to the medieval Aristotelian-Thomist metaphysical synthesis, resisted all modern cognitive heresies, and continued to claim absolute rights to the control of education. The same critique had to be less relevant wherever religion had freed itself from its ties to medieval scholasticism, either to establish new ties with the new science (the Newtonian synthesis in England and Scottish commonsense realism in America), or to abandon the external objective world of nature and society altogether and find a place in the interior subjective world of the human heart (the various forms of pietist and romantic religion).[62]

Once science was free to proceed "as if" God did not exist, however, it turned its own method to the analysis of the hypothesis of God. The first "scientific" explanations of the origins of the first primitive religion, from which all later religions were supposed to have sprung, concluded that the genealogy of religion could be traced back either to the fears and impotence of primitive humanity in the face of the superior forces of nature; to the first bubbling and stammering attempts of the human mind to understand its own psyche, its own dreams and visions; or to the attempts of the first social groups to understand and represent themselves. Religion was therefore either primitive physics (naturism) or primitive psychology (animism) or primitive sociology (totemism), all of which would inevitably be replaced by the corresponding modern scientific paradigms.[63] With the replacement of religious worldviews by scientific ones, science would become, in Weber's formulation, the final carrier of the universal process of disenchantment which religion itself had initiated by progressively freeing itself from magic. In the final act of this process, scientific worldviews themselves would succumb to the process of secularization as science, accepting its own self-limitations, disenchanted its own "charisma of reason." At the end of the process, science's own self-misconceptions, as the path to *true* art, to *true* nature, to God, or to happiness, would reveal themselves as so many illusions.[64]

While the cognitive critique of religion was directed against the truth claims of religious worldviews, the practical-political critique was directed against the ideological functions of religious institutions. In their struggles against the absolutist alliance of throne and altar, the philosophes came almost naturally to an alternative explanation of the historical origins of revealed religion. Fascinated by ancient mystery religions and by their own personal experiences with esoteric initiations into secret Masonic societies or forced underground into conspiratorial societies, the philosophes arrived at an explanation of religion as a grand historical conspiracy between priests and rulers to maintain the people ignorant, subject, and oppressed. Voltaire's *écrasez l'infâme* served as declaration of war against the church and all ecclesiastical institutions. The radical Enlightenment reveled in exposing sacred texts as forgery, sacred practices as contagious pathologies, religious founders as impostors, and priests as slothful hypocrites, imbeciles, or perverts. The same methods which Catholic rationalism had applied to popular religious superstitions and which sectarian Protestantism had turned against Catholic popery were now turned against revealed religion and any form of clericalism. Of the three forms of religion analyzed by Rousseau—"the religion of man," "the religion of the citizen," and "the religion of the priest"—it is the third which "is so evidently bad that it would be losing time to demonstrate its evils."[65] Indeed, the presence or absence of anticlericalism is the best indicator of the suitability as well as the effectiveness of the political critique of religion in any given country.

All the branches of the Enlightenment agreed that this "religion of the priest," the Roman church and all established churches, was bound to disappear with the fall of the ancien régime and the establishment of political liberties. But some currents of the Enlightenment balked at what they feared to be the consequences of a society without religion. A conservative tradition, best represented by the deist Voltaire, who was mindful of the consequences atheism and libertine discourse could have upon his own servants, upheld the ancient theory of double truth, wanting to preserve the ancient distance between the agnostic educated elites and the superstitious masses. The liberal tradition, while favoring the "religion of man," was tolerant of any religion as long as it was properly disestablished from the state and separated from the economy—as long as it was privatized. In such a form, liberal statesmen and entrepreneurs concurred, religion was even useful. Generally, enlightened liberal thinkers had no difficulty in finding modern religious reality faithfully depicted in Gibbon's celebrated passage on ancient religion: "The various modes of worship which prevailed in the Roman world, were all considered by the people, as equally true; by the philosopher, as equally false; and by the magistrate, as equally useful."[66]

Another current, which will culminate in Durkheimian sociology, mindful of the anomic and unsolidary consequences of a society governed solely by utilitarian norms and egoist self-interest, postulated the need for a new secular "civil religion" to play a societal, normative-integrative function. Only the radical materialists, Holbachian or Marxian, followed the logical consequences of their atheism. The Holbachians were convinced that the secular sovereign through the proper administration of pain and pleasure could do without the need for religious legitimation or normative integration. Not the priest but the hangman was the ultimate guarantor of social order.[67] Marx, recognizing that religion was not only the ideology of the oppressor but also "the sigh of the oppressed creature" and "the inverted consciousness of an inverted world," argued that the need for state repression, the need for religious consolation, and the need for false consciousness would last as long as their common source, class societies, endured. It was "the task of history" to carry to completion the process of secularization initiated by capitalist development, to construct a fully rational, socialist society which would "strip off its mystical veil" and "offer to man none but perfectly intelligible and reasonable relations to his fellowmen and to Nature."[68]

Marx's critique of religion, however, already proceeds from "the anthropological turn of the religious question."[69] This anthropocentric turn was first developed by the Left Hegelians, most systematically in Feuerbach's theory of religion as "projection" and "self-alienation," was continued in three different directions by Marx, Nietzsche, and Freud in their critiques of religion, and came together once again in the early Critical Theory of the Frankfurt school.[70] It is perhaps not surprising that the subjective, aesthetic, and moral critique of religion would emerge and be most effective in Lutheran Germany, while the cognitive and political critiques had thrived in Catholic France and somewhat belatedly and in milder form in Anglican England. After all, it was Luther who in his pamphlet *The Freedom of a Christian* had created a radical chasm between the realm of freedom and the realm of unfreedom, assigning freedom to the "inner" man, to the "inner" sphere of the person, while the "outer" person was irremediably subject to the system of worldly powers.[71] The external world of society and nature was literally left to the Devil, while religion underwent a visible process of subjective internalization. By withdrawing to the inner subjective expressive sphere, by becoming a pietist religion of the heart, Lutheranism and all modern forms of expressive religion became relatively immune to the scientific critique of religious worldviews and to the political critique of ecclesiastical institutions. The sphere of politics was indeed the sphere of violence and evil. As a state church, the Lutheran church also partook of this sphere, but Lutheranism introduced the principle of a double morality, a secular one for the outer sphere of the "office" and a Christian one for the "inner" sphere of the person, so that the freedom of "inner religion" was assured.[72]

If, as Engels pointed out, the publication of Feuerbach's *The Essence of Christianity* was received with such a general enthusiasm and the book had such a liberating effect upon its readers, certainly upon the

Left Hegelians,[73] it was because it expressed in the most simple and unambiguous terms a widely shared but not yet verbalized experience: that the essence of Christianity is humanity, that theology is anthropology, and that the object of religion, God, is nothing but the expression of the essence of man. Feuerbach insists that the point of departure of his atheism is not the cognitive positivist postulate that "religion is an absurdity, a nullity, a pure illusion," nor the political anticlerical postulate that religion is a priestly conspiracy or that the Gospels are a forgery and "the life of Jesus" a myth but, rather, the recognition that religion itself teaches us atheism, since "religion itself. . .in its heart, in its essence, believes in nothing else than the truth and divinity of human nature."[74] Moreover, he added, he was not inventing anything since "theology has long since become anthropology." Luther had already shifted the interest from God's ontological essence to what God is for man, that is, to Christology, and Schleiermacher had reduced religion to mere "feeling." The consequences of such a reduction could only be, as Hegel pointed out in his critique of Schleiermacher, that religion, god, and the religious experience all would dissolve into mere subjectivism.[75] Indeed, any theology that begins with human subjective states cannot but produce anthropological statements. Feuerbach could, therefore, conclude that religion is "the solemn unveiling of a man's hidden treasures, the revelation of his intimate thoughts, the open confession of his love secrets."[76]

"To enrich God, man must become poor; that God may be all, man must be nothing."[77] This being the secret of divine omnipotence and human impotence, it was time to reclaim as their own the self-alienated essence which humans had projected onto heaven. It was time to stop the sensual renunciation, the self-denial, religious asceticism in all its forms. For the young Marx, "It was now no longer a question of the struggle of the layman with the *priest outside himself,* but rather of his struggle with his *own inner priest,* with his *priestly nature.*"[78] If, as Feuerbach said, "religion is the dream of the human mind," then not the positivist critique of theology but the psychoanalytic interpretation of dreams is the adequate method of critique of religion. It was time, as Freud said, to recognize that religious illusions expressed powerful human desires longing to be fulfilled, that "as a universal obsessional neurosis" religion was based on the *repression* and *displacement* of *instinctual impulses.* It was time for humanity to "come of age," to abandon its infantile narcissism, to accept *the reality principle,* to reconcile itself with *culture* and to overcome all the *discontents* that result from the deprivations and instinctual controls which culture demands.[79]

Through his own method of deep psychological introspection, Nietzsche arrived at similarly radical but different conclusions. It was no longer a question of mere scientific atheism and the maturity required to do without religion and without surrogate paternal authority. The naked truth unveiled by the *genealogy of morals,* much harder to accept than Freud's *reality principle* and all the scientific *facts,* was that the entire structure of modern civilization, its rational secular moralities, and its religion of humanity were nothing but a secularized form of Judeo-Christianity—the *cleverest revenge* of that *priestly caste* which had proven to be unmatched *wizards* as carriers of the contagious *hysteria of the ascetic ideal* and as *diverters of the course of resentment.*[80] Precisely, for that reason, the infinite ocean left empty by *the death of god* could not simply be filled by humanity. Only the birth of the *superman,* in possession of a transmoral conscience *beyond good and evil,* could surmount nihilism and avert the impending catastrophes modern societies were facing.

All the thinkers of the nineteenth-century German Enlightenment and anti-Enlightenment, in reacting against Hegel's last-ditch effort to establish a Christian-philosophical synthesis, simply took for granted, like Feuerbach, that

Christianity has in fact long vanished, not only from the reason but from the life of mankind, that it is nothing more than a *fixed idea,* in flagrant contradiction with our fire and life assurance companies, our railroads and steam carriages, our picture and sculpture galleries, our military and industrial schools, our theaters and scientific museums.[81]

In such a world, whatever residual religion, if any, still remains becomes so subjective and privatized that it turns "invisible," that is, marginal and irrelevant from a societal point of view.

The Privatization of Religion Thesis

The most elaborate and systematic formulations of the privatization of religion thesis are to be found in the works of Thomas Luckmann and Niklas Luhmann. The point of departure and main assumptions of the privatization thesis are that the process of secularization has largely run its course, that the process is most likely "irreversible," and that the consequences of this process for the Christian or any other religion are the ones which Wolfgang Schluchter has summarized into two theses:

(1) As far as the world views are concerned, largely completed secularization means that religious beliefs have become subjective as a result of the rise of alternative interpretations of life, which in principle can no longer be integrated into a religious world view.

(2) As far as the institutions are concerned, largely completed secularization means that institutionalized religion has been de-politicized as a result of a functional differentiation of society, which in principle can no longer be integrated through institutionalized religion.[82]

These two related theses were first elaborated systematically by Luckmann and later reformulated by Luhmann in the language of systems theory.

In *The Invisible Religion,* Luckmann radicalized the thesis of secularization by arguing, first, that traditional religious institutions were becoming increasingly irrelevant and marginal to the functioning of the modern world, and that modern religion itself was no longer to be found inside the churches.[83] The modern quest for salvation and personal meaning had withdrawn to the private sphere of the self. Anticipating later analyses of narcissism and of the "new religious consciousness," Luckmann argued that "self-expression" and "self-realization" had become the "invisible religion" of modernity. Luckmann's explanation is tied to theories of institutional and role differentiation. Modern differentiation leads to a sharp segmentation of the various institutional domains whereby each domain becomes an autonomous sphere governed by its own "functionally rational" internal norms. The person qua person becomes irrelevant for the functionally rational domains, which come to depend increasingly on abstract, impersonal, replaceable role performances. Since the individual's social existence becomes a series of unrelated performances of anonymous specialized social roles, institutional segmentation reproduces itself as segmentation within the individual's consciousness.

Since religious institutions undergo a process of differentiation and institutional specialization similar to that of other institutional domains, religious roles also become specialized, "part-time roles" within the individual conscience. The more the performance of the nonreligious roles becomes determined by autonomous "secular" norms, the less plausible become the traditional global claims of religious norms. Consequently, "a meaningful integration of specifically religious and nonreligious performances and norms with their respective jurisdictional claims remains a problem."[84] In principle there are several typical solutions to the problem, from (a) "a prereflective attitude in which one shifts from 'secular' to religious performances in routine fashion" to (b) a reflective reconstitution of individual religiosity after some search to (c) the adoption of competing "secular" value systems.[85] Crucial is the fact that the individual can and thus has to choose at least implicitly one of those solutions. Irrespective of the choice, the solution will be, therefore, an individualistic one. The free choice, in turn, determines the consumer attitude that the "autonomous" individual manifests vis-à-vis a widened range of options. As a buyer, the individual confronts a wide assortment of "religious" representations, traditional religious ones as well as secular new ones, manufactured, packaged, and sold by specialized service agencies, out of which the individual constructs and reconstructs—either alone or in congregation with like-minded selves—a necessarily precarious private system of ultimate meanings.

Significant for the structure of the modern world is the fact that this quest for subjective meaning is a strictly personal affair. The primary "public" institutions (state, economy) no longer need or are interested in maintaining a sacred cosmos or a public religious worldview. In other words, modern societies do not need to be organized as "churches," in the Durkheimian sense, that is, as moral communities unified by a commonly shared system of practices and beliefs. Individuals are on their own in their private efforts to patch together the fragments into a subjectively meaningful whole. Whether the individuals themselves are able to integrate these segmented performances into "a system of *subjective* significance" is not a relevant question for the dominant economic and political institutions—so long at least as it does not affect their efficient functioning adversely. In any case, it is amply evident that capitalist markets and administrative states can live with a lot of individual and social "anomie" before reaching a Durkheimian crisis of social integration. Luckmann shows, moreover, how the modern sanctification of "subjective autonomy" and the retreat of the individual to the private sphere serves de facto to legitimate and reinforce the "autonomy of the primary institutions." In this respect, Durkheim was correct in viewing "the cult of the individual" as a social product, as the new social form of religion which modern societies have created for themselves. But as Luckmann points out, "By bestowing a sacred quality upon the increasing subjectivity of human existence it supports not only the secularization but also what we called the dehumanization of the social structure."[86] Luckmann concludes by noting pessimistically that even though one may view such "dehumanizing" modern trends as undesirable, they may have become nonetheless "irreversible."

Niklas Luhmann's systems theory elaborated further Luckmann's functionalist thesis. Luhmann's theory distinguishes between three different *forms* of differentiation of society (segmentation, stratification, and functional differentiation). In so doing it offers a convincing answer to the problem posed by Durkheim's theory of the *division of labor*. Working within the Durkheimian tradition, Luhmann shows that functionally differentiated modern societies do not require and are unlikely to have the kind of normative societal "positive" integration postulated by Durkheim.[87] Thus, any theory of modern religion which postulates the likelihood of the "birth of new gods" or the "return of the sacred" or "religious revivals" or the existence of a "civil religion" on the basis of society's functional need for normative integration is based on untenable premises. Luhmann's theory of functional differentiation is also well situated to explain why the privatization of religion is a dominant trend in modernity. Indeed, when viewed from such a perspective, Durkheim's sociology of religion becomes to a large extent irrelevant to an understanding of religion in the modern world.

The theory and the thesis of privatization become problematic, however, when they are applied in such a way that the thesis of privatization, from being a testable and falsifiable empirical theory of dominant historical trends, is turned into a prescriptive normative theory of how religious institutions ought to behave in the modern world. Schluchter's discussion of "the irreversibility of secularization" may serve to illustrate the dangers implicit in such a use of the theory of functional differentiation. On the basis of the two theses stated above Schluchter asks two questions:

(1) Is there a legitimate religious resistance to secular world views that is more than a refusal to accept the consequences of the Enlightenment?

(2) Is there a legitimate religious resistance to de-politicization, a resistance that is more than a clinging to inherited privileges?[88]

My answer to both questions, on the basis of the empirical evidence I am going to present in the five case studies, is an unconditional yes. This does not mean that the evidence supports the thesis of the reversibility of secularization. It only means that both questions are formulated in such a way that they prejudge the relationship between secular worldviews and Enlightenment and the relationship between religious politicization and threats to functional differentiation. A theory which is not flexible enough to account for the possibility that some secular worldviews may actually be anti-Enlightenment and that religious resistance in such cases may be legitimate and on the side of Enlightenment is not complex enough to deal with the historical "contingencies" of a yet unfinished modernity and of a not yet completed secularization.

Indeed, the theory should not start with the premise that "there must be a fundamental tension and conflict between a religious and a secular world view, between religious and secular humanist conduct."[89] We may say with some confidence that currently, at least in America, both religious "fundamentalists" and fundamentalist "secular humanists" are cognitive minorities, that the majority of Americans tend to be humanists, who are simultaneously religious and secular. The theory of secularization should be reformulated in such a way that this empirical reality ceases to be a paradox. If, as Schluchter himself recognizes, the tension has lessened and "the old front lines have largely crumbled," it is not only because the Enlightenment has lost some of its fundamentalist anti-religious edge, as a result of the disenchantment of its own charisma of reason. The rapprochement has been reciprocal, for religion has often served and continues to serve as a bulwark against "the dialectics of enlightenment" and as a protector of human rights and humanist values against the secular spheres and their absolute claims to internal functional autonomy.[90] Indeed, religion could even serve as a bulwark against the claims of systems theory that humanist self-referential conceptualizations are theoretical anachronisms; that is, religion could stand against all posthumanity and posthistory theses.

The theory of secularization should also be complex enough to account for the historical "contingency" that there may be legitimate forms of "public" religion in the modern world, which have a political role to play which is not necessarily that of "positive" societal integration; that there may be forms of "public" religion which do not necessarily endanger modern functional differentiation; and that there may be forms of "public" religion which allow for the privatization of religion and for the pluralism of subjective religious beliefs. In order to be able to conceptualize such possibilities the theory of secularization will need to reconsider three of its particular, historically based—that is, ethnocentric—prejudices: its bias for Protestant subjective forms of religion, its bias for "liberal" conceptions of politics and of the "public sphere," and its bias for the sovereign nation-state as the systemic unit of analysis.

Unlike secular differentiation, which remains a structural trend that serves to define the very structure of modernity, the privatization of religion is a historical option, a "preferred option" to be sure, but an option nonetheless. Privatization is preferred internally from within religion as evinced by general pietistic trends, by processes of religious individuation, and by the reflexive nature of modern religion. Privatization is constrained externally by structural trends of differentiation which force religion into a circumscribed and differentiated religious sphere. Privatization is mandated ideologically by liberal categories of thought which permeate modern political and constitutional theories.

Indeed, it is only by questioning the liberal private-public distinction as it relates to religion, and by elaborating alternative conceptualizations of the public sphere, that one can disentangle the thesis of privatization from the thesis of differentiation and thus begin to ascertain the conditions of possibility for modern public religions.

2   Private and Public Religions

> Binary distinctions are an analytic procedure, but their use-
> fulness does not guarantee that existence divides like that.
> We should look with suspicion on anyone who declared
> that there are two kinds of people, or two kinds of reality
> or process.—Mary Douglas[1]

Of all social phenomena none is perhaps as protean and, consequently, as unsusceptible to binary classification as religion. Of all dichotomous pairs of relational terms few are as ambiguous, multivocal, and open to discursive contestation as the private/public distinction. Yet the private/public distinction is crucial to all conceptions of the modern social order and religion itself is intrinsically connected with the modern historical differentiation of private and public spheres. As inaccurate as it may be as an empirical statement, to say that "religion is a private affair" is nonetheless constitutive of Western modernity in a dual sense. First, it points to the fact that religious freedom, in the sense of freedom of conscience, is chronologically "the first freedom" as well as the precondition of all modern freedoms.[2] Insofar as freedom of conscience is intrinsically related to "the right to privacy"—to the modern institutionalization of a private sphere free from governmental intrusion as well as free from ecclesiastical control—and inasmuch as "the right to privacy" serves as the very foundation of modern liberalism and of modern individualism, then indeed the privatization of religion is essential to modernity.[3]

There is yet another sense in which the privatization of religion is intrinsically related to the emergence of the modern social order. To say that in the modern world "religion becomes private" refers also to the very process of institutional differentiation which is constitutive of modernity, namely, to the modern historical process whereby the secular spheres emancipated themselves from ecclesiastical control as well as from religious norms. Religion was progressively forced to withdraw from the modern secular state and the modern capitalist economy and to find refuge in the newly found private sphere. Like modern science, capitalist markets and modern state bureaucracies manage to function "as if" God would not exist. This forms the unassailable core of modern theories of secularization, a core which remains unaffected by the frequent assertions of critics who rightly point out that most people in the modern world still, or yet again, believe in God and that religions of all kinds, old and new, manage to thrive in the modern world.

Theories of secularization, however, have greater difficulty in answering those critics who point out that the modern walls of separation between church and state keep developing all kinds of cracks through which both are able to penetrate each other; that religious institutions often refuse to accept their assigned marginal place in the private sphere, managing to assume prominent public roles; that religion and politics keep forming all kinds of symbiotic relations, to such an extent that it is not easy to ascertain whether one is witnessing political movements which don religious garb or religious movements which assume political forms.[4]

Thus, while religion in the modern world continues to become ever more privatized, one is also witnessing simultaneously what appears to be a process of "deprivatization" of religion. To deal with this paradox, we need to examine once again the various meanings of the distinction between private and public religions. Without trying to develop an exhaustive and universally valid classificatory scheme, the following conceptual clarification has a threefold aim: (1) to serve as a conceptual tool in the interpretation of what could be called "varieties of public religion" in the modern world; (2) to reveal the extent to which theories of secularization double as empirically descriptive theories of modern social processes and as normatively prescriptive theories of modern societies, and thus serve to legitimize ideologically a particular historical form of institutionalization of modernity; and (3) to examine whether public religions may not play a role in redrawing the contested boundaries between the private and the public spheres in the modern world.

On the Private/Public Distinction

In "The Theory and Politics of the Public/Private Distinction," Jeff Weintraub has reconstructed four major ways in which distinctions between "public" and "private" are currently made in social analysis:

(1) The liberal-economistic model . . . which sees the public/private distinction primarily in terms of the distinction between state administration and the market economy.

(2) The republican-virtue (and classical) approach, which sees the "public" realm in terms of political community and citizenship, analytically distinct from *both* the market and the administrative state.

(3) The approach, exemplified for example by the work of Ariès (and other figures in social history and anthropology), which sees the "public" realm as a sphere of fluid and polymorphous sociability.

(4) A tendency . . . in certain kinds of economic history and feminist analysis, to conceive of the distinction between "private" and "public" in terms of the

distinction between the family and the market economy (with the latter becoming the "public" realm).[5]

Some of the terminological disagreements may be due to the difficulties of fitting the reality of modernity, which at least since Hegel has been known to be tripartite—family, civil/bourgeois society, and state—into the binary and dichotomous categories of "public" and "private," which to a large extent derive from the dualistic differentiation of the ancient city into *oikos* and *polis*. The novelty of modernity derives precisely from the emergence of an amorphously complex, yet autonomous sphere, "civil society" or "the social," which stands "between public and private" proper, yet has expansionist tendencies aiming to penetrate and absorb both. The actual empirical boundaries between the three spheres, moreover, are highly porous and constantly shifting, thus creating interpenetrations between the three. Indeed, each of the three spheres may be said to have both private and public dimensions.[6]

Since social reality itself is not dichotomous, the use of binary categories leads necessarily either to the clear delimitation of one of the poles, leaving the rest of reality as an amorphous residual category, or to the clear delimitation of the two extreme poles, leaving a no less amorphous residual sphere between public and private.[7] Those conceptions, for instance, which begin with a clear delimitation of the private sphere, understood either as the sphere of the individual self or as the intimate sphere of domestic and personal relations, tend to place all the rest into an undifferentiated category of "the public." Erving Goffman's sociology may serve as an extreme illustration. What Goffman calls "the field of public life" embraces the entire realm of face-to-face interaction, including the "face-to-face interaction within a private domestic establishment."[8] The private sphere proper is restricted to the "backstage," where the individual can relax unobserved before donning the theatrical personae which the public self will play in the strategic performance of "interaction rituals" in public places. By contrast those liberal conceptions which begin with a delimitation of the public sphere as the governmental public sector tend to group all other spheres into an undifferentiated "nongovernmental" private sector.[9]

But some of the conceptual differences between the various positions are not solely terminological, nor are they simply due to different perceptions as to where the actual empirical boundaries lie in reality itself. To a large extent they reflect, as Weintraub points out, "deeper differences in theoretical (and ideological) commitments."[10] In other words, they are normative counterfactual critiques of the actual historical differentiation between the public and private spheres in the modern world, as well as

ideological critiques of the conceptual reifications which serve to legitimate modern historical trends. Among the recent critiques one could
mention: (a) classical/republican critiques of the modern tendency to
reduce the political to the governmental sphere of the administrative
state, a tendency which contributes to the dissolution of the "public
sphere" proper;[11] (b) republican virtue critiques of modern utilitarian
individualism with its tendency to reduce the public interest to the aggre-
gation of individual private interests, or to privatize morality, reducing it
to subjectivist emotivism or solipsist value-decisionism;[12] and (c) feminist
critiques of the dichotomy between a male, public, political, and immoral
realm and a female, private, apolitical, and moral realm.[13]

Against those evolutionary theories which prefer to interpret what I
call the "deprivatization" of modern religion as antimodern fundamentalist reactions to inevitable processes of modern differentiation, I argue
that at least some forms of "public religion" may also be understood as
counterfactual normative critiques of dominant historical trends, in
many respects similar to the classical, republican, and feminist critiques.
The public impact of those religious critiques should not be measured
solely in terms of the ability of any religion to impose its agenda upon
society or to press its global normative claims upon the autonomous
spheres. In modern differentiated societies it is both unlikely and undesirable that religion should again play the role of systemic normative integration. But by crossing boundaries, by raising questions publicly about
the autonomous pretensions of the differentiated spheres to function
without regard to moral norms or human considerations, public religions
may help to mobilize people against such pretensions, they may contribute to a redrawing of the boundaries, or, at the very least, they may
force or contribute to a public debate about such issues. Irrespective of
the outcome or the historical impact of such a debate, religions will have
played an important public role. Like feminist critiques or like republican
virtue critiques of modern developments, they will have functioned as
counterfactual normative critiques. Besides, one does not need to accept
the normative premises of such religious critiques in order to recognize
that they may help to reveal the particular and contingent historical
character of modern developments and to question the normativity of
modern facticity.

Private and Public Religions from the Perspective of
Religious Differentiation

Some aspects of the modern differentiation between private and public
religions already appear within the social scientific study of religion as

the distinction between "individual" and "group" religiosity at the interaction level of analysis; as the distinction between "religious community" and "community cult" at the organizational level of analysis; and
as the distinction between "religion" and "world" at the societal level
of analysis.[14]

"Individual and Group Religiosity"

Religion . . . shall mean for us *the feelings, acts, and experiences of individual
men in their solitude, so far as they apprehend themselves to stand in relation
to whatever they may consider the divine.*—William James[15]

Religion is not an arbitrary relation of the individual man to a supernatural
power; it is a relation of all the members of a community to the power that has
the god of the community at heart.—Robertson Smith[16]

One could hardly find two apparently more incompatible positions.
William James and the individualist school insist that "personal religion"
is primordial, while all the institutional aspects of religion—"worship
and sacrifice, procedures for working on the dispositions of the deity,
theology and ceremony and ecclesiastical organization"—are secondary.[17] Stretching his methodological individualism somewhat, one could
perhaps place Weber in this camp, since Weber also views individual
charisma, "the personal gift of grace," as the essential and elementary
form of religious life, while religious roles and institutions he analyzes
as the result of "routinization of charisma."[18] However, Weber's own
theory of charisma implies that the personal power of charisma can be
confirmed and maintained only by the recognition of others. Charisma,
in this sense, is an eminently intersubjective—social—category. It ex-
presses a relation between leaders and followers, which is the foundation
for the transformation of charisma into institutional religion. Without
its institutionalization into some kind of elementary charismatic community, personal charisma remains an autistic, sociologically and historically irrelevant experience.

By contrast, the collectivist school of thought, best represented by W.
Robertson Smith and Émile Durkheim, insists that religion is always a
group, a collective, affair; that there is no religion without "a unified
system of beliefs and practices . . . which unite into, one single moral
community." Durkheim recognizes that there is scarcely a society without "the private religions which the individual establishes for himself
and celebrates by himself," but he insists that "these individual cults are
not distinct and autonomous religious systems," that individual religion
either is simply derived from group religion or is no religion at all,
but magic. Indeed, the presence or absence of a church is, according to

Durkheim, what helps define both religion and magic: there is no religion without a church; there is no church of magic.[19]

All attempts so far to reduce religion to one of the two poles while excluding or explaining the other as a derivation of the former have been unsatisfactory. The attempt to solve the problem by ordering both forms of religion in an evolutionary sequence, which normally runs from primitive, collective religion to modern, individual religion, has proven equally problematic, irrespective of the fact that one can show clear historical trends in this direction. Malinowski showed conclusively that "even in primitive societies the heightening of emotions and the lifting of the individual out of himself are by no means restricted to gatherings and to crowd phenomena."[20] While Durkheim may have been correct in stressing the public nature of primitive cults, he failed to recognize that "much of religious revelation takes place in solitude." Against Durkheim, Malinowski shows that the *religious* and the *collective* are not necessarily coextensive; that much religion is individual and private, while much collective effervescence and many public ceremonies have no religious meaning.[21]

"Community Cults versus Religious Communities"

The primeval cult, and above all, the cult of the political association, have left all individual interests out of consideration. . . . Thus, in the community cult, the collectivity as such turned to its god. The individual, in order to avoid or remove evils that concerned himself—above all, sickness—has not turned to the cult of the community, but as an individual he has approached the sorcerer as the oldest personal and "spiritual adviser." . . . Under favorable conditions this has led to the formation of a religious "community," which has been independent of ethnic associations. Some, though not all, "mysteries" have taken this course. They have promised the salvation of individuals *qua* individuals from sickness, poverty, and from all sorts of distress and danger.—Max Weber[22]

A similar distinction between public "community cults" and private "religious communities" is drawn by Robertson Smith when he writes that "religion did not exist for the saving of souls but for the preservation and welfare of society" and that "it is only in times of social dissolution . . . that magical superstition . . . invade[s] the sphere of tribal or national religion."[23]

The two types of religion correspond to two different types of community with different membership entry rules. In the case of community cults, the political and religious communities are coextensive. Consequently, one is born into community cults and membership in both the sociopolitical and the religious community coincides.[24] Durkheim, following Robertson Smith and Fustel de Coulanges, correctly viewed the god of the community cult as the symbolic representation and sacralization of the community. Incorrectly, however, he presented as a general, universal theory of religion what in fact turns out to be a particular theory of one of its forms.

Religious communities, by contrast, are constituted in and through the association and congregation of individuals in response to a religious message. Originally, at its inception, the religious community is separate from and not coextensive with the political community, although it may soon also assume a political form. The most developed form of religious communities, "salvation religions," represents an individualized and usually privatized form of religion which is primarily constituted through the personal relationship with the savior, the personal God, the prophet, or the spiritual adviser. They are "twice-born" religions which presuppose the experience of "a sick soul" in need of redemption, of a "divided self" in need of "unification."[25] Because they release the individual from particularistic, ascriptive ties, salvation religions are potentially conducive to the formation of universalistic religious communities through processes of ever wider fraternization (and sororization).[26]

Strictly speaking, those are analytical ideal types. While one may find both types of religion side by side in some societies, normally most religions will be mixed types presenting some combination of elements from both. Usually religions perform social as well as psychological functions and meet collective as well as individual needs. But in certain historical periods or stages of development as well as in particular cultures and religious traditions, one form may clearly predominate over the other. Neither the typological variations nor the dynamics of transformation could be discussed properly, though, without entering into the systemic level of analysis to take into account the process of differentiation of the religious and the political spheres, as well as the internal process of rationalization of the religious sphere. It is unnecessary to retrace here the ground so painstakingly explored by Max Weber in this area. Only a few critical remarks are in order:

It should be obvious that the form of the community cult will be determined primarily, other things being equal (something that rarely happens in history), by the type of political community: clan, tribe, confederation, kingdom, empire, republic, nation-state, and so on. But we would lose ourselves trying to cover all the possible variations and combinations. After Weber's work, it is even more obvious that the form of the religious community is determined primarily, again other things being equal, by the content and structure of the religious message itself and by the dynamics of the ideal and material interests of those groups and strata to which the religious message is originally addressed. But the truly relevant dynamics historically emerge when the two forms—the dynamics of community cult formation and the dynamics of religious community formation—meet, fuse, interpenetrate, and repel each other in all kinds of combinations.

The Christian "church" is only one particular historical type of combination of religious community and political community, which emerged out of the complex encounter of the Christian religious community and the Roman imperial state structure. This is a truism, which needs to be repeated, however, since sociologists still tend to use the typology developed by Weber and Troeltsch as general ideal types, applicable to other times and places, when "church" and "sect" are strictly speaking "historical" ideal types, which are misleading when applied uncritically to non-Western contexts and are equally misleading when applied to modern times after the emergence of an altogether different and radically new form of political community, the modern state. The early Christian church was a particular, almost typical, form of congregational "religious community" or "salvation religion," organized around the soteriological-eschatological cult of Christ, which after a period of clear separation from the Roman political community and confrontation with the Roman imperial structure was adopted by the Roman Empire as its "community cult."[27] Afterwards, with the disintegration of the Western Roman Empire, the Christian religious community itself adopted the political machinery and the administrative and legal structure of the imperial state, becoming in the process a salvation religion with the political structure of an imperial state.

Such a "church," such a particular combination of salvation religion and political community, is unlikely to appear anywhere else, even though Islam and Buddhism, the other two great universalistic salvation religions, have developed their own various combinations of political and religious communities.[28] All modern territorial national churches cease to be sociologically speaking a "church" the moment they cease being compulsory, coercive, monopolistic "sacramental grace institutions." This happens either when the church loses its own means of coercion and enforcement, or when the state is no longer willing or able to use its means of coercion to maintain the compulsory and monopolistic position of the church. Indeed, the moment heretical "sects" and "apostasy" are officially tolerated within the same political community, or the principle of religious freedom becomes institutionalized, even the still established state church ceases being, strictly speaking, a "church." The differentiation of religious community and community cult re-emerges once again, but now along a separate modern secular state which no longer needs a religious community cult to integrate and maintain the political community. The precariousness of "established" national churches (Lutheran, Anglican, Catholic, and Orthodox alike) in the modern world is understandable, caught as they are between a secular state which no longer needs them as community cults and people who prefer to join religious communities, if and when they want to satisfy their individual religious needs.

Islam is the unique historical case of a religion which was born simultaneously as a religious charismatic community of salvation and as a political community. This was expressed in the dual religious and political charisma of its founder, Muhammad, as God's messenger and as political and military leader. It is even more literally expressed by the fact that the Islamic era begins not with the birth or death of a founder or with the date of revelation but, rather, with the *hijra,* or migration, which marks the foundation of the Islamic political community in Medina ("the City"). The *umma,* the Islamic community, has seen itself most of the time as simultaneously a religious community and a political community, the community of believers and the nation of Islam. But it is totally inaccurate to argue that Islam has no differentiated religious and political spheres. Indeed, the history of Islam could be viewed as the history of the various institutionalizations of the dual religious and political charisma of Muhammad into dual and differentiated religious and political institutions.[29]

Understandably, the foundational myth of any charismatic community has a special paradigmatic power in the historical transmission of traditions, particularly when the foundational myth can avail itself of the force of God's revelation. Rebellions, reformations, revolutions, and all kinds of historical changes can be introduced in the name of the foundational myth, while claiming to be reverting to the pristine purity of origins, to a time before any accommodation to the world had taken place. Like other religions, Christianity also had to find its own accommodation to modernity and to the differentiation of the secular spheres. But Christianity, particularly sectarian Protestantism, could eventually embrace both modernity and secularization as a return to the primitive church, when an exclusive religious community of salvation was organized separate from the political community. Similarly, the Catholic "reformation" in the twentieth century has taken the form of a conscious rejection of "Constantinian Christendom."[30]

Religion and "World"

Know that you can have three sorts of relations with princes, governors, and oppressors. The first and worst is that you visit them, the second and the better is that they visit you, and the third and surest that you stay far from them, so that neither you see them nor they see you.—Abu Hamid Muhammad al-Ghazzali

This statement by the twelfth-century Muslim theologian captures most succinctly the basic options, as well as the typical and traditional attitude of all salvation religions toward the world of politics, and toward the "world" in general. Buddhists, Christians, and Muslims may read the statement differently, since their original paradigmatic attitude as well as the historical experience these religions have accumulated through the ages may vary significantly. Nonetheless, the three basic options remain and, if made to choose, the three great "world religions" would probably rank the three options in the same order. They fear most, perhaps because they know how frequently they have found themselves unable to resist it even in the modern era, caesaropapism in any form, that is, the "world"'s control and use of religion for its own purposes, most frequently to legitimate political rule and to sanctify economic oppression and the given system of stratification.

The second option, theocracy, the power to influence and shape the world according to God's ways, is always preferable. It is also a very tempting option which even the most otherworldly religions have often found difficult to resist. The will to power of ascetic religion and its power to shape and transform the world while trying to transcend it can be found in the most unexpected places, from the mountains of Tibet to the deserts of Utah. But ultimately all theocratic attempts tend to succumb to the paradox of unintended consequences. The more religion wants to transform the world in a religious direction, the more religion becomes entangled in "worldly" affairs and is transformed by the world. The third option, distance, detachment, and separation, is the one which ultimately tends to prevail and which both religious and worldly people tend to prefer, since it protects the world from religion and religion from the world. None of the three options, however, can permanently resolve the tension between "religion" and "world."

Taking a lofty view of world history while being conscious that such a perspective flattens out all the "differences," one may easily discern two great "axial" shifts in the relation between religion and world. The first axial shift, well noticed by Karl Jaspers and used by Max Weber as the foundation for his world-historical sociology of religion, was the wave of world renunciation which beginning roughly around the sixth century B.C. shook one ancient civilization after another, from India to China, from the Near East to Greece.[31]

The new attitude of world rejection took hold first of intellectuals and elites, of philosophers and prophets. But later, this attitude of devaluation and relativization of this world for the sake of a higher one became democratized and popularized by the new salvation religions, which emerged as the most consequential world-historical result of the axial shift. At least in the case of the Mediterranean basin, this widespread shift from public to private religion, from community cult to mystery and salvation religions, from civic man to inward man, from objectivist to subjectivist philosophy, has been amply documented by historians of ideas and social historians. Peter Brown has explained the paradoxical and revolutionary triumph of Christianity in the ancient pagan world as "the surprisingly rapid democratization of the philosophers' upper-class counterculture by the leaders of the Christian church."[32]

But the inward turn of religion toward the private individual for the sake of salvation is full of public paradoxes and external consequences in the world. Precisely when religion wanted to leave this world alone, the powers of the world could not afford, it seems, to leave religion alone. Jesus' message to abandon the messianic hopes of a worldly kingdom and to find "God's Kingdom" in one's "inner heart" threatened the core of Judaism as a public covenanted religion. The "scandal of the cross" was the punishment for such a public crime. The Roman imperial state, which had abandoned its old republican civil religion, which had incorporated all kinds of foreign gods into its pantheon, which permitted its subjects to pursue privately the most exotic of religions and mystery cults, could not allow that the most private, world-indifferent, and humble of religions, Christianity, would refuse to participate in the only community cult left, the worship of the emperor. Thus, Christians had to meet public persecution.

The Christian "inward" turn toward "otherworldly individualism" had other external, unintended consequences in the world. Otherworldly asceticism showed its Janus face in the combination of world abnegation and world mastery. Historical sociologists starting from very different premises, from Max Weber to Louis Dumont, from Norbert Elias to Michel Foucault, have amply demonstrated that inner discipline has a greater "civilizing" effect than any this-worldly reward or any external discipline and punishment effected by the powers of this world. Certainly, the unique establishment of a "*Civitas Dei*" in this world, of a Roman church with real and significant worldly power, which pretended to rule the world directly or indirectly, was of crucial importance. Some observers have insisted that the historically unique character of the modern state cannot be understood unless one sees it as a secularized, "transformed church." In any case, the story ended paradoxically with an unprecedented commitment of the Christian individual to the world, with a new transformation of the outerworldly individual into the innerworldly individual, with the rise of the modern individual.[33]

Whether one views the joint rise of the modern state and modern capitalism as being codetermined by this new Christian attitude or

whether one sees the new Protestant innerworldly attitude as being determined by the emergence of the modern world system, there is no doubt
that it marks a new axial shift in the relation between religion and world.
Eventually, the world forced religion to withdraw to a newly created
and, for the first time in history, "institutionalized" private sphere. The
new territorial national churches, one after another, were subjected to
royal absolutist control and, despoiled of their large holdings by secularization laws, had to ingratiate themselves more and more with the rising
bourgeois classes. The same dual process will become evident throughout
eighteenth-century Europe: Erastianism, regalism, caesaropapist control
from above, which transformed all branches of Christianity into "established" but impotent community cults of the new nation-states, and a
new pietist turn inward, which liberated the modern individual from the
external, ritual, and sacramental control of the church and transformed
the various denominations ever more into private "religious communities."[34]

Protestantism, used here as an analytical model without entering into
the very significant internal variations within it, pioneered this process
and helped to shape the particular form the process of institutionalized
differentiation of the spheres has taken so far.[35] In this respect, Protestantism set a powerful historical precedent to which other world religions
had, and still have, to respond in their own ways. For centuries, the
Catholic church fought quixotically both the modern innerworldly turn
and the modern differentiation of the spheres as heretic windmills. Finally, with Vatican II came the "official" belated recognition of the legitimacy of the modern world. Throughout the world, Catholicism has been
turning innerworldly with a vengeance. Yet the Catholic church, while
accepting the modern principle of "religious freedom" and thus ceasing
to be for all practical purposes a "church" in the Weberian sense,[36]
continues nonetheless to uphold the "church" principle of an ethical
community. Modern Catholicism wants to be both an innerworldly and
a public religion. But can there be a modern form of public religion that
does not aspire to being an "established," state or societal, church?

Private and Public Religions in the Modern World

Using as an analytical framework the four different ways of conceptualizing the "private/public" distinction examined by Jeff Weintraub, one
could draw in principle four different binary combinations of "private"
and "public" religions. Without aiming to present an exhaustive typology, the resulting types incorporate the threefold distinction between
individual and group religiosity, religious and political community, and

religious and worldly/secular spheres, while illuminating the basic options religions have under conditions of modern differentiation, that is, in the modern differentiated secular world.

Individual Mysticism versus Denominationalism

Beginning with Goffman's sociological rather than political distinction between the private "backstage" sphere of the self and the field of "public life," where face-to-face interaction takes place—a distinction that is clearer than the one drawn by Weintraub from Ph. Ariès's social history—one could distinguish between private individual religiosity, the religion of the private self, and all the public forms of associational religion. This distinction corresponds roughly to the one drawn by Thomas Luckmann between invisible religion and church religion, as well as to the typological distinction between what Ernst Troeltsch called "individual mysticism," or "spiritual religion," and the typically modern form of voluntary, individualistic, and pluralistic religious association, "the denomination." Although it has no place in Troeltsch's tripartite typology, the modern denomination is bound to diffuse and absorb, if not to supersede, what in his view were the two traditional forms of organizational religion, "the church" and "the sect."[37]

It is a commonplace of sociological analysis that the modern differentiation of autonomous spheres leads irremediably to a pluralism of norms, values, and worldviews. Max Weber attributed "the polytheism of modern values" to this differentiation.[38] Undoubtedly, the differentiation of the spheres leads to conflicts between the various gods (Eros, Logos, Nomos, Mars, Leviathan, Mammon, the Muses, etc.). But this conflict can be institutionalized and contained through systemic functional differentiation.[39] In any case, this is not the true source of modern polytheism. If the temple of ancient polytheism was the Pantheon, a place where all known and even unknown gods could be worshiped simultaneously, the temple of modern polytheism is the mind of the individual self. Indeed, modern individuals do not tend to believe in the existence of various gods. On the contrary, they tend to believe that all religions and all individuals worship the same god under different names and languages, only modern individuals reserve to themselves the right to denominate this god and to worship him/her/it in their own peculiar language. Rousseau's "religion of man . . . without temples, altars or rituals," Thomas Paine's "my mind is my church," and Thomas Jefferson's "I am a sect myself" are paradigmatic "high culture" expressions of the modern form of individual religiosity.[40] Deism, the typical fusion of individual mysticism and enlightenment rationalism, is recognizable in all three expressions. "Sheilaism" is the name Robert Bellah et al.

have given to the contemporary "low culture" expression, after one of the people they interviewed actually named her own "faith" after herself, "my own Sheilaism": "I believe in God. I'm not a religious fanatic. I can't remember the last time I went to church. My faith has carried me a long way. It's Sheilaism. Just my own little voice." The interviewers add, "This suggests the logical possibility of over 220 million American religions, one for each of us."[41] The cultic form of modern polytheism is not idolatry but human narcissism. In this particular sense, the cult of the individual has indeed become, as foreseen by Durkheim, the religion of modernity.

While sensing that individual mysticism was the religion of the future, Troeltsch could not anticipate its organizational form: "Since it arose out of the failure of the real ecclesiastical spirit, it finds it difficult to establish satisfactory relations with the churches, and with the conditions of a stable and permanent organization."[42] In America, however, individual mysticism found a fertile soil. Evangelical pietism, "the religion of the heart," was the vehicle which served to spread individual mysticism, democratizing and popularizing it, as it were, throughout American Protestantism whereas denominationalism, the great American religious invention, became its organizational form. Indeed, pietism occupies in the modern transformation of religion the same place MacIntyre attributes to emotivism in the transformation—dissolution—of traditional moral philosophy.

The doctrinal basis of denominationalism had already emerged with the First Great Awakening. But as in Europe, the institutional structure of established churches and sectarian dissent, even though already highly pluralistic, did not permit it to crystallize. First, constitutional disestablishment and, then, the Second Great Awakening transformed Protestant churches and sects alike into denominations. By the 1830s, evangelical Protestantism, organized denominationally, had become de facto the culturally, though not politically, established American civil religion. Following World War II, Catholicism and Judaism were added to the system. "Protestant-Catholic-Jew" became the three respectable denominational forms of American religion. The great religious experimentation of the 1960s left the denominational gates wide open; and by 1970 with the *Welsh* decision, the Supreme Court, which has always regulated the rules of entry into the free, competitive, denominational religious market, basically let in any faith willing to play by the rules.[43] It is the denominational structure of the religious subsystem which transforms all religions in America, irrespective of their origins, doctrinal claims, and ecclesiastical identities, into denominations.[44]

In his comprehensive study of "society and faith since World War II,"

The Restructuring of American Religion, Robert Wuthnow documents in detail the weakening of internal denominational ties, the lessening of interdenominational conflicts and prejudices, and the increasing organization and mobilization of religious resources across rather than through the denominations. He interprets this evidence, however, as "the declining significance of denominationalism," when it could actually be interpreted as a further indication of the logic of denominationalism.[45] From its inception in the First Great Awakening, denominationalism has never meant an absolute exclusive allegiance to one's particular denomination. Those "born-again" souls who have "experienced" individually the redeeming power of the "New Light" have always tended to feel closer fellowship with kindred spirits in other denominations than with "Old Lights" in their own.[46] Once the denominations become particular vehicles for individual religious experience, the external organizational form and the doctrinal content of the particular denomination become ever more secondary. People no longer need to switch denominations to find their own faith, or to join kindred fellows in interdenominational social movements. While this development may indicate the declining significance of the denominational churches, it can also be interpreted as the triumph of the denominational principle.

Even typologically classical sects like Protestant fundamentalism or the classical church, the *Una, Sancta, Catholica, et Apostolica* Roman church, are externally constrained and, more important, internally induced to function as denominations. The myriad "independent" fundamentalist churches and preachers, each and every one of them holier and more fundamentalist than the other, proclaiming "their own" literalist interpretation of the fundamentals of the same Christian faith, contained in the same text, the Holy Bible, attest to the power of modern individualism. The individual, private reading of any text forms a very shaky ground for doctrinal fundamentalism. When those myriad fundamentalist atoms leave their self-imposed private sectarian seclusion in order to organize themselves publicly into a Moral Majority or, in what amounts to the same thing, when those individual resources are skillfully mobilized by political entrepreneurs for collective action, fundamentalism becomes just another denomination.

The Catholic church is exposed to similar internal and external pressures. Recent visits of the pope to the United States have shown conclusively that American Catholics are more than ever willing to express publicly and effusively their union with the "vicar of Christ" and their loyalty to the Holy See. But like other modern individuals, American Catholics seem to reserve for their own consciences the ultimate inalienable right to decide which doctrines from the traditional deposit of faith are truly essential. Even when Catholics accept voluntarily the authority of certain teachings as dogma or authoritative doctrine, the interpretive problem, or leeway, still remains. The meaning and relevance of any written or oral text for any given context still requires interpretation. Increasingly, moreover, it is individuals who are doing the interpretation. Thus, bumper stickers to the contrary, *Roma dixit*, or the fact that God has spoken loud and clear, by no means settles the matter. The history of the great religions of *The Book*, Judaism, Christianity, and Islam, whether or not they have hierocratic ecclesiastical institutions or authoritative schools of interpretation, indicates that they are all caught in the same doctrinal interpretive quagmire. Whenever modern structural differentiation and religious individualism are introduced, the same logic of denominationalism can be found at work. In any case, in the United States one religious organization after another—Protestant churches, Protestant sects, Catholicism, Eastern Christianity, Judaism, Eastern religions, and, lately, Islam—has become a denomination, both internally and vis-à-vis one another. The question that needs to be addressed, however, is whether the denomination, as the modern, voluntary form of religious association based on religious freedom and religious pluralism, can also assume a different kind of "publicity," a political one, in modern differentiated societies.

Established versus Disestablished Religions

Within the liberal political tradition the distinction between private and public religions has always been clearly drawn in terms of the constitutional separation of church and state. In accordance with the liberal tendency to limit the public sphere to the governmental public sector with all the rest lumped into a great "private" sector, established state churches are designated as "public" religions whereas all other religions are considered to be "private." Since the liberal conception tends to conflate and confuse state, public, and political, the disestablishment of religion is understood and prescribed as a simultaneous process of privatization and depoliticization. In the liberal conception religion is and ought to remain a private affair. The liberal fear of the politicization of religion is simultaneously the fear of an establishment which could endanger the individual freedom of conscience and the fear of a deprivatized ethical religion which could bring extraneous conceptions of justice, of the public interest, of the common good, and of solidarity into the "neutral" deliberations of the liberal public sphere.

The incongruence in the liberal conceptualization becomes immediately apparent in the paradoxical contrast between the highly depoliticized and privatized religion of the Established Church of England (or of any national state church which accepts Erastian principles) and the public and political posture of free, congregational, "leveling," nonconformist sects or of any disestablished religion ready to clash with an unjust and sinful state. Even more paradoxical from a liberal political perspective has to be Tocqueville's perceptive and, at least for its time, largely accurate statement that "religion in America takes no direct part in the government of society, but it must be regarded as the first of their political institutions."[47]

The liberal rationale for disestablishment is as valid and unimpeachable today as it always has been. Historical pressures for the separation of church and state emerged from the dual dynamics of internal religious rationalization and the secular state's emancipation from religion. From religion itself came the sectarian demand for "religious freedom." As Georg Jellinek showed conclusively, the modern principle of inalienable human rights originated with the radical sects and was first institutionalized constitutionally in the Bills of Rights of the various American states.[48] Without this religious sectarian input one may reach the principle of religious "toleration," but not necessarily the principle of religious "freedom." Indeed, before becoming the enlightened liberal principle of "freedom of thought," the pressure for toleration more often than not found its historical source in *raison d'état,* in the modern state's exigency to emancipate itself from religion.[49]

The dual "no establishment" and "free exercise" clause of the First Amendment to the U.S. Constitution incorporated this dual historical rationale for separation. This duality has continued to this day to be the source of contestation since, as Thomas Robbins has shown, it can lead to very different interpretations of the principle of separation.[50] A "strict separationist" reading, based on radical sectarian, libertarian, or liberal "neutrality" principles, consistently rejects not only any government support but also any government regulation of religion. The "benevolent separationist" reading, by contrast, based either on the principle of historical tradition and "original intent" or on the functionalist argument of the positive societal functions of religion, rejects government regulation but demands general government support of religion. At the opposite pole, the "secularist" reading, suspicious of religion's negative functions, favors government regulation of religion while denying religion any government support. Finally, even when it accepts formal separation, the "statist" interpretation is also consistent with caesaropapist principles in favoring both government support and government's absolute control of religion.[51]

The limits of the liberal conception derive from its tendency to conceive of all political relations, religious ones included, too narrowly in terms of juridical-constitutional lines of separation. But the problem of the relation between religion and politics cannot be reduced simply to the clear-cut issue of the constitutional separation of church and state. While disestablishment and separation are necessary to guarantee the freedom of religion from the state, the freedom of the state from religion, and the freedom of the individual conscience from both state and organized religion, it does not follow that religion must be privatized in order that these freedoms be guaranteed. Here again it is necessary to make a clear distinction between the legal principle of separation and the liberal normative prescription of privatization. The soundness of the liberal principle of "separation" finds perhaps its best indirect confirmation in the fact that the Catholic church has accepted it after having rejected it obstinately as incompatible with the "church" principle. Indeed, given this incompatibility, the final Catholic recognition of the religious legitimacy of the modern principle of freedom of conscience, a principle which Catholic doctrine now sees grounded in "the sacred dignity of the human person," had to be accompanied by the surrender of its identity as a compulsory institution. The Catholic church in Vatican II, by adopting the principle of "religious freedom," officially ceased being a "church" in the sociological sense of the term. Yet the Catholic church still refuses to accept the related liberal principle of absolute privatization of religion and morality.

There is a sense in which the liberal principle of privatization is also unimpeachable. Insofar as the legal principle of separation is based not solely on *raison d'état* principles or on liberal principles of toleration as necessary conditions for a modern differentiated and pluralist social order but on the very principle of freedom of conscience, which is the foundation of the inviolable "right to privacy"—without which there can be neither a modern democratic state nor a modern civil society— then the "deprivatization" of religion presupposes the privacy of religion and can only be justified if the right to privacy and freedom of conscience are also legally protected from religion.[52] In other words, from the normative perspective of modernity, religion may enter the public sphere and assume a public form only if it accepts the inviolable right to privacy and the sanctity of the principle of freedom of conscience.

This condition is met and, therefore, the deprivatization of religion can be justified in at least three instances:

a) When religion enters the public sphere to protect not only its own freedom of religion but all modern freedoms and rights, and the very right of a democratic civil society to exist against an absolutist, authoritarian state. The active role of the Catholic church in processes of democratization in Spain, Poland, and Brazil may serve to illustrate this instance.

b) When religion enters the public sphere to question and contest the absolute lawful autonomy of the secular spheres and their claims to be organized in accordance with principles of functional differentiation without regard to extraneous ethical or moral considerations. The Pastoral Letters of the American Catholic bishops questioning the "morality" of the arms race and of the state's nuclear policies, as well as the "justice" and inhuman consequences of a capitalist economic system, which tends to absolutize the right to private property and claims to be self-regulated by unchecked market laws, exemplify this second instance.

c) When religion enters the public sphere to protect the traditional life-world from administrative or juridical state penetration, and in the process opens up issues of norm and will formation to the public and collective self-reflection of modern discursive ethics. The public mobilization of the so-called Moral Majority and the Catholic public stand on abortion in support of "the right to life" are examples of this third instance.

In the first instance religion would serve in the very constitution of a liberal political and social order. In the second and third instances religion would serve to show, question, and contest the very "limits" of the liberal political and social order. At the very least, the deprivatization of religion might serve to question the empirical validity of the thesis of privatization of modern religion and, more important, it might force the theory of privatization to question its own normative foundations in the liberal model of the public sphere and in the rigidly juridical separation of the private and public spheres.

Public Civil Religions versus Private Religious Communities

The modern concept of "civil religion," from its inception in Rousseau's work to its elaboration by Robert Bellah, is intimately linked to the classical republican virtue tradition and its mistrust of the modern liberal political tradition. In Bellah's theory of American civil religion this republican tradition became fused with the Calvinist tradition of the covenanted religious and political community and with the Durkheimian normative functionalist tradition and its conception of a moral, functional individualism counterposed to an egoist, utilitarian, and dysfunctional one.[53]

When it comes to religion, the classical republican tradition would distinguish between, on the one hand, public civil religions functioning as the cult of the political community and, on the other hand, private domestic cults, associational community cults, and individual privatist religions of salvation. The tension here would be between the particularism of an ethical community which integrates all citizens into a political cult coextensive with the political community and competing allegiances to either more primordial or more universalistic forms of community. Most corrosive of republican civil religions are those soteriological religious tenets which liberate the individual from absolute allegiance to the political community, freeing the self to choose individual, innerworldly or outerworldly, roads to salvation or to join other individuals to form wider, universalizable religious communities that transcend the particularism of the political community, be it a city-state or a nation-state. Indeed, the problem for the republican tradition is how to politicize religion, how to harness the integrative power of religion without exposing itself to the threat of theocracy, which, if triumphant, would eliminate the autonomy of the political sphere. Even when successful, however, Erastianism and all similar attempts to exert secular control over the religious institutions will lead to the impairment of religion. The field will be open either for iconoclastic prophetic critiques of political idolatry or for privatistic soteriological withdrawal.

Rousseau's discussion "Of Civil Religion" exemplifies vividly all these dilemmas.[54] He begins with the recognition that the old undifferentiated fusion of "the gods" and "the laws" of the state was destroyed by the Christian introduction of "a kingdom of the other world" and could no longer be reconstructed. The dualist political structure of medieval Christendom which replaced the political system of antiquity introduced not only "the most violent despotism" but also a "double power," a principle of dual sovereignty which resulted in "a perpetual conflict for jurisdiction which has made any system of good polity impossible in Christian States." In formulating his own proposal for a modern polity, Rousseau starts with the premise that "no State has ever been established without having religion for its basis." But he decides that none of the three existing forms of religion satisfies the conditions for a "good polity." The "religion of the priest," Roman Catholicism, is politically useless and evil. Internally, it "gives to mankind two codes of legislation, two chiefs, . . . requires from them contradictory duties, and prevents their being devout men and citizens at the same time." Externally, moreover, transnational ecclesiastical institutions transcend the territorial limits, the political community of citizenship, and the normative sovereignty of the modern nation-state. Hence, they cannot produce loyal subjects.[55]

By contrast, the "religion of the citizen" would undoubtedly produce loyal subjects through the sacralization of the state and the nation. But it "is also evil," because it is "founded in error and falsehood" and it leads to intolerant national chauvinism and sanguinary jingoism. Finally, the "religion of man" is "holy, sublime and true," as it transforms all the human race into "brothers." But politically it is useless, since, "having no particular connection with the body politic," it does not add anything either to the legitimacy of the laws or to the "great bonds of particular societies." Furthermore, it undermines republican virtue by replacing in "the hearts of the citizens" their attachment to the state with their own private mundane or supramundane concerns.[56] In the end, Rousseau solves the dilemma by affirming simultaneously and inconsistently the modern right of religious freedom and freedom of opinion, which no sovereign has the right to abridge or control, and the need for "a purely civil profession of faith, the articles of which it is the business of the Sovereign to arrange, not precisely as dogmas of religion, but as sentiments of sociability without which it is impossible to be either a good citizen or a faithful subject."[57]

Durkheim's attempt to solve the Hobbesian problem and Rousseau's political dilemmas through a sociological theory of normative societal integration based on a scientific secular morality which could serve as the civil religion of modern societies only reproduced the same old unresolved tensions using a new sociological language. Robert Bellah's theory of American civil religion has the advantage of being empirically grounded, as it starts from the premise that historically the American polity appears to have had something like a civil religion. However, even if one accepts the premise that indeed there was a time when the American polity was integrated through a civil religion made up of a peculiar combination of biblical/Puritan, republican/Enlightenment, and liberal/utilitarian religious/moral principles, it was already obvious at the time of Bellah's formulation of the theory that whatever was left of this civil religion was becoming increasingly irrelevant. Bellah himself soon came to recognize that the national "covenant" had been "broken" and that no ordinary jeremiad could put the old covenant together again. Moreover, the very triad of principles which jointly constitute the American civil religion, and which are in some respects not unlike Rousseau's three religions, again illustrate the same dilemmas. Can the republican, the biblical, and the modern individualist traditions be combined without undermining each other? Can American civil religion be anything other than the patriotic cult of the manifest imperial destiny of the American nation or the cult of a nation made up of individuals pursuing their own private utilitarian forms of religion? Both would undermine republican virtue. A more committed republicanism would prefer to banish religion to the private sphere and to pursue the secular religion of politics.[58]

As long as civil religion is conceptualized either politically at the state level as a force integrating normatively the political community or sociologically at the societal level as a force integrating normatively the societal community, such a civil religion is unlikely to reappear in modern societies. Moreover, if and when there is extant something like a civil religion, it will be more likely than not the adaptation of a living tradition to modern conditions. In any case, to postulate the existence of such a civil religion on the functionalist ground that modern societies "need" such a civil religion is theoretically untenable and normatively undesirable. What needs to be examined is the different ways in which religions, old and new, traditional and modern, may play public roles, eufunctional and dysfunctional, in the public sphere of civil society. Consequently, the concept of "civil religion" ought to be reformulated from the state or societal community level to the level of civil society.

Following Alfred Stepan, one may conceptualize the modern "polity" as consisting of three differentiated arenas: the state, political society, and civil society.[59] Following the "discursive" model of "public space," one may conceptualize the "public sphere" as a constitutive dimension of each of these three arenas of the polity.[60] In principle, religion could be located, as it were, in each of these three public spaces of the polity. There may be "public" religions at the state level, the "church" being the paradigmatic example. There may be "public" religions at the political society level, as in all instances when religion becomes politically mobilized against other religious or secular movements, or institutionalized as a political party competing with other religious or secular parties. The whole range of Catholic counterrevolutionary movements from the time of the French Revolution to the Spanish Civil War, which David Martin has aptly characterized as "reactive organicism"; the political mobilization of religious minorities reacting to or proacting against different types of *Kulturkampf* coming from the state or from other religious or secular movements or parties; structural systems of religious-political "pillarization," such as those characteristically developed in Belgium or Holland; the church's mobilization of the laity through "Catholic Action" to protect or advance the church's interests and privileges; the system of Christian-Democratic parties which crystallized after World War II in Catholic and, to a lesser extent, in Lutheran countries; and the recent electoral mobilization of the New Christian Right—all these cases could be viewed as different types of "public" religion located at the level of political society.[61]

It is one of the central theses of the present work that, at least in Western Europe, this historical epoch, the "age" of reactive organicism, of secular-religious and clerical-anticlerical cultural and political warfare, of Catholic Action, of religious pillarization, and of Christian Democracy has come to an end.[62] Reactive organicism was the church's response to the French Revolution as well as to the nineteenth-century liberal revolutions, while Catholic Action and Christian Democracy were the church's response to the emergence of secularist and laicist, particularly socialist, mass parties at the turn of the century. Both were defensive reactions to what was rightly perceived as a hostile, modern, secular environment. If the church today no longer seeks to reenter the state through the mobilization of the laity in order to regain control over society, it is to a large extent due to the fact that the church no longer feels threatened by a hostile secular state or by hostile social movements. The disappearance of anticlericalism from everyday politics in Catholic countries is perhaps the most telling indicator of this historical transformation.

A mutually reinforcing dynamic of recognition and rapprochement between religion and modernity has taken place, bringing to a close the conflictive cycles opened up by the Enlightenment critique of religion. On the one hand, the critical recognition of the dialectics of enlightenment and the postmodern self-limitation placed upon the rationalist project of secular redemption have led to a rediscovery of the validity claims of religion and to a recognition of the positive role of the Catholic church in setting limits to the absolutist tendencies of the modern state, whether in its Polish communist variant or in its Latin American "national security" variant. On the other hand, the Catholic *aggiornamento,* that is, the innerworldly turn of the church, the religious revaluation of secular reality, its prophetic commitment to the principles of freedom, justice, and solidarity in the social and political order have made superfluous precisely those aspects of the Enlightenment critique of religion which were still relevant not long ago in places like Spain or Brazil.

Most important, the Catholic church has largely renounced its own self-identity as a "church," that is, as a territorially organized, compulsory religious community coextensive with the political community or state. This change in self-identity, stimulated by the further secularization of a modern state which no longer needs religious legitimation, has led to a fundamental change in the location and orientation of the Catholic church from one centered and anchored in the state to one centered in civil society. It was this voluntary "disestablishment" of Catholicism, this change of self-identity, which permitted the Catholic church to play an active role in processes of democratization from Spain to Poland, from Brazil to the Philippines.

The most significant development which has emerged from recent transitions to democracy in Catholic countries is the fact that, despite finding itself in a majority position with unprecedented prestige and influence within civil society, the Catholic church everywhere has not only accepted the constitutional separation of church and state and the constitutional principle of religious freedom, but also abandoned its traditional attempts to either establish or sponsor official Catholic parties, which could be used to defend and advance politically the ecclesiastical privileges and claims of the church. The church appears to have accepted not only disestablishment from the state but also disengagement from political society proper. This does not mean, however, that Catholicism becomes necessarily privatized or that the church is no longer likely to play any public role. It only means that the public locus of the church is no longer the state or political society but, rather, civil society.

"Home" versus "Work": The Private Feminine Sphere of Religion and Morality versus the Public Masculine Sphere of Work and Legality

Finally, one could also apply to the religious field the distinction drawn by feminist critics and some modes of economic analysis between the public sphere of "work" and the private domestic sphere. Semantically, of course, the antonym of "work" is not "home" but "leisure." The distinction nonetheless describes the actual modern historical process of separation of the work-place from the household. Moreover, it plays a critical function in drawing attention to a dual process constitutive of modernity. It shows, in the first place, that under modern conditions of commodity production only the sphere of salaried employment is recognized as "work," thus excluding from consideration and reward (power, status, wealth) the entire sphere of human and social reproduction, from parturient "labor" to child rearing to the entire gamut of domestic activities connected with the reproduction of the labor force, all of them activities in which female exertion and work are preponderant.[63] Additionally, it points to the fact that under modern capitalist conditions the sphere of leisure itself has been commodified and transformed into the autonomous sphere of industrialized "mass culture," the sphere where cultural objects are produced, distributed, and consumed.

When applied to the religious field, the distinction between "public" work and "private" home immediately shows the ambiguous place of religion in the modern world. On the one hand, one could say almost categorically that religion belongs to the sphere of culture. Historically, religion has been, as attested by anthropological, cultural historical, and civilizational analysis alike, "the core" of culture. Some of the best sociological analysis of religion has shown that religion in the modern world like the rest of culture is also exposed to forces of commodification. "The pluralistic situation," writes Peter Berger, "is, above all, a *market situation*. In it, the religious institutions become marketing agencies and the religious traditions become consumer commodities."[64] Indeed, in the United States the "salvation" department may be one of the most diversified and profitable sectors of the entire mass culture industry. Yet it is symptomatic of the uncertain place of religion in the modern world that theories of modern culture and the newly established field of the sociology of culture tend to ignore religion altogether. It is understood, at least tacitly, that by culture one means exclusively "secular" culture.

It is the feminist critique of the public male/private female split which perhaps illuminates best the deep meaning of the modern privatization of religion. To say that "religion is a private affair" not only describes a historical process of institutional differentiation but actually prescribes the proper place for religion in social life. The place modernity assigns to religion is "home," understood not as the physical space of the household but as "the abiding place of one's affections" (Webster's). Home is the sphere of love, expression, intimacy, subjectivity, sentimentality, emotions, irrationality, morality, spirituality, and religion. This domestic sphere, moreover, is the female sphere par excellence. Indeed, Ann Douglas has appropriately described the historical process of privatization of religion which took place in the first half of nineteenth-century America as a process of "feminization."[65]

As feminist critics and moral philosophers have pointed out, the feminization of religion and morality had impoverishing effects on both the private and the public realm.[66] Religion, like moral virtue, became so sentimentalized, subjectivized, and privatized that it lost not only public power but also intersubjective public relevance. Exempt from public discursive rationality and accountability, religion as well as morality became simply a matter of individual, private taste. While premodern societies tended to coerce public expressions of religion, from collective "Actos de Fe" in the public square to public and communal penance, modern societies by contrast tend to banish any public display of religion. Actually, the privatization of religion reaches the point in which it becomes both "irreverent" and "in bad taste" to expose one's religiosity publicly in front of others. Like the unconstrained exposure of one's private bodily parts and emotions, religious confessions outside the strictly delimited religious sphere are considered not only a degradation of one's privacy but also an infringement upon the right to privacy of others.

The consequences for the public sphere of "work" were equally significant. Politics and economics became literally "amoral" spheres, realms from which moral or religious considerations ought to be excluded. In the process, the "public sphere" itself became impoverished. Seyla Benhabib has shown that the liberal model of "public dialogue" and its "neutrality" rule impose certain "conversational restraints," which tend to function as a "gag rule," excluding from public deliberation the entire range of matters declared to be "private"—from the private economy to the private domestic sphere to private norm formation.

Yet, as Benhabib points out, "The model of a public dialogue based on conversational restraint is not neutral, in that it presupposes a moral and political epistemology; this in turn justifies an implicit separation between the public and the private of such a kind as leads to the silencing of the concerns of certain excluded groups."[67] Furthermore, the principle of "dialogic neutrality" tends to ignore the "agonistic" dimension of politics and fails to recognize that "all struggles against oppression in the modern world begin by redefining what had previously been considered 'private', non-public and non-political issues as matters of public concern, as issues of justice, as sites of power which need discursive legitimation."[68]

By incorporating the practical experience of the women's movements and feminist theoretical concerns reflexively into her political theory, Benhabib is able to show not only the limits of the liberal model of "public space" but also the extent to which Habermas's "discursive model" has inherited unnecessarily some "dubious distinctions from the liberal social-contract" that seem to be at odds with a more radically proceduralist reading of the theory. In the case of liberalism, the crucial need to maintain a clear differentiation between the spheres of legality and morality, in order to protect precisely all modern individual freedoms and the right to privacy, led to an overjuridical conception of the public and private divide.

The same justifiable concern, Benhabib argues, leads Habermas to establish overly rigid boundaries between "public issues of justice" and "private conceptions of the good life," "public interests" and "private needs," and "public matters of norms and private matters of values."[69] The issue, of course, cannot be the elimination of those boundaries which are necessary to protect modern freedoms and to structure modern differentiated societies. What is at issue is the need to recognize that the boundaries themselves are and need to be open to contestation, redefinition, renegotiation, and discursive legitimation. According to Benhabib, "If the agenda of the conversation is radically open, if participants can bring any and all matters under critical scrutiny and reflexive questioning, then there is no way to predefine the *nature* of the issues discussed as being ones of justice or of the good life itself prior to the conversation."[70] This should include all boundaries: private and public, moral and legal, justice and the good life, religious and secular. It should also include the boundaries between all the functionally differentiated systemic spheres: state, economy, civil society, family, religion, and so forth.

What I call the "deprivatization" of modern religion is the process whereby religion abandons its assigned place in the private sphere and enters the undifferentiated public sphere of civil society to take part in the ongoing process of contestation, discursive legitimation, and redrawing of the boundaries. In the 1980s, religion throughout the world was in the forefront of various forms of public collective action, agonic as well as discursive, often on both sides of every contested issue, itself being both the subject and the object of contestation and debate. The issue, therefore, cannot be whether religion essentially is good or bad for politics, functional or dysfunctional for the social system, historically progressive or regressive. Social scientists, both as practical actors and as theorists who are also engaged in making "distinctions" and drawing boundaries, will need to develop analytical and normative criteria to differentiate the various forms of public religion and their possible sociohistorical consequences. But above all, social scientists need to recognize that, despite all the structural forces, the legitimate pressures, and the many valid reasons pushing religion in the modern secular world into the private sphere, religion continues to have and will likely continue to have a public dimension. Theories of modernity, theories of modern politics, and theories of collective action which systematically ignore this public dimension of modern religion are necessarily incomplete theories.

II

Five Case Studies:
Analytical Introduction

The following case studies examine five different stories of the transformation of public religions on the roads to modernity. Each of the empirical studies has two sections. The first, the historical section, reconstructs in a highly schematic way the markedly different patterns of secularization and the histories of structural relations between church, state, and society in two types of settings. The second, the contemporary section, analyzes the various public roles the different religions have assumed in the last decades.

The two types of settings are territorial national churches and competing denominations within a free and pluralistic religious market. The first three case studies of Catholicism in Spain, Poland, and Brazil present three different stories of three typical territorial national churches which, despite their common Catholic doctrines, rituals, and ecclesiastical structures, evince markedly different patterns of church, state, and societal interrelations. Although structured around the same central categories, each of the stories is meant to stand on its own. Instead of imposing a common analytical framework upon the different histories, I have tried to let the stories illustrate the different and changing meaning of the central analytical categories.

Sociological categories are, by nature, historical and phenomenological. They are historical because the social reality they are supposed to help analyze is historical. As reality changes historically, the meaning of the categories used to analyze this reality must change accordingly. They are phenomenological because social scientists share most of their fundamental categories with social actors who are constantly defining and redefining the meaning of those sociological categories. The attempts of social scientists to insulate their categories from historical change and from the changing phenomenological meanings given by the actors is futile and illusory. Such a state of affairs naturally makes for very imprecise categories and for imprecise science. But in sociology categorial and scientific precision is usually bought at the price of interpretive relevance. The problem is particularly acute for comparative-historical sociology.

"Church" is the central analytical category of the present comparative-historical study. It should be obvious that the historical reality and the phenomenological meaning of "church" in, let us say, sixteenth-, nineteenth-, and twentieth-century Spain, Poland, and Brazil are radically different. It would be pointless, therefore, for a comparative-historical study of this nature to begin with a definition of what a church is.

Indeed, there is a tension throughout the study between (a) the sociological, ideal-typical, category of church as defined by Max Weber and Ernst Troeltsch, a definition which they derived from the specific historical reality of the post-Constantinian imperial Roman church; (b) the phenomenological-doctrinal self-definition of the relevant collective actors who constitute the church as an ecclesiastical institution—and here it is important to keep in mind that the Catholic church is both a transnational institution which transcends any particular national society and a national institution deeply embedded in the different histories and structures of particular countries—and (c) the historically changing reality of national churches, particularly the changing structural location of the church in relation to state and society.

From the particular perspective of this study, that is, from the perspective of churches as "public" religions, it is the third meaning, the changing structural reality and the changing relational character of churches, that is most relevant. The most important conclusion one may draw from a comparative-historical analysis of the Spanish, Polish, and Brazilian churches is that the structural location any church occupies between state and society determines to a large extent the form which such a church assumes as a public religion. Insofar as churches are compulsory institutions, in Weber's sense of the term, they are by definition state-oriented institutions. Either they themselves control the means of compulsion, in which case they are theocratic state institutions, or they must rely on the state to protect their compulsory status. This means that as long as the church aspires to be a compulsory institution it is the different and changing nature of the state that determines above all the different and changing nature of the church.

From this perspective, the two most important transformations in the period under study were, first, the emergence of the modern system of centralized absolutist states and the related emergence of national territorial churches and, second, the emergence of the secular state with its claims of separation from the church and liberation from the religious-normative type of integration of the political community. The Spanish Catholic church may be viewed as the paradigmatic example of an established church of a multinational imperial state which violently resisted its disestablishment from the liberal state and which was able to reassert, also with violence, its status as the established church of a Catholic state.

The Polish Catholic church offers the paradigmatic example of a state church manqué, that is, of a territorial national church in search of a nation-state, assuming the symbolic representation and the religious-normative integration of the nation in the absence of the state, protecting the nation from disjunction and foreign occupation, and resisting the imposition of a secular state that attempted to disestablish the church from the nation.

The Brazilian Catholic church may be viewed as a typical example of a colonial church which was mainly the caesaropapist administrative arm of an imperial-colonial state, later transformed into the established church of a liberal-positivist state, which reemerged after disestablishment aspiring to become a national church in alliance with the populist state and its project of national development.

In a second, different setting the United States represents the paradigmatic and historically first model of the separation of church and state. Perfect separation entails the constitutional abolition of the church and its transformation into a religious denomination. Constitutionally, in the eyes of the law, every religious association, irrespective of its self-definition, has the same denominational status. Denominations must per force be society oriented and become voluntary, competitive religious associations. From now on, it is their relation to society that will primarily determine their nature. Evangelical Protestantism emerged as the transdenominational hegemonic civil religion of American society. Catholicism emerged as the sectarian territorially organized national denomination of immigrant Catholic ethnics.

The so-called Catholic *aggiornamento* of the 1960s, culminating in the Second Universal Vatican Council, officially redefined the self-identity of the Catholic church. That is, the relevant collective actors, which in the case of a hierarchic episcopal church are the representative bishops of the global church, publicly redefined their own identity as a church. From the perspective of this study the most important consequence of this collective redefinition of the situation was the transformation of the Catholic church from a state-centered to a society-centered institution.

Thus, while the historical sections of the case studies could be construed as evidence that in determining the type of public religion, religious doctrines, that is, self-definitions, do not matter and structural location is everything, the contemporary sections show that an official change in religious doctrine, that is, in the self-definition of the relevant collective actors, may significantly affect the structural location of any given church. Prior to Vatican II, the Spanish, Polish, and Brazilian Catholic churches occupied very different structural/positions in what were also very different political regimes. After the council all three churches, and other national Catholic churches throughout the world, began to assume a similar structural position and to play similar positive roles in challenging the respective authoritarian regimes and facilitating the transition to democracy. Four documents of Vatican II form the core of the new collective self-definition of the church and have given the main direction to the generalized reformation of national Catholic churches: *Dignitatis Humanae, Gaudium et Spes, Lumen Gentium,* and *Christus Dominus.*[1]

From a world-historical perspective, the Declaration on Religious Freedom, *Dignitatis Humanae,* is perhaps the most consequential and the most radical departure from tradition. It establishes the very conditions of possibility for a *modern* type of Catholic public religion. Without this declaration every other document would have been for all practical purposes meaningless. The recognition of the inalienable right of every individual to freedom of conscience, based on the sacred dignity of the human person, means that the church abandons its compulsory character and becomes a "free church." Truth can no longer be imposed, nor is it permissible to coerce individual consciences to follow external dictates. The immediate historical consequences of the declaration were (a) the acceptance of the modern principle of disestablishment and separation of church and state; (b) the contestability of any Catholic party or political movement officially sponsored by the Catholic church; and (c) in the long run the incompatibility of a dogmatic conception of authoritative tradition and the principle of freedom of conscience.[2]

In terms of the internal transformation of Catholicism, particularly of its economic and political ethics (in Weber's sense of the term), the most radical departure from tradition with equally visible world-historical consequences was the Pastoral Constitution on the Church in the Modern World, *Gaudium et Spes.* This document represents the lifting of the Catholic *anathema* that was hanging over modernity and the final acceptance of the legitimacy of the modern *saeculum,* of the modern age and of the modern world. This process of secularization in its spatial dimension entails a change from an otherworldly to an innerworldly orientation. From now on, action on behalf of peace and justice and participation in the transformation of the world will become not an added but a constitutive dimension of the church's divine mission. In its temporal dimension, the legitimacy of the modern age entails the acceptance of the principle of historicity and the church's obligation to discern "the signs of the times." It is no longer a question of the church teaching the world eternal truths and upholding the objective moral order ontologically inscribed in natural law, but of the church accepting the task of having to appropriate the meaning of the Gospel in and through historical interpretation.

Ecclesiologically, the Dogmatic Constitution on the Church, *Lumen Gentium,* radically altered the self-identity of the church as a religious institution by placing at the beginning of the text the definition of the church as "the People of God," where everyone, the laity and the clergy, shares, unequally to be sure, in the same priesthood of Christ. Only then does there follow a discussion of the episcopate and of the hierarchic division of labor within the church. Similarly, discussions of the function of the laity in the church and of the universal calling to sanctity precede the discussion of "the religious" and of their function and calling.

Finally, the Decree on the Bishops' Pastoral Office in the Church, *Christus Dominus,* stresses the collective, collegial nature of the episcopate as successors to the college of the Apostles, who in communion with the pope exercise jointly the pastoral and magisterial office of the entire church. The decree also recommends that the institution of synods and councils of the early church be renewed, and it mandates the establishment of national and regional episcopal conferences. The most important implication of the last two documents, *Lumen Gentium* and *Christus Dominus,* is the very redefinition of just who constitutes the relevant collective actors with the authority to define the collective self-identity of the church.

As shown by the ideological struggles taking place within the church since the accession of Karol Wojtyła to the Papacy, and particularly since the accession of Cardinal Ratzinger to the old post of modern "grand inquisitor," there is much room for disagreement among the relevant collective actors over the correct theological interpretation of those texts. But sociologically speaking, the sociohistorical consequences, intended or unintended, unleashed by the publication and the widespread internalization of the message of these documents are undeniable. There is no better confirmation than the very emergence of a project of Catholic "restoration" based on the premise that these sociohistorical consequences were the unexpected and undesired result of a misinterpretation of the original Vatican intent.[3]

If before it was the nature of the state that was crucial in determining the character of the church, once the church ceases to be or no longer aspires to become a compulsory institution, it is the nature or the model of society held by the relevant social actors that determines the changing character of the church as a public religion. The role of the Catholic church in processes of democratization in Spain, Poland, and Brazil was different not only because of the diverse nature of the authoritarian regimes but also because of the different nature and models of society in the three countries. Following Guillermo O'Donnell, the categories of "civil society," "nation," and "the people" are used in the three comparative-historical studies as alternative contested models of society and as alternative principles and structures of mediation between state and society, and between church and society.[4]

The Spanish Catholic church has finally accepted disestablishment from the state and the reality of a pluralist civil society. The question is whether under such conditions the church can still find any role as a public religion. The Polish Catholic church played a crucial role in legitimating the emergence of a Polish civil society. The question is whether the church is willing to give up completely its historical identity as a state church manqué and to become disestablished from the nation. If in Poland the tension is that between nation and civil society as structuring collective identity principles of society, in Brazil the tension is between the principles of civil society and "the people." The Brazilian Catholic church's adoption of a new identity as "the People's Church" was crucial in facilitating the transition to democracy. But with the institutionalization of a democratic political regime, this identity found itself in tension with the reality of a pluralistically structured civil society and with the reality of the elitist, professional structures of mediation of political society.

The Catholic aggiornamento also had fateful consequences for American Catholicism. From its inception Catholicism in the United States had been a minority sect, at times persecuted, at times barely tolerated, that was compelled by circumstances to keep its religion private and that strove to assimilate its ethnic immigrants while protecting their separate faith and to become accepted as an American denomination. The Vatican redefinition challenged the American Catholic church to question its Americanism, to abandon its private posture, and to assume the identity of a public denomination.

Placing the study of Evangelical Protestantism in a comparative-historical context within the study of the transformation of Catholic churches to modernity is particularly instructive in a dual sense. It helps to view the sectarian withdrawal of Protestant fundamentalism as the typical reaction of a church which resists its disestablishment from civil society and refuses to become just another private denomination. Furthermore, a look at the parallel trajectory of the Catholic and evangelical denominations in twentieth-century America helps to understand the contemporary evangelical revival and its public reemergence as a form of evangelical aggiornamento.

3   Spain: From State Church to Disestablishment

The centuries-long Christian *Reconquista* of the Iberian Peninsula from the Muslim conquerors led to an early identification of religious and national identity. But it was the formation of the early modern Spanish state under the Catholic kings that led to the identification of church and state and to the transformation of Spanish Christianity into the church militant. Religious mobilization played a crucial role in the making of the Spanish state. Indeed, the belatedly introduced Inquisition (1481) was bound to play a state-making function, becoming the first truly national, unified, and centralized state institution. The expulsion of Jews, Muslims, and Moriscos from Spain took place within a typical pattern of popular pressure from below and religious mobilization from above.[1]

In order to reintegrate itself with Europe, Spain shed its two unwanted religions precisely at a time when Europe itself was being cut asunder by the Protestant Reformation and the Catholic Counter-Reformation. The Counter-Reformation put an end to Spain's enthusiastic economic, political, and cultural experiments in early modernity. The Hapsburg monarchy, the Universal Church, and the American colonial empire all combined to sacrifice the incipient Spanish nation-state to the ideal and material interests of the "Universal Christian Monarchy," a historical project at odds with the emerging international system of European states.[2]

The church militant went on fighting Islam in the Mediterranean and in Asia, pagans in America, and heretics in Europe. Spain had turned the concept of religious crusade against Christian Europe. The defeat of Spain's quixotic imperialism led to its bitter isolation from the emerging modern Europe. Crown and church together decided to preserve within the Spanish dominions the universalist and Catholic ideal of political and religious unity that they had failed to maintain by force in Europe. Unlike other European nations, Spain would not recover from the general seventeenth-century crisis.[3]

The Bourbons in the eighteenth century began the slow process of reorientation toward Europe. But the task of catching up was made complicated by the fact that those forces opposing the "enlightened" reforms refused to accept the view that the difference between Spain and Europe was one of quantifiable "backwardness," insisting that there was a qualitatively unreachable cleavage between two mutually exclusive civilizations. When the typical sixteenth-century conflict between "ancients" and "moderns" reemerged in eighteenth-century Spain, it began to resemble the form it would take in Eastern European countries, particularly in Russia, and in non-Western civilizations resisting Westernization.[4]

In eighteenth-century Spain the conflict first emerged within the church itself between a reformist wing led by the Augustinians and enlightened clerics, protected by enlightened despotism, and a traditionalist wing led by the Jesuits and the Dominicans. What the ultramontane Jesuits were most against was Bourbon regalism and the puritan Jansenism of the reformers, while the scholastic Dominicans were obstinate in their opposition to the introduction of modern philosophy and modern science into Spanish universities. The expulsion of the Jesuits from the Spanish dominions in 1776, following a series of urban "riots" in Madrid for which the Jesuits were conveniently blamed, marked the temporary triumph of reformist Gallican caesaropapism. But the French Revolution and Napoleon's intervention in Spanish politics shattered the "enlightened" model of elite-controlled reform from above, took away the "aura" from the absolute monarchy, and brought in its place modern forms of political conflicts and collective action.[5]

The church played a crucial role in the mobilization of the Spanish people against the Napoleonic invasion. The War of Independence, led locally in many instances by guerrilla priests, was fought as a religious crusade against "the impious hosts of Satan." The traditional identification of Catholic faith and Spanish nation was thereby strengthened. Meanwhile, cut off from the rest of Spain, self-appointed political elites met in Cádiz to draft the 1812 Liberal Constitution, which proclaimed the sovereignty of the nation. More than the measures dismantling the ancien régime, such as the abolition of seigneurial jurisdictions and the disentailment of the lands of the church, it was the abolition of the Inquisition in 1813 that gave rise to the fiercest polemics between Liberales and Serviles in the Cortes de Cádiz. Prominent liberal clerics led the attack on the Holy Office. Indeed, the clergy, with its ninety-seven deputies, constituted almost one-third of the Constituent Assembly. But the church hierarchy and the rural clergy reacted against the attempts to dissolve the Inquisition and were able to redirect their diatribes from the French invaders to the internal heretics, the liberal *afrancesados*. Catholic Spain now turned the concept of religious crusade against liberal Spain. The phenomenon of "the two Spains," a Catholic Hispanic Spain facing a liberal Europeanizing one, was born.[6]

In 1814 the people of Madrid staged an enthusiastic welcome to the restored absolutist king, shouting "Long live the fetters," thus mocking the slogan of the liberal Enlightenment, "Let's break the fetters." At the beginning of the nineteenth century the church, that is, its hierarchy and most of its clergy, stood with the crown and ordinary people against reformist liberal elites. The absolutist restoration forced Spanish liberals into exile or underground into Masonic lodges and conspiratorial secret societies. There took place the typical Latin fusion of liberalism and anticlericalism, as well as the typical Iberian fusion of liberalism and praetorian politics.[7]

The early identification of nation and religious faith that had facilitated early modern state formation and had spared Spain the religious civil wars of early modern Europe now became an impediment to modern nation building and transformed modern political conflicts into religious warfare. The three civil wars of modern Spain—the First Carlist War (1833–40), the Second Carlist War (1870–76), and the Spanish Civil War (1936–39)—all started as antimodern counterrevolutions and were sanctified by an embattled Catholic church as religious crusades against godless liberalism or atheistic communism. As a counterpart, the burning of churches and convents and the killing of clerics and nuns was to become a typically recurrent feature of Spain's modern political upheavals from the 1830s, when the first public outbursts of fierce anticlericalism occurred in Madrid and in other major cities, to the 1930s.[8]

Spanish developments per se were not unique. They represent an extreme version of what David Martin has termed "the French (Latin) pattern" of secularization. In this pattern, according to Martin,

such revolutionary explosions become endemic, and religion as such is frequently a political issue. Coherent and massive secularism confronts coherent and massive religiosity. . . . One ethos confronts an alternative ethos, particularly where the elite culture of the secular Enlightenment acquires a mass component and achieves a historicized ideology i.e. Marxism.[9]

What was unique about Spanish developments was, first, the triumph of Catholic reactive organicism over modern secularism in the Spanish Civil War and, second, the fact that this protracted religious-political conflict between "ancients" and "moderns" assumed in Spain the form of a civilizational conflict between a Catholic Hispanic Spain and a liberal Europeanizing one.

In the 1830s, by embracing Carlism and rallying the peasantry of

Northern Spain against the new constitutional monarchy, the church managed to alienate most social forces in the country. The state's response was to disentail the lands of the church, to abolish the tithe, and to dissolve the monastic orders. The quick sale of the lands of the church at auction provided the Spanish Treasury with the needed revenues to fight the Carlist insurrection, but it frustrated the old liberal project of creating a landowning peasantry loyal to the liberal regime. The properties fell into the hands of conservative landowners, who from now on were bound to the liberal cause by their material interests. Thus, the "betrayed" liberal revolution consolidated the "latifundist" agrarian capitalism of Central and Southern Spain, while the church lost its rural economic base as well as its ties with the rural proletariat that developed there. Simultaneously, however, since the legitimist Carlist cause became fused with peripheral Basque and Catalan nationalism, the church's support of Carlism also consolidated the church's strong presence in those regions.[10]

By mid-century, expropriation had left the Spanish church destitute. The closing of monasteries and the dissolution of the male religious orders had brought to an end the influence the church had exerted through education and beneficence. Save in the North, the church found itself forsaken, divorced from the state and from the ruling classes. The dramatic decrease in the size of the clergy, from approximately two hundred thousand in 1808 to fifty-six thousand in 1860, despite Spain's sharp overall population increase, is a telling indicator of the secularization of Spanish society.[11]

The church, however, soon began its reconquest of Spanish society through a renewed alliance with the liberal oligarchic state. The 1851 Concordat brought about a détente between church and state. It entailed the final recognition of the liberal regime by the Vatican in exchange for a gradual and partial reestablishment of Catholicism. The 1868 "Glorious Revolution" brought a second, briefer and more superficial, disestablishment. But the 1874 *Restauración* resecured the alliance between church and state.[12] Bourgeoisie and landowners, their revolution safely accomplished, found it opportune to reconcile themselves with a needy church. The new ruling class attained respectability and obtained an important ally in blocking the political demands of radical democrats and the socioeconomic demands of the lower classes. The bourgeoisie was brought back into the church's bosom, adopting a mainly external form of cultural Catholicism while refusing to concede to the church any control over private conscience or private morality. Spanish Catholicism, while maintaining its mass base in the landowning peasantry of the North, became an increasingly urban and "bourgeois" institution. Meanwhile, the growing rural and urban proletariat was becoming increasingly "de-

Christianized." In its eagerness to bring its strayed sheep back into the fold, the church had abandoned the larger flock. At the turn of the twentieth century, in the chronic conflicts between capital and labor and between oligarchic *caciquismo* and mass democracy, the Spanish church stood firmly, with but a few exceptions, on the side of capital and *caciquismo*.[13]

But the Spanish liberal state also had to pay dearly for the legitimation of the Catholic church. From now on, the state would have to support the clergy economically, thereby feeding lower-class resentment against the state and against a church which had become part of the state administration. But more important, the liberal state ceded to the church control over public and private education, thus giving up the best instrument it had to build a modern nation and to shape the mind of its citizenry. Clerical education, both directly and indirectly, reinforced the tendency of religious, class, and ethnic-national identities to become more important than any all-Spanish national identity. Moreover, the reestablishment of the confessional state also reinforced the old identification between the "official" Spanish nation-state and the Catholic faith at a time when large sections of the population were abandoning the church and adopting militant atheism. Not surprisingly, anticlerical and antistatist ideologies grew contemporaneously.[14]

The alliance between the state and the Catholic church came to an end during the Second Spanish Republic (1930–36). The Republic instituted the separation of church and state, took over from the church control of public education, and enforced the privatization of Catholicism and the laicization of Spanish society. When the Republican leader Manuel Azaña proclaimed in the Republican Cortes that Spain had ceased being Catholic, he was only stating polemically the new constitutional reality. But in the context of the aggressive anticlericalism and laicism of the Republic, the Catholic church understood the proclamation as a call to arms. The church stopped short of voicing its unloyal opposition to the new republican regime publicly, but it became evident that the Spanish Catholic church was not willing to accept the liberal principles of separation of church and state, state control of public education, freedom of conscience, religious freedom, and the privatization of Catholicism. Unwilling to accept the loss of its privileges, apprehensive of the officially condoned anticlerical attacks, and fearful of the more serious threats posed by the impending socialist revolution, the Catholic church joined the military uprising enthusiastically and sanctified the sanguinary civil war as a religious crusade of liberation. The violent and unrestrained religious persecution in many areas of the Republican zone confirmed the church's worst fears of the militant atheism of the Spanish left. The church's response, however, was to condone and all too often to sanctify an even more violent and indiscriminate official repression in the Nationalist zone.[15]

Victory in civil war brought the absolute triumph of Catholic Spain over "the other Spain." Catholicism became once again the official state religion. The church regained all its institutional privileges and was offered the modern administrative means to enforce its religious monopoly and to impose the unity of faith and nation. Through state coercion, Spanish society became Catholic again. Though often used as a derogatory term, Nacional-Catolicismo serves as the most apt shorthand analytical characterization of the Franco regime. While the regime adopted many of the external manifestations of fascism in its ideology, organization, and symbolic paraphernalia, it is no exaggeration to say that the Catholic church constituted the main institutional and ideological pillar of the regime.[16]

The church gave the regime the original ideological legitimation of the civil war and its main initial source of mass popular mobilization. After the war, once the regime began demobilizing, Catholicism became the source of its diffused legitimation and the basis for its authoritarian "mentality." Catholic corporatism became the only slightly coherent ideological and formative principle of the regime. Catholic lay organizations, first the elitist Asociación Católica Nacional de Propagandistas (ACNdP) and later the even more elitist Opus Dei, provided the Francoist state with its most important administrative cadres. When, following the defeat of the Axis powers, the regime found itself boycotted and shunned as an international pariah, the church through its links with the Vatican and other Catholic churches provided the regime with its first basis for international legitimation.[17]

It was at least part of the official rhetoric to portray the regime as the ideal Catholic model of church-state relations and as the exemplification of the Catholic "third way" between liberal democratic capitalism and totalitarian socialism. Franco himself in his public speeches and particularly in his writings appropriated the typical Catholic antimodern philosophy of history, declaring that the civil war had been a crusade against Masonry (his personal bête noire), the French Encyclopedia, and all their modern derivations—liberalism, capitalism, and socialism. Modern liberal Spain, from the eighteenth-century Enlightenment to the Second Spanish Republic, was to be repressed and forgotten. The "New Spain" was to forsake all its ties with a decrepit modern world. Modeling itself after the great imperial age of the Catholic kings and the Counter-Reformation, it was to resume Spanish history where it had left off prior to the introduction of the foreign heresies that had precipitated its decline.[18]

Given this fusion of church and state, of Catholicism and regime, the slow but progressive distancing of the church from the regime which began in the early 1960s and the open conflict and final break between the two in the 1970s were important in the legitimation crisis and the final dissolution of the regime.[19] A purely instrumental explanation of those changes as a conscious strategy of institutional adaptation on the part of the church would be patently inadequate. Even if one were to privilege such an interpretation, it would still be necessary to explain what made it possible for the Spanish church to abandon its traditional reactive organicism and to adopt for the first time in its modern history such a rational future-oriented strategy of adaptation to changed circumstances.[20] The conjunction of three interrelated processes could serve to explain in part the change in orientation by the Spanish Catholic church from a state-centered to a society-centered strategy.

The Internal Transformation of Spanish Catholicism

To a large extent, the massive re-Catholicization of Spanish society after the civil war was rather superficial, as it was mainly the result of administrative coercion and public pressure. As the coercion and the pressure diminished progressively, the Catholic revival petered out. But some aspects of the revival were genuine and would have a deep effect both on the transformation of Spanish Catholicism and on the relationships of church, state, and society.[21] Among the manifestations of the Catholic revival which pointed to internal changes within Spanish Catholicism were the following:

• The emergence for the first time in modern Spanish history of groups of autonomous and respectable lay Catholic intellectuals who came to play an important critical role in the otherwise extremely impoverished intellectual discourse of Franco's Spain and would serve to mediate the chasm between the "two Spains." Figures like Aranguren, Laín Entralgo, and Tovar are paradigmatic here. For the first time as well, lay Catholic intellectuals had an impact upon the theological discourse of Spanish Catholicism.[22]

• The emergence of two modern, that is, innerworldly, Catholic religious movements that would come to play an important role in Franco's Spain and that would spread beyond Spain to become the first modern contribution of Spanish Catholicism to the Universal Church. The Cursillos de Cristiandad was the first historical manifestation within Spanish Catholicism of a Catholic type of evangelical revivalism and born-again Christianity. Similarly, the Opus Dei was the first manifestation within Spanish Catholicism of a militant type of Protestant ethic. Particularly the Opus Dei, the secretive lay Catholic movement/organization, proved very successful after the civil war in recruiting young upwardly mobile elites through its new message of sanctification of professional work and ascetic dedication to one's professional calling.[23]

• The emergence, also for the first time in Spanish history, of a genuine social Catholicism springing from Catholic Action. Groups within the Catholic workers' movement, Hermandades Obreras de Acción Católica (HOAC) and Juventudes Obreras Católicas (JOC), became radicalized in the 1950s and progressively began to confront both the Catholic hierarchy and the regime.[24]

Structural Transformations of the Regime

In 1956 there took place in the University of Madrid a series of violent clashes between Catholic and Falange students fighting for control of the student movement. The student conflicts paralleled the power struggles that were taking place within the state administration between Catholic and Falange leaders. Both groups were trying to determine the direction of the new economic policies needed to overcome the economic impasse reached by the regime, once the import-substitution model of industrialization appeared to be exhausted. Unexpectedly, Franco dismissed the leaders of both warring factions and called Opus Dei members into the government. The Opus Dei "technocrats" introduced radical changes in the economic policies of the regime by pursuing an aggressive policy of export-oriented economic growth, the rationalization of the state administration, and the integration of Spain into the world capitalist system.[25]

The replacement of Catholic Action elites, close to the Catholic church's hierarchy, which had served the regime since its inception, by parvenu elites from the Opus Dei, a sectarian movement within Spanish Catholicism viewed suspiciously by the church as well as by the economic, political, and cultural establishment, had the unintended consequence of facilitating the progressive distancing of the church and other established elites from the regime. Out of power, the displaced elites adopted a posture of semiloyal, semidemocratic opposition to the regime and began to serve as a mediating link with the more radical democratic opposition. Furthermore, technocracy, development ideologies, and ideologies proclaiming "the end of ideology" came to replace Catholicism as the basis for the ideological legitimation of the regime. Some of the displaced Catholic elites also adopted genuinely Christian Democracy, establishing links with European Christian Democracy.[26]

As the social consequences of the new stabilization policies introduced by the technocrats became clear, some Catholic bishops from the South, first individually and later collectively, began in their pastoral letters to criticize openly the social policies of the regime. In this respect, although the radicalization was milder in the Spanish case, the bishops from the latifundist South played a similar role to the one played by the Northeast bishops in the radicalization of the Brazilian church. Bishop Añoveros came to occupy within the Spanish church and in the eyes of the regime a position similar to the one occupied by Dom Helder Câmara in the Brazilian church. Similarly, although it was less severe in the Spanish case, state repression directed against Catholic priests and laity opposing the regime led moderate sectors of the church to close institutional ranks and to confront the regime openly while also protecting the new opposition movements emerging from civil society.[27]

The acute secularization of Spanish society that accompanied the rapid processes of industrialization and urbanization was viewed at first with alarm by the church's hierarchy. Slowly, however, the most conscious sectors of Spanish Catholicism began to talk of Spain no longer as an inherently Catholic nation to be reconquered anew but rather as a *país de misión*. Catholic faith could no longer be compulsorily enforced from above; it had to be voluntarily adopted through a process of individual conversion. With the official adoption of the new Vatican policies, Spanish Catholicism for the first time ceased resisting modern processes of secularization. Slowly the church learned to come to terms with secularization and even to view them as a "sign of the times."[28]

External Transformations of Catholicism

At the Second Vatican Council, the Spanish bishops probably constituted one of the most conservative blocs of the assembled Catholic hierarchy. Prior to the council some sectors of the Spanish clergy and laity had begun their own process of *aggiornamento*. But their demands had found little resonance within the hierarchy. Now the official policies coming from Rome gave the modern sectors of Spanish Catholicism the leverage they needed to pressure the hierarchy and to confront the regime.[29]

The promulgation of the encyclical *Pacem in Terris* (1963) marked a turning point. The Christian Democratic sector—gathered around the ex-minister of education Ruiz Giménez and their influential journal *Cuadernos para el Diálogo*—now took the lead in demanding the institutionalization of the rule of law, the transformation of the regime into an Estado de Derecho (Rechtsstaat), and the protection of the human, civil, and political rights of the Spanish people. Ironically, some of the same Catholic groups and individuals who in the 1950s had represented the regime at home and abroad as a model of Catholic order now took the leadership in questioning the legitimacy of the regime. Moreover, the privileged exemption from state censorship which Catholic publications had gained after the war could now be used to criticize the regime and to defend general principles of freedom of expression and freedom of the press.[30]

The transformation of Spanish Catholicism was both sudden and extensive. The change in language from Latin to the vernacular was accompanied by a more significant change in the content of Catholic discourse. Even a superficial comparison of the Catholic publications of the 1950s with those of the 1960s reveals the difference.[31] The training of priests in the seminaries underwent a radical overhaul. Scholasticism was abruptly dropped and replaced with modern philosophies and modern theologies. A new generation of priests avidly embraced the new direction, taking a confrontational attitude vis-à-vis their own older colleagues, their hierarchy, and their confused flocks.[32] Spanish popular religiosity, already weak when compared with that of Poland, was unable to survive the iconoclastic onslaught of the new liturgy and the new pastoral practices. Active Catholic cadres and some sectors of the laity, particularly among the middle classes, felt comfortable with the new *Catolicismo conciliar,* but many Catholics were not able to make the transition and stopped practicing altogether. Most young priests, and even some older ones, felt increasingly uncomfortable with their traditional roles as sacramental mediators and searched for personally and socially relevant pastoral practices, usually adopting various forms of social service and political activism. Religious vocations, a traditional avenue of social mobility, became much less popular and the secularization of the regular and secular clergy increased dramatically. The number of seminarians, for example, decreased from 8,397 in 1961/62 to 2,791 in 1972/73; around four hundred priests left the clergy annually between 1966 and 1971; and one-third of Spanish Jesuits left the order between 1966 and 1975.[33]

Throughout the 1960s, the Spanish church was sharply divided along generational lines between a majority of bishops and a large minority of priests over sixty years of age, on one hand, and a minority of bishops and a majority of priests under forty years of age, on the other. The Vatican's intervention in Spanish affairs, by changing the organizational structure and the composition of the Spanish episcopate, tipped the balance of forces in favor of the new Catholicism. By 1970, the reformers had gained control of the newly created National Conference of Bishops, which had replaced the older Conference of Metropolitans. At first, by refusing to give up its right of presentation of bishops, the Franco regime had presented a serious obstacle to Vatican attempts to renovate the Spanish episcopate. But the Vatican managed to circumvent this obstacle by forcing older bishops to retire, who thereby lost their right to vote in the National Conference, and by nominating younger auxiliary bishops with the right to vote. By nominating auxiliary bishops, the Vatican was able to exclude the regime's intervention in their nomination. Of the seventy bishops who constituted the Spanish episcopate in 1966, 65 percent were sixty years of age or older and only five were auxiliary bishops. By 1973, there were seventy-seven bishops, seventeen of which were auxiliary bishops, while the number of bishops sixty years of age or older had decreased to 40 percent of the total.[34]

Two events make the year 1971 a turning point in the transformation of the Spanish church. That year Cardinal Tarancón, who represented a majority of moderate bishops, was elected president of the National Conference. From now on the church would openly demand the liberalization and democratization of the regime. Nothing perhaps better captures the dissociation of the Catholic church from the Franco regime than the famous incident in 1973 when, at the funeral of the president of the government, Carrero Blanco, who had been killed by ETA, the Basque terrorist organization, the extreme right shouted to the presiding cardinal, "Tarancón al paredón" ("up against the wall"). At the very moment when the Spanish left abandoned its historical anticlericalism, it was being adopted by the Spanish right, resentful of the betrayal of a church that, after having been so pampered by the regime, was now abandoning it.[35]

The other important event of 1971 was the convention of the First Joint National Assembly of Bishops and Priests, which produced the celebrated public confession of sin for the role played by the church in the Spanish Civil War. The famous text read: "We humbly recognize our sin and ask for forgiveness, for we did not know how to become true 'ministers of reconciliation' among our people, torn by a fratricidal war."[36] This policy of reconciliation was probably the most important contribution of the Spanish Catholic church to Spain's transition to democracy.

The Role of the Church in the Transition

If the dissociation of the church from the Franco regime contributed to the regime's crisis of legitimation, the church's support of the democratic opposition contributed to the strengthening of civil society. The role of the church in the process of democratization can be analyzed at three different levels.

The Militancy of Catholic Activists in the Democratic Opposition

From the late 1950s on, Catholics played an active role in the emergence of the new democratic opposition movement. One finds *engagé* Catholics among the leadership of the whole spectrum of opposition parties, from the monarchists to the extreme left. Some developments have primarily symbolic significance. For instance, the theocratic, monarchist Carlist movement, which from the 1830s to the 1930s had provided the shock troops of counterrevolutionary Catholicism in all three civil wars, became radicalized in its opposition to the regime and adopted a "socialist" platform. Some of the most radical underground opposition groups, like the Castroist Frente de Liberación Popular (FLP) and the Trotskyist Organización Revolucionaria de Trabajadores (ORT), had Catholic origins. None of these groups, however, were able to survive the transition to electoral democratic politics. Of much greater historical relevance was the fact that for the first time in Spanish history Catholics joined and played an active role in the historical parties of the left, the Socialist party (PSOE) and in the Communist party (PCE). Indeed, the fusion of the Catholic and the secular left in the underground opposition to the regime was an important factor in the disappearance of anticlericalism from Spanish politics.[37]

Worker priests and lay activists who came from the Catholic workers' movement of the 1950s also played a central role in the emergence of the new working-class movement of the 1960s and in the establishment of the new semiclandestine trade unions, Comisiones Obreras and Union Sindical Obrera (USO).

Catholic activists also played an important part in the reemergence of the Catalan and Basque nationalist movements in the 1960s. But this fact is less remarkable, since the Catholic church historically had always supported the nationalist movements in both regions, maintaining a close alliance there with society against the centralist Castilian state.

The Church's Protection of the Democratic Opposition

Even in the worst periods of Francoist repression, the norms and values of civil society and the democratic traditions of liberal Spain were preserved and transmitted through the family, the working class, and intellectual networks. The moment state repression eased in the early 1960s oppositional activities against the regime proliferated throughout the country and in all spheres of society. In this respect, the democratic opposition movement in Spain emerged independently of any support from the institutional church.[38] Unlike in Poland or Brazil, the Spanish church did not need to become "the voice of the voiceless" or the very promoter of the reconstitution of civil society. But the church contributed to the consolidation of the democratic opposition in two ways:

a) By offering religious legitimation for the democratic principles upon which the activities of the opposition were based—freedom of expression, freedom of association, civil and political rights—the church undermined the repressive policies of the regime and thereby strengthened the opposition. The regime's traditional portrayal of the democratic opposition as the work of an external, mainly Communist conspiracy against Catholic Spain became no longer credible and, therefore, the repression now appeared simply as the expression of an illegitimate system of power based on naked force. When the regime introduced its first liberalization measures in the 1960s, the opposition was emboldened and it increased its confrontational activities. When the regime tried to put a lid on oppositional activities in the late 1960s by reverting to more repressive policies, it proved no longer able to regain control of public order. In addition, it lost most of the diffused legitimacy the regime may still have had among Spain's silent majority.

b) By offering its religious buildings, its churches and monasteries, as a relatively protected sanctuary where interregional, interclass, and interparty sectors of the opposition could meet, the church helped to coordinate and to unite diverse sectors of the democratic opposition into a unified movement of civil society against the authoritarian state. Notorious incidents when the police entered church buildings where important clandestine meetings were being held—such as national conventions of Comisiones Obreras or the assembly of the democratic opposition of Catalonia—only served to discredit the regime even further, by showing the entire population that the democratic opposition enjoyed the support of the church.

The Role of the Church in National Reconciliation

Much more important than its role in providing a physical space where the opposition could meet was the role of the church in providing a symbolic space for the reconciliation of all Spaniards. The religious-secular cleavage had played such a destructive role in modern Spanish politics because, by superimposing itself upon the other two major cleavages—the class conflict between capital and labor and the regional conflict between the hegemonic Castilian center and the nationalisms of the periphery—it had made all of them untractable. The Catholic church's final acceptance of the legitimacy of the modern world and the abandonment by the Spanish left of its traditional anticlericalism put an end to the religious-secular cleavage in modern Spain, thus making the other conflicts more susceptible to the politics of negotiation and compromise. Indeed, the spirit of compromise, the search for consensus, and the willingness to enter pacts became among the most remarkable characteristics of the Spanish transition. Semantic connotations such as *reconciliación, concordia, tolerancia, acuerdo, pacificación,* and *convivencia* all appear again and again in the political discourse of the democratic transition, in campaign speeches as well as in parliamentary debates. The immediate need to defend a transition still threatened by the danger of military coups and by the terrorism of the right and the left partly explains the willingness to compromise exhibited by most political forces. But only the more remote background of the collective memory of the negative experience of the civil war and of the system of exclusion which followed it may explain the fact that the politics of consensus, so characteristic of the Spanish transition, became almost an end in itself.[39]

The two great historical pacts of the democratic transition reflect this politics of consensus. The Moncloa Pact (1977), mediated by the government and the main political parties, though mainly symbolic, was the first historical compromise between capital and labor. Of greater historical relevance, however, was the constitutional pact one year later between the main political forces. The constitutional pact made possible the drafting of a constitution which, for the first time in Spanish history, was not the imposition of the will of the victors in the political struggle over the vanquished but, rather, the end result of an exacting process of responsible backstage negotiation between representative political elites.[40]

Throughout the transition the Catholic church played a low-key, yet positive, backstage role. Even though the church was still able to have written into the 1978 constitution a paragraph recognizing "the sociological fact" that the majority of the Spanish population was Catholic, the Spanish Catholic church finally accepted officially and without apparent misgivings the reality and, more important, the principles of separation of church and state, and of religious freedom.[41] Equally important was the decision not to sponsor any "Catholic" party or to support directly any of the Christian Democratic parties. A genuine desire for religious peace; the realization that the Catholic community, the clergy included, had become pluralistic politically and would not support any monolithic Christian party; and the fear that such an officially sponsored party could have become a minority party and thus would have undermined the church's claim that Catholicism was Spain's national religion—all these factors probably contributed to the political neutrality of the church during the transition. None of the three competing Christian

Democratic parties was able to survive the 1977 elections. In a sense, the political neutrality of the church during the transition meant that the Spanish Catholic church not only had accepted its separation from the state but also had abandoned its traditional attempts to enter political society through the mobilization of the Catholic laity.

Ultimately, the entire process amounted to the recognition of the voluntary principle of religious allegiance. The Spanish church has accepted the fact that it is no longer a church in the Weberian sense of being an obligatory monopolistic community of faith coextensive with the nation. The Catholic faith has ceased being, de facto as well as in principle, a national faith. At last, the principles of religious faith, national identity, and political citizenship could be uncoupled in Spain. Moreover, the constitutional recognition that Spain is a multinational state has in and of itself undermined the very principle of a unitary Spanish nation. The various nations making up the Spanish state have become institutions within a pluralistically organized civil society. By recognizing both, the fact and the principle of a pluralistically organized civil society, the church has become a denomination, a powerful one to be sure, but a denomination nonetheless, functioning within civil society.[42]

Opinion surveys after the successful consolidation of democracy indicate that the Spanish population also has internalized these principles. In 1984 an overwhelming majority of Spaniards (86 percent) still considered themselves Catholics.[43] But the number of practicing Catholics is much lower, tending to oscillate around 38 percent of the population. The number of Spanish youth who are practicing Catholics also seems to be decreasing noticeably. The number of youth attending Sunday mass has dropped from 62 percent in 1975 to 35 percent in 1982.[44] It is also evident that there no longer exists a religious cleavage which may serve to polarize either social classes or political electoral choices. Practicing Catholics are distributed relatively evenly throughout the Spanish population: they constitute 44 percent of the upper middle class, 38 percent of the lower middle class, and 34 percent of the working class. This is probably the most dramatic historical change when contrasted with pre–civil war trends. Similarly, though still unevenly, practicing Catholics tend to be distributed along the entire Spanish electoral spectrum.[45] Twenty-five percent of those who voted the Socialist party into power in 1982 were practicing Catholics.[46] In this respect, there is currently no longer a Catholic vote susceptible of political mobilization by the church.

Besides, the church not only can no longer regulate the public morality of the Spaniards; it also can no longer take for granted its control over the private morality of the Catholic faithful. According to a 1984 survey, 65 percent of Spaniards approved of the use of contraceptives; 54 percent would accept married priests; and smaller majorities showed approval of divorce (47 versus 40 percent) and premarital sexual relations (45 versus 41 percent).[47] It is not surprising, therefore, that the Catholic church failed to block or amend, through institutional corporatist pressure or through Catholic mobilization, the new legislation introduced by the Socialist government on precisely those issues the church still considers to fall within its own particular sphere of competence, namely, religious education, divorce, and abortion. The same survey showed that a majority of Spaniards thought that the church should not exert influence over the government (43 versus 32 percent); that the church does not have adequate answers either to the needs and problems of the individual (43 versus 39 percent) or to the problems of family life (49 versus 34 percent); and that the church's claim to moral authority is not based on a knowledge of reality (41 percent versus 27 percent).[48]

One may thus conclude that in Spain religious faith and morality are becoming privatized. Spain not only has joined the European Community but also has apparently adopted the general European pattern of secularization. It remains to be seen whether the Catholic church will reinforce these trends by retreating to the cure of souls and by concentrating on the protection of what it considers to be its institutional corporatist interests, or whether the church will be able to use its remaining institutional and moral weight to become a critical moral voice that, by participating on an equal basis in Spain's public debates, may help to enliven the public sphere of Spain's civil society.

On some of the occasions when the Catholic church joined Spanish public debates, its participation remained largely ineffective, among other reasons because it was unable to frame its discourse in such a way that it could not easily be dismissed either as a conservative partisan critique of the Socialist government or as an empty traditionalist critique of modern secular culture. The Catholic church's public condemnations in the summer of 1990 of the amorality prevailing in Spanish culture and of the widespread corruption in Spanish politics, at a time when the Socialists were afflicted by public scandals, may have added to the disapproval rate of the Socialist administration and to the general disaffection from politics, but it did not further any serious public debate about the meaning and nature of private and public morality in modern societies. Similarly, the pope's more recent criticism of Spain's "de-Christianization" and moral degeneration into "neopaganism" was perceived as a traditional religious critique of secular culture, even though the pope insisted that it was misleading to identify the church's critique with its hardened antimodern positions of the past.[49] In both instances, moreover, the Socialist government's defensive overreaction helped to frame the issue as a lingering reflex of the clerical-anticlerical cleavages so typical of past Spanish politics. Significantly, even critical theologians, such as Casiano Floristán and Enrique Miret Magdalena, feeling embattled by the restorationist pressures emanating from the Vatican, were unable to elevate the partisan dispute to a serious public debate and tended to dismiss the church's critiques either as a return to the condemnations of heretical modernism or as nostalgia for the lost neo-Christendom.

4   Poland: From Church
of the Nation to Civil Society

As in Spain, "frontier" conditions in Catholic Poland led to an early identification of religious and national cultural identity. This identity has been maintained and reinforced by subsequent developments.[1] Polish Catholicism has been repeatedly at the forefront of Catholic expansion or Catholic defense against other religions in Eastern Europe, to wit, different versions of paganism, Orthodoxy, Islam, Protestantism, and, finally, atheistic Communism. This gave Polish Catholicism its particular "militant" character. But like medieval Spain, where the three Abrahamic religions had been able to develop patterns of religious coexistence and creative civilizational encounters, *Polonia semper fidelis* served also as the setting for unique experiments in religious tolerance. The factor determining whether the direction taken is militancy or tolerance seems to be the identification of church and state. Indeed, Poland's failure to develop an early modern centralized state may be the single most important factor in explaining the divergence in Spanish and Polish Catholic developments. In Poland the Szlachta democracy of the federalist "republic of nobles" frustrated both centralized absolutism and the identification of church and state. Early modern Poland became a haven for dissenting faiths fleeing generalized religious warfare in Europe. Even after the Counter-Reformation reasserted Catholic hegemony in Polish culture and the war with Sweden awakened a strong anti-Protestant reaction, Poland still constituted a striking example of religious tolerance.[2]

Catholic Poland, like Catholic Ireland, is an example of a Catholic country which, in the absence of the typical fusion of absolutism and caesaropapism, deviates significantly from what David Martin has termed "the French-Latin pattern of secularization."[3] In both cases religion was strengthened by becoming the focus of resistance to a conqueror. Church and nation became identified at a time when the Catholic church was the only institution capable of cutting across the partition of Prussian, Russian, and Austrian Poland. During the nineteenth century, Catholicism, romantic nationalism, and Slavic messianism fused into a new Polish civil religion. At first, this process was restricted primarily to the gentry and the intelligentsia. But in the 1870s, the threat Bismarck's Kulturkampf posed to the linguistic and religious identity of the Polish peasantry pushed this group into the nationalist cause.[4]

Remarkably enough, the fusion of the Polish national and Catholic identities even took place in the face of reactionary Vatican policies which consistently supported the conservative monarchies and condemned the Polish uprisings. But the Vatican's "betrayal" was offset by the dedication of the radical lower clergy, by the farsighted leadership of a few hierarchs, and by the emergence toward the end of the nineteenth century of a Polish version of "social Catholicism." The formation of collective status and class identities, ideological positions and political groups, was refracted by the national question. Nineteenth-century Poland avoided the typical patterns of conflict between the Catholic church and the secular liberal state, between the church and a secular humanist intelligentsia becoming increasingly anticlerical, and between the church and a socialist workers' movement turning first anticlerical and then militantly atheistic. The typical positive correlation of education, industrialization, urbanization, and proletarianization with secularization either did not obtain in Poland or was significantly attenuated.[5]

When the first phase of industrialization took place, most of the state and capital was in foreign hands. Therefore, the church could not be perceived as legitimating either state domination or capitalist exploitation. As a result the first generation of Polish workers was neither de-Christianized nor denationalized, certainly not to the extent that was common elsewhere. On the contrary, there was frequently a fusion of class, religious, and national identity.

Polish Independence and the End of Polish "Exceptionalism"

With the establishment of a Polish independent state after World War I, the unity of the nation against foreign enemies began to dissolve. There appeared the standard cleavages between classes, parties, and ideologies while the chauvinism of every nationalism in power began to show its ugly face in its treatment of the Jewish and Ukrainian minorities. The unity between church and nation also began to dissolve, and there appeared splits between a conservative hierarchy and the more radical lower clergy. Moreover, though the church did not share state power and often found itself in conflict with the Polish state, its leanings toward Dmowski's nationalist Endecja served to alienate the other political parties and to antagonize the religious and national minorities. Anticlericalism, though a mild one by Latin standards, also began to emerge. It appeared in the quarrels between the nonconfessional Polish state and the church, represented symbolically in the feud between Marshall Piłsudski and Metropolitan Sapieha. It appeared among large sectors of the intelligentsia, which had finally incorporated the Enlightenment critique as well as the positivist and Marxist critiques of religion. This anticlericalism was perhaps best represented by the remarkable and little-known Polish school of the sociology of religion. It appeared, as was to be expected, within the socialist left and even within the peasants' movement led by Wincenty Witos.[6]

Had these trends continued, they might have put an end to Polish exceptionalism. But they were cut short by World War II and by the renewed experience of partition, foreign occupation, and unified historical resistance. National solidarity was once again strengthened by the extreme ordeal, and the Polish church found itself once more on the side of the nation, suffering more than its share of the brutal Nazi repression and supporting the underground both physically and spiritually. Any grudge Poles may have had against their church was soon forgotten.

The Catholic Nation versus the Communist State

All attempts by the Communist regime to sever the links between Catholic church and Polish nation ended in failure. It is true that the odds were against the new regime. The church's prestige was at an all time high, and its identification with the nation was reinforced by the fact that as a result of the eradication of the Polish Jewry, the massive Polish-Ukrainian resettlements, and the redrawing of Poland's borders, almost the entire population of post–World War II Poland was, at least formally and for the first time in modern Polish history, homogeneously Catholic.[7] By contrast, the prestige of the Polish Communists had never been high, the practical liquidation of the entire Communist party by Stalin did not help matters, and its replacement, the Polish Workers' Party, was, like the regime, marked by the original sin of foreign conception.[8]

Nevertheless, the regime could count on the nearly universal yearning for a clear break with the past, on the widespread acceptance of radical social reform, and on the delusions of large sectors of the intelligentsia.[9] Above all, the regime could count on power: the power to coerce, the power to suborn, the power to manipulate. Yet the regime's goal of attaining total power was frustrated again and again by the resistance of a church which, on the one hand, was willing to recognize the regime, to render unto Caesar what was Caesar's, even to lend it support and legitimacy for the sake of the nation and the requirements of the Polish *racja stanu*—something which was repeatedly stressed by Cardinal Wyszyński—while, on the other hand, the church showed a dogged determination to deny Caesar what the church claimed was God's, that is, control of the church and of the religious sphere. The consistent position of the church contrasted markedly with the utter lack of consistency in the state's policies toward the church, its strategies being marked by purely tactical considerations.[10]

The ultimate goal of the regime was clear, and it never ceased proclaiming it: the complete elimination of the church and of religion from Polish life. But it was also understood that like the final phase of communism, this goal was still far away and all kinds of detours might be needed in order to reach it. All the strategies of forced secularization from above, used relatively successfully first in the Soviet Union and then throughout Eastern Europe, were also variously tried in Poland, albeit with little success.[11]

Neutralization and control through the official incorporation of the church into the state failed. Unlike the Orthodox church, the Catholic church proved relatively immune to socialist caesaropapism. Neither the creation of "patriotic priests" nor that of "progressive Catholics," neither the support given to the schismatic Polish National Catholic Church nor the attempt to deal directly with the Vatican and thus bypass the unyielding Polish hierarchy, was able to either divide the church or undermine its prestige.[12]

The strategy of coercion also failed. The amount of repression needed to terrorize the whole nation would have been staggering even by Stalinist standards. The selective repression of representative bishops, priests, and nuns only served to turn them into martyrs or national heroes, as attested by the triumphal popular acclamation with which the release of Cardinal Wyszyński was received.[13]

Socialist resocialization also failed. The attempt to establish a new civil religion and to create a new "socialist man," an attempt which was far from successful elsewhere in Eastern Europe, was a total failure in Poland. In spite of the state's control of all official means of communication, education, and socialization, the church and the Polish family were able to serve as effective counteragencies of socialization, and together they successfully defended the right of all Poles to a religious education. All attempts to rewrite Polish history and to depict the church as an enemy of the nation and an enemy of the people backfired.[14] The official propaganda machine lost all its credibility, and the church became the cherished trustee of the nation's history, culture, and traditions, and of the collective memories of the Polish people.[15]

The marginalization of religion to a private religious sphere also ultimately failed because neither church nor state could agree on the boundaries or accept the customary limits.[16] Neither Catholic principle nor

Polish tradition could be easily reconciled with a conception of religiosity borrowed from bourgeois Protestantism and restricted to the private and unmediated relationship between the individual conscience and God, adorned at most by an Orthodox conception of ceremonial ritual, spiritually edifying but restricted to sacred places. Neither could Soviet socialism recognize in earnest the right of an autonomous sphere to exist, where "antisocialist" that is, antisystem norms and values, could develop. Such a model of autonomous differentiation of the spheres, borrowed from bourgeois modernity, implied the recognition of a pluralism of norms and values which was simply irreconcilable with "the leading role of the party."

Finally, secularist planning through economic development also failed to bring the expected results. The hopes of the Gierek era that economic development, borrowed from the West materially and ideally, would have the same secularizing effects in Poland it had apparently had in the West were also unrealized.[17] It is true that the model of economic development itself failed. But even before its failure had become obvious, the evidence of progressive secularization was ambiguous at best.

Marxist sociologists of religion had been collecting every promising sign indicating that the laws of secularization were also operating in Poland.[18] But at the end of the Gierek era most indicators seemed to point rather to a reverse process of desecularization:[19]

There was an absolute and relative increase in the number of bishops, priests, nuns, seminarians, and so forth, when compared with pre-Communist Poland.

There was a progressively accelerating increase in the number of parishes, churches, Catholic periodicals, and publications.

Indicators measuring the religious beliefs of the population, which had always remained inordinately high, even showed some tendency to rise, most significantly among the young.

The figures on religious practice were even more overwhelming, since even those who did not consider themselves "believers" participated in religious ceremonies as a symbolic opposition to the regime.

Clearly the church had won the war of secularization as well as all the main battles. Every time there was a direct confrontation between the Catholic church and the Communist regime over the control of religious education, over the control of ecclesiastical appointments, over the curriculum in the seminaries, over the millennium celebration, even over constitutional revisions, the regime had to withdraw and the power and the prestige of the church were enhanced in the process.

Cardinal Wyszyński was no doubt the individual most directly responsible for the church's victory. Historically, during interregnums or whenever the Polish throne became vacant, the Primate of Poland had served as Interrex, as actual or symbolic regent. Unofficially for almost forty years, Cardinal Wyszyński symbolically filled the office of Interrex certainly as effectively as any other Primate in Polish history. In a sermon at the Warsaw Cathedral on 7 February 1974 elaborating on his conception of the relations between church, nation, and state in Poland, Cardinal Wyszyński revealed his explanation of the victory of the church, namely, the primacy of the relationship between church and nation over that between church and state:

From the beginning there has been true cooperation in Poland between the Church and the Nation—and often cooperation between the Church and the State as well. Of course the dimension of the increasing links between the Church and the Nation are one thing, and the cooperation between the Church and the State another. The nation, after all, is a permanent phenomenon, like the family, from which the nation is born. The proof of this permanence is the fact that, despite the persecutions and the increasing struggle it has been subjected to in defense of its independence, living on the borders of (various) cultures, languages, faiths and rites, the nation has nevertheless survived until today. The Church, supporting the Polish nation so that it would not be destroyed, has helped it to survive. . . . There have been moments when the state fell silent, and only the Christ's Church could speak out in the Polish nation. It never stopped speaking out, not even when, in the time of the partition, the state was forced into silence. . . . It is the particular merit of the Church never to have stopped working, even in the most difficult situations. We ought to realize this when we speak of establishing correct relations between the Nation and the Church, between the State and the Church in our country.[20]

The structure of beliefs and practices of Polish Catholicism was formed for the most part during the Counter-Reformation and has remained virtually unchanged until the present.[21] Some of the most salient characteristics of this structure are the following:

• The public ceremonial, highly sacromagical character of the typical Polish rituals: pilgrimages (Częstochowa), processions (Corpus Christi), passion plays (Kalwaria Zebrzydowska).[22]

• The highly centralized hierarchic structure of the church, with the Primate at the top, in its unique dual role as head of the Polish church and Interrex, thus symbolizing the union of church and nation.[23]

• The prominent position of the clergy, with a prestige and influence perhaps unequaled in the Catholic world, functioning as sacerdotal and sacramental mediator between the sacred and the profane, and between

God and the Polish people, but also functioning as mediator, representative, and guide of the community in its social functions.[24]

• The Marian devotion and the two most representative Polish national cults, Częstochowa and Kalwaria. Particularly, Our Lady of Częstochowa at Jasna Góra serves as the national shrine of Polish Catholicism and as the symbolic fortress of the nation against foreign invasions. The icon of the Black Madonna has for many years been associated with historical and collective memories of national suffering, resistance, and final triumph.

Our Lady of Częstochowa was most effectively made into an impressive symbol of national and Catholic resistance to the Communist regime when, upon his release from prison, Cardinal Wyszyński mobilized the church and the nation to implement the Marian program he had conceived while imprisoned: the rededication of the nation to the "Queen of Poland" in 1956 at the 300th anniversary of King John Kazimierz's vows; the yearly vows of the Great Novena culminating in the 1966 millennium celebration; the annual procession of the Black Madonna to every single town in Poland, leading up to the celebration of the ninth centenary of the martyrdom of Saint Stanislaw in 1979.

Every attempt by the authorities either to stop the religious manifestations or to undermine them by staging parallel secular manifestations failed. Again and again the allegedly totalitarian regime's power of mobilization was dwarfed by the church's power of mobilization. The Marian program was not only able to keep the Catholic population mobilized for over twenty years around religious issues. It also symbolically linked in a dramatic way Polish sacred and secular history, the fusion of church and nation, and the ambiguous relationship of church and nation to the state. Indeed, it illustrates in paradigmatic fashion the power of religious beliefs and rituals to serve the cause of national integration by re-creating the bonds of national solidarity.

The Conflict between Church and State

The conflictive relations between church and state in Socialist Poland are usually analyzed from the perspective of institutional relations in terms of periods of confrontation, amelioration, accommodation, mediation, and so forth.[25] I would like to use a different approach and view those relations from the perspective of the principles of resistance which informed the church's actions. In my view one can distinguish three such principles of resistance corresponding roughly to three different phases in church-state relations. Those would be the principle of religious resistance, the principle of national resistance, and the principle of civil resistance.

The Principle of Religious Resistance

From 1948 to 1956 the church was fighting for its own survival as an independent religious institution. Naturally, corporatist self-interests predominated over any other concern. Yet corporatist self-interests were transcended the moment the struggle became a struggle for religious freedom, a universalistic principle, against the totalitarian tendencies of an atheistic yet theocratic state which wanted to impose its own secular religion upon its subjects.[26] The "Polish October," when Polish workers rose up demanding "bread and God," was the turning point in this phase. The church attained recognition and the right to autonomous existence in exchange for its support of the embattled Gomulka government. But the struggle against the totalitarian tendencies of the state had to be renewed continuously beyond 1956, since it became clear that the state would make concessions only in times of weakness when it needed the church's support but was not ready to institutionalize any of those concessions permanently.

The Principle of National Resistance

Having ensured its own institutional survival, the church could now attend to its traditional role as the nation's keeper. The new autonomous space gained by the religious institution could be used in defense of the nation. The pulpit, the religious classroom, the seminaries, pastoral letters, the Catholic University, the Catholic press—all became autonomous spaces where the collective national identity and the traditions and values of Polish culture could be preserved and transmitted. But the activities of the church were not restricted to this traditional form of "organic work" in times of partition or foreign occupation. From the very beginning, the church had played a very active role in the "Polonization" of the Western territories despite the Vatican's reluctance to recognize the new Polish-German boundaries. Soon the church began to challenge the state directly by reminding it repeatedly that the defense of national sovereignty is the primary duty of the state toward the nation. The clear implication was that the state was either violating or neglecting its national duties and that this was also the reason for its lack of legitimacy. The series of accusations and counteraccusations that followed was a reflection of the battle over the minds of the Poles in which both church and state were consciously engaged. The state accused the church of appropriating intolerably sovereign functions of the state in trying to represent the nation both externally (in the conflict over the Polish bishops' letter of reconciliation to the German bishops) and internally (in the conflict over the 1966 millennium celebrations). The Poles tipped the balance decidedly in favor of the church when they attended in great masses the celebrations of the millennium of Polish Christianity rather than the competing celebrations of the millennium of Polish statehood.

The Principle of Civil Resistance

Having established its own right to defend both religious rights and the rights of the nation, the church slowly began to expand its protection into new areas of human rights, civil rights, and workers' rights. At first, these new rights were defended in connection with the rights of the nation, as if to imply that civil rights were derived from national rights or, at least, that the duty of the Polish church to protect human and civil rights was derived from its role as the nation's keeper. Progressively, however, the church began to use a new language of universal rights, detached from any particular religious or national tradition. Furthermore, the right and duty of the Polish church to defend those rights was no longer grounded on the national character of the Polish Catholic church but, rather, on the universal mission of the church of Christ.

The precipitating factor in steering the Polish church in the new direction was probably the "Polish December," which consolidated the typical pattern of food price increases, workers' protests, and changes in party leadership.[27] The episcopate's letter of 29 December 1970, addressed to "All compatriots of our common Motherland," already resembles the type of Chartist manifesto the church's public pronouncements will increasingly display from this time on.

The recent events have made it amply apparent that the nation's right to existence and independence must include: the right to freedom of conscience and freedom of religious life . . . , the right of our nation to free cultural activity . . . , the right to social justice . . . , the right to truth in social life, to truthful information and to freedom of expression . . . , the right to material conditions . . . , the right of citizens to be treated without abuse, unfair injury or persecution. Both the central authorities and the entire state administration, and especially those charged with the maintenance of order in society, are responsible for the assurance of these rights. All citizens of the state are to share in this responsibility.[28]

The church's call for civic responsibility materialized in 1976 in the widespread public reaction against the announced amendments to the constitution. Obviously, the authorities not only had failed to assume their responsibility in guaranteeing those rights but also were planning to write their violation into the constitutional law of the land. The church joined in the public reaction against the attempt to link constitutionally the entitlement of rights to the fulfillment of duties, against the attempt to limit Polish sovereignty constitutionally, and against the attempt to inscribe into the constitution the actual division between the leaders and the led.

This resistance against further state incursions marks the starting point of the movement for the self-defense and self-organization of society. These civic actions, promoted first by intellectuals and protected and supported by the church, crystallized that same year in the foundation of the Workers Defense Committee (KOR) and would culminate in the emergence of Solidarity in its triple dimension as a national, a democratic, and a workers' movement. The new dialogue between the church and the left, and the coming together of Catholic and secular intellectuals in KOR, was to be of crucial significance for the emergence as well as for the character of Solidarity.[29]

The Normative Challenge to the Authoritarian and Totalitarian Tendencies of the Modern State

One could view the new civil defense role of the Polish church as a natural extension of its historical role of national defense. But it is important to stress that this extension implied a qualitative change and was influenced by general developments in the Roman Catholic church. Indeed, it is striking how similar the language of the Pastoral Letters of the Polish episcopate, written from the early 1970s on, is to the language of the letters of the Spanish and Brazilian episcopates.[30] Of course, this similarity in language derives from the fact that all of the letters have a common source, namely, recent papal encyclicals—*Mater et Magistra, Pacem in Terris, Populorum Progressio*—and the documents of the Second Vatican Council, particularly the Constitution of the Church in the World, *Gaudium et Spes*.[31]

It is undeniable that throughout the Catholic world, from the mid-1960s on, the church or at least some sectors of the church have been highly vocal in their defense of human, civil, and social rights against authoritarian states and economically oppressive regimes.[32] In many Catholic countries—for instance, in Spain or Brazil—this new stance entailed a radical change in church-state relations or in the class alliances of the church. In the case of Poland the qualitative nature of the change passed largely unnoticed since it appeared as a continuation of the established pattern of church-state conflict and church-nation alliance. The slogan was still the same: "Let Poland be Poland." But the meaning of what Poland ought to be had changed.

In *The Church and the Left*, Michnik correctly argues that the Pasto-

ral Letters of the Polish bishops and the pronouncements of the pope
provided religious legitimation for the model of a modern, differentiated,
pluralistic, and self-regulated society. He notes, of course, that this is
also the model of society pursued by the secular left and seems to be
struck by the fact that the church appears to have assumed some of the
central norms and values of modernity and the Enlightenment.[33] The
tone of surprise in Michnik's analysis has to do with the fact that at
least up to 1968, the Polish left and much of the rest of the world
had regarded the Polish church as reactionary, ultraconservative, and
antimodern.[34] As in all caricatures, there was a kernel of truth behind
the obvious distortion. According to Michnik, it was only in the course
of their involvement in the political opposition that secular intellectuals,
"far removed from the Church," "were discovering that the Church was
itself a source of democratic and humane values."[35]

In explaining the new dialogue between the church and the left, Michnik stresses in a characteristically self-critical fashion the process of rethinking on the part of the left which permitted the rediscovery of the
Christian roots of modernity. Some Catholic critics reacted rather
harshly to the call for dialogue, at times even questioning the right of a
secular intellectual like Michnik, who was tainted by his past association
with the regime, to pass what they viewed as condescending moral judgment on the church. But in fact, Michnik was being overtly generous
with the church, because at the time he omitted stressing the obvious fact
that it had taken the Catholic church centuries to accept the legitimacy of
modernity or to uncover the Christian roots of many of the modern
developments it had persistently opposed. Had this been the position of
the church all along, the Enlightenment critique of religion would have
been superfluous.

Indeed, the process of rethinking within the church, the *aggiornamento* which made the new dialogue possible, was as drastic as the one
undertaken by the Eastern European left with respect to its Marxist
creed.[36] But the reluctance of the Catholic church to acknowledge any
fundamental change in position and the fact that Cardinal Wyszyński
remained at the helm throughout this period have served to obscure the
nature of these changes. Undoubtedly, as Michnik points out, even a
traditional Catholic church has an antitotalitarian potential. But a look
at other Catholic churches in Eastern Europe shows that only in Poland
was this potential truly actualized.[37]

It is true that the impact of the Vatican *aggiornamento* upon Polish
Catholicism was not as sudden, radical, extensive, or definitive as in
Spain. This was the case partly because of the different church-state

relations in the two places and because of the embattled character of Polish Catholicism. On the one hand, not being an established state church, the Polish church had found it easier to unburden itself earlier of much of the dead weight of the ancien régime. Thus, change did not need to be as radical in Poland as in Spain. Ironically, Stalinist nationalization had also helped to free the church from its remaining historical ties to the conservative propertied classes. Moreover, the Vatican II proclamation of the principle of religious freedom and the implicit call for separation of church and state it entailed were received in Poland as a prop in the church's struggle against the atheist regime, while in Spain they struck at the very core identity of the Catholic regime. On the other hand, being as embattled as ever, Polish Catholicism could not afford sudden changes. Hence, it maintained some of the rigidity and conservatism which had served so well to preserve the Polish cultural identity through the ordeal of the partitions.

One could add that Polish Catholicism had also been undergoing its own internal process of *aggiornamento*. Given the exceptional fusion of religious, class, and national identities, modern Catholic social doctrines had found a natural resonance in Poland.[38] For all his rigidity and conservatism, Cardinal Wyszyński had been an outspoken defender of "social Catholicism." His vision of the church of the masses, of "the people," was undoubtedly rooted in traditionalist paternalism, but it served to keep ordinary people within the fold. On their part, sectors of the lay Catholic intelligentsia, organized in Catholic clubs and around Catholic publications such as *Tygodnik Powszechny, Znak,* and *Więż*, had been receptive to modern Catholic currents from abroad, such as humanism and personalism.[39] As in Spain, one of the most important effects of the Second Vatican Council was the support it gave to lay Catholic intellectuals in their traditional quest for autonomy from clerical control.

It is important to remember that, before becoming pope, Cardinal Wojtyła had played a prominent role within the Polish church. It was not by chance that he was elected pope by his peers.[40] He had had a few important interventions during Vatican II. In one of them he joined the American bishops in defending the principle of religious freedom. He was the main force behind the movement for post-Council reform in Poland. Himself an intellectual, he found it easier than Cardinal Wyszyński to develop close ties with reform-minded Catholic intellectuals, particularly with the *Znak* group, which often internalized the Council's message sooner and deeper than did much of the Polish hierarchy. As cardinal of Kraków he had promoted the "Oasis" or "Light-Life" Movement, the first revivalist-evangelical movement within Polish Catholicism. As pope he is the sign of the mutual influences, interdependencies, and contradictions between the global Roman Catholic church and Polish Catholicism.[41]

Although modern Catholicism has recognized the autonomy of the secular spheres, it does not accept the claims of these spheres to have detached themselves completely from morality. Consequently, it does not accept the relegation of religion and morality to the private sphere, insisting on the links between private and public morality. It resists the radical individualism that accompanies privatization and stresses the collective and communal—the ecclesial—character of the proclamation of faith and of religious practices, while simultaneously upholding the absolute rights of the individual conscience. Thus, it simultaneously affirms dogma and freedom of conscience. It also maintains an organicist conception of society that demands that all its parts work toward the common good and be subordinated to higher moral principles. In this sense, it maintains the principle of communal ethical life.

Superficially this may appear to be a reassertion of medieval Thomist organicism. The influence of neo-Thomism on twentieth-century Catholic theology would seem to support such a view. But there is a fundamental break with Thomist organicism. The "common good" is no longer tied to a static ontological view of natural law, itself tied to a conception of a natural social order. The church's claim that it is the depository of the common good is no longer tied to its expertise in a divinely prescribed natural law but, rather, to its "expertise in humanity." It is the transcendent, divinized humanity revealed in Jesus Christ that serves to ground the sacred dignity of the human person, as well as the absolute values of human life and freedom. The church escapes the nominalist critique of the traditional ontological conception of natural law by embracing the historicism implicit in the biblical message.

With some lingering neo-Thomist strains, this is the core of Karol Wojtyła's theology, equally visible in his pre-papal writings as in his papal pronouncements. In addition, Wojtyła has developed a personalist philosophical anthropology, informed by the work of Max Scheler, which is consistent with this theology but is not derived from it. This permits him to maintain both the religious particularity and the anthropological universality of the Christian message.[42] Striking in his papal pronouncements, particularly in those dealing with issues of public morality, is the fact that they are not addressed to Catholics as faithful members of the church, obliged to follow specific particular rules of the Catholic moral tradition. He addresses every individual qua member of humanity, challenging each one to live up to universal human norms, which are derived from the universal human values of life and freedom.

These absolute values serve to ground both the sacred dignity of the human person and the inalienable rights to human autonomy and self-determination. The fact that the pope also ties these allegedly universal norms and values to a particular religious tradition is certainly bound to affect the reception of these universalistic claims by non-Christians. But at the same time, in places where this particular religious tradition is still alive, it will probably serve to sanctify and legitimate modern norms and values as Christian ones.[43]

Only after the Catholic church officially and unequivocally embraced the principle of religious freedom and freedom of conscience at Vatican II could it develop a modern normative position. The traditional position and attitude of the Catholic church toward modern political regimes, once it realized it would have to live with them, had been that of neutrality toward all "forms" of government. It is true that the church had rarely failed to express its preference, and the Catholic "affinity," for hierarchic and corporatist over republican and liberal democratic "forms" of government. But the church also repeatedly stressed that if necessary it would learn to tolerate the latter and coexist with it. Above all, the church always asked the faithful to "obey" the rightful authorities. So long as the policies of those governments did not infringe systematically upon the corporate rights of the church to religious freedom, *libertas ecclesiae,* and to the exercise of its functions as *mater et magistra,* the church would not question their legitimacy. Only in those instances, and even then most rarely, would the church resort to the use of its traditional doctrine of lawful rebellion.[44] The assumption of the modern doctrine of human rights entails, however, not only the acceptance of democracy as a legitimate "form" of government, but the recognition and acceptance of the normative foundations of modern democracy. In other words, it implies the recognition that modern democracy is not only a "form" of government but also a type of polity based on the normative universalist principles of individual freedom and individual rights.

One can surely see a continuity between the contemporary Catholic defense of human and civil rights against the modern authoritarian state and traditional Catholic critiques of tyranny and despotic rule. One can even view contemporary church-state conflicts as a continuation of the traditional Catholic struggle against the absolutist claims of the secular state. Against the arbitrary rule of the tyrant and against claims of *raison d'état,* the church has always argued that the legitimacy of the state ought to be subordinated to the common good. But there is a fundamental difference between the traditional opposition to immoral rule because it violates "natural law" and the natural social order, and opposition to modern authoritarian rule because it violates the dignity of the human person and the rights to freedom, autonomy, and self-determination. The first conception of the common good can serve to defend a traditional social order from radical social change. The second conception presents a prophetic challenge to the established authoritarian order and may serve to legitimate a modern civil society. In Poland, this modern legitimation of human rights reinforced an already powerful political tradition based on the defense of the traditional historical liberties of the Polish gentry and an equally powerful cultural tradition in which the martyrdom of Saint Stanislaw reminds every Pole that there is a higher moral law and a higher principle of legitimation than *raison d'état*.

The Catholic Church and the Rise of Solidarity

Uniquely among Eastern European societies, Poland has been able to preserve two autonomous institutions from the totalitarian grasp of the Socialist state: the Catholic church and private agriculture. This was to be the most valued heritage of the 1956 "Polish October," when the church was to play a crucial role against state penetration in a dual sense:

a) It served as a refuge against the complete Sovietization of Polish society first by defending its own institutional self-preservation as an autonomous church and then by extending its protection increasingly to other areas and sections of society: peasants and farmers, national culture and traditions, lay Catholic groups, students, workers, and intellectuals, human rights, and finally the right of society as a whole to self organization.

b) The second important role of the church was that of being, in Michnik's words, "the most perfect model of the coexistence of an independent social institution with state power."[45] Andrew Arato has argued rightly that Michnik's own program of democratization, spelled out in his 1976 essay "New Evolutionism," can be interpreted as the extension and generalization of the institutional model of church independence, aiming to include other groups and institutions in a dual system of autonomous societal pluralism and monolithic state power.[46]

There were other ways in which Polish Catholicism contributed to the emergence of Solidarity. The striking image of the Gdansk shipyard workers on their knees partaking of Holy Communion manifested the extent to which traditional popular Polish religiosity, with its typical undifferentiated fusion of sacred and profane time and space, has survived the thrusts of modern Polish history. Catholic intellectuals associated with the Catholic Intellectual Clubs (KIKs) also played an important role part first in the foundation of KOR and later as official and unofficial advisers to the movement. Finally, there was the impact which the election and the visit of a Polish pope had on public opinion and on the Polish collective consciousness.[47]

After Solidarity

While few would question the positive role of Polish Catholicism in the emergence of Solidarity, the role the church and Polish Catholicism played thereafter in the martial law period, in the reemergence of Solidarity, and in the transition to democracy has been much more ambiguous.[48] The ease with which the church, following the establishment of martial law, reverted to its traditional role as mediator between the Communist state and Polish society should serve as at least a warning signal of the threats the institutional power of the Polish church poses to a fully autonomous civil society.

Given the fact that within the structure of People's Poland the church tended to attain its greatest influence precisely when both state and society needed its mediation, it was almost natural for the church to fall into "the mediation syndrome."[49] Under martial law, the church intervened to protect society from state repression and to demand from the state the protection of individual human and civil rights, but it stopped short of demanding the institutionalization of full political rights. The state, in turn, needed the church's mediation in order to obtain from society at least passive compliance so that the state of emergency could be "normalized." By working together with the state toward such a normalization, the church adopted a policy of political "realism," which basically implied accommodation to present reality as the point of departure for efforts to improve conditions in the future while relegating Solidarity and its ideals to the historical past.[50]

One can only speculate whether it was considerations of institutional self-interest or, rather, a realistic accommodation to a lesser evil that had greater weight in the church's position. Martial law may have been deplorable, so the official argument went, but it was necessary in order to save the Polish nation either from the threat of external aggression or from the danger of internal disintegration and civil war. Polish civil society had to be sacrificed for the sake of the Polish nation. There is no doubt that the patriotic appeal to save the Polish nation found a deep resonance in the collective conscience of the Polish episcopate. However, it is equally evident that from the point of view of institutional self-interest, martial law was good for the church. Never had the churches in Poland, already full under normal conditions, been so crowded as in

the martial law period. At the same time, however, the church's constructive cooperation with the regime paid off. Never had it been so easy for
the church to obtain state permits to build new churches.

If in the 1960s church and state had been consciously engaged in a
battle over the mind of Polish society, during the martial law period
state and society were engaged in a battle over the mind of the church.[51]
The "affair" Popiełuszko illustrates the complex interrelations and the
tug-of-war between the three.[52] Radical priests like Popiełuszko, who
had unambiguously sided with society against the state, were impeding
the regime's project of "normalization." By re-creating sacramentally the
collective effervescence of the original experience of Solidarity, they were
helping to keep the movement alive as well as preserve its norms and
values.[53] Having failed in its attempts to silence Popiełuszko through
personal threats, blackmail, and slander, the regime began to pressure
the church hierarchy to restrain the radical priest, arguing that such an
extremist political use of religion was impeding the normalization of
state-society relations and endangering the gains already achieved in
church-state relations. The church passed along the state's pressure, add-
ing its own heavier hierarchical pressure by demanding institutional obe-
dience over any other allegiance. Even after Popiełuszko's murder by
the secret police, at first the hierarchy went along with the game of
normalization and tried to arrange for a private family burial, seeking
to avoid the kind of public political manifestation of Solidarity into
which the people would convert his funeral. It was the people, not the
church hierarchy, who made Popiełuszko into a Polish and Catholic
martyr.[54]

Similarly, Solidarity was kept alive and reemerged politically with the
round-table talks of 1989, in spite of the fact that the church, at least
the hierarchy, seemed to have accepted its relegation to the past. Due to
the extreme hierarchic centralization of the Polish church, the kind of
open internal conflicts, indeed, the hegemonic struggles between the various groups and tendencies within the episcopate which were so visible in
Spain and in Brazil, could neither develop fully nor manifest themselves
publicly in Poland. For the same reason, the character and personality
of the individual at the top of the hierarchy, the Primate, play an extraordinary role in setting the tone, as well as the direction, of the church's
policies. There seems to be general agreement that upon the nomination
of Józef Glemp as Primate in 1981, the Polish church began to move in
an increasingly nationalist and fundamentalist direction.[55] It is pertinent
to add, however, that in this respect as in many others, the presence of
a Polish pope in Rome complicates the issue. One can easily imagine
that without such a higher presence the Polish church might have taken
an even more nationalist and fundamentalist direction.

The electoral triumph of Solidarity and the collapse of the Communist state have opened up a completely new chapter both in church-state and in church-society relations in Poland. There is a whole series of new fundamental questions which will need to be addressed and resolved constitutionally, institutionally, and culturally. Some of these questions are as follows:

a) Once a legitimate democratic Polish state has finally emerged, recognized by Polish society as its national state, will the church willingly relinquish its historical role as the nation's keeper or will the church continue competing with the state over the symbolic representation of the Polish nation?

b) Will the church fully accept the principle of separation of church and state, and will the church permit public issues to be resolved through institutional democratic channels, such as free electoral choice and open legislative and public debate, or will the church try to impose the Catholic confession upon state and society by curtailing or bypassing those channels and by using its enormous corporate power to restrict the electoral choices or to censor public debates?

c) Which form of social integration or solidarity principle will the church promote, that of "civil society" or that of "nation"? Will the church accept the principle of self-organization of an autonomous civil society, based on the plurality and heterogeneity of norms, values, interests, and forms of life, or will the church promote the principle of a homogeneous Polish Catholic national community?

Given Catholic principle, Polish tradition, and the reality of the institutional power and corporate influence of the church in Polish culture and society, it is hard to imagine that Polish Catholicism could soon become privatized. Undoubtedly, Catholicism in Poland will continue being a public religion for the foreseeable future. The suggestion that the Catholic church ought to accept the liberal principle of privatization is in this case unrealistic, normatively unjustified, and tactically perhaps counterproductive. There are clear signs that the Polish church already feels embattled by what it views as the advancing forces of liberalism. Indeed, warriors and spectators alike seem to agree that the main ideological battle taking place today in Poland after the defeat of socialism is that between Catholicism and liberalism. As long as these remain the main terms of engagement, one cannot but sense that the historical stage is being set in Poland for the compulsive reenactment of the vicious cycles of the nineteenth-century French-Latin pattern of secularization. Even looking back only as far as Poland's interwar period as a historical precedent, one can anticipate conflicts between the church and the secular state as well as new forms of ideological and political polarization in Polish society along religious-secular lines. Ironically, full-fledged anticlericalism may also emerge and take root in Poland at a time when it has practically disappeared from most Catholic countries.

Not surprisingly, the Polish Catholic church has rejected the liberal principle of privatization as a self-interested secularist prescription for the marginalization of religion into public irrelevance. Since the church has made clear that it plans to maintain a public presence in Poland, the decisive and still open question is at which level of the polity the church will choose to make its public presence felt. Will it want to intervene and play a public role at the state level? Will it mobilize its resources for battle in political society? Or will it limit itself willingly to playing a role in the public sphere of an open and differentiated civil society? Judging from the ambiguous and relatively restrained interventions of the church in Polish politics since 1989, those questions remain open.

One may at best give inconclusive answers recognizing that apparently the hierarchy is still grappling with those issues in its traditional secretive ways, is tentatively trying to shape circumstances and outcomes in an optimum "Catholic" direction without provoking a backlash, and is slowly learning to adjust to the new democratic order. Ironically, the newly gained *libertas Ecclesiae,* public recognition, and greater freedom of action seem to demand from the church greater self-restraint, more responsibility and public accountability for its influential interventions in the public sphere, and, ultimately, less maneuverability and authority than it had under the Communist regime. At this point, one can only point out some of the dilemmas facing the church in its public interventions at each of the three levels of the polity.

Cardinal Glemp has repeatedly expressed his preference for a confessional Catholic state. In 1984 he wrote a sympathetic introduction to a new edition of Roman Dmowski's 1927 pamphlet *Church, Nation, and State,* in which the leader of Endecja had advocated an authoritarian National-Catholic regime.[56] In 1988 in an internal document of the Polish episcopate, leaked out and published in *Aneks,* Glemp defended the traditional Catholic position against the principle of religious freedom and separation of church and state, arguing like the traditionalists did at Vatican II that the church cannot tolerate falsehood or recognize that error has the same rights as truth.[57] In 1991 Primate Glemp presented an ambiguous public proposal to repeal the constitutional separation of church and state on the dubiously democratic grounds that the rule of the Catholic majority would require the constitutional recognition of the religious confession of the majority of Polish citizens. But in the face of some public resistance and, apparently, the disapproval of the Vatican, the church did not press the issue. For the time being, at least, it appears that the Polish Catholic church has resigned itself to accepting the constitutional separation of church and state. Irrespective of its preferences, the Polish hierarchy could hardly publicly defend a position that goes against the new doctrine of religious freedom proclaimed at Vatican II, against the repeatedly expressed views of the Polish pope, and against general historical trends in Europe and throughout the Catholic world.

But the formal acceptance of constitutional separation does not necessarily mean that the Polish church is ready to refrain from intervening in state affairs privately through corporatist avenues. In the fall of 1990, under obvious pressure from the church, the Ministry of Education of Mazowiecki's Solidarity government put religious education back into the public school curriculum. This administrative act was unconstitutional, at least technically, since de jure the old constitution was still in force. But, more important, it contradicted the spirit of the yet to be written democratic constitution by removing administratively such a crucial issue from public debate.

The church's heavy pressure was equally evident in the passage by the Solidarity-controlled Senate in 1991 of a bill de-legalizing—that is, criminalizing—abortion. Again significant was the way the bill was passed, practically without debate—only one female senator dared to raise some questions—all senators virtually echoing the official Catholic position. One can suspect, as did the majority of Poles who according to opinion surveys oppose the criminalization of abortion, that the fear of the electoral consequences of contradicting the church on this issue weighed heavily on senatorial minds.[58]

The fundamental question is the extent to which the church is ready to refrain from using its extraordinary corporate power to bypass the normal democratic process by establishing itself as an extraconstitutional and extraparliamentary *tutelary power* over certain *reserved domains* of policymaking, such as religion, education, and family morality. The church has the right and duty to let its voice be heard publicly on this or any other issue, as long as it respects the rights of others to express contrary views publicly. But if the church does not exercise self-limitation in the use of its corporate power, preferring to withdraw those issues from the discursive public sphere of parliament or civil society, democracy in Poland could attain a *"perverse institutionalization."*[59]

The so far sporadic and ambiguous interventions of the church in the sphere of political society also make unclear the extent to which the church is ready to restrain itself from intervening in this sphere. The 1990 presidential campaign made public the existing cleavages within Solidarity and within Polish civil society. It also made it obvious that the old "us" versus "them" identification no longer worked. And despite all the attempts to discredit Prime Minister Mazowiecki and other Catholic intellectuals as "crypto-Jews," it also became evident that the political divisions in Polish society do not run solely along Catholic-secular lines. The October 1991 parliamentary elections showed even more clearly the limits and dilemmas of the church's intervention in political society. As in Spain and Brazil, the church in Poland throughout the transition refrained from organizing or sponsoring a Catholic party. At first, in the October parliamentary elections, it avoided endorsing any of the five competing Catholic parties, which eventually formed an electoral coalition. The church's vague appeal to the voters at the last minute to vote for "Catholic" candidates was largely ineffective and probably counterproductive. Even if the appeal helped to add a few percentage points to the votes obtained by the Catholic League, it would not be strategically wise for a national church to identify itself with an electoral coalition that was able to obtain only 9 percent of the votes in a very crowded electoral field in an election in which a majority of the Poles abstained from participating.

Even if the Polish church sought to, it is unlikely that it could organize or sponsor, much less control, a large majoritarian Catholic party. Only the unlikely emergence of a threatening secularist anti-Catholic front would compel diverse Catholic forces to coalesce into a Catholic or Christian-Democratic front. Barring such a development, which only irresponsible interventions of the church in political society could facilitate, one can expect Catholic groups to be distributed, as they presently are, across the spectrum of the Polish party system. Under such conditions it would be unwise on the part of the church to side with any particular political formation. The political mobilization of Catholics across parties for some presumably nonnegotiable "Catholic" issue, such as abortion, would most likely provoke the countermobilization of an anticlerical coalition which would reproduce the turn-of-the-century Latin pattern of secular-religious cleavages.

Even assuming, however, that the church will refrain from directly intervening in political society, this should not necessarily bar it from active intervention in the public sphere of civil society. The church has the right and the duty to speak up publicly on any issue it considers of public relevance, from the evil of abortion (perhaps a lesser evil) to the personal and societal need for religious and moral education (freely and pluralistically organized) to the need to establish norms of solidarity and perhaps institutional mechanisms to limit and counter market laws and state administrative measures which are blind and impervious to human needs and to the damage they produce in the social fabric and in the lifeworld. As the pope did in his June 1991 visit to Poland, the church is also entitled to urge the Poles to avoid and resist what is seen as the Western European path of secularization, materialist and hedonist consumerism, utilitarian individualism, and liberalism. The fundamental question is whether the church will strive for Catholic hegemony in the public sphere to stifle and silence dissonant voices or whether it will respect the right of these voices to be heard publicly. Here much depends on the courage of Polish intellectuals, particularly Catholic intellectuals, to express their differences of opinion publicly, especially when their opinions differ from those expressed by the church's hierarchy.[60]

Even in Poland, where the hierarchic, centralized, and clericalist nature of the Catholic church, along with traditional elements of Catholic culture, would seem to press in the direction of Catholic hegemony, one finds strong countervailing forces. Once the need for a unified societal resistance against the Communist state disappeared, Polish society exhibited an increasing pluralism of interests, norms, and values, belying any notion of a homogeneous Catholic national community.[61] Any attempt to impose Catholic solutions on societal problems not only may open up religious-secular cleavages; given the increasingly pluralistic nature of Polish Catholicism, it could also lead to internal conflicts and divisions within the Catholic community and the church.[62] The often stated discrepancy between the strong hold the church appeared to have over the public mind of the Poles on so-called national issues and the much weaker hold it appeared to have over the consciences of individual believers on issues of private morality clearly indicates that Polish Catholicism historically has served more as a public civil religion than as a private religion of individual salvation. As an example, the high rates of abortion in Catholic Poland indicate that, for all kinds of reasons, abortion has become a normal method of birth control. The state certainly promoted abortion, perhaps even trying to embarrass the Catholic church by showing how weak an influence the church may have over the private morality of the Catholic Poles. Given the scarcity of modern forms of contraception and their proscription by the church, as well as the views expressed in public opinion polls by the majority of Poles, the stage seems to be set for the emergence of conflicts between the church and large sectors of Polish society. If the church maintains its uncompromising attitude and insists on enforcing Catholic morality publicly, there is still a danger that the institutionalization of some form of Polish National-Catholicism could serve as an obstacle to the consolidation of an open and pluralist Polish civil society. It could also open the way for the kind of religious-civil warfare endemic to the Latin pattern of secularization. If the thesis presented in this book is correct, however, the Polish Catholic church could learn to accept modern secularization, that is, the relatively autonomous differentiation of the secular spheres, without necessarily resigning itself to the decline or the privatization of Catholicism in Polish civil society.

5   Brazil: From Oligarchic Church to People's Church

Like the rest of the Latin American Catholic church, Brazilian Catholicism is a historical outgrowth of the militant Catholicism of the Iberian Peninsula.[1] But from the outset there were some fundamental differences between Portuguese colonization and Spanish colonization that contributed to the establishment of two different forms of Catholicism within the same basic model of colonial Christendom.[2] The central institution governing church-state relations, the Padroado or Patronato Real, was basically the same in both cases.[3] The series of royal privileges that the Portuguese and Spanish crowns obtained from the Papacy, as a reward for their militant zeal in reconquering the Iberian Peninsula from Islam, transformed both colonial churches into ideal-typical exemplars of Catholic caesaropapism. As observed by Lloyd Mecham, "Never before or since did a sovereign with the consent of the Pope so completely control the Catholic Church within his dominions."[4]

Both churches became administrative dependencies of the state, allowing the crown to establish near absolute political, economic, and even doctrinal control over the ecclesiastical institution. The *placet,* that is, the right of the crown to censor all ecclesiastical bulls, letters, and documents, including papal ones, de facto severed any direct links between the colonial churches and the Vatican. Only after independence, in the nineteenth century, did the Vatican begin to reassert its influence over the Latin-American national churches. In the case of Brazil this process was even slower than in the rest of Latin America. Only with the proclamation of the First Republic in 1890 was the Brazilian church able to free itself from state control and to establish close links with the Vatican.[5]

Even though the institution of royal patronage was basically the same in both cases, the administrative presence of the state and particularly of the institutional church in colonial Brazil was never either as intensive or as extensive as it was in Spanish America. While Spanish colonialism soon assumed the form of an administratively controlled process of intensive and extensive colonization, aiming to reproduce in the periphery the basic institutions of the colonial center, Portuguese colonialism maintained the basic characteristics of a mercantile empire much longer. Similarly, while the rapid and extensive Christianization of Spanish America was the result of an intensive joint administrative effort of church and state, the evangelization of Brazil was left to the initiative of the religious orders, particularly the Jesuits. Consequently, the institutional presence of the church in colonial Brazil was extremely weak. Up to 1676 there was only one diocese for the entire territory, and neither the Portuguese crown nor the state church showed any inclination to establish either parishes, universities, or seminaries for the training of a practically nonexistent secular clergy. Other than the missionary zeal of the Jesuits and other religious orders, only the autonomous self-organization of *irmandades,* the lay brotherhoods which tended to reproduce in the colony popular Portuguese religiosity, can explain the existence of a modern Catholic Brazil.[6]

In this respect, two of the distinguishing characteristics of Brazilian Catholicism, the weak institutional penetration of Brazilian society by the church and the dynamic self-reproduction of different forms of "quasi-Catholic" popular religiosity autonomously from clerical control, have their historical origins in Brazil's colonial reality. One could further argue that the Popular Church and the ecclesial base communities (CEBs) that emerged in the 1970s as the organizational form of such a church are structurally linked to these two distinguishing characteristics of Brazilian Catholicism. They are the result of a dual process of strategic adaptation of an institutionally weak church to its changing environment and of the transformation of autonomous popular religiosity in a modern direction.

Prior to the eighteenth century, the institutional weakness of the colonial church had been largely the unintended result of benign neglect and of the casual disinterest of the Portuguese crown in religious affairs. But with the spread of Enlightenment ideologies and the adoption of an aggressive Gallican regalism by the Portuguese state, the colonial church now was weakened even further as the result of interested state policies. The expulsion of the ultramontane Jesuits from the Portuguese dominions in 1759 in particular delivered a severe blow to the Brazilian church, from which it would only begin to recover toward the end of the nineteenth century.

In Spain and its colonies, the similar triumph of Gallican regalism had been only temporary, interrupted as it was by the French Revolution, by the wars of independence, and by the ensuing conflicts between the liberal state and the church that emerged throughout the nineteenth century in the Iberian Peninsula and Latin America. In Brazil, by contrast, independence actually led to a reinforcement of state control over the church. Perhaps nothing better illustrates the unique evolution of nineteenth-century Catholicism in Brazil than the peculiar fusion of Catholicism and Freemasonry, under the mantle of a caesaropapist state, which adopted first liberalism and later positivism as its guiding ideology. Brazil's emperor, Pedro I, was simultaneously the first ecclesiastical authority and Grand Master of the Order; Father Diogo Feijoo, minister of justice and regent, was the main enforcer of Brazilian Gallicanism; numerous priests and bishops were also Masons; and the Catholic *irmandades* became centers of Masonic activity.[7]

The first conflict between church and state in Brazil took place in the 1870s precisely over Freemasonry. What made the conflict possible was the emergence of a few bishops in Brazil who had studied in France and for the first time began to look to the Vatican, rather than to the state, as their source of authority. Pius IX had been trying to reassert papal doctrinal and institutional authority over the national churches. In 1864 came the promulgation of *Quanta Cura,* the encyclical attacking Masonry, and of the *Syllabus,* which among the long list of "modern errors" included national churches, the *placet,* the precedence of civil law over canon law, and civilian control of religious affairs. Not surprisingly, Pedro II chose not to give his imperial *placet* to the publication in Brazil of both papal texts, since they attacked Brazilian conditions so directly. In 1870, the First Vatican Council, which was attended by seven of the eleven Brazilian bishops, proclaimed the dogma of papal infallibility. The conflict between church and state broke out soon thereafter, in 1874, over the attempts by two Brazilian bishops to follow the Vatican, by demanding that their priests abjure Masonry and that the Catholic *irmandades* expel all Masons from their midst. The state's response was to imprison both bishops. The reaction from political elites, society, and even the Brazilian church was practically nonexistent.[8]

In 1889 a military coup overthrew the empire and established the First Republic. The conditions of the Brazilian state church had become so deplorable that, when the republic decreed the separation of church and state in 1890, the Brazilian bishops, while rejecting the principle of separation, welcomed the reality as a liberation from state control that would give the church the religious freedom it had never enjoyed as a state church. In their Pastoral Letter of March 1890, the bishops came to the sobering conclusion that the "pretended patronage" had actually been a form of "state oppression" that had almost destroyed the church.[9] After almost four hundred years of state patronage, the Catholic church in Brazil had merely thirteen bishops and about seven hundred priests for a nominally Catholic population of 14 million. Moreover, the level of internal discipline and the moral conduct of the Brazilian clergy deviated greatly from European Catholic standards.

Its newly gained freedom allowed the Brazilian church to begin a process of internal reform and dramatic institutional growth. But the loss of state protection, including economic support, forced the church to rely for the first time on its own resources in an officially secular and politically hostile environment. The church became painfully aware of its extremely weak presence in a nominally Catholic society. With Vatican support and the importation of European clergy, there also came the Romanization and Europeanization of the Brazilian church in its general outlook and strategies. The church adopted the neo-Christendom model and the mobilization strategy of Catholic Action, which were then being adopted throughout Europe.[10]

The new vision and the new strategy were formulated most consistently in the famous 1916 Pastoral Letter of Dom Sebastião Leme, archbishop of Recife and Olinda, later of Rio de Janeiro. According to Dom Leme, who until his death in 1942 was the most prominent leader of the Brazilian church, it was the lack of religious education at all levels of society that explained the paradox of a church without influence in a nominally Catholic country. The solution he proposed, which he was able to implement rather successfully, was the typical strategy of Catholic Action, namely, to reconquer society by Christianizing its elites. The education of activist Catholic elites would permit the church to gain a stronghold in the most important institutions, particularly in the state, wherefrom the church could extend its religious education to the rest of society. As Bruneau observes, "The solution for Leme lay in a pressure group strategy, to re-enter public life and from this position use power to promote influence."[11]

Thus, less than twenty years after it had welcomed the separation of church and state, the Brazilian church, impelled by the perception of institutional weakness, began to search for a new alliance with the state. Modeling itself after the European churches, which were becoming urban middle-class institutions, the Brazilian church chose to ignore the immense majority of the population, the lower rural classes and their unorthodox popular religiosity. The ruling oligarchic elites on their part, having adopted positivism as their ideology, were ignoring the church. The church had to rely on the formation of middle-class lay Catholic elites to serve as carriers of the Catholic Action project.

The cornerstone of this project was the Centro Dom Vital. Created in 1922, the Centro brought together an impressive generation of Catholic intellectuals who later, for many years, would play prominent roles in Brazil's public life. At first, most of them adopted the kind of Catholic corporatist nationalism then in vogue throughout the Catholic world. Some, like Gustavo Corção and Plínio Corrêa de Oliveira, remained prominent leaders of the Brazilian Catholic right. Others, like Alceu de Amoroso Lima and Hélder Câmara, influenced by French Catholic thinkers such as Jacques Maritain and Emmanuel Mounier, began in the 1940s to adopt a more progressive form of social and political Catholicism, thus anticipating and influencing the progressive turn the entire Brazilian church would later take.[12]

The 1930 military coup which brought Getúlio Vargas to power also brought the state closer to the church. Dom Leme became Vargas's close personal friend and occasional adviser. Though personally an agnostic, Vargas realized the important role the church could play in the kind of state-organized middle-class populist nationalism he was projecting.[13] Furthermore, a few strategically organized massive demonstrations of popular religiosity in 1931 and the success of the Catholic Electoral League (LEC) in the 1933 elections for the Constituent Assembly had proven that the church had already amassed considerable mobilization resources.[14]

Mainwaring has noted that "the 1934 Constitution met LEC's principal demands, including state financial support for the Church, prohibition of divorce and recognition of religious marriage, religious education during school hours, and state subsidies for Catholic schools."[15] Vargas's assumption of dictatorial powers and the creation of the corporatist authoritarian Estado Nôvo in 1937 brought church and state even closer together. While Brazilian Catholicism was not as entangled with the Vargas authoritarian regime as the Spanish church was with the Franco regime, nonetheless Catholic ideologists also celebrated the Estado Nôvo as the model of the Catholic "Third Way."[16]

Thereafter, until the late 1960s, the Brazilian church followed basically the general developments of the Brazilian state and of Brazilian society.[17] In the 1970s, however, a new Brazilian church emerged, the People's Church, which not only became the main force of opposition to the bureaucratic-authoritarian regime, supporting the reconstitution of civil society against the state, but also began to sponsor the radical transformation of Brazilian society. What explains this transformation of the Brazilian church from its traditional pattern of orientation to the state to a new orientation toward society? There seems to be a deceptively simple answer to this question. Precisely because the new bureaucratic-authoritarian regime had created a chasm between state and society, the church, forced to choose between the two, threw its lot with society against the state.[18]

Three issues are crucial for an understanding of the distinguishing characteristics of the Brazilian transformation. An analysis of the three issues also serves to put into question each of the premises of a purely strategic-instrumental institutional analysis. These three issues are the following:

1. the hegemonic struggles within the church
2. the church's prophetic stand against the National Security State and its model of economic development
3. the People's Church and the CEBs

The Hegemonic Struggles within the Church

Ralph Della Cava's analysis has convincingly shown that the transformation of the Brazilian church, rather than being the intended result of an institutional strategy of adaptation, is best understood as the largely unintended outcome of a complex process of interaction and hegemonic struggles between the various individual and collective actors within the Brazilian church.[19] To a large extent, the transformation needs to be viewed within the larger context of the general transformation of the Latin-American Catholic church, which in turn has to be seen as the Latin-American version of the general process of Catholic *aggiornamento*.[20]

There is general agreement that the 1968 Medellín conference of Latin-American bishops marks a turning point in this transformation for two reasons: first, because it served to legitimate and to give official impetus to a process which had already started from below but now assumed a dynamic of its own; second, because to a large extent it generated the very phenomenon of a Latin-American church as a continent-wide institution with a differentiated regional identity, and as a transnational social movement made up of transnational cadres and collective actors with a common discourse and a collective project of historical transformation. Any comparative analysis of the Latin-American national churches shows that it is misleading to make facile generalizations about Latin-American Catholicism, for the differences between the various national churches there are much greater and more striking, for instance, than those between the various Western European national churches.[21] Nonetheless, today it is impossible to understand the developments of the particular national churches without taking into account the new reality of a Latin-American church. The study of the Brazilian church is of special relevance in this respect, because it is the largest Catholic church in the world, it played a leading role in the general transformation of the Latin-American church, and it is the only place where the project of radical transformation was, at least for a while, officially institutionalized at the top of the church's hierarchy.

In Brazil, as in the rest of Latin America, the initial impetus for change came as an institutional reaction to the perception of external threats which the rapid changes in Latin-American societies were posing to the church as an institution. Precisely in order to coordinate and direct the institutional response to those threats, the National Conference of Brazilian Bishops (CNBB) was created in 1952, as the personal initiative of then Msgr. Hélder Câmara, with the support of his close personal friend Msgr. Giovanni Montini, later Pope Paul VI, who was working at the time at the Vatican's Secretariat of State. Under the energetic leadership of Hélder Câmara and with the help of a small group of activist bishops, unrepresentative of the more conservative Brazilian episcopate, the CNBB became a kind of Joint Chiefs of Staff of the Brazilian church, planning and implementing a strategy of institutional and social change, very much in alliance with the reformist strategies of economic development which were promoted by the Brazilian state after Vargas's democratic return to power in 1951. Out of this close collaboration of church and state emerged two church-initiated and state-financed projects of social change: SUDENE, the regional development program for the Northeast, and MEB, the national program of literacy training and social and political mobilization through *conscientizaçao*. MEB, in particular, was destined to play a crucial role in the radicalization of Catholic Action cadres.[22]

The 1962 *Plano de Emergência para a Igreja do Brasil*, prepared by the CNBB, identified secularization, Marxism, Protestantism, and spiritism as the four main threats facing the Brazilian church.[23] The first three were the threats commonly identified by most Latin-American churches in the 1960s. The fourth, spiritism, refers broadly to the various forms of Afro-Brazilian religion and to Kardecism.[24] But the institutional response of the CNBB that was adopted as the official strategy of the Brazilian church was neither a conservative reaction nor a defensive adaptation to external changes but, rather, an offensive proactive promotion of radical social change. Moreover, while the CNBB in conjunction with the government was promoting a strategy of radical reform from above, the radical Catholic left and its party, Popular Action (AP), were competing with the Marxist left to become the vanguard of revolutionary change.

Conservative bishops, however, felt increasingly apprehensive and suspicious of the progressive leadership assumed by a CNBB that in their eyes did not represent the majority of the episcopate. Fearful of Marxist infiltration and critical of the calls for greater autonomy coming from

Catholic lay cadres, they began to curtail radical activism and to regain clerical control of the Catholic youth organizations (JUC, JEC, and JOC).[25] Meanwhile, the Catholic right was mobilizing upper- and middle-class women through "family and rosary marches" against the "Bolshevik peril," thus creating the social base for the 1964 military coup.[26] The 1964 military coup, which put an end to all projects of radical reform from above as well as from below, was followed by an internal coup within the Brazilian episcopate which displaced the small group of progressive bishops from the leadership of the CNBB. In their first joint declaration after the military coup, the Brazilian bishops thanked God and the armed forces, "who heeded the prayers of millions of Brazilians and delivered us from the communist peril."[27] In the next elections for all the CNBB positions, which ironically took place in Rome in the midst of the Vatican Council sessions, a coalition of conservative and moderate bishops defeated the progressive slate, the Central Commission was expanded from seven to thirty-seven members, and the whole administrative structure was decentralized, thus making the CNBB more representative of the entire episcopate but also diffusing its leadership role.[28]

It is even more significant, therefore, that by the early 1970s the CNBB, now representative of the entire Brazilian episcopate, had again begun to assume a leadership role, directly confronting the authoritarian regime and advocating and promoting radical social change. As Ralph della Cava observes, "A new hegemonic group— . . . the People's Church (Igreja do Povo)—had through an ongoing struggle come to prevail within Brazilian Catholicism."[29] This time, however, it was no longer a small group of progressives assuming the leadership of the church but, rather, the majority of moderate bishops and the entire Brazilian church that was being radicalized by the policies of the National Security State and its model of economic development.

The Prophetic Stand of the Brazilian Church

Even though such an analysis would tend to miss the dynamics of faith and religious motivation which led the CNBB leadership and radical lay Catholics to embrace social and political activism as a form of religious "engagement" and of Christian witness, nevertheless an instrumentalist analysis of the adoption by the CNBB leadership of a strategy of social reform prior to the 1964 military coup could be at least partly justified. One could certainly argue that by promoting social reform at a time when such projects were emanating from the state and from the left, the church was simply either trying to ride the crest of reform or competing with other groups and institutions to maintain its influence. Indeed, although the church had been an early advocate of agrarian reform, it took the formation of the socialist Peasant Leagues and of the communist *sindicatos* for the church to begin to organize its own project of peasant mobilization.

But such an analysis would be incongruent when applied to the church's support of social and political change in postcoup Brazil. When the Brazilian church under military rule again began to advocate social reform, it stood alone against the current, facing the ire of the state and experiencing in its own right the violence of the system. First to speak up was the traditionally progressive Northeast church, which had never been completely silenced. Then came the Amazon church, which gained its regional identity and its voice when it began resisting the savage, state-organized, capitalist penetration and colonization of the Amazon, a process which was bringing havoc to Indian and peasant communities and uprooting all forms of life that were standing in its way. Finally came the loud protest of the traditionally conservative church of the industrial South, particularly of São Paulo, which was galvanized both by the state terror spread chaotically by paramilitary death squads or administered efficiently in the infamous torture chambers of the Second Army Command, and by the increasing pauperization which was spreading through the rapidly growing concentric circles of São Paulo's slums. The Brazilian church became "the voice of the voiceless" after 1968, once the Fifth Institutional Act had finally institutionalized the National Security State and the ensuing repression had at last silenced society.[30]

One could still argue that with its courageous stand the church was trading present troubles for future influence. Undoubtedly, the Brazilian church acquired for the first time the kind of prestige and influence in Brazilian society it had never had before, when the church stood close to the corridors of power. But to view the church's stand as an institutional strategy or as a calculated risk is rather farfetched. The victims of state terror belie such an analysis. The church has always known, since it first experienced Roman state terror, that the blood of martyrs fertilizes church growth. But it is hard to conceive that the church would advocate or promote martyrdom as a strategy of institutional growth. Institutional analysis ought to be able to distinguish between power sought as an strategic goal and influence that comes as the unintended consequence of virtuous conduct, even when remembering with Nietzsche that the will to power lurks everywhere, even in the most humbling act of meekness.

Only an analysis which views the church's stand against the state as the assumption of a *prophetic* role can offer a convincing interpretation of the transformation of the Brazilian church. Of course, the entire institution never assumed a prophetic role and the readiness of moderate or even conservative bishops to confront the state can be easily explained as the expression of esprit de corps, or of institutional and corporatist self-interest. Many moderate and conservative bishops began to speak up only when they saw the repressive arm of the state reaching their own diocesan priests or their episcopal colleagues. Yet corporatist self-defense or solidarity cannot be the whole explanation, for the same bishops failed to speak up in 1964, after the military coup, when the brunt of the state's repression was directed at radical Catholics, including some priests. Besides, when the Brazilian bishops took a public stand in the early 1970s, they were not defending the privileged rights of sacred persons but, rather, the sacred dignity of the human person. It was the realization that the National Security State had gone too far, that it was overstepping the boundaries of the traditional moral order, that despite its rhetorical defense of Christian civilization its totalitarian tendencies were endangering not only the autonomy of the church but fundamental human values, that made even reluctant bishops take a public stand.[31]

The leadership role taken by the most outspoken sectors of the Brazilian church against the authoritarian state and its model of economic development was in any case certainly prophetic. "Prophetism" was not unique to the Brazilian church. It emerged everywhere throughout Latin-American Catholicism.[32] What distinguished the Brazilian case was the fact that in Brazil prophetism was more generalized and became institutionalized at the top. Weber's explanation of the emergence of ancient Hebrew prophecy may provide at least an approximate explanation of the emergence of contemporary prophetism.[33] Weber attributed the emergence of prophecy in ancient Israel to the joint existence of four conditioning factors:

1. an ethical-prophetic religious tradition, that is, the conception of a monotheistic transcendental God who intervenes in history;
2. "free" intellectuals, that is, intellectuals detached or alienated from the powers that be;
3. the massive proletarianization of the peasantry;
4. an international context of imperial power struggles.

These four conditions were also present in Latin America in the 1960s, and they may help to explain the emergence of liberation theology there, not only as a form of intellectual discourse but as a social movement.[34]

1. The history of the three Abrahamic religions shows that the ethical-prophetic component within the Jewish-Christian-Muslim traditions is always there, lying dormant, waiting to be reawakened when conditions are suitable. The renovation of Catholic theological discourse that ac-

companied the *aggiornamento* brought this tradition to life. The natural-
istic, ontological scholastic tradition was replaced by a biblical historicist
theology. The rediscovery of the old conception of the church as "the
people of God" and of secular history as the history of salvation found
deep resonance in Latin-American conditions. The paradigmatic prophetic texts of the biblical tradition—Exodus, the Prophets, and the
Gospel—were rediscovered and read, in many instances for the first time,
with new eyes. Also rediscovered was Latin America's own prophetic
tradition, that of Fray Bartolomé de las Casas and other missionaries and
visionaries who, as defenders of the Indians, had stood against colonial
exploitation.[35] Brazil also had its own tradition of millenarian socio-
religious protest.[36]

2. Although there are significant variations in church-state relations
throughout Latin America and although Brazil is an extreme case in this
respect, Brazil's experience, analyzed above, can be generalized to the
rest of Latin America.[37] Again, the timing and historical details of the
process vary significantly—timing and historical details being of crucial
relevance in determining whether the prophetic tradition will take hold
in one country or not. But the general outline of the historical process
can be reconstructed ideal-typically in the following way: for over four
hundred years, the Latin-American church stood bound to the state and
to the oligarchic classes. Unlike in Brazil, however, in many Latin-
American countries, after independence, the liberal and positivist state
separated itself from the church. But this only led a forsaken church to
seek closer ties with conservative parties and oligarchic classes in order
to obtain new protection and regain access to the state. In any case, at
the turn of the twentieth century, throughout most of Latin America,
Brazil here being the main exception, the Catholic church found itself
bound to the oligarchic state. As the oligarchic state entered into crisis
and was replaced by other forms of state differently throughout Latin
America, the church was forced to reassess its political and class alliances. Christian Democracy and alliances with various forms of populism became the typical responses of the church.[38] In some cases, notably
Mexico and Uruguay, a secular state with its own sources of legitimation
showed little interest in entering alliances with the church.[39] In other
cases, notably Colombia, the oligarchic alliance was remarkably able to
survive while adjusting to new state forms.[40] When in the 1960s both
Christian Democracy and populism entered their own kinds of crisis or
were simply proscribed by the new bureaucratic-authoritarian regimes,
the church was forced once again to reassess its state relations and its
class alliances.[41] This forced liberation from old ties made the church
free to establish altogether new relations. The process was particularly

critical where the crisis of the oligarchic state, or of the rural oligarchic social order which had survived the fall of the oligarchic state, coincided with the crisis of Christian Democracy and populism. This was the case in Brazil, Peru, and Central America, precisely the places where liberation theology emerged and took hold as a social movement.[42]

But it was not only the church as an institution that was freed from old ties. Even more important was the fact that church intellectuals—priests, pastoral agents, lay activists—were freed from their traditional religious roles by the dual influence of modern secularization and Catholic *aggiornamento*. As traditional pastoral and sacramental roles and the personal identities that went with them were put into question, church intellectuals were forced to reassess their personal lives and commitments and became free to adopt new, more "relevant" roles and to develop new, more satisfying identities. Existing surveys of the Latin-American clergy in the 1960s in places as diverse as Chile, Colombia, Bolivia, and Brazil detected very clearly this crisis in personal and role identity. In this respect, outer "secularization," the massive and rather sudden departure of priests and nuns, and inner "secularization," the adoption of social and political activism by many of those who remained, were parallel and closely related phenomena.[43]

Moreover, of all church intellectuals, the ones who experienced this crisis most severely and the ones most likely to assume prophetic roles were those who had lived in two worlds, either because they were foreign priests in Latin America or because they were Latin-American priests who had studied abroad. A quick look at the list of the thirty to forty individuals most influential in the development of liberation theology will show that well over half of them fall within one of the two categories. Similarly, half of the priests who joined the Christians for Socialism movement in Chile were foreign-born. But this does not make liberation theology less autochthonous, as some critics have tried to argue.[44] It was not the ideas, brought mostly from Europe, that were in themselves radical but their confrontation with Latin-American conditions that made them so. That the experience of "backwardness," which requires the knowledge and confrontation of two worlds, can serve as a radical impulse should not be surprising. When the roots of backwardness are found in colonial or imperial oppression, the impulse for liberation becomes even stronger. If one adds the sense of guilt or ethical responsibility that derives from viewing oneself as a privileged intellectual of a church which for so long aided in the oppression, then the personal determinants impelling individuals to assume prophetic roles or to become organic intellectuals of the oppressed fall easily into place.[45]

3. The proletarianization of the peasantry is, of course, a global phe-

nomenon which always accompanies capitalist penetration. Throughout Latin America in the 1960s proletarianization assumed massive forms, but only in some cases does it appear to be structurally connected with the emergence of prophetism. Again, the already mentioned cases of Brazil, Peru, and Central America are paradigmatic. Conditions for a fusion of proletarianization and prophetism seem to be particularly ripe when (a) proletarianization coincides with a situation in which there are no available channels of mobilization (parties, trade unions, etc.); (b) the capitalist penetration that produces proletarianization is state-organized and attempts at mobilization meet with violent state repression; and (c) there is a popular religiosity which can be tapped by pastoral agents for religiously based mobilization.

4. Liberation theology emerges in Latin America at the same time and for the same reasons as the "imperialism and dependency" discourse. Some of the common reasons were the experience of peripheric dependency from the capitalist center; the frequent American imperialist interventions in Latin-American politics, mostly to topple nationalist, populist, or democratic regimes; the role of the United States in providing the ideology, the training, the weapons, and the support of the "new professionalism" of the Latin-American armed forces and of the National Security State; the Cuban revolution and the fatal mirage of impending revolution it created throughout Latin America on both the left and the right. Latin America, like the rest of the Third World, became the theater for the hegemonic struggles between the two superpowers and the systems and ideologies they represented, capitalism and socialism. Many intellectuals and religious individuals, whether leftist or rightist, also tended to see the hegemonic struggle in light of the history of salvation, as a Manichaean struggle between good and evil. The fact that national rulers and oppressors were perceived as puppets of external imperialist powers made them even more illegitimate and open to prophetic condemnation.

The Church of "the People" and the CEBs

It is not possible to understand the transformation of the Brazilian church without taking into account the historical process which Gustavo Gutiérrez has called "the eruption of the poor in history."[46] The church, like the Brazilian state and the Brazilian elites, had largely ignored and excluded the rural masses. The rural oligarchic structure of entire Northern, Northeastern, and Central Brazil had been left practically untouched by Vargas's middle-class and industrial working-class populism and by the process of economic development and state transformation it had unleashed.[47] Up to the mid-1950s, when the first Peasant Leagues emerged, the rule of the "colonels," the local patrons who also doubled as political bosses, had gone unchallenged.[48] Heeding the Gospel's words that "the poor will always be with you," the church had taken the poor for granted and like the state and the rest of society had concentrated most of its ecclesiastical resources in the more developed South. From 1950 on, however, when the first call for agrarian reform by Dom Engelke, bishop of Campanha, Minas Gerais, was heard, "the agrarian question" would assume greater and greater relevance in the church's vision, until it became the single most important factor in the transformation of the very identity of the church as the Igreja do Povo.[49] It was the new attention given to the agrarian question with all its ramifications that led to the church's discovery of "the people" and to the church's assumption of the "preferential option for the poor."

Many factors played a role in this process.

a) The newly gained perception of what Dom Engelke called "the subhuman condition" of rural workers.[50] Dom Engelke was by no means a radical bishop, but slowly the discovery of the poor radicalized the bishops of the Northeast and the Amazon. Their collective pronouncements became increasingly more radical, attacking not only the subhuman conditions but also what they saw as the structural causes of those conditions. By the early 1970s they were openly calling for the "overcoming of capitalism" and the "socialization of the means of production."[51]

b) The perceived threat the emergence of the "ligas camponesas" in the late 1950s—organized by the Socialist Francisco Julião—presented to the tenuous hold the church had over the popular Catholicism of the rural population. The Natal movement and the church's involvement in rural unionization were a direct response to this perceived threat. Soon, though, the Catholic rural *sindicatos* became the largest and most active in the field, assuming a dynamic of its own and leading to the radicalization of all involved, that is, the base, the leadership cadres, and the hierarchy. The violent repression which followed the 1964 military coup destroyed the peasant movement, but the Northeastern bishops continued speaking up, condemning state repression and advocating social reform. By courageously drawing the ire and repression of the state upon themselves, Northeastern bishops, pastoral agents, and Catholic activists initiated the dynamics of church-state confrontation which led in the early 1970s to the break of the Brazilian church with the authoritarian regime.[52]

c) The Movement for Grass-roots Education (MEB), which played a crucial role not only in the social and political radicalization of Brazilian

Catholicism, but in changing the very institutional identity of the Brazilian church. By adopting Paulo Freire's ideas and methods of *conscientização*, what had started as a school radio program to teach literacy and catechism in Sutatenza, Colombia, was transformed into a national program of popular political education and mobilization of those who had been excluded from participation in the extremely elitist Brazilian society. By linking personal with social transformation as the very goal of education, the illiterate poor learned to see their personal ills as part of larger societal structures. The slow assimilation of Freire's pedagogy by the students and, more important, by the teachers themselves was as important as the lessons in political mobilization. According to E. de Kadt, around two-thirds of the MEB's leadership cadres had some Catholic Action background and over half of the cadres had belonged to one of the radical youth movements (JUC or JEC). Most of them were already familiar with Freire's ideas, but it was trying to implement them that made the difference. The populist faith in the people's own ability to organize themselves and to transform their own lives and society may have been naive, but it had a profound effect upon the Catholic elites that were working with ordinary people, upon the self-understanding of the church as a "church of the people," and upon the creation of a whole series of grass-roots organizations within the church and within society. MEB was the only movement of civil society able to survive military repression, which it did by falling under the protection and the ecclesiastical control of the hierarchy. The movement was depoliticized and given a more religious orientation, but it served as a link with the newly emerging CEBs.[53]

d) The rapid proletarianization which followed the increasing capitalist penetration of rural Brazil. This proletarianization presented the church with two different types of challenges. First, the church was forced to confront the human and social consequences of a rapid process of economic growth which i) disrupted the life-world of peasant and Indian communities, led to even greater latifundist concentration, and increased the pauperization and social inequalities of rural Brazil;[54] ii) led to rapid urbanization and to the proliferation of urban slums throughout Brazil, where new urban marginal classes where amassing without housing, without work, and without the most basic utilities;[55] and iii) increased even further the national income inequality, already one of the highest in the world, as well as the appalling regional differences in income and wealth between the industrial South and the rural Northeast.[56]

The church's response, particularly that of the regional churches of the Northeast, the Amazon, and São Paulo was (a) to help organize, support, and protect Indians, rural and urban workers, squatters, peasants, and small farmers in their struggles against landowners, capitalists, and state and local authorities; (b) to set institutional structures within the CNBB, such as the Indian Missionary Council (CIMI), the Land Pastoral Commission (CPT), the Workers Pastoral Commission (CPO), and the Justice and Peace Commission in order to help coordinate all the activities, to gather and publicize information, and to present reform proposals; and (c) to confront the regime directly with the publication of collective pastoral letters criticizing in the harshest possible terms the institutionalized terrorism of the National Security State, its constant violation of human and civil rights, the widespread use of torture and assassination, and the "Brazilian model of development." The Brazilian model, as one of the harshest documents put it, "means a 'development' that enriches only a small minority. . . . For the poor, the system offers a future of increasing marginalization. For the Indians it offers a future of death."[57]

But increasing proletarianization and urbanization presented the church with a second type of problem, this one challenging the very institutional identity of the church. In increasing numbers the new urban poor were joining Protestant sects, particularly Pentecostalism, and various Afro-Brazilian syncretic religions, particularly, Umbanda.[58] Moreover, it was becoming painfully obvious to the church that it could no longer count on the traditional clerical means of evangelization and pastoral care to confront the new challenges. This was the context within which the first experiments in ecclesial base communities as alternative forms of pastoral care began in the mid-1960s. Soon, however, the Brazilian church learned to make virtue out of necessity, and by the early 1970s the experimental stopgap measures had become an alternative model of church, officially promoted from above.

A quick look at the demographics of the Brazilian church should give an idea of the dimensions of the challenge. In the mid-1960s Brazil had a population of 80 million, 93 percent of which was nominally Catholic. To take pastoral care of this population, there were around 250 bishops (the largest episcopate in the world), around 12,500 priests (over 40 percent of them foreign), and around 4,600 parishes (with approximately 17,000 Catholics per parish, while in the United States, West Germany, and Portugal the number of Catholics per parish was approximately 2,000). Most of the ecclesiastical resources, like the economic ones, were heavily concentrated in the South. While the number of inhabitants per priest in Santa Catarina and in Rio Grande do Sul was around 4,150, in the Northeast, where Pentecostalism and Umbanda were spreading most rapidly, the number oscillated between 11,000 in Rio Grande do Norte and the extreme 29,600 in Maranhão. In addition, there was little hope for improvement in the future. Between 1967 and 1977, 2,300 priests (ca. 20 percent) left the priesthood, while the traditional vocational sources, seminaries, and foreign priests were dwindling.[59]

By the early 1980s, Brazil's population had reached 130 million, the number of bishops had increased to 360, and the number of priests had stayed around 13,000 while there were roughly 80,000 new ecclesial base communities. As Leonardo Boff, the most important and original Brazilian liberation theologian, has observed, a new "ecclesiogenesis" had taken place. The ecclesial base communities had "reinvented" the Brazilian church.[60] But it would be a serious error to interpret the growth of the CEBs simply as a function of the shortage of priests. Other Latin-American churches experienced similar shortages, and yet neither the hierarchy there promoted the CEBs nor did they take root from below. Today, with 360 bishops and 38 priests per bishop, the Brazilian church is probably the top-heaviest in the world, yet it is also perhaps the least hierarchic, the least clerical, and one of the most democratic internally at all levels.[61]

The shortage of priests was certainly important in giving impetus to the early experiments, but the CEBs could neither have grown as they did nor taken the form they took without (a) the decision of the hierarchy to promote them, fully conscious that they were promoting an alternative model of church; (b) the full commitment of the pastoral agents who initiated and continued guiding them and who saw them not only as alternative forms of religious community but even more as popular organizations where the people could develop humanly, socially, and politically, indeed, as the self-organization of society from below; and (c) the existence of a resilient Catholic popular religiosity which had been able to reproduce itself for centuries with minimum clerical control. It was not so much an ecclesiastical strategy of institutional survival as a conscious decision to transform the church's identity and to become the church of the people by directing the attention and resources of the church to the lower classes. In Brazil, "the preferential option for the poor," a concept which originated in the Brazilian church and was assumed by the Latin-American church at Puebla, ·became to a larger extent than anywhere else a true commitment.[62]

Guillermo O'Donnell has argued that "nation," "civil society," and "lo popular" can be viewed as three alternative principles and structures of mediation between state and society.[63] While "nation" is the principle of organization of a homogeneous societal community organized politically through the state against other nation-states and against the internal "other," the enemy within, "lo popular" or, rather, "lo nacional-popular," as it appears in Argentinian Peronist political discourse, is the principle of organization of a homogeneous societal community organized politically through the state against internal and external oligarchies. As political movements geared to conquer the state or already organized through the state, both nationalism and populism tend to be undemocratic insofar as the structure of mediation of national or popular interests is usually organized through the plebiscitarian relationship of the leader and the masses and through corporatist representation. In the case of Argentinian populism, in the first phase of Peronismo, the three corporations representing "nacional-popular" interests were the unions, the army, and the church.

What is significant about the new populism, the new trade unionism, and the new social movements that emerged in Brazil in the late 1970s, all three of them with organizational and ideological roots in the CEBs, is the fact not only that they were directed against the nationalism of a National Security State that excluded both civil society and the people from political participation, and against an economic nationalism that measured development solely by the growth of the gross national product, but also that they broke with much of the elitism and the statism of traditional Brazilian populism.[64] In the new political discourse, "the people" served both as the principle of self-defense of society against the state and as the principle of self-organization of society autonomously from the state. In this respect, it was akin to the principle of organization of Polish Solidarity. In both cases civil society, a concept which also assumed a central role in the new political discourse, was conceived as "a political space" autonomous from the state. Hence, the concept of civil society was consciously opposed to traditional ideas of the relations between state and society. The emphasis on "the people" was directed against the traditional elitism of Brazilian political society and its structures of mediation and representation of interests, which had excluded the majority of the people from participation. In this respect, both concepts, that of civil society and that of "the people," were not so much principles of mediation between state and society as principles of self-organization of society without mediations and without the state, principles of direct communitarian democracy with strong affinities with Christian anarchism.[65]

While incorporating some aspects of the concept of civil society, the concept of "the people" maintains an ambiguous tension with traditional conceptions of civil society. As Rubem César Fernandes has pointed out,

The movement for the construction of civil society turns highly ambiguous since, while being oriented towards the defense of the autonomy of the individual (and of groups of individuals associated freely), it maintains at the same time the idea of a collective social identity, which encompasses society as a whole. In Brazil, this entity is called "the people," in Poland "the nation."[66]

In both cases the church assumed a central role of symbolic representation, as the nation's keeper in the case of Poland, and as "the people of God" in the case of Brazil.

This ambiguous tension became manifest throughout Brazil's transition. Nobody can question the crucial role of the Brazilian church in the process of democratization. When both civil society and political society were silenced and repressed, the church became their voice and assumed their defense. In their collective Pastoral Letter "I heard the Cry of My People" the bishops of the Northeast spoke as courageously as any prophet has ever done:

Repression is increasingly needed to guarantee the functioning and security of the associated capitalist system. The legislature has no authority; urban and rural unions are forcefully depoliticized; the leaders are persecuted; censorship has gotten worse; workers, peasants and intellectuals are persecuted; priests and activists in the Christian churches suffer persecution. The regime has used various forms of imprisonment, torture, mutilations, and assassinations.[67]

São Paulo's cardinal, Dom Paulo Evaristo Arns, became the spokesman and leader of the national campaign for civil and human rights, and publicized worldwide the regime's systematic use of torture.[68] The role of the CEBs in the emergence and growth of the new social movements has also been amply documented.[69]

But as the *abertura* proceeded and the electoral competition assumed a dynamic of its own, which the regime could no longer control even by constantly changing the rules of the electoral game, the church seemed to be distancing itself from the process. It is true that the church encouraged political participation, urged the people to vote, and publicized the different political options, trying to be neutral, while being accused of favoring the parties of the left, particularly the new Workers' Party (PT). As in Spain, the decision to remain neutral and not to promote any Christian party was a constructive one. There was certainly pressure on the church from the Vatican to depoliticize, to leave politics to the politicians, and to concentrate on its pastoral duties. But besides that, there was the residual ambiguity of the "People's Church" toward the state, toward political society, and toward political elites which, while claiming to represent the people, most likely would continue reproducing the mechanisms of exclusion.

The Dilemmas of Catholic Democratization

The successful transition to democracy and the ensuing institutionalization of political society lead per force to a relative privatization of Catholicism. Everywhere, once the phase of consolidation of democracy begins, the church tends to withdraw from political society proper, leaving this realm to professional politicians. A dual dynamic seems to be at work.

On the one hand, there are the unavoidable structural constraints imposed by the establishment of a liberal democratic political system and the concomitant institutionalization of a democratic political society with its characteristic elitist structures of mediation and representation. Everywhere, once the phase of consolidation begins, the political hour of a civil society, united in opposition to an authoritarian state, tends to come to an end. Even if the church wanted to resist this structural trend, it is unlikely that it would be able to maintain the highly prominent political role of the transitional phase.

On the other hand, however, these structural trends have been reinforced by the new policy directives coming from the Vatican and by the conservative project of "restoration" associated with the Papacy of Karol Wojtyła and led by Joseph Cardinal Ratzinger, the prefect of the Sacred Congregation for the Doctrine of the Faith. The pope's repeated warnings to priests and pastoral agents to concentrate on their pastoral duties, while leaving the political sphere to the laity; the censoring and suspension of progressive theologians and clerics, from Spain to Brazil, from Germany to the United States; the attempt to coopt, temper, and spiritualize the discourse of liberation theology and the practices of the basic Christian communities; and, above all, the Vatican's attempt to regain centralized control of the National Conference of Bishops through the nomination and appointment of conservative and moderate bishops—all these processes have worked in the direction of the privatization of Catholicism.[70]

Furthermore, unlike Spanish or Polish Catholicism, which face no serious religious competition, Brazilian Catholicism is forced to confront the religious competition coming from evangelical Protestantism as well as from Afro-Brazilian religions. During the last thirty years Protestantism, particularly the Pentecostal churches, has continued its steady expansion in Brazil and has become indigenous and self-reproducing to such an extent that nowadays it needs to rely less than Catholicism on religious personnel from abroad.[71] Similarly, Afro-Brazilian religions, particularly Umbanda, and spiritism, particularly Kardecism, have continued growing and ever larger sectors of the nominally Catholic population participate simultaneously in Catholic, Afro-Brazilian, and spiritist religious practices. Much of the competition, moreover, is centered around the same religious clientele, the large rural and urban marginal sectors of the Brazilian population. Thus, in addition to the pressures coming from the institutionalization of political society and from the Vatican, the very dynamics of religious competition impel the Brazilian church to concentrate on its pastoral role.[72]

Vatican pressure and the open support given to the more moderate and conservative sectors of the hierarchy through episcopal nominations and appointments have, temporarily at least, silenced the more progressive sectors of Brazilian Catholicism.[73] Ironically, in his trip to Brazil in October 1991, the pope expressed public support for agrarian reform, apparently trying to legitimate once again the church's public involvement in social and political issues.[74] But the papal voice found little public resonance.

Today, the Catholic church in Brazil can no longer be a state church, nor can Catholicism any longer claim to be the national faith. Additionally, given the constraints of *raison d'église* and the organizational imperatives of the church in the modern world, one cannot expect the Catholic church to support one party or one partisan option in Brazilian political society.[75] Nor can the self-designation of the church as "*A Igreja do Povo*" or its "preferential option for the poor" still have the connotation it received in the first phases of liberation theology, when its discourse was informed by the traditional populist rhetoric of "people" versus "oligarchy" and by the Marxist vision of the impending class struggle. Ironically, large sectors of the Brazilian poor are showing a preference for "evangelical" Protestantism while large sectors of the middle classes have become estranged from the "populist" church. But given the political and economic realities of the Brazilian democratic order, it is unlikely that the Brazilian church will withdraw permanently to the privatized sphere of the spiritual care of souls. Despite universal suffrage and the legal obligation to vote, half of Brazil's adult population can be characterized at best as second-class citizens, barely able to eke out a meager subsistence at the margins of the Brazilian economy. The church can still be or may again become "the voice of the voiceless," of those whose views and interests do not find institutional representation in Brazilian political society.

6   Evangelical Protestantism: From Civil Religion to Fundamentalist Sect to New Christian Right

The public reemergence of Protestant fundamentalism as a social movement in the 1980s raises three fundamental questions for sociological analysis. The first question, why here and not elsewhere? derives from the fact that among advanced Western industrial societies only in the United States has there appeared a religious fundamentalist movement of societal importance.[1] The second question, why now? derives from the fact that from the 1930s to the 1970s the fundamentalist wing of evangelical Protestantism had been a relatively pietistic, withdrawn, and virtually ignored sector of American Protestantism. Finally, what are the possible implications and consequences of the unexpected entrance of religious fundamentalism into the public sphere of a modern society?

The First Disestablishment: The Secularization of the State

The "exceptionalism" of the American fundamentalist phenomenon needs to be viewed in terms of the historically peculiar process of secularization in America. From independence to the present, American Protestantism has gone through three consecutive processes of disestablishment. The first disestablishment, the constitutional one, constructed the still disputed "wall of separation" between the Protestant churches and the American state. This disestablishment brought about the separation of the state from ecclesiastical institutions and the dissociation of the political community of citizens from any religious community. But the secularization of the state did not bring in its wake either the decline or the privatization of religion. On the contrary, as is widely recognized today, the constitutional protection of the free exercise of religion created the structural framework for the emergence and the unprecedented expansion of what Martin Marty has called "the crazy quilt of Protestant denominationalism." At a time when continental European Christianity was mostly retreating, unable to withstand the waves of industrial, political, and cultural revolution, American Christianity was "awash in a sea of faith." Evangelical revivalism became the organizational principle and the common denominator of all the religious groups competing in the Protestant denominational religious system. By the 1830s, evangelical Protestantism had become established de facto as the American civil religion, that is, as the public religion of American civil society. The homogenization of the main Protestant denominations made possible the launching of a transdenominational evangelical crusade to "Christianize" the people, the social order, and the republic.[2]

Given this historical development, the principle of religious liberty enshrined first in the Virginia Statute on Religious Liberty and then in the First Amendment becomes even more remarkable. The establishment of any particular church at the national level was certainly precluded by the territorial distribution and the relatively equal strength of the three colonial churches at the time of independence: Congregational, Presbyterian, and Anglican. But either multiple religious establishments or the establishment of a generalized Christian (i.e., Protestant) religion could have been an outcome had it not been for the active collaboration of Jefferson, Madison, and dissenting Baptists in Virginia. This "Jeffersonian moment," bringing together republican deism and radical-pietist sectarian Protestantism, was both fragile and brief.[3] But it was able to create a revolutionary constitutional reality which, thanks to the progressive sacralization of the Constitution, was able to withstand the wide gap between the *pays constitutionel* and the *pays real*, as well as the repeated Protestant crusades to put God or Christ in the Constitution, to define America as a Christian nation, and to protect Christianity as the common law of the land. Some New England states maintained their established Congregational churches for several decades, and despite article 6, section 3, of the Constitution, most state constitutions maintained for even longer periods of time clauses disqualifying non-Protestants, non-Christians, or atheists from public office.[4]

It is true that the religious factor has been an important ingredient of American politics from the very origins of the American party system.[5] But properly speaking, public religion in America has not functioned at the level of mobilized political society. Even though the fusion between party and denominational allegiance has generally been important, the American party system was not organized along strict denominational or secular-religious cleavages, as was the case in many European countries. If, as Tocqueville said, "religion in America . . . must be regarded as the first of their political institutions,"[6] this is due to the role which religion played in the public sphere of civil society. The established ministry of the New England Standing Order could not prevent the election of Jefferson to the presidency, much less the rise of Jacksonian democracy, but its nativist attacks against deism, infidelity, and foreign revolutionary conspiracies along with the revivalist enthusiasm of the Second Great Awakening were effective in derailing the American Enlightenment and in Christianizing post factum the republic.[7]

The democratization of the aristocratic republic and the democratization of Christianity went hand in hand and had similar effects upon political and religious culture.[8] Andrew Jackson, though a strict separationist, was the first "evangelical" president. Evangelical Protestantism soon attained hegemonic control over the public discourse of American civil society. Except for the Unitarian liberalism of Harvard, a new synthesis of Calvinist faith, Scottish commonsense realism, and the evangelical religion of the heart became entrenched in one Protestant college after another and maintained its cultural hegemony over the "life of the mind" until the last quarter of the nineteenth century.[9] This cultural hegemony was not restricted to the culture of the elite. Through the public school, the common school, and the Sunday school movements, it encompassed the entire public realm of education and religious instruction, and it extended to the mass media and to societies and movements for moral and social reform. Indeed, evangelical societies established the framework for all forms of American voluntary societies and evangelical revivalism became the cradle of American social movements.[10]

The Second Disestablishment: The Secularization of the Life of the Mind and the First Mobilization of Protestant Fundamentalism

The "second disestablishment" cannot be traced back to one single event or to a series of events, but the final outcome is clear: the secularization of American higher education and the loss of Protestant cultural hegemony over the public sphere of American civil society. For two important reasons, however, one could choose the Civil War as the initial milestone in the process. Civil war and reconstruction created the structural conditions for the rapid process of capitalist industrialization and urbanization that radically and irrevocably altered antebellum American society.

The new industrial society needed new institutions of higher learning. The traditional Protestant colleges and universities shed or marginalized their divinity schools, their original nuclei, as they entered upon the modern process of academic and scientific specialization. The opening up of public lands for state land-grant colleges speeded up the process. The natural sciences, particularly Darwinism, the newly emerging social sciences, and the cultural-historical sciences with their new epistemologies and critical methods of interpretation presented explanations of nature, society, and human culture that were often in conflict with established Protestant worldviews.[11]

The new urban, industrial America was no longer shaped predominantly by Protestantism. Finding the new city a largely foreign, unregenerate, and dangerous environment, evangelical Protestantism never tried very hard to conquer it.[12] Undoubtedly, evangelical Protestantism learned to adapt to the new environment and to prosper in it, as did most other privatized forms of religion. But for the most part, urban revivalism no longer tried to Christianize the new urban environment, contenting itself with saving souls from it. When the liberal wing of evangelical Protestantism, the Social Gospel movement, tried to "Christianize the social order," it soon realized that it would have to compete not only with sinful resistance but with secular and non-Protestant movements and organizations.[13] The masses of newly arrived non-Protestant immigrants could no longer be assimilated on Protestant terms.[14] Moreover, the split of Protestantism into what Martin Marty has called "a two-party system" made any attempt at Protestant cultural hegemony impossible. Actually, the split was a double one. There was, first, the ideological-theological split between public liberal Protestantism, which was becoming less and less evangelical, and private conservative evangelical Protestantism. But second, within evangelical Protestantism, there was the internal racial cleavage between white and black denominations. Attempts at Protestant cultural hegemony in urban America became futile. Even in those rare cases in which Protestants became a majority, ideological and racial cleavages made Protestant hegemony unfeasible.[15]

The second important reason why the Civil War marks a turning point in the second disestablishment is precisely because it anticipates this dual internal cleavage within American Protestantism. In the South, the crucibles of religion and race, which have always been the key factors in American "exceptionalism," were fused together inextricably.[16] More firmly than anywhere else, evangelical Protestantism became the uncontested civil religion of the South. At the time of the Civil War, the South was 90 percent Protestant. Furthermore, southern Protestantism was 90 percent Baptist and Methodist. Paradoxically, defeat in the Civil War allowed white southern evangelical Protestantism to remain the established civil religion of the South until the recent "third disestablishment."[17]

American Protestantism has always had to live with the tension that has resulted from the various attempts to integrate its four primary components. New England Puritan Calvinism contributed the political establishmentarian theology of the covenant and the postmillennial impulse to transform the world and to realize God's kingdom. At the opposite pole, there was the dissenting, separatist Baptist tradition, a tradition which could either turn in an antinomian, radical sectarian, and antiestablishmentarian direction or, when trying to avoid any entanglement with the world, withdraw into privatized, pietist religion. Scottish Presbyterianism and its transformation into Princeton theology contributed the impulse toward intellectual rationalization and Reformed theological orthodoxy, at times in creative dialogue, at times in militant opposition to the thought of the age. Finally, there was the evangelical, pragmatist, individualist, perfectionist, and universalist contribution of Methodism to American Protestantism. With its disregard for theological speculation, its universal calling to holiness, its Arminian optimist faith in the spiritual abilities of ordinary people, its quantitative criteria of pastoral success, its impulse toward the rationalization of revival techniques, and its drive toward ecclesiastical bureaucratic centralization, Methodism blended best with life on the frontier and with the spirit of the age.[18]

Serious theological differences, which had already begun to emerge in the 1830s, led to formal organizational splits between the northern and southern branches of the three main evangelical denominations (Methodist, Baptist, and Presbyterian). As southern evangelicalism progressively repressed its original impulse to condemn the "evil" institution of slavery, accommodated itself resignedly to worldly realities, and finally learned to lend Christian justification to the system of slavery, it also lost the impulse to transform the world and became ever more otherworldly, concentrating on the all-important business of saving white and black souls. Burdened by "bad faith," southern evangelicalism never manifested as unequivocally as its northern counterpart a postmillennial faith in progress.[19]

Defeat and victory in the Civil War only reinforced the divergent trends. Old time religion in the South became even more suspicious of worldly entanglements, finding theological justification for such a position in the tradition of strict Baptist separation of church and state. Victorious Yankee Protestantism, by contrast, became ever more committed to the postmillennial faith in the progressive realization of the millennium and in the manifest destiny of Christian America. As the second disestablishment proceeded apace, however, the conservative wing of northern evangelical Protestantism began to waver and to lose faith in urban, industrial America. The turnaround from postmillennialism to premillennialism and from social reform to rescue mission, which is noticeable in urban revivalism from Charles Grandison Finney to Dwight L. Moody, is the best indication of a transformation that prepared the ground for the emergence of fundamentalism.[20]

In his first inaugural address in 1829, President Andrew Jackson had stated his "belief" that

man can become more and more endowed with divinity; and as he does he becomes more God-like in his character and capable of governing himself. Let us go on elevating our people, perfecting our institutions, until democracy shall reach such a point of perfection that we can acclaim with truth that the voice of the people is the voice of God.[21]

The source and emphasis of Finney's "perfectionist" revivalist preachings may have been different, but he evinced a similar postmillennial optimism when in 1835 he prophesied that "the millennium can come in three years" if Americans "do their duty." With the help of the Holy Spirit, human effort could pave the way for "the creation of a new heaven and a new earth." When William Miller, leader and founder of the premillennial Adventists, predicted that the end of an increasingly corrupt world would come in 1843, Finney retorted that revival successes were "evidences" that "the world is not growing worse but better."[22]

Dwight L. Moody, Finney's great successor as a midwestern urban revivalist, manifested a typical disinterest in theological speculation, rationalized even further the well-proven revivalist techniques, imparted Victorian middle-class respectability upon urban revivalism, and pioneered the organization of independent evangelical "empires." But he also preached the "infallibility" of the Bible and gave paradigmatic expression to the new otherworldly, premillennial impulse in the famous passage from his sermon "The Second Coming of Christ": "I look upon this world as a wrecked vessel. God has given me a lifeboat and said to me, 'Moody, save all you can.' " In a later sermon he added that "a line should be drawn between the church and the world, and every Christian should get both feet out of the world."[23]

Looking at urban America from the vantage point of his Illinois Street Church in Chicago, Moody no longer saw "a City upon the Hill" but Sodom. George Marsden calls Moody the "progenitor of fundamentalism," because in Moody he already finds anticipated the three main doctrinal components that will come together in the religious fundamentalist movement of the 1920s: Darby's dispensational premillennialism, Keswick holiness teachings, and Princeton's Reformed orthodox emphasis on "sola Scriptura."[24]

Protestant fundamentalism emerged at the turn of the century as a modern antimodernist reaction against the "second disestablishment": against the disestablishment of evangelicalism from the emerging liberal Protestant main-line churches, against the disestablishment of Protestantism from American education, and against the disestablishment of the

Protestant ethic from American public life. Militant fundamentalism fought its battles on three fronts: against the liberal-modernist heresies within the northern evangelical denominations, against the teaching of Darwinism in the public schools, and against "rum and Romanism" in urban America.

The inerrancy of the Bible had been a traditional, taken-for-granted belief for most Protestants, who had always relied on Scripture as the foundation for the central Protestant doctrine of "sola Fide." But like the "infallibility" of the pope, the "infallibility" of Scripture was turned into a fundamentalist dogma only when Scripture was challenged by modern trends and ideas. Above all, the new methods of "higher biblical criticism" threatened to undermine the foundation upon which anti-traditional, antitheological American evangelical Protestantism had been built. Higher criticism had placed "hermeneutics" at the center of the theological enterprise, and in the process it had challenged both the central tenet of orthodox Reformed faith in the "return to Scripture" and the naive, historyless illusion, best exemplified by the Disciples of Christ, that evangelical Protestantism was a faithful return to the original primitive church. By rejecting mediating traditions, American Protestantism had tried to skip all the intermediate centuries of ecclesiastical corruption and confounding scholastic interpretations.[25]

Behind evangelical "primitivism" one can find the populist, anti-intellectualist, commonsensical rejection of learned church doctors and the romantic-pietist and pragmatic predilection of experiential proof over reasoned knowledge. Paradoxically, however, with the incorporation of dispensational premillennialism into fundamentalism what triumphed was neither an orthodox traditionalist nor the commonsensical, literal reading of the Bible, but a relatively new, esoteric, yet popular school of interpretation which understood Scripture as a text full of hidden meanings and of scientific and historical facts, (past, present, and future), whose revelation was open to ordinary people initiated in "millennial arithmetic." In time, after fundamentalism had become a sectarian subculture, separate not only from main-line liberal Protestantism but also from the wide world of conservative evangelicalism, not "the fundamentals" of the faith, which were shared by most conservative Protestants, but dispensationalism became the most visible badge of fundamentalism.[26]

But in the 1920s, it was around the defense of the principle of "sola Scriptura" that premillennialists and orthodox Reformed theologians could unite into a fundamentalist front against liberal, modernist heresies. The particular "fundamentals," chosen rather arbitrarily, were not as important as the fact of proclaiming some "fundamentalist" tenet, some taboo boundary which could not be trespassed. The publication of *The Fundamentals* (1910–15) had the same purpose as the pope's condemnation of the modernist heresy (1907). Conservative theologians were trying to arrest the modernist impulse of their liberal colleagues to adapt to the modern, secular world, or, as liberals would say in their own modernist theological language, to assume faithfully the historicist task of incarnating eternal, universal Christian truths ever anew in particular, historically changing forms.[27] Devoid of the pope's hierarchic authority and without means of doctrinal enforcement, the twelve-volume publication could not have the same effect as the papal proclamation. Religious and secular literati for the most part ignored it, but the free distribution of 3 million copies gave a name and a communications infrastructure to the emerging movement.

The theological "fundamentalist controversy" of the 1920s took place primarily within the northern Presbyterian and Baptist denominations in major urban centers (New York, Philadelphia, Chicago).[28] Therefore, it was not a conflict between rural and urban, southern and northern America, but a conflict within urban northern Protestantism over what Richard Niebuhr called the relation of "Christ and Culture."[29] Beneath the theological debate there was the basic question whether American Protestantism should accept graciously and embrace, or rather reject and oppose, its disestablishment from modern, urban, secular America. Marsden indicates that for those evangelicals who for whatever ideal or material reasons could no longer feel at home in modern America, "the experience of displacement was especially traumatic."[30]

But before retreating to their self-imposed religious and cultural ghetto, fundamentalist leaders tried to mobilize behind their banner widespread popular sentiments against Darwinism by turning the controversy over evolutionism into a direct confrontation between Protestant supernaturalist faith and modern naturalist science. Originally, the fundamentalist and evolutionist controversies had been separate. Militant premillennialists were the ones, according to Marsden, who eagerly embraced the antievolutionist crusade and tried to use it to expand the fundamentalist movement. In William J. Bryan they found an eager leader of a populist crusade to pit the Bible and the popular faith of ordinary Protestant Americans ("the Rock of Ages") against Darwin and the idle speculations of Godless intellectuals ("the age of the rocks"). In the South and in rural and small-town America they found a constituency ready to be mobilized for the crusade to ban the teaching of evolution from public schools.

Ultimately, the attempt to put evolutionism and modern science on trial backfired. The movement could pass antievolutionist laws in a few southern and border states. It could win the Scopes trial in Tennessee. But it lost the broader public and the larger battle. Marsden writes, "In the trial by public opinion and the press, it was clear that the twentieth century, the cities, and the universities had won a resounding victory, and that the country, the South, and the fundamentalists were guilty as charged."[31] Following the trial, the fundamentalist movement collapsed and, once banished from public view, most intellectuals assumed that it had been relegated to the dustbin of history. A theology which could trace its immediate origins to Princeton and which had spokesmen as distinguished as Machen J. Gresham now became associated with rednecks, with hillbillies, and, in the words of H. L. Mencken, with the "gaping primates of the upland valleys."[32] Along with Pentecostalism and other evangelical sects, fundamentalism became the religion of the disinherited.[33]

The discredit suffered by the fundamentalists served to enhance the public respectability of their religious antagonists. Liberal Protestants and their churches now became "main-line."[34] But above all, the discredit served to confirm liberal intellectuals in their secular prejudices. For many intellectuals, not only fundamentalism but Christianity and religion were put on trial in Dayton, Tennessee, and found guilty by association. Mencken defined Christendom as "that part of the world in which, if any man stands up in public and solemnly swears that he is a Christian, all his auditors will laugh."[35] The "monkey trial" brought out into the open a reality that had already been painfully clear to Protestant leaders in the aftermath of World War I. The failure of the interchurch campaign had marked the "loss of innocence" and the "moment of truth for Protestant America."[36] Evangelical Protestantism had ceased being the public civil religion of American society.

Nothing illustrates this better, perhaps, than the failure of Protestantism to react to the Great Depression. No public voices were heard, and there was no religious revival. Along with the economy, religion was undergoing its own "depression."[37] After the war, both religion and the economy underwent a typical cyclical revival, and the "Christianization" of the American people continued apace, but the character of Christianity had changed. Religion had become increasingly privatized, and Protestantism had become just another denomination. The Protestant churches and other denominations could, and often did, still enter the public sphere. But they were no longer established there. They had to compete not only among themselves but, most important, with secular rivals. The "Methodist Age" and the "Protestant Era" had come to an end.[38]

But for a few more decades one element from this era survived the disestablishment of Protestantism from the cognitive sphere and from public opinion. The most endearing and enduring inheritance from Puritanism, the Protestant ethic, continued to dominate public morality, the American way of life, and, one could add, "the American self."[39] Evangelical Protestantism not only had democratized Calvinist thought but also had democratized its culture of self-control, industriousness, and the renunciation of pleasure. "Temperance," the most ancient of virtues, defined as "habitual moderation in the indulgence of the appetites and passions," had always been one of the four Christian "cardinal virtues" along with prudence, justice, and fortitude. Puritan asceticism made it into *the* cardinal virtue.

As part of its nativist campaign, the New England federalist clergy was fond of founding "benevolent" societies with such names as the Connecticut Society for the Suppression of Vice and the Promotion of Good Morals and the Massachusetts Society for the Suppression of Intemperance. Soon these societies became national and transdenominational.[40] The pattern traced by Joseph Gusfield in the temperance movement reappears in other single-issue movements.[41] As part of its mission to Christianize and civilize "the common man," the New England clergy established the American Temperance Society (1826) to promote moderation in drinking. Evangelical revivalism radicalized this impulse and turned it into an ascetic movement of inner self-control. Temperance turned into total abstinence and became the moral badge of evangelical Christians. Of all the sins of the flesh and of all the moral vices, intemperance became the most visible mark of the unregenerate, of "the other." And there could be no greater sign of depravity than the profanation of the Puritan Sabbath. It was to be expected that Catholics and Jews would fall into the category of "the other." But even industrious German Lutherans could not be admitted into the family of evangelical Christians as long as they continued to enjoy their beer and their Sunday celebrations.

Faced with the obstinate external resistance of the unregenerate to mend their ways, the temperance movement turned into "prohibition" and sought to ban the immoral conduct of drinking through coercive legislation. Prohibition was the last of the pan-Protestant crusades that was able to mobilize religious and secular, conservative and progressive, fundamentalist and modernist, rural and urban Protestants in defense of the American way of life. It was not so much the threat of loss of status, as the threat of disestablishment and loss of hegemony, that made this crusade so symbolic. For the last time in history, the Protestant pietist Republican coalition came victoriously together in the 1928 presidential campaign against the Catholic "liturgical" Democratic coalition.[42]

The New Deal consolidated the immigrant, Democratic coalition. But paradoxically, despite repeal of the Eighteenth Amendment, it also consolidated, at least temporarily, the Protestant ethic. The welfare state, World War II, and the post–World War II economic boom made possible the rapid assimilation of the non-Protestant immigrant population into "*the* American way of life." As Will Herberg has pointed out, by the mid-1950s, Protestant-Catholic-Jew had become the three denominational forms of a new American civil religion that had the Protestant ethic and faith in America's millennial role as its moral and doctrinal core. The election of a Catholic president and the inaugural address of that president, John F. Kennedy, were viewed as confirmation of the thesis.[43] But the celebration of the new national consensus did not last very long. The welfare state and consumer capitalism fed "the cultural contradictions" which undermined the Protestant ethic irrevocably.[44] By the mid-1960s there were numerous indications that a "third disestablishment," the disestablishment of Protestantism from the American way of life, was under way. From now on, "the American way of life" would be characterized by the plurality of ways of life, by what could be called moral denominationalism. The disestablishment of the Protestant ethic brought about the secularization of public morality and the emergence of a pluralistic system of norms and forms of life. From the first to the third disestablishment, the interpretation of the First Amendment was progressively extended from the constitutional protection of the "free exercise of religion"; to freedom of inquiry, thought, and speech; to freedom of conduct.

The Third Disestablishment: The Secularization of the Lifeworld and the Second Mobilization of Protestant Fundamentalism

Considering the amount of journalistic and social-scientific commentary it has provoked, one could perhaps concur with Jeffrey K. Hadden's claim that Protestant fundamentalism "is destined to become the major social movement in America during the last quarter of the twentieth century." But one should not discount the opposite claims of those who either question the very newness of the New Christian Right or have implied that, if not perhaps fully an invention of the mass media, certainly the strength and significance, actual and potential, of the New Christian Right has been blown out of proportion by friend and foe alike.[45]

Of the various theoretical-analytical models for the study of social movements, the "resource mobilization" perspective can best both reconcile these seemingly contradictory claims and explain how the infrastructural resources of Protestant fundamentalism could be organized so quickly and unexpectedly into a full-fledged social movement.[46] A summary account could run as follows. What started at the turn of the century as a movement within the organizational network of the transdenominational revivalist sector of northern Protestantism soon turned into a bureaucratic insurgency aiming to take over the organization of several denominations. Unmasked by Harry E. Fosdick's sermon "Shall the Fundamentalists Win?" they failed in their coup d'etat, lost the confrontation with the modernists, and either seceded or were forced out of the denominations. Thus began the fundamentalist "long march."

A few fundamentalist sects survived as scattered islands under siege in the sea of urban liberal Protestantism. Most of them retreated to rural and southern areas, where they could create their own separatist archipelagoes or swim almost unnoticed in the sea of conservative evangelical Protestantism. The leaders concentrated on the task of expanding the network of Bible conferences, Bible colleges and institutes, Bible publishing houses, and evangelical empires. A few firebrands, like Carl McIntire and Billy James Hargis, ventured into the world of Cold War politics, but few of the rank and file followed them. Most evangelical entrepreneurs concentrated on their old line of business, the saving of souls at home and the establishing of missions abroad, while waiting for the Second Coming. Recurrent schisms and strict separatism from apostate evangelicals and from the world became successful product differentiation strategies and marketing techniques. Rigidly doctrinaire, fundamentalists nonetheless continued the old evangelical tradition of pastoral pragmatism. Always searching for innovation and the constant rationalization of revivalist techniques, they were among the first to recognize and exploit the potential of televangelism. Soon they gained a virtual monopoly of the religious airwaves and became experts in the latest fund-raising techniques. As in the case of the Catholics a century before, the establishment of Christian schools, which had seemed at first a purely defensive reaction against their bête noire, secular humanism, soon turned into a bonanza. The congregational, educational, and recreational evangelical lifeworld became increasingly self-sufficient and self-reproducing. Indeed, while other sectors in the religious industry seemed to be headed for long-term decline, the evangelical sector and, particularly, the fundamentalist wing continued experiencing uninterrupted growth.[47]

By the mid-1970s, business was booming. After a long hiatus, the United States once again had an evangelical president, and 1976 became "the year of the evangelical." Having been alerted by the Catholic church's organization of the right-to-life movement, issue entrepreneurs and professional organizers from the New Right (Paul Weyrich, Richard Viguerie, and Howard Phillips) saw a golden opportunity to carry out the long-awaited conservative revolution and grand party realignment through the mobilization of a transdenominational religious right.[48] While trying out issues and moral concerns with which to coopt this balky "conscience constituency" and its untapped infrastructural resources, these men concentrated on their forte. As Paul Weyrich said: "Organization is our bag. We preach and teach nothing but organization."[49] Through the intermediation of Edward McAteer and Robert Billings, they gained access to the fundamentalist world. Evangelical preachers soon became their best pupils.

By 1979 the three key social movement organizations (SMOs) of the New Christian Right (the Moral Majority, Christian Voice, and the Religious Roundtable) were in place. The cooptation of Jerry Falwell as president and founder of Moral Majority, Inc., in June 1979 was the key to the entire venture. In one month Moral Majority had raised $1 million, one-third of the projected first-year budget. Six months later, polls indicated that 40 percent of Americans, close to 80 percent in the South and Southwest, had heard of the Moral Majority, although most did not like what they had heard. In one year the organization claimed to have three hundred thousand members, including seventy thousand ministers. The impact of the New Christian Right in the 1980 and in posterior elections is still being debated. But clearly the movement, if not driving the Reagan revolution, as some of the leaders claimed, was at least riding on its coattails. In 1987, one year before Reagan's departure from the White House, Falwell abandoned politics to rededicate himself full time to the management of his gospel conglomerate, which was then experiencing a fall in revenues. But Falwell's departure only precipitated the fall of a movement whose decay analysts had previously noticed.

While the resource mobilization perspective can offer a plausible account of how movements get organized and how they grow and decay, the perspective, particularly its "organizational tributary," is less helpful in explaining why people would want to start a movement in the first place.[50] The grievances and motives that move people to collective action, the will to power, the desire for recognition and inclusion—these the theory considers to be constant and, as such, they can be taken for granted. When in short supply, moreover, they can easily be manufactured from above. Apparently, only the lack of environmental opportunities, the scarcity of resources, and deficits in organizational technologies stop people from getting organized. Overreacting to the emphasis older theories had placed on grievances, relative deprivation, and beliefs in explaining the rise of social movements, the resource mobilization perspective prefers either to ignore them or to view them simply as resources waiting to be organized.

But fundamentalist separatists present an interesting quandary for the theory. Why would people who have obviously mastered the organizational techniques and have marshaled plenty of resources in the evangelical line of business prefer to stay out of the mobilizational game? To argue that for fifty years the fundamentalists had been patiently building the infrastructure waiting for the right moment to strike seems a bit contrived. Additionally, there is not much evidence that the rate of profit in the old line of business was falling, forcing the televangelists to look for new business opportunities elsewhere or, inversely, that success encouraged them to expand and diversify. Breaking the most fundamental of fundamentalist rules, strict separation, would expose one to the accusations of apostasy and compromise. In the fiercely competitive televangelist market such an accusation could bankrupt even the most solvent of businesses.

Once somebody has made the decision to organize, the role of outside, professional, social movement expertise becomes crucial. But first one has to explain the decision itself, the "change of mind and heart." It is true that Republican political entrepreneurs had noticed the evangelical "conscience constituency" at least since the Eisenhower presidency. But the costs and the political risks of mobilization had seemed too high. Known for their stubborn independence, evangelicals preferred to stay aloof and go about their own business or, worse, they were too hot to handle. In a two-party system, their "bigotry" and "fanaticism" could easily become a political liability. When in 1976 Jerry Falwell, a proper and successful televangelist with impeccable fundamentalist credentials, began to organize "I love America" rallies in front of state capitols across the nation, New Right political entrepreneurs finally found somebody from the Religious Right with whom they could talk business. Falwell became the movement's key resource.[51]

There was only a minor problem. In 1965 Falwell had stated emphatically the reasons why a fundamentalist could not get involved in politics:

We have few ties to this earth. We pay our taxes, cast our votes as a responsibility of citizenship, obey the laws of the land, and other things demanded of us by the society in which we live. But, at the same time, we are cognizant that our only purpose on this earth is to know Christ and to make Him known. . . . Believing in the Bible as I do, I would find it impossible to stop preaching the pure saving gospel of Jesus Christ and begin doing anything else—including fighting communism or participating in civil rights reforms.[52]

One could perhaps discount such talk as the convenient rhetorical criticism by white southern Baptists of black clergy activists, were it not for the fact that the statement was fully consistent with what fundamentalists had been saying and doing for decades. It served, moreover, to indict not only fellow evangelist Martin Luther King, Jr., but also fellow fundamentalist Carl McIntire. The fact is that upon entering public life a decade later, Falwell was forced to admit that Martin Luther King had been right, that he had changed his mind, that he now saw that his earlier interpretation of the inerrant Bible was wrong, that he had some ties to this earth after all, and that he had a Christian moral imperative to organize a movement fighting communism abroad and feminist and gay rights reforms at home.

Naturally, there was no need for the political entrepreneurs to be overly concerned with Falwell's qualms of conscience. They could only welcome the fact that he had come to his senses and become their ally. From their organizational perspective, they needed to worry about only three things. First, Falwell himself had to feel comfortable with his own account and with his new identity so that he would put all his evangelical energies into the new mission. Second, to avoid becoming a general without an army, he would have to either find fellow fundamentalists who had gone through the same process of conversion or convince his fundamentalist constituency that, even though he had misled them before, now they should believe him, have the same change of heart he had had—develop also a new identity—and follow him. And third, he would have to neutralize the rear guard attacks from fellow unconverted fundamentalists who would surely accuse him of treason while haranguing his troops to switch camps.[53]

Unless resource mobilization theory prefers to adopt the perspective of professional organizers, who being interested primarily in results do not care much about what moves people to action, it will have to decide how to treat Falwell's "change of mind and heart."[54] Fundamentalist separatists present an interesting problem because they are not simply "free riders" or draft dodgers. They are conscientious objectors. Moreover, to a much larger extent than was the case in the civil rights movement, the fundamentalist churches were not just an infrastructural resource to be used by the organizers. The churches and their "conscience constituencies" were the movement.

Confronted with Falwell's conversion and that of his followers, one can do one of three things. One can disregard all subjective motives as irrelevant "pre-texts." One can impute some "real" motive or structural external force, hidden to the actor but known to the scientific observer. Or one can seriously take into account the actor's definition of the situation. I assume that the choice one makes among these three alternatives will be determined to a large extent by prejudgments about how people act, by methodological presuppositions about the tasks and nature of social science, and by implicit theories of the present.

For those who prefer the third alternative, the interpretive task is made easier by the fact that Jerry Falwell has published two accounts of himself, his motives, his goals, and the fundamentalist tradition to which he belongs. One of the texts, *The Fundamentalist Phenomenon* (1981), is a self-portrait of fundamentalism mainly for outsiders. It depicts fundamentalists' origins and history, their family tree, their beliefs, their customs, their claims, their aims.[55] The other text, *Listen, America!* (1980), is the manifesto of the founder of the Moral Majority.[56] Like all manifestos, it derives its special texture from its strategic character. It is both a call to arms to potential supporters and a public warning to potential adversaries. While any manifesto may have some element of deceit built into it, if it is to be effective, the gap between the private and the public persona, and the gap between the authors' true beliefs and worldview and the public messages sent to friends and adversaries, cannot be too wide.

Listen America! is a straightforward presentation of the worldview, grievances, motives, intentions, and goals of Jerry Falwell and, one may assume, of the core of the movement he organized and led.[57] The book is divided into three distinct parts. Parts I and II, about equal in size, form the bulk (90 percent) of the book and are directed at the public at large. Part III, "Priority-Revival in America," is directed primarily at fellow evangelical Christians.

Part I, "Liberty—Will We Keep It?" is a standard manifesto of the Old Right of the Grand Old Party advocating less government intervention in the economy, fewer taxes, larger defense budgets, the transfer of government functions to state and local governments, supply economics, and greater private initiative to take care of common societal needs and social problems, from education to welfare, from crime to unemployment. Its familiar message is that uncontrolled government spending, runaway inflation, and a weakened defense posture against communism are threatening, as never before, America's freedom. The 1980s are portrayed as a "Decade of Destiny." The threat of national catastrophe is imminent. But it is not too late to "turn America around." The text is interspersed with quotations from Milton Friedman, William Simon, Margaret Thatcher, Edmund Burke, Benjamin Franklin, Henry Kissinger, retired generals, the *Book of Proverbs* and other biblical texts, *Readers' Digest,* and *U.S. News & World Report.* It tells the standard historical reconstruction of a Puritan, Christian, Republican America, "One Nation under God," and of America's millennial role as the leader of "the free world." Nothing in the first part of the book is of much help in trying to understand the emergence of the New Christian Right. But it can help to explain why the New Christian Right would join the Reagan revolution.

Part II, "Morality—The Deciding Factor," can be viewed as the manifesto of the New Christian Right. On the one hand, the structure of the text is typically evangelical. Revivalists have always been consummate practitioners of the Jeremiad, a style inherited from the Hebrew prophets, turned into an art form by the Puritans, later to become a standard rhetorical form of American public discourse.[58] Grievances are actually built into the fundamentalist worldview. One need not tell a fundamentalist how bad things are. Fallen nature, a covenant broken beyond repair, an American nation forsaken by God and turned into Babylon, a world beyond redemption in this dispensation until the Second Coming—these are the very raisons d'être of separatist fundamentalism. More startling, even threatening to their separate existence, is to find one of their own preachers telling them that fundamentalists could and should do something about how deplorable things are, that there is still time and hope for a national revival, and especially that they should join hands with other Americans, even with apostates, papists, and non-Christians, to remedy things and save America.

Such a Jeremiad, which undoubtedly serves as the subtext, would probably not go very far in moving people, least of all fundamentalists, to action. But Falwell's is not just a standard evangelical sermon. Falwell tries to show that something radically new has happened, that new historical developments are changing the external, taken-for-granted sinful world beyond recognition, that these external forces are encroaching upon the separate fundamentalist lifeworld, and that therefore fundamentalists and the old silent majority, who would like to see their traditional world defended or restored, should act jointly to reverse historical trends before it is too late.

The style and tone of the text are not very different from that of a down-to-earth public moralist, informed by a conservative reading of Durkheimian sociology, who accumulates page after page of empirical data, taken from national newspapers, showing increasing rates of suicide, crime, drug abuse, divorce, teenage pregnancy, abortion, and the like, all proving that society is reaching intolerable levels of anomie, normlessness, and social disintegration. The subheadings indicate the primary "concerns" of the movement: the family, children's rights, the feminist movement, the right to life, homosexuality, television, pornography, education, rock music, drugs and alcohol. The "grievances" listed under each of the subheadings all have the same structure.

1. First, they specify a concrete event or specific time period to which they trace the origins of the threatening change:

In the past twenty years a tremendous change has taken place [in the structure of the family] (p. 121).

For the past two decades psychologists have told parents not to spank their children (p. 140).

The Equal Rights Amendment strikes at the foundation of our entire social structure. . . . ERA came out of Congress on March 22, 1972 (pp. 151, 154).

Experts estimate that between 5 million and 6 million babies have been murdered since January 22, 1973, when the U.S. Supreme Court, in a decision known as *Roe v. Wade,* granted women an absolute right to abortion on demand during the first two trimesters of pregnancy (p. 165).

Not too many years ago the word "homosexual" was a word that represented the zenith of human indecency. . . . This is no longer true (p. 181).

About 1955, *Playboy* magazine brought sex into American drugstores. . . . Today *Playboy* has approximately 100 competitors. The year 1969 was a watershed one because the courts. . . . The literature that was once underground began to surface (p. 199).

Until about thirty years ago . . . Christian education and the precepts of the Bible still permeated the curriculum of the public schools (p. 205).

Drug addiction was once confined to back alleys, to vacant lots, and to the inner city. Today from the posh offices of prestigious businessmen to the playgrounds of junior high schools, millions of Americans are taking drugs (p. 232).

2. Next, the culprits are identified. They are always either organized minorities (secular humanists, feminists, gay rights activists) or some branch of the federal government (Supreme Court, Congress, Internal Revenue Service):

Most Americans remain deeply committed to the idea of the family as a sacred institution. A minority of people in this country is trying to destroy what is most important to the majority (p. 122).

Feminists are saying that self-satisfaction is more important than the family. . . . At the foundation of the women's liberation movement there is a minority core of women (pp. 124, 150).

Militant homosexuals march under a banner of "civil rights" or "human rights . . . " demanding to be accepted as a legitimate minority (p. 183).

Our government is trying to enact laws that I feel are contrary to the traditional American family (p. 130).

It is our government that has attacked the family's role as a primary educator of children. The Internal Revenue Service is now seeking to control private and Christian schools. HEW has undertaken the redrafting of textbooks to purge traditional moral concepts. Court decisions have all but mandated the replacement of religion with secular humanism (p. 131).

Prayer and Bible reading were taken out of the classroom by our U.S. Supreme Court. Our public school system is now permeated with humanism (p. 205).

3. Next, Falwell's text points out the historical results and consequences of these organized attacks: on the one hand, relativism, the emergence of "the permissive society," the abandonment of clear moral standards, and the proliferation of alternative life-styles, and, on the other hand, the penetration by federal bureaucracies of the traditional lifeworld:

We are very quickly moving toward an amoral society where nothing is either absolutely right or absolutely wrong. Our absolutes are disappearing (p. 117).

Sexual promiscuity has become the life style of America (p. 123).

There is a movement for legislation that would deem homosexuals as "normal." Homosexuality is now presented as an alternate life style (p. 181).

The family-oriented programs [on television] are often telling you to accept divorce as a natural alternative, and to accept controversial life styles (p. 189).

We are willing to accept what is abnormal as normal. . . . Readily available, pornography is subconsciously telling our children that this is acceptable. . . . The Court would not even prescribe methods to guide a community . . . the jury decided it could not agree on a standard of obscenity (pp.200–202).

Students are told that there are no absolutes and that they are to develop their own value systems. Humanists believe that . . . moral values are relative, that ethics are situational (p. 206).

Children are taught . . . that the traditional home is one alternative. Homosexuality is another. Decency is relative (p. 210).

The Domestic Violence Prevention and Treatment Act could establish a federal bureaucracy to intervene in matters relating to husband and wife (p. 131).

We reject public policies or judicial decisions that embody the children's liberation philosophy: that children have rights separate from those of their family and/or parents (p. 135).

Section 2 of the Equal Rights Amendment would mean federalizing vast powers that states now have (p. 157).

Christian parents have found the need to remove their children from the public educational system and to begin educating them in Christian schools. . . . Christians simply want to educate their children in the way that they see fit. . . . Recently the Internal Revenue Service has attacked Christian schools (pp. 218–21).

4. Finally, the text states what the goals of the movement are:

To provide leadership in establishing an effective coalition of morally active citizens who are (a) prolife, (b) profamily, (c) promoral, and (d) pro-American (p. 259).

[We advocate the passage of family protection legislation which would] counteract disruptive federal intervention into family life and encourage the restoration of family unity, parental authority, and a climate of traditional authority . . . and reinforce traditional husband-and-wife relationships (p. 136).

We must stand against the Equal Rights Amendment, the feminist revolution, and the homosexual revolution (p. 19).

It is the Christian school movement and the restoration of voluntary prayer in public schools that will provide the most important means of educating our children in the concepts of patriotism and morality (p. 223).

Right living must be re-established as an American way of life. . . . The authority of Bible morality must once again be recognized as the legitimate guiding principle of our nation (p. 265).

The social-scientific student of social movements should not take the actor's definition of the situation at face value. One should examine the definition to see whether it makes sense when tested against commonsensical, taken-for-granted, ordinary definitions and against established social-scientific interpretations of the same reality.[59] At first sight, at least, the actor's definition in this case seems perfectly plausible. Looking at the series of antecedent events or environmental changes mentioned, one could perhaps argue about the relative significance of any of them and add some neglected ones like technological, economic, and demographic changes; one could surely debate the positive or negative meaning of those changes; but as a whole Falwell's enumeration is consistent with standard historical and sociological accounts of the period. With respect to the culprits, one may detect in the fundamentalist account a certain paranoid or Manichaean style and a penchant for conspiracy theories. Without denying human agency or purposeful behavior, social scientists like to stress somewhat more complex, impersonal structural forces (in undermining traditional gender roles and family structures, for instance). Secular intellectuals may also have some difficulty identifying "secular humanism" as an organized social movement or as a collective actor. After all, those labeled "secular humanists" do not see themselves in such a role. But at least indirectly, the self-definition of the fundamentalist mobilization as a countermobilization, that is, as a reaction to the threat posed by the mobilization of organized minorities, is fully consistent with standard explanations found in the resource mobilization literature.[60] Besides, if one discounts the fact that fundamentalists tend to be blind to the threats that markets and their beloved free enterprise system pose to their traditional lifeworld,[61] their identification of centralized state penetration as a threatening development is also consistent with established social-scientific explanations, even though in their grievances they tend to lump together processes of administrative colonization and processes of juridical penetration of the lifeworld.[62]

Their diagnosis of the present situation as one characterized by the increasing differentiation of morality and legality, by cultural and moral relativism, by multiplicities of forms of life, and by the crisis of foundationalism is also fully consistent with classical theories of cultural modernity and with more recent theories of postmodernity. It is also consistent with the thesis presented here, which from the long-range perspective of the relationship of Protestantism and American culture views this process as a third disestablishment, as the disestablishment of the Protestant ethic and the emergence of a legally protected pluralistic system of norms in the public sphere of American civil society.

From this perspective, the political mobilization of Protestant fundamentalism and its organization into the New Christian Right may be viewed as a typical reactive defensive movement to protect the separate fundamentalist lifeworld from external threats. Once again the actor's definition of the situation is most emphatic: "Something had to be done now. The government was encroaching upon the sovereignty of both the church and the family."[63] To explain such a mobilization, one does not need to recur to any process of conversion. It was simply a matter of survival, and in such an emergency even fundamentalists can relax their doctrinal rigidity.

When sovereignty (or its perception) is at stake, the transition from a reactive defense to a proactive offense is easy and almost imperceptible. The need to restore the status quo ante, to "return to moral sanity," to reestablish the American way of life and the normal conditions under which fundamentalists may go back to their normal separate business of saving souls, also becomes easily understandable. The restorationist project in this case would still be only an attempt to conserve the traditional structures. To a certain extent, one could argue that the disestablishment of the Protestant ethic in the outside world presented a much greater threat to the survival of fundamentalism as a Protestant sect than the encroachment of government bureaucracies upon its separate subculture. Fundamentalism can live with sin and apostasy in the outside world.

Actually, fundamentalism needs them to maintain its own self-identity as the true Christian church. Even in its most separatist posture of sectarian rejection of the world, Protestant fundamentalism has always understood itself as the Calvinist church of the elect. But fundamentalism cannot survive in a world devoid of shared moral meanings and standards, in a postmodern world in which it would become just another quaint subculture, like that of the native Indians or the Amish, to be added to the "gorgeous mosaic" of American cultural pluralism.

It is when it becomes evident that a mere defensive offensive is no longer possible, because the lost world can no longer be brought back, that the project of restoration turns into something else, either into counterrevolution or into public involvement in the construction of new shared normative structures. In any case, fundamentalism at this point ceases being a privatized, separate religious enclave and reenters American public life as a public religion with claims upon the public sphere of civil society. It is at the precise moment when public involvement is defined as a "moral imperative" that one can speak of the conversion of a fundamentalist.

Once again, the actor's definition of the situation offers the most evident clues of this personal change. The most revealing passages are those in which Jerry Falwell tries to explain to fellow evangelists why he, "a Fundamentalist—big F!" while upholding "the fundamentals" and maintaining personal separation from a sinful society and ecclesiastical separation from other evangelicals, nonetheless feels a moral imperative and a Christian responsibility to get involved and urges them to do the same. It is evident that Jerry Falwell has rediscovered the ties to this earth that he had denied in 1965. Those ties are

- the ties of generational solidarity binding parents to succeeding generations

It is not just a question of dealing with our generation but with the generations to come. Our children and our grandchildren must forever be the recipients or the victims of our moral decisions today (p. 255).

- the ties of Christian solidarity binding fundamentalist Christians not only to their communities but to the Christian tradition

The history of the church includes the history of Christian involvement in social issues. . . . In America, outstanding evangelical preachers such as Charles G. Finney, Albert Barnes, and Lyman Beecher called on Christians to feed the poor, educate the unlearned, reform the prisons, humanize treatment for the mentally ill, establish orphanages, and abolish slavery (p. 261).

- the ties of political solidarity binding citizens to their political communities

We must insist that equal education and employment opportunities are available to all Americans regardless of sex, race, religion, or creed. Fundamentalists have been woefully negligent in addressing this issue. We can no longer be silent on this matter, which is so crucial to millions of our fellow Americans.[64]

- the ties of human solidarity binding every individual to the entire family of humankind

Millions of human beings are starving to death all over the world. . . . I am convinced that we Christians who have so much must be our "brother's keeper" in the poverty-stricken regions of the world. . . . While liberal theologians have been talking and theorizing about world hunger, we have been raising millions of dollars to feed starving people.[65]

In the political rebirth of Protestant fundamentalism one can find four different postures: a defensive reaction to protect the lifeworld of fundamentalists from outside encroachment, a proactive offensive to restore the American way of life, a counterrevolutionary theocratic impulse to impose biblical morality upon the nation, and a proactive involvement in the public affairs of the nation. At different times, in different sectors, and at different stages of the movement any one of the postures may take ascendancy. Each of them is in tension with the others, and Protestant fundamentalism has not made up its mind which public identity it should assume. It is not yet fully clear, therefore, what kind of public impact the deprivatization of Protestant fundamentalism would have upon American public life.

The Public Impact of the Deprivatization of Protestant Fundamentalism

My main interest in this work is neither in Protestant fundamentalism as a religious denomination, that is, as one of the branches of evangelical Protestantism, nor in the political mobilization of the New Christian Right and the consequences it would have on electoral politics or on the American party system. My main interest is in Protestant fundamentalism as a public religion and in its potential impact on the public sphere of American civil society. The following, somewhat speculative, analysis will examine possibilities rather than facts and will proceed by drawing out, as it were, conclusions from the logic of the argument developed so far in this chapter and throughout the book. On the basis of a critical reconstruction of some of the assessments of the protestant fundamentalist phenomenon found in the literature, one could distinguish between the negative threats public fundamentalism could pose and the positive contributions it could make to the public sphere.

The Threat of Restoration

There is little doubt that the political project of mobilized fundamentalism involved some kind of restoration. The words "restore," "return," "reestablish" appear frequently in the public statements of Jerry Falwell and other leaders of the Moral Majority.[66] It is also well known that restoration in the strict sense of the term is a historical impossibility, and certainly it is rarely a project aiming simply at conserving a given tradition. Nevertheless, it is important to understand the point in time, or the established order, that serves as a model or a principle of any project of restoration. To which status quo ante would the mobilized Moral Majority like to return? To a time before the first, before the second, or before the third disestablishment? Do the fundamentalists want to restore a Protestant established church, a Protestant civil religion, or the Protestant ethic?

The reestablishment of a Christian theocracy. There is a radical wing of Protestant fundamentalism, the "reconstructionists," whose project it is to establish a Christian theocracy modeled after Calvin's Geneva and Puritan Massachusetts. In fact, the reconstructionists reject any differentiation between religion, law, and morality, or between the religious and the political community, and would like to establish a Christian "dominion" and a social order ruled by Hebrew Mosaic law. Gary North, head of the Institute for Christian Economics in Tyler, Texas, is their main theologian-ideologue. His project is to establish the intellectual and doctrinal foundations for a Christian alternative to the modern secular order, from Christian science to Christian economics, from Christian law to a Christian state. For North, any kind of pluralism, religious or moral, cultural or political, is equivalent to polytheism and, therefore, is idolatrous.[67] But the reconstructionists represent only a fringe group within the hodgepodge of fiercely independent religious enterprises constituting the separate world of fundamentalism. In their orthodox Calvinism they are the radical heirs of the Princeton Reformed Presbyterian wing of the fundamentalist alliance of the 1920s. Many observers have noticed a generalized rediscovery of the Calvinist theological heritage among evangelicals, from the Charismatic Pat Robertson to the Baptist Jerry Falwell. Given their insignificant numbers, the only threat posed by the reconstructionists would be in terms of the theological-ideological influence they might be having upon a younger generation of fundamentalists who are abandoning premillennialism for a new postmillennial project to Christianize the social order and realize God's kingdom.

The mainstream of Protestant fundamentalism that was mobilized by the Moral Majority has repeatedly disclaimed any theocratic intention and proclaimed their sacred respect for the Constitution and for the principles of disestablishment and free exercise of religion. Given their unquestioned patriotism, their sacralization of the free enterprise system and the American way of life, their congregational structure of sectarian nonconformist, independent churches, and their Baptist reverence for the separation of church and state, there is no reason to doubt their sincerity when they state that the "Moral Majority strongly supports a pluralistic America. While we believe that this nation was founded upon the Judeo-Christian ethic by men and women who were strongly influenced by biblical moral principles, we are committed to the separation of Church and State."[68]

Despite the alarmist warnings emanating from the ACLU and other countermobilized secularists that Protestant fundamentalism poses a threat to "our civil liberties," it certainly does not pose a threat to the free exercise of religion. In any case, even if they wanted to, something which is doubtful, fundamentalists certainly do not have either the power or the numbers to undermine the principles of the religious clauses of the First Amendment. Protestant fundamentalism neither wants to nor could become an established church.

The reestablishment of Protestantism as a civil religion. A much stronger argument could be made for the notion that, if they could, Protestant fundamentalists would gladly reestablish the cultural hegemony of evangelical Protestantism and re-Christianize the Constitution, the republic, and American civil society. In their writings, one finds constant references to the Judeo-Christian, biblical origins and intentions of the founding fathers, as well as frequent criticisms of what they see as a recent secularist reading of the First Amendment. In their view, Jefferson's "wall of separation" was meant to protect the free exercise of authentic religion from any state encroachment and to impede the establishment of any particular church. It was not meant to promote a secular, neutral state or to extend the free-exercise-of-religion principle to include freedom from religion. Diffused, generalized, transdenominational, biblical, Judeo-Christian religion should not only predominate in civil society but be able to penetrate the wall and permeate the state and all republican institutions.

This attempt to re-Christianize the enlightened deism of the founding fathers and the Constitution, an attempt which to be sure is modeled after the successful precedent of nineteenth-century evangelical Protestantism, would not have to be taken too seriously were it not for the fact that it coincides with a general attempt on the part of neoconservative intellectuals to appropriate and revise the "original intent" of the authors of the constitutional texts in a similar direction.[69] Given these concerted efforts, one should reiterate the simple fact that, if anybody could claim direct paternity of the spirit and the letter of the Virginia Statute on Religious Liberty and of the First Amendment, it would have to be Thomas Jefferson, James Madison, and John Leland and that, whatever their true religious attitudes may have been, the original intent of the free exercise clause was most clearly and emphatically stated by the deist Jefferson and the radical sectarian Baptist Leland, and in almost identical language: "It does me no injury for my neighbour to say there are twenty gods, or no god. It neither picks my pocket nor breaks my leg" (Thomas Jefferson). For Leland, the First Amendment permitted "every man [to] speak freely without fear, maintaining the principles that he believes, [and to] worship according to his own faith either one god, three gods or no god or twenty gods, and let government protect him in doing so."[70]

But the very foundation of the Moral Majority, not as a trans-denominational pan-Protestant social movement organization but as a transdenominational Judeo-Christian coalition attempting to include, in Falwell's words, "Catholics, Jews, Protestants, Mormons, Fundamentalists," would seem to indicate that Falwell did not believe that the reestablishment today of nineteenth-century Protestant hegemony was either desirable or possible.[71] Obviously, if external developments and internal cleavages had made the continuation of this hegemony no longer possible at the turn of the century, much less would its restoration be possible today when secular forces, non-Protestant religious groups, and internal cleavages within Protestantism have if anything grown much stronger.[72] But if an all-Protestant crusade could no longer work after the apostasy of liberal Protestantism, could a marriage of convenience with those religious groups which had been so despised by evangelical Protestantism in the nineteenth century work? Only if such a majority of religious conservatives and "moral" Americans could be put together would the fears be justified of those who feel that, whatever else it may entail, the legally protected disestablishment of the Protestant ethic from American civil society constitutes a gain in civil liberties.

The reestablishment of the Protestant ethic as the American way of life. That the reestablishment of Protestant morality and of the traditional American way of life forms the core of the fundamentalists' project of restoration is obvious from their statements and from the publicly stated goals of the movement. That this is what the fundamentalists want has also been acknowledged by sympathetic neoconservative intellectuals. In the words of Nathan Glazer, resurgent fundamentalism is "a 'defensive offensive,' meant to get us back to, at worst the 1950s, and even that is beyond the hopes, or I would think the power, of Fundamentalist faith."[73]

One may well understand the high hopes of the "moral majoritarians" and even the sympathies of neoconservative intellectuals, whether Catholic or Jewish. More difficult to understand are the inflated misperceptions, shared by sympathizers, adversaries, and many social scientific analysts, of the potential power of the fundamentalists. The hopes and fears regarding the impact of fundamentalism were based on the following assumptions: that the fundamentalists constituted a "disciplined, charging army"; that the moral majoritarians could put together an all-evangelical coalition under the fundamentalist banner; that anybody who, according to surveys, believed in the fundamentals or declared to have had a born-again experience could be counted as part of the Moral Majority constituency; that given their alleged moral conservatism, Catholics would become likely allies, turning the coalition into a New Christian Right; that one could even add a battalion of militant Mormons and a company or two of conservative Jews who, though perhaps numerically unimportant, were nonetheless of great strategic value in the propaganda war to allay the fears of influential minorities and to be able to rebaptize the campaign as a "Judeo-Christian" operation; that when the hour of battle arrived, most "true" religionists would join forces in a united front against the evil forces of modern, secular humanism. Anyone who knew something about any of these potential constituencies also knew how unfounded these assumptions were.[74] A well-organized, vociferous minority, whose unexpected mobilization caught everybody by surprise but whose very loosely defined potential constituency never reached 20 percent of the population, had miraculously become, in the minds of many, a threatening majority.

The Hope of Revival

Even if the goals of restoration of the Moral Majority were always beyond reach, one could still conceive the possibility that the political reemergence of Protestant fundamentalism could have positive, though unintended and perhaps for the actors even undesired, consequences. These great expectations can be grouped into three types: the hope for yet another "great awakening" contributing to a national revival, the hope for an evangelical revival leading to a grand Protestant party realignment, and the hope for revitalization of "the naked public sphere."

Another great awakening? Since part III of Falwell's *Listen America!* places "Revival in America" as a top priority for the movement and for the nation, it is not surprising to find social scientists asking whether the revival of evangelical Protestantism could have such an impact upon the nation. In his essay "Another Great Awakening?" Phillip Hammond brings together two related schools of thought: William McLoughlin's theory of "revitalization," which assumes that great awakenings are the normal, cyclical procedure through which societies renew and reform themselves, their culture, and their shared values, and Tocqueville's observations concerning the importance of religion, religious voluntarism, and the related participation in all kinds of voluntary associations for American democratic culture and institutions. One can easily perceive Bellah's theory of "civil religion" as a tacit subtext linking both lines of inquiry.[75]

Hammond harbors no illusions about the potential of the evangelical revival and clearly answers his own question in the negative. But the fact that the question itself is raised indicates that American intellectuals may share some central assumptions and expectations with evangelical revivalists. To be sure, they expect not evangelical Protestantism but a different kind of civil religion to play this function. Nonetheless, the striking assumption that America needs or is likely to have an awakening, and that this awakening may re-create American civil religion, is there. After sorting out the evidence, Hammond concludes, "In short, the current religious fervor is not itself an awakening, but it very likely is an element of a larger movement destined to become an awakening."[76] In my discussion of civil religion in chapter 2, I have indicated why I find such an assumption empirically unfounded and normatively undesirable.

The revival of evangelical Protestantism? Probably the most significant long-term impact of the public reemergence of Protestant fundamentalism will play itself out in some eventual realignment within the internal denominational boundaries of American Protestantism. The boundaries between fundamentalist and evangelical Protestantism have always been fuzzy and porous. Often only the self-proclaimed posture of separatism has served to identify to oneself and to others one's pure fundamentalism. With the general evangelical revival of the 1970s and the public reemergence of fundamentalism, the boundaries have tended to disappear altogether. On this issue, there is clearly disagreement among the experts.[77] There is general agreement, though, that whatever else it has been, the public reemergence of Protestant fundamentalism has been part of a much more complex, multivalent, and multidirectional general evangelical revival.

Three trends, apparently pulling in different directions yet interrelated and not fully incompatible, have been noticed. First, there is the newly gained prominence and centrality of fundamentalists within the wider world of conservative evangelical Protestantism. Their most daring moves have been the organizational takeover of the two main conservative Protestant denominations, the Southern Baptist Convention and the Lutheran Church, Missouri Synod.[78] While in the 1920s the failure of the organizational takeover of the liberal denominations led to the formation of a social movement, in the 1980s the energies, resources, and organizational lessons of the failing social movement were redirected into denominational coups d'etat. Does this mean that the main conservative denominations are going fundamentalist (something which seems unlikely) or, rather, that the fundamentalists are reentering the main denominations?

A second trend, carefully documented by James Davison Hunter, has been the at times almost imperceptible but persistently accumulative process of liberalization, secularization, and accommodation of evangelical Protestantism to modernity. Attitudinal surveys of faculty and students in evangelical colleges and seminaries confirm this trend.[79] Hunter's studies are one of the most important confirmations of the continued validity and usefulness of the theory of secularization, particularly considering that one can show a clear correlation of evangelical secularization with processes of industrialization and urbanization in the South and in other areas where evangelicals tended to predominate, as well as with processes of occupational and educational mobility among evangelicals. As evangelicals become less and less disinherited, their religion changes accordingly.[80]

The only problem I find in the thesis is that Hunter maintains a rather straightforward version of the thesis of secularization, whereby, first, confronted with the outside forces of modernity, religion's only choice is either futile resistance or accommodation, which ultimately entails capitulation, and, second, accommodation—that is, secularization—necessarily means privatization. If one begins with a radical separation between an external, modern, secular world and a besieged traditional religious enclave, then, indeed, the choice is a stark one. Ironically, the modern traditionalist and the secular scientist seem to share the same view of what constitutes true religion and of what the options are. If one follows an entirely different line of thought, going from Hegel to Parsons, which views the modern secular world itself as the externalization and institutionalization of religion in the world, then the evaluation of what constitutes secularization will be radically different. There is a position in between which assumes that religion is always embedded in the world and that what Hunter and orthodox evangelicals call authentic traditional evangelical religion is itself nothing but the accommodation of nineteenth-century religion to the world. One could call this process the ever renewed encounter and accommodation of religion and the world.

However one wants to evaluate the present accommodation of evangelicalism and modernity, it is clear that the contemporary revival does not entail the privatization of religion. On the contrary, some observers have noticed a third long-term trend, "a great reversal," from private separation and indifference to public involvement and concern for the world.[81] If the trend continues, it will radically alter the two-party system of American Protestantism, which, according to Martin Marty, emerged at the turn of the century.[82] The division between private, traditional, evangelical churches and public, modernist, liberal churches may be coming to an end. Intellectually and politically, evangelicals form the most lively sector of present-day American Protestantism.[83] Like Catholics, they are undergoing their own process of *aggiornamento*. Given the congregational rather than episcopal character of their churches, the process cannot take the form of a sudden, unified and uniform, authoritative policy change from above. It is working itself out in the most diverse directions, most of them patently innerworldly and postmillennial, despite the frequent assertions of evangelicals that doctrinally they still are premillennialists. Moreover, within the evangelical tent, the range of public commitments, from the liberation theology of Ronald Sider and Jim Wallis to the radically neoorthodox public posture of Charles Colson to the theocratic establishmentarian temptation of Jerry Falwell, is as wide and as difficult to categorize within traditional left-right dimensions as the one found within Catholicism.[84]

The revitalization of the public square? The most articulate defense of the positive contribution the public reemergence of Protestant fundamentalism may bring to the public sphere of American civil society is the one offered by Richard Neuhaus in *The Naked Public Square*. Neuhaus is right that there was a very strong public bias, buttressed by social science theories, legal-constitutional interpretations, and liberal-secularist ideologies, against letting religion into the public sphere. Most religions accepted this bias and stayed outside the public sphere. Neuhaus's own life history, however, shows that again and again churches, the clergy, religious groups, and religious constituencies circumvented this bias and were able to enter the public sphere and have an impact upon it. But Neuhaus is not right in implying that the fundamentalists were excluded from what Martin Marty has called "the republican banquet."[85] They voluntarily withdrew and stayed out of it for religious reasons. When they returned unexpectedly, other guests were first startled and some, considering the fundamentalists' public manners "uncivil," thought that they should be left out. But the fundamentalists have set shop in the public square, and many of them plan to stay. Some have established their businesses very close to government buildings and party headquarters. Throughout the 1970s and 1980s conservative evangelicals and fundamentalists established more religious lobbies than did their liberal competitors.[86] The New Christian Right has also established its electoral credentials as a bona fide faction of the right wing of the Republican party. If all they wanted was inclusion and recognition, they have earned it. But their very success underscores their status as a moral minority. Furthermore, now that they have a seat in the republican banquet on equal terms with all the other guests, what are they going to do with their voice? Neuhaus states the fundamentalist dilemma as follows:

The religious new right . . . *wants to enter the political arena making public claims on the basis of private truths.* The integrity of politics itself requires that such a proposal be resisted. Public decisions must be made by arguments that are public in character. . . . Fundamentalist morality, which is derived from beliefs that cannot be submitted to examination by public reason, is essentially a private morality. If enough people who share that morality are mobilized, it can score victories in the public arena. But every such victory is a setback in the search for a public ethic.[87]

Besides the normative issues raised by the entrance of religion, particularly a fundamentalist one, into the public sphere of modern secular society and the threats it poses to the integrity of politics, one might consider the basic dilemmas facing any religion, particularly a fundamentalist one, which wants to enter the competitive field of modern democratic politics and to score victories there.

The logic of fundamentalism has greater affinities with an "agonic" than with a "discoursive" model of the public sphere.[88] But even modern agonic electoral politics has certain rules of engagement which are inimical to fundamentalism. The name Moral Majority already signaled simultaneously the fundamentalist claim to hegemony, the choice of electoral mobilization as the road to power and public influence, and an implicit willingness to submit the cognitive, practical, and moral validity claims of fundamentalism to the discretion of the ballot box and to the principle of majority rule. Mobilizational and electoral success, however, require not only strategic adjustment to the rules and dynamics of the organizational society and electoral politics but also ideological compromises, which tend to undermine fundamentalist principles and identities. A well-organized militant minority taking advantage of the element of surprise or using stealth methods can score early victories. But the successful mobilization of fundamentalism soon called forth the countermobilization of its opponents. Moreover, in order to join an electoral majority it became necessary to enter into electoral alliances and to fill a circumscribed and subordinated niche as a faction of a broad Republican party coalition. Soon it also became obvious that the very goal of legislating fundamentalist morality could hardly be reconciled with the kind of normative compromises and parliamentary horse trading that are usually required for legislative success.

The discoursive model of the public sphere is even more incompatible with fundamentalism. The logic of open public discourse implies that modern societies, while protecting the free exercise of fundamentalism in the private sphere, procedurally cannot tolerate fundamentalism in the public sphere. Fundamentalism has to validate its claims through public argument. This presents fundamentalists with a stark choice. Those who accept the rules of engagement in the public sphere and begin to argue with their neighbors will have to abandon their fundamentalism, at least procedurally. Their claims that their normative wares are the only genuine ones or are more valuable than those of their denominational competitors will be exposed to open appraisal, to the typical plausibility tests, and to the bargaining adjustments regnant in an open pluralist market of ideas.[89] Undoubtedly, some shoppers will stop by and may appreciate or even buy their antiques. Many others will look at fundamentalism with nostalgia and admit that the fundamentalists have got a point, but will look for more "contemporary" answers to the fundamentalists' questions. But "true" fundamentalists, who prefer not to compromise their ideas or to expose their fundamentals to public discoursive validation and to a probable "plausibility crisis," will most likely abandon the public square and return to their isolated hamlets, where they can protect the worth of their sectarian wares uncontested, only to find out that government inspectors and regulators will not leave them alone and that televangelist and secularist competitors will come peddling their merchandise in their very living rooms. Unable to become an established church or to remain a separate sect, fundamentalism is destined to become just another denomination.

7   Catholicism in the United States: From Private to Public Denomination

Catholicism in the United States of America has been shaped for the most part by four factors:[1]

1. Catholicism in the United States has been a minority religion in a predominantly Protestant country. This means that, structurally, in terms of its relation vis-à-vis the hegemonic Protestant culture, Catholicism has functioned as a *sect* and has been treated as such.

2. The Constitution, however, offers this minority religion, at least formally, equal protection under the law. This means that, systemically, in terms of the place of Catholicism within the pluralistic, free religious market, as regulated by the dual clause of "no establishment" and "free exercise" of religion, Catholicism has become just another, indeed the largest, religious *denomination*.

3. Internally, American Catholicism has been shaped by the consecutive waves of immigration of Catholics from various European nations. For the most part, the various Catholic immigrant groups, usually organized along national parish lines, have kept their Catholic-ethnic allegiance while also becoming a single American-Catholic ethnic group. This means that, congregationally, Catholicism in America has functioned as a multiethnic, territorially organized *national church*.

4. Catholicism in the United States has always had to live with the dynamic tension that has resulted from being both Roman and American. What this means is that, ecclesiologically, in terms of its internal doctrinal, ritual, and organizational structure, the American Catholic church has always been a member of the transnational, universal *Roman Catholic church*. Consequently, American Catholics have always had to prove their absolute allegiance to the American civil religion in order to

The first, historical part of this chapter is a condensed version of an earlier, more elaborate historical reconstruction, "Roman, Catholic, and American: The Transformation of Catholicism in the United States," *International Journal of Politics, Culture, and Society* 6, no. 1 (1992).

be admitted into the national covenant, without putting into question
their equally absolute allegiance to Rome. Not surprisingly, the American Catholic church has become the most "American," that is, patriotic,
of all American denominations and the most Roman of all the national
Catholic churches.

Thus, Catholicism in America has functioned simultaneously in four
different ways: structurally as a sect, systemically as a denomination,
congregationally as a territorial national church, and ecclesiologically as
a member of the Universal Church.[2]

The Catholic Minority in a Protestant Country

Catholicism has always been a minority religion in a predominantly
Protestant country, but the relative position of the Catholic minority
vis-à-vis the Protestant majority and the relative position of the Protestant majority vis-à-vis American culture have changed dramatically from
independence to the present.[3]

In 1789, the inaugural year of the Constitution and of the first Catholic diocese (in Baltimore), there were approximately thirty-five thousand
Catholics within an American population of 4 million. Massive immigration, from the 1830s on, changed the relative size of the Catholic minority dramatically. By 1850, the Catholic population stood at 1.7 million,
making the Catholic church the largest religious denomination in the
United States—slightly ahead of the largest Protestant denomination, the
Methodist church, which had been an even tinier religious minority at
the time of independence. By 1910, there were 16 million Catholics in
a population of 92 million. Just after World War II, the number of
Catholics reached 25 million, a number as large as that of the membership of the six largest Protestant denominations combined (Methodists,
Southern Baptists, Presbyterians, Episcopalians, United Lutherans, Disciples of Christ). By 1980, there were 50 million Catholics in a total
American population of 222 million.[4] According to American Institute
of Public Opinion (AIPO) surveys, the number of people declaring themselves Protestants declined from 69 percent of the American adult population in 1947 to 57 percent in 1985, while the number of Catholics
rose during the same period from 20 percent to 28 percent.[5]

Numbers by themselves do not make either churches or sects. It is the
attitudinal and structural relations between the religious groups and the
relations of those groups to the dominant culture that make the difference. Actually, the category "Protestant" masks fundamental differences
and at times mutual intolerance between the various Protestant groups.

In colonial America, however, all Protestant groups, irrespective of doctrinal or ecclesiastical differences, shared a virulent antipopery. All viewed the Catholic church as the "Anti-Christ" and the "Whore of Babylon." Indeed, at times, the external enemy, Catholicism, was the only thing that could cement internal Protestant unity.

The Second Great Awakening, with its Protestant crusade to Christianize America, established the foundation of the American denominational religious system. By the late 1820s, that peculiar fusion of what Perry Miller called "romantic nationalism" and "romantic evangelicalism" was completed.[6] The Protestant nativism which had first been directed against republican deism soon turned against Catholicism. In 1830—the year in which the first anti-Catholic newspaper, *The Protestant*, appeared in New York—Lyman Beecher, the father of the "New School" of New England Calvinism, inaugurated his series of anti-Catholic sermons, linking Catholicism and despotism as the enemies of American republican principles.[7] As Irish immigration accelerated, Protestant nativism acquired social and political forms to become the American Republican party of the 1840s and the Know-Nothing movement of the 1850s. The Reverend Horace Bushnell, the father of American liberal theology, warned Protestant America: "Our first danger is barbarism, Romanism next."[8] He could have added, "Both happen to be Irish." Following the "Bloody Monday" nativist riots of 6 August 1855 in Louisville, Kentucky, Abraham Lincoln warned that if the Know-Nothings came to power, the Declaration of Independence would read, "All men are created equal except Negroes, foreigners and Catholics."[9] But the Know-Nothings soon disappeared as the moral energies of the Protestant crusade became absorbed in the antislavery movement and in civil war.

Nothing illustrates better the sectarian isolation of American Catholicism, perhaps, than the fact that, with a few exceptions, Catholics preferred to watch the abolitionist debate from the sidelines, viewing it mainly as an internal Protestant issue, indeed as a dangerous Protestant crusade which was ripping the nation asunder. American Catholics failed to see the connection so clearly made by Lincoln between their status and that of the enslaved American Negroes. When civil war arrived, the Catholic church in the North and that in the South loyally supported their respective patriotic causes. But unlike every major Protestant denomination, the American Catholic church did not split into northern and southern branches.

From the 1880s to the 1920s, a familiar combination of themes emerged: foreign immigration on an even larger scale; an evangelical revivalist crusade and a Social Gospel movement to once again Christianize America and save the world for democracy; progressive reform movements: temperance, woman suffrage, and child labor legislation; anti-Catholic nativism, which found expression in the foundation of the American Protective Association in 1887; the expansion of the Ku Klux Klan in the South; and campaigns for laws restricting immigration. Not surprisingly, Catholics saw themselves as the targets of yet another Protestant crusade. Progressive Protestants, by contrast, tended to view Catholics as the main obstacle to reform. Revivalists like Billy Sunday never tired of warning their congregations of the menace the "hordes" of "foreigners" were posing to Christian America and of blaming "the foreign vote" for blocking Prohibition. Only "a great Anglo-Saxon majority," Sunday warned, could overcome this "foreign influence."[10] The sense of menace felt by Protestant nativism was not totally baseless. According to Jay P. Dolan, "By 1890 the Catholic urban population . . . outnumbered the urban population of all other religious denominations combined."[11]

But the old evangelical consensus around a Christian America had begun to dissipate. To the right, the fundamentalists lost faith in America ever becoming Christian without apocalyptic divine intervention and adopted a radical version of premillennial sectarianism. To the left, liberal Protestants began to drop the qualifier "Christian" from the American mission and adopted a secular postmillennial vision of progress.[12] Evangelical Protestantism lost its cultural hegemony and became disestablished, opening the way for the formation of a new national covenant, a new civil religion that eventually would incorporate Catholics, Jews, and secular humanists. But before breaking apart permanently, the old evangelical coalition came together again to win the last Protestant crusade, Prohibition, and just one more time, briefly, at Al Smith's 1928 presidential campaign, to block the entrance of popery into the White House.[13]

For all practical purposes anti-Catholic nativism died with this election. To be sure, Protestant-Catholic conflicts flared up in the 1940s and 1950s. But those were no longer the clear church-sect, majority-minority conflicts of the past. They were the first signs of normal interdenominational conflicts.[14] Old Protestant prejudices have lingered on, particularly among fundamentalist and sectarian Protestants, and, as an atavistic intellectual and class prejudice, among liberal upper-class Protestants in the Northeast.[15] But in a deservedly celebrated book in the mid-1950s, Will Herberg wrote that Protestant-Catholic-Jew had become the three denominational forms of being American.[16] The election of a Catholic to the presidency in 1960 was the best confirmation of the thesis. Before being allowed into the White House, however, John F. Kennedy had to prove his worthiness before an association of Protestant ministers in Houston.

A Catholic Denomination in a Free Religious Market

The *Ark* and the *Dove,* setting sail to America in 1634, could serve as befitting a symbol of Catholic Maryland as the *Mayflower* was of Puritan New England. While the covenanted Puritans were to be "a City upon a Hill," lord proprietor Cecil Calvert instructed his governor and commissioners that "all Acts of Romane Catholique Religion be done as privately as may be" and that Catholics "be silent upon all occasions of discourse concerning matters of religion."[17] Not surprisingly, given the disabilities under which they had to function in most of the colonies, Catholics welcomed with enthusiasm the radically new constitutional arrangement inscribed in the First Amendment. In a letter to Rome in 1783, Catholic priests wrote that "in these United States, our Religious system has undergone a revolution, if possible, more extraordinary, than our political one."[18]

It is customary to distinguish the "republican" from the "immigrant" phase of American Catholicism and to attribute two radically different styles of Catholicism to both phases.[19] The characterization which David O'Brien has presented of the republican American Catholic is very much akin to Bernhard Groethuysen's masterful characterization of the eighteenth-century, self-made French Catholic "bourgeois." Both types represented the style of successful Catholic laymen, faithful to the church but fully at home in the world, who had learned to segregate rigidly, in the liberal tradition, their political, economic, and religious roles. They urged the church to "stick to religion," while they "engaged in economic and political life with no direct and little indirect reference to religious faith."[20]

Bishop John England of Charleston, in his address to Congress on 8 January 1826, answering Protestant critics offered the classic legitimation of liberal republicanism:

Our answer to this is extremely simple and very plain; it is that we would not be bound to obey it, that we recognize no such authority. I would not allow to the Pope, or to any bishop of our church, outside this Union, the smallest interference with the humblest vote at our most insignificant balloting box. He has no right to such interference. You must, from the view which I have taken, see the plain distinction between spiritual authority and a right to interfere in the regulation of human government or civil concerns. You have in your constitution wisely kept them distinct and separate.[21]

He concluded by offering his vision of the place he wanted Catholicism to occupy in the American republic and in the pluralist, denominational religious system:

We desire to see the Catholics as a religious body upon the ground of equality with all other religious societies. . . . We consider that any who would call upon them to stand aloof from their brethren in the politics of the country, as neither a friend to America nor a friend to Catholics. . . . We repeat our maxim: Let Catholics in religion stand isolated as a body, and upon as good ground as their brethren. Let Catholics, as citizens and politicians, not be distinguishable from their other brethren of the commonwealth.[22]

But John England's vision would not be realized, at least not until the 1960s. The competing vision of a Christian America, zealously pursued by evangelical Protestantism, and the system of Protestant denominationalism that ensued did not allow for the acceptance of Catholicism as just another American denomination. Moreover, the massive immigration of impoverished Irish Catholics made them clearly distinguishable, by class and ethnicity, from their fellow citizens and presented the Catholic hierarchy with radically new challenges. A very different type of Catholic church, the immigrant church, with a new type of episcopal leadership, emerged in the 1840s.

Most commentators have viewed Bishop John Hughes of New York as the most forceful and articulate representative of the new immigrant Catholic church. Two incidents, in particular, serve to illustrate the immigrant style. Following the "Philadelphia riots" of May and July 1844, when plans for a nativist rally in New York City were announced, Bishop Hughes demanded a meeting with Mayor Robert Morris to warn him that, "if a single Catholic church is burned in New York, the city will become a second Moscow."[23] Thereafter, the Catholic bishop of New York—and bishops of other cities where Catholic immigrants would constitute a majority of the working class—would be a power to be reckoned with by politicians and elected officials. It was John Hughes who inaugurated what Andrew Greeley has called "the self-image of the bishop as the father and protector, of a flock not able to take care of itself and surrounded by hostile enemies."[24]

The republican Catholic style had been based on the model of autonomous Catholic individuals who entered the public sphere not as Catholics but as indistinguishable citizens, in order to participate in the advancement of the public good. The immigrant Catholic style, by contrast, was based on the premise of the collective organization and mobilization of Catholics as a group—distinguishable from other groups by religion, class, and ethnicity—in order to advance their particular group interests.

The church, with the bishop as "church boss," became a vehicle for the protection, self-organization, and mobilization of Catholic immigrants. Once Irish-Catholics began to control the urban political machines, the power of the local bishop became naturally enhanced. While Bishop Hughes actually failed in his attempts to create a Catholic party under his control, nonetheless he taught the immigrants that a militant and politically united Catholic bloc, normally tied to the Democratic party, could best defend their interests.

Having failed in his efforts to get the Protestant King James Version of the Bible out of the public school, in 1841 Bishops Hughes campaigned for state funding of Catholic schools, provoking in the process a Protestant nativist reaction. When both major parties, Whigs and Democrats, refused to support his efforts, Bishop Hughes entered his own candidates. The Catholic ticket was defeated, but it obtained sufficient votes to persuade the New York state government to take over the administration of the city's public schools from the private, mainly Protestant, Public School Society. If Bishop Hughes could not get state aid for Catholic education, at least he would remove Protestant education from the public schools. Furthermore, a separate Catholic parochial school system now seemed more justified than ever and Hughes became its most decisive champion. "To build the school-house first, and the church afterwards" became his famous dictum.

To keep the faith of the immigrants, protecting them from Protestant America while helping them take their rightful place as a "separate but equal" ethnic and religious group in American society, became the central task of the immigrant church. The repeated controversies surrounding public and parochial schools became the most evident signs of the different visions which Protestant and Catholic had of America and of the role religion was to occupy in public life. With the creation of the parochial school system, the Catholic church was serving notice that it had its own agenda of Americanization. The Catholic perception that the public school system was an agent, first, of Protestantification and, then, of secularization led to the creation of a system of Catholic education unparalleled in the entire Catholic world.

The church and all its institutions would play a crucial function in the assimilation—Americanization—of the Catholic immigrant, but it was done on Catholic terms. Out of the most varied national groups, there emerged one single Catholic religious body that stood distinctly apart from all other religious bodies and from the dominant American culture. At the end of the nineteenth century, "Americanists" such as Bishops Gibbons, Ireland, Keane, and Spalding resisted the separatist trend, but the conservatives were able to prevail with the aid of the

Vatican. The pope's condemnation of the Americanist heresy (1899), followed by the condemnation of the Modernist heresy (1907), had a chilling effect on an emerging liberal Catholicism and on all attempts to integrate American Catholicism into American culture.[25] The issues were similar to those which led to the split between fundamentalist and modernist Protestantism, but in the case of American Catholicism, Vatican intervention served to enforce unity within a divided hierarchy while imposing the conservative position upon the entire church.

The first half of the twentieth century marks the golden age of the "proud and glorious isolation" of American Catholicism from the contemporary world, a withdrawal into a separate cultural ghetto not unlike the sectarian withdrawal of fundamentalism from the emerging secular American culture. The Catholic counterculture and countersociety were built around the neighborhood ethnic parish with its distinct form of "devotional Catholicism," the Catholic school system (from elementary school to college), a distinct Catholic worldview based on a refurbished "neo-Thomism" and a mythical view of the Catholic Middle Ages, separate Catholic mass media, and myriad Catholic voluntary associations (religious, professional, and recreational).[26]

The safe cultural haven lasted until the mid-1950s, when some Catholic intellectuals became disaffected with the "complacency in mediocrity" of the Catholic intellectual ghetto.[27] But the carefully built Catholic subculture was undermined by more powerful structural forces. World War II, the G.I. Bill, and the general economic boom had set American Catholics on a new journey of emigration and geographical, educational, and occupational mobility, away from the working-class, urban, ethnic neighborhoods into more highly educated, higher-income, and middle-class all-American suburbs.

At last, after a long and unexpected detour, John England's liberal republican vision was being realized. American Catholics were joining the American mainstream—indeed, more than any other group they were beginning to define middle America—and were entering public life not as Catholics, in defense of their particular group interests, but "as citizens and politicians," more and more indistinguishable from other Americans. Whether intentionally or not, John F. Kennedy's famous speech before the Protestant ministers in Houston was almost a replica of John England's address to Congress.[28]

Kennedy offered the classic liberal position of radical separation between the private religious and the public secular spheres. Religious views are the individual's own affairs, and they ought to be irrelevant in public affairs or in the exercise of public secular roles. Churches ought to stick to religion and not meddle in public matters. Actually, historical precedent, trends, and pressures in this direction were such that, had the

Vatican Council and developments in global Catholicism not interfered, probably this liberal position would today be the de facto official position of the American Catholic church. Instead, we have witnessed in the late 1970s and 1980s a new style of "public Catholicism" that is clearly distinguishable from both the "liberal republican" and the "immigrant" styles, and has no established precedent in the history of American Catholicism.

The Immigrant Church: From a Multinational to an American National Church

Congregationally, the fundamental characteristic of a church is that of being a territorially organized religious body which claims compulsory and universal membership. The sect, by contrast, is a religious association based on voluntary and selective membership. The compulsory attribute is a historically specific aspect of the post-Constantinian Christian church which was tied to a particular structural dualism of spiritual and temporal power, which de facto no longer exists in today's Catholic world and in principle was abandoned by the Catholic church with the Declaration of Religious Freedom at Vatican II.

The fundamental and remaining difference, therefore, is that the church aspires to universal membership and, consequently, welcomes saints as well as sinners, while the sect aspires to be an exclusive association of saints. Sociologically, this is translated into the principle that usually, under normal circumstances, individual members are born into the church or, more precisely, are incorporated into the church as members of a natural community into which they are born—that is, family, ethnic group, nation, and so forth. The members of the sect, by contrast, join the sect qua individuals after a selection process.

The Catholic church in the United States has always been a church insofar as its membership has been composed, for the most part, of individuals who were incorporated into the church as members of larger ethnic-national groups. Indeed, before it functioned as a national American Catholic church, the immigrant church functioned as a church of disparate ethnic Americans. Related to this immigrant nature of the Catholic church in America, that is, to being the result of the transplantation of disparate parts to a new environment out of which a new body had to be formed, there have emerged recurrently in the history of American Catholicism four series of problems or tensions in need of constant resolution:

a) The tension between a multinational and an American national church.

b) The tension between the traditional church principle of prescribed membership and the voluntary denominational principle dominant in the American religious environment.

c) The tension between the traditional episcopal, clerical, and authoritarian governance structures of the church and the democratic, lay, and participatory principles which permeate the American polity.

d) The tension between episcopal sovereignty and the need for a centralized national church structure.

E Pluribus Unum

From the very beginning the fundamental problem of the Catholic church in America has been how to form a unified body out of disparate and scattered Catholic parts.[29] In order to maintain institutional growth and fulfill its pastoral duties, the Catholic church in America has always had to cater to the most diverse linguistic, cultural, and spiritual needs of its people. In order to maintain institutional unity, however, the church hierarchy has had to ensure that the most diverse Catholic groups would become one single American Catholic church. This tension between the pastoral and the institutional demands has not always been easy to resolve. The same conflicts that emerged first between the French cultured, aristocratic hierarchy and *la canaille irlandaise* would reappear with every new immigrant group. Jay Dolan has put it most concisely: "Brownson wanted the Irish to become American; Ireland cajoled the Germans; and Mundelein worked on the Polish."[30]

The 1916 religious census indicates that six national groups—the Irish, Germans, Italians, Polish, French Canadians, and Mexicans— accounted for 75 percent of the 16 million Catholics. Eastern European peoples—the largest being Slovaks, Czechs or Bohemians, Lithuanians, and Ruthenian-Ukrainians—made up most of the rest. All in all, American Catholics were organized along national parish lines, speaking twenty-eight different languages.[31]

In the context of the general American experience, immigration and national and linguistic diversity are per se not noteworthy. Noteworthy, however, is the fact that unlike every other major religious body in America, Christian or Jewish, which fell prey to the dynamics of American denominationalism and split along national, linguistic, doctrinal, regional, class, or racial lines, the Catholic church in America has been able to keep the overwhelming majority of Catholic immigrants and their descendants within one single American Catholic church.[32] This is perhaps the most persuasive evidence that the American Catholic church functions as a territorially organized national church for ethnic Catholics and, simultaneously, that the Roman Catholic church transcends all national churches.

With the immigration-restriction laws of the 1920s, the American Catholic church began to lose its immigrant, multinational character, giving way to a rapid process of Americanization and assimilation of the various Catholic ethnics into one single Catholic group distinct from Protestants and Jews. Being overwhelmingly an urban population, American Catholics were particularly affected by the post–World War II process of suburbanization. They left the ethnic neighborhoods and national parishes in large numbers to join all-American suburbs and all-Catholic parishes. The demographic move to the West and the South had similar consequences. By the 1960s the assimilation of American Catholics was nearly complete.[33]

Religious Community versus Community Cult

As Catholicism immigrated to America it had both to compete with Protestant denominationalism and to adopt, at least partially, some of its principles in order to succeed.[34] The uprootedness which accompanied emigration meant that "faith" could no longer be taken for granted. It had to be actively and voluntarily "kept" or "revived." In this respect, Catholicism in America also assumed, constitutionally and phenomenologically, the denominational shape of a "free church." Concurrently, however, uprootedness and a foreign environment only exacerbated the need for community, while Protestant nativist hostility served to reinforce ethnic and Catholic solidarity. For the immigrant, the national parish served to re-create, in fact, often to create for the first time, the lost world of the home country. The *parish mission* was the form which Catholic evangelical revivalism took in nineteenth-century America.[35]

Ordinary Catholicism was shaped, practically until the shock of Vatican II, by the persistence of devotional Catholicism. But throughout the twentieth century, Catholic devotion became less communitarian and more privatistic. The Depression and the New Deal created the conditions in the 1930s for the golden age of "social Catholicism."[36] But the religious revival of the post–World War II era brought back an even more privatist, devotional, and legalist religion. However, there were some minoritarian countermovements, all pointing to a new type of Catholicism, no longer centered around the parish, lay in orientation, and characterized by various combinations of individual commitment, inner-worldly spirituality, communitarian orientation, and public philosophy.[37]

One can also observe a transformation of the Catholic community orientation toward progressively higher levels of generality: from the village community, to the ethnic neighborhood and national parish, to the American Catholic community, to the American national community, and after Vatican II to the world community. Ironically, the total commitment to America, which was once the hallmark of liberal Catholicism against the particularism of the national ethnic parish, later became characteristic of conservative Catholicism.[38] Precisely at the time when Catholicism had finally become American and American Catholics had become faithful followers of the American civil religion, transformations in world Catholicism offered broader, more universalistic perspectives which challenged the nationalist particularism of the American civil religion.

People of God or a Bishops' Church?

Any viable institutional structure for the Roman Catholic church in America would have to take into account three determining factors: the American circumstance, appropriate relations between the three main actors—hierarchy, clergy, and laity—and relations with Rome. The American circumstance was, of course, shaped by the two determinant experiences of independence and republicanism, experiences which inevitably had spilled over onto the sphere of religion.[39] Four issues in particular had to be resolved: the need to have a bishop ordinary as the head of the church; the need to define who had the right to nominate bishops; the need to define who had the right to nominate pastors; and the need to define who had rights over church property. Only the first American Catholic bishop, John Carroll, was elected by the American clergy. Thereafter, Rome would reserve for itself the right to choose the American hierarchy.[40]

The need to establish clear norms that would regulate the institutional relations between hierarchy, clergy, and laity became evident in the conflicts of "trusteeism" in Saint Peter's Church in New York City between 1785 and 1790.[41] The divergent interests of the hierarchy, the clergy, the laity, and the various social strata within the laity led to a series of conflicts, pitting priest against priest, clergy against laity, the trustees against ordinary people, and all against the bishop. The crisis came to a head when a priest, Father Nugent, with the support of "people of little importance and Irish," took control of the church away from the more prosperous trustees and denied John Carroll's episcopal authority, arguing that his jurisdiction was invalid in New York because he had received it from a foreign court, Rome. Bishop Carroll, who had earlier opposed the trustees' use of the civil courts to remove another priest, now deemed it necessary to check this act of open clerical rebellion against ecclesiastical authority "even by recourse to civil authority."[42]

The New York court ruled against the priest, de facto recognizing the right of the Catholic church in the United States to establish its own internal ecclesiastical discipline. When this discipline failed, the church could make use of secular courts to remove recalcitrant pastors. Later, in defending the American system of "no establishment" and "free exercise of religion" against European critics, American bishops would always argue that the system gave the church the kind of *libertas ecclesiae* it had never had when it was under the alleged protection and patronage of Christian princes. At the end, both the clergy and the laity were left out of the system of governance of the American church. Faced with a rebellion from their inferiors, the bishops showed their willingness to accept the monarchical rule of the pope in exchange for the pope's support of their own monarchical rule in their dioceses.[43] The American Catholic church became, to an extent unequaled in the entire Catholic world, a bishops' church.

Episcopal Sovereignty versus a National Synodic Church

The tension and conflicts between a monarchic and a synodic church are as old as the church itself. The tensions have reemerged ever anew with changing sociohistorical circumstances. As a bureaucratic imperial system, the church has always been exposed to the tension between centripetal and centrifugal forces that is typical of such systems.

John Carroll's plan for an American church had been that of a collegial body of the clergy under the spiritual authority of an ordinary bishop. But the daunting task of literally building the initial institutional structures (American bishops would always be primarily "brick and mortar" bishops) and the pressing need to reassert some episcopal hierarchic discipline frustrated the plan. After his death, Carroll left a collection of mostly undistinguished prelates, narrowly absorbed in the problems of their own dioceses, who established the long-lasting tradition of a church based on local episcopal sovereignty, devoid of any collective, centralized, or federated national structure, authority, or vision.[44]

Undoubtedly, the narrow local focus of the bishops' vision was also conditioned by the very nature of the American political system in the nineteenth century. Since politics were centered on the local and state level—this being particularly the case of those issues like education, morality legislation, and the like, which absorbed most of the bishops' attention—it is not surprising that even those bishops inclined to political activism tended to concentrate their efforts on the local and state level. It was also at this level that they had political clout.[45] In this respect, the American Catholic church could be characterized as a diocesan rights church in a states rights political system.

But even after the process of bureaucratic centralization and nationalization of government in Washington forced the Catholic hierarchy to establish there parallel administrative, policy, and lobbying agencies, most bishops continued resisting jealously any encroachment upon their local episcopal sovereignty. Indeed, as Dolan points out, the high point in the conception of the bishop as absolute ruler came toward the end of the nineteenth century after the "symbolic apex" of papal absolutism with the declaration of papal infallibility in 1870. Following the legislation of the 1884 Baltimore Council, "Each bishop became Pope in his own diocese."[46]

The slow process of redirecting the Catholic church's attention from local to national politics began in the early decades of the twentieth century. The turning point was the founding of the National Catholic War Council in 1917 as a contribution to the national war effort. The founding of this council marks in many respects the beginning of "social Catholicism."[47] For the first time, there was some institutional commitment on the part of the church to social and political action. In 1919, the council released the *Program of Social Reconstruction,* an important text most of whose policy recommendations would be incorporated later into New Deal legislation. But this so-called bishops' program was in fact a text written by Father John A. Ryan that was appropriated by the bishops as their program.[48]

In 1919 the national orientation and the new "social Catholicism" were reinforced by the transformation of the War Council into the National Catholic Welfare Council (NCWC), which, in addition to creating a permanent administrative structure, called for annual meetings of all American bishops. But most bishops received the new structure with indifference and a group of conservative bishops made an almost successful appeal to Rome to kill the idea. They were able, at least, to change the name from "council" to "conference," just to make clear that it was not a synodic body that could encroach upon the episcopal sovereignty of the individual bishops. It was only a deliberative body with no binding power, which could safely be ignored.

Nothing illustrates better than these two incidents the difference between the "social Catholicism" of the interwar period and the new form of "public Catholicism" that emerged in the 1980s. Social Catholicism had emerged as the initiative of a minority of activist bishops and, above all, clergy who took the social doctrines of the church seriously. Many of them came from the progressive Midwest and found in those doctrines the source for a Catholic "Social Gospel." Most bishops, however, were only reluctantly tolerant of their activities. Moreover, like presidential candidate Al Smith, most ordinary "devout Catholics from childhood" would have replied that they "never heard of social encyclicals."[49] Father John A. Ryan, "the Right Reverend New Dealer," may have been well known and influential in the corridors of Washington and among ACLU members, but certainly he was less well known and much less popular among ordinary Catholics than his archrival Catholic social activist, populist radio priest, and profascist corporatist Father Charles Coughlin.[50]

Being Catholic and American

At the very moment when Catholicism had finally become American, the Vatican *aggiornamento* reopened the old vexing question of the relationship between being Catholic and being American. Actually, now for the first time, American Catholicism was forced to confront modernity. It was no longer a question of being simultaneously a traditional Catholic and a modern American and, thus, proving pragmatically that there was no incompatibility between both forms of being. Now the question was how to modernize, how to update, the old traditional Catholicism itself.

The fact that Catholicism could adapt so well to American conditions without ever confronting modernity is indeed striking. Tocqueville offered a plausible explanation:

The Catholic priests in America have divided the intellectual world into two parts: in the one they place the doctrines of revealed religion, which they assent to without discussion; in the other they leave those political truths which they believe the Deity has left open to free inquiry. Thus the Catholics of the United States are at the same time the most submissive believers and the most independent citizens.[51]

Catholics had learned to compartmentalize rigidly two spheres of life, the religious and the secular. Catholicism was restricted to the religious sphere, while Americanism was restricted to the secular sphere. American Catholics were Roman Catholics in church and ethnic Catholic Americans in the world. Besides, this segmentation seemed to be fully in harmony with the alleged "wall of separation" established by the First Amendment. Actually, the First Amendment not only protected politics from Catholic interference. It also protected Catholicism from the external interference of free public inquiry.

Against the accusations of the incompatibility of Romanism and Republicanism, American Catholics repeated persistently in self-defense that they were Roman in spiritual matters, and only in spiritual matters, and republican, and therefore, American, in civil matters. Evangelical Protestants, who never made such a separation since their goal was to Christianize the republic, remained unconvinced. They could only view such an argument as a contrived subterfuge. Evangelical Protestants knew instinctively that there was something about "Romanism" that was ultimately incompatible with "modern" republican principles. But not being fully "modern," they were unable to frame the issue in terms of the relationships between modernity, freedom of inquiry, and religious dogma and kept repeating the old unfounded arguments about the threats of "foreign" Roman intervention to republican institutions or the incompatibility between Catholicism and democracy.[52]

Granted that Catholics were dogmatic about the authoritative tradition of the church. But nineteenth-century evangelical Protestants were no more willing to let free critical inquiry enter and question Scripture than Catholics were ready to let free inquiry question the authority of tradition. Bishop John Hughes saw clearly through the Protestant conceit. Being a strict Catholic separationist, that is, a republican in civil matters and a dogmatic absolutist in spiritual matters, he could not accept the American civil religion. He would not accept any of the Protestant claims about a Christian America, nor the attempt to teach Protestantism in the common schools through the subterfuge of nonsectarian Christianity. If America was to be Christian, then there was no reason why it should assume the Protestant rather than the Catholic version of Christianity.[53] Later on, however, "Americanists" such as Cardinal Gibbons and Archbishop Ireland found perfect harmony between Catholicism and the American civil religion. Their task, according to Archbishop Ireland, was that of "teaching laggard Catholics to love America, teaching well-disposed non-Catholics to trust the Church."[54] In a speech at the 1884 Third Plenary Baltimore Council, trying to convince laggard conservative bishops, Bishop Ireland said:

There is no conflict between the Catholic Church and America. I could not utter one syllable that would belie, however remotely, either the Church or the Republic, and when I assert, as I now solemnly do, that the principles of the Church are in thorough harmony with the interests of the Republic, I know in the depths of my soul that I speak the truth.[55]

But the conservative bishops remained unconvinced. Bishops Corrigan of New York and McQuaid of Rochester, knowing the official Catholic doctrine on church and state and on religious freedom, could accept the notion that, "under the circumstances," the church could accommodate itself to American conditions. This was known in Catholic parlance as "the antithesis." But "the thesis," the ideal situation, could only be an established church in a confessional state.[56] The church as the depositor of divine truth could not accept the notion that error has the same rights as truth.[57] During the "Americanist" controversy, the issues were never discussed openly in these terms. But this was the central issue. Everything else was secondary.

The "Americanists" held the American truths to be self-evident. But their great failing, indeed, the historical failing of American Catholicism, was their inability to offer reasoned intellectual arguments for those truths, arguments that could be translated into Catholic theological language and, thus, challenge directly the traditional teachings of the church on this issue. They were able to offer impassioned confessions of their faith in the American system. They also defended the American proposition on pragmatic, utilitarian grounds, showing how beneficial the American system had been for the Catholic church, how the church had greater freedom and greater success in America than in allegedly Catholic countries.[58] But they could not offer theological rationales for democracy, freedom of religion, and disestablishment.

When the condemnation of the Americanist heresy came, they fell silent. Publicly, having expected much worse, they felt exonerated and would repeatedly state that they had never held the opinions condemned by the Holy Father in *Testem Benevolentiae* (1899). As far as they were concerned, therefore, "Americanism" was a nonheresy. But they never dared to defend publicly the truths they held so deeply. The effects of the condemnation on American Catholicism would be long-lasting. It would be necessary to wait another fifty years until a Catholic theologian, John Courtney Murray, at last offered theological arguments for the American truths, challenging in the process the Catholic "thesis."[59] At Vatican II, all American bishops stood up in unison to defend not only the practice but the principle of religious freedom.[60]

The Declaration On Religious Freedom, *Dignitatis humanae,* came at a moment when the tensions of being both American and Catholic had totally disappeared. The anti-Communist crusade of the Cold War era made this possible. This was a crusade all freedom-loving people could join, those fighting for republican freedom and those fighting for the freedom of the church. Rome and the republic could at last be allies.[61] Albeit for different reasons, Catholic liberals like John F. Kennedy and conservative Catholics like Cardinal Spellman both shared the conviction that there could be no conflict between the Catholic church and the American republic—for President Kennedy because there was a wall of separation between private faith and the modern secular world, for Cardinal Spellman because Catholicism and American patriotism had become undistinguishably fused in the American civil religion.[62]

These were the two minds of American Catholicism at the beginning of the Vatican Council. As the Roman *aggiornamento* reached American shores, it became obvious that both types of Catholicism were being challenged by a new understanding of the relation between religion and the world. Both the liberal wall of separation and the civil religion fusion were put into question. Private faith could no longer leave secular public matters alone. Nor could spiritual truths ignore the "signs of the times" or be immune to freedom of inquiry. But an eschatological dimension also warned not to identify any social order with God's kingdom. A new tension, this time voluntary and purposeful, between Catholicism and Americanism emerged. For the first time, the Catholic faith dared to challenge American public affairs. In doing so, however, the Catholic faith could no longer avoid exposing itself to public scrutiny, public debate, and public contestation.

American Public Catholicism after the Vatican Aggiornamento

Three events above all exemplify the new type of public Catholicism: the 1983 Pastoral Letter, *The Challenge of Peace: God's Promise and Our Response;* the 1986 Pastoral Letter, *Economic Justice for All: Catholic Social Teaching and the U.S. Economy;* and the public interventions of the American bishops in the politics of "abortion" after the 1973 *Roe v. Wade* Supreme Court decision and their involvement in electoral politics since the 1976 presidential elections.[63] The three events can be characterized as different types of public speech acts, that is, the American bishops speaking out on abortion, nuclear warfare, and the economy. In discussing the three events it is helpful to differentiate three moments: (a) the historical background behind the speech acts; (b) the nature and character of the speech acts as public events; and (c) the reactions and the intended and unintended public consequences.[64]

The Background to the Bishops' Public Intervention

It is a widely shared assumption that Vatican II led to a radical transformation of American Catholicism.[65] The best way of describing this transformation would probably be to call it a "radical reform from above coming from abroad." Confirming evidence for such a thesis can actually be found in two works which try to offer alternative explanations of the emergence of American "public" Catholicism.

In *Catholic Bishops in American Politics,* Timothy Byrnes argues that the bishops' role in the contemporary American political process can only be explained satisfactorily as a reaction to two fundamental changes in the American political system: the "expansion of the federal government's authority and initiative" at the expense of state and local power and a "shift in the partisan alignment of the national party system" that has led to a "more fluid and volatile competition between the parties" and to the "discovery of religion as a tool of political mobilization and coalition building."[66]

Undoubtedly, these two changes determined the historical context within which the public actions of the American bishops took place. Particularly, the 1973 Supreme Court decision protecting the right of women to abortion served as a catalyst for the active involvement of the Catholic church in national anti-abortion politics. Catholic support of the right-to-life movement was probably the single most important factor in alerting the New Right to the mobilization potential of conservative religious groups in its project to bring about a major party realignment. In turn, the political emergence of the New Christian Right and its role in the Reagan "revolution" forced the more liberal sectors of the Catholic church to rethink their political strategy, to avoid being identified with single-issue movements, and to incorporate their opposition to abortion in a broad pro-life political strategy, Cardinal Joseph Bernardin's "seamless garment," that included opposition to nuclear policies and the support of "economic justice for all." In this respect, the American political context within which the bishops had to frame their public involvement gave added urgency to the need to write the pastoral letters.

But as Byrnes himself clearly shows, the original impulse and the spirit as well as the letter of all the public interventions of the American bishops can be traced directly to Roman directives and texts: to the documents of Vatican II, to papal encyclicals, and to ordinary synods. The particular form taken by attempts to implement the new doctrines could not help but be shaped and colored by the given American political context.

If there is no doubt that the impulse for the new type of public Catholicism came from abroad, it is even more obvious that this new Catholicism has to be understood as a "reform from above." Naturally, liberal sectors of American Catholicism, which in different ways had anticipated many of the Vatican reforms, welcomed those reforms and tried to push them as fast and as far as they could. But it is farfetched to view what Joseph Varacalli calls "the establishment of Liberal Catholicism in America" as the result of the rise of a "New Catholic Knowledge Class."[67] To explain the transformation of American Catholicism as the rise of a new class makes little sense unless one is willing to argue that the bishops themselves were the vanguard of the new class. In such a case, however, the new class paradigm is hardly illuminating. A theory of ideological transformation of the old ruling class would be much more appropriate.[68]

There are, however, two insights from Varacalli's use of "new class" theory which are relevant. Undoubtedly, the Vatican *aggiornamento* and its reception in the United States took place in the midst of a radical restructuring of American society. The storm that, according to John

Tracy Ellis, broke over American Catholics in about 1966 came on top of the shocks associated with the move of the urban ethnic working class to join "the new American society."[69] Being the most blue collar, the youngest, and the most anti-Communist of all American groups, Catholics could not but be deeply affected by the educational and occupational revolution associated with the coming of postindustrial society, by the youth revolt and the counterculture of the 1960s, and by the anti–Vietnam War movement. There is no doubt that a new and activist intellectual stratum emerged within American Catholicism in the 1960s, whose members were to be found among bishops, priests, nuns, and laity alike and who became the carriers of the new Catholicism. But the neoconservative version of the thesis, which views the process as the rise of a new knowledge class usurping power from the old bourgeois class, is simply irrelevant in the Catholic context.[70]

There is also little doubt that theologians and other Catholic intellectuals played a crucial role in the Catholic reformation. One only needs to recall the role of the "periti" in Vatican II, or the role of a small group of Latin-American theologians in the Medellín Conference. Similarly, Varacalli has stressed the role played by liberal Catholic intellectuals and by the professional bureaucrats who came to control the newly established National Conference of Catholic Bishops/United States Catholic Conference (NCCB/USCC), particularly its Advisory Council. The aim of Varacalli's study is to show that the ten-year (1973–83) bicentennial program, "A Call to Action: Liberty and Justice for All," was "conceived out of the bosom of the Advisory Council of the NCCB/USCC."[71] But Varacalli has to admit that the elaborate three-stage bicentennial program was a direct response of the American bishops to Paul VI's encyclical *Call to Action* (1971) and to the 1971 Synod of Bishops' *Justice in the World,* which pronounced that "action on behalf of justice and participation in the transformation of the world fully appear to us as a constitutive dimension of the preaching of the Gospel, or in other words, of the Church's mission for the redemption of the human race and its liberation from every oppressive situation."[72]

Conservative Catholics are entitled to believe that these and similar statements by popes and by the bishops of the entire church constitute a dangerous deviation from Catholic tradition, a secularization that transforms the otherworldly transcendent Gospel into an immanent Catholic Social Gospel. There would be good empirical grounds for such a belief. But given the source of such public statements, conservatives have a harder time offering empirical evidence that the activism of liberal Catholics constitutes a misinterpretation of Vatican II and a deviation from official teachings. Given their respect for the infallibility of such teachings, conservatives cannot possibly argue in public that recent official teachings were erroneous.

The conservative thesis, central to the "Catholic Restoration" aggressively pursued by Cardinal Ratzinger, that the expansion of the role of the theologians and other Catholic intellectuals led to an illegitimate usurpation of the church's magisterium from the bishops has to be viewed as part of a revisionist attempt by the Vatican to regain centralized doctrinal control by reinterpreting the "correct" meaning of Vatican II.[73] The ideological struggles taking place within the church today are not primarily those between a conservative hierarchy and a liberal laity, nor even those between bishops and dissenting theologians. They are struggles within the hierarchy and within the laity over the correct magisterium of the church.[74]

The same dogmatic respect for tradition that constrains any liberal reform, and that impedes the possibility that any reformist pope will wake up one day and declare the teachings of his predecessor erroneous or no longer valid, equally constrains conservative popes and members of the Roman Curia in their restorationist projects.[75] In this respect, the official teachings proclaimed by Vatican II and by subsequent papal and synodal declarations can no longer be easily excised from the Catholic tradition nor can the reforms instituted by the Vatican *aggiornamento* be easily reversed. At most, a conservative hierarchy may attempt to appropriate the exclusive interpretation of the meaning of those teachings or may attempt to control the process of reform from above, to "freeze" the *aggiornamento* at one particular period of time, or to quell the spirit and impulse for reform. Under present historical circumstances, however, short of abandoning the universalist claims of the church and withdrawing to a fundamentalist sectarian posture, such attempts are likely to fail. The present Vatican project of once again centralizing the control of doctrinal teaching through the replacement of liberal bishops with conservative ones throughout the world is at best a process fraught with contingencies whose outcome not even a long-reigning and powerful pope could control.

Episcopal Speeches as Public Events

Taking into account the character of the speech writers, the styles of discourse, the claims to validity of the speeches, and the stated purpose of the speech, one has to differentiate between, on one hand, the pastoral letters on war and peace and on the economy and, on the other, the bishops' statements on abortion, as being two significantly different types of public discourse.

The pastoral letters. The pastoral letters *The Challenge of Peace* and

Economic Justice for All were texts approved democratically by a two-thirds majority of the National Conference of Catholic Bishops, which reflected the consensus reached by this collective body after a long process of public, collective deliberation and consultation, with wide community participation.[76] Indeed, taking into account the scope, the depth, and the systematic nature of the public deliberations, one may say that the most relevant characteristic of the letters from a public point of view was the very process through which they were written. They may be viewed perhaps as an empirical approximation of the institutionalization of discourse ethics at a general civil society level.[77] Certainly, from a Catholic perspective they represented a radical departure from traditional modes of doctrinal and moral teaching. Nothing illustrates this better than the hostile reaction of Cardinal Ratzinger: "It is wrong to propose the teaching of the bishops merely as the basis for debate; the teaching ministry of the bishops means that they lead the people of God and therefore their teaching should not be obscured or reduced to one element among several in a free debate."[78]

Naturally, the episcopal deliberations did not approximate an "ideal speech situation." After all, the speakers were hierarchs who claimed to be the authoritative teachers of a particular moral tradition with universal validity claims. However, from the outset, the bishops acknowledged different levels of normativity and validity claims in their statements. There is one unquestioned fundamental value, the sacred dignity of the human person, which they assume as the revealed, but also as the rationally self-evident, foundation of their system of morality. From this universal value there follow certain general norms and moral principles which also have universal validity claims. But when it comes to the application of these general norms to particular circumstances or to the translation of principle into public policy, the bishops admit that this requires practical prudential judgment and that only degrees of approximation to moral certainty are attainable. Ultimately, in such cases the individual conscience has to make the final moral decision.

Moreover, the same texts are written with two different audiences in mind, the Catholic faithful and the general public, to which correspond two different claims of authoritative teaching. To Catholics, the texts are presented as authoritative moral doctrinal texts which, taking into account the different levels of normativity mentioned above, the faithful have a moral duty to accept as authoritative guides when making their own personal ethical decisions. But even here the bishops leave some room for rightful dissent. To the general public, the pastoral letters are presented as documents for public reflection and deliberation which should have the function of helping to establish collective norms with which to evaluate the morality of public policies and of economic structural practices.

The 1983 Pastoral Letter *The Challenge of Peace* represented a radical departure from the past in a dual sense. Prior to the Vietnam War, the American bishops had never tried to apply systematically the Catholic "just war" moral tradition to American circumstances. Furthermore, the American Catholic church had traditionally offered unquestioning support for the foreign policy and the war aims of the American state from the revolution to the Vietnam War.[79] World War I and World War II served to reinforce American Catholic patriotism.[80] During the Spanish Civil War, a brief divergence from American foreign policy emerged when the Catholic hierarchy and a majority of American Catholics supported Franco's Nationalist uprising, but World War II and particularly the anti-Communist crusade of the Cold War allowed Catholics to realign themselves securely within the American patriotic camp to such an extent that sectors of the Catholic right could appoint themselves as inquisitorial guardians of Americanism.[81]

When President Kennedy initiated the American intervention in the Vietnam War, he could count on full and unquestioning Catholic support, notwithstanding the existence of a small but significant Catholic pacifist left, best represented by the Catholic Worker movement.[82] In the early days of the war, Catholics were generally more hawkish than the rest of the population. From 1966 on, however, public opinion surveys show that Catholics became consistently and increasingly more dovish than Protestants and the general population, at a time when the Catholic hierarchy was still supporting the war.[83] Only in 1971, in the *Resolution on Southeast Asia,* after other religious leaders and most Americans had condemned the war, did the bishops finally come to the conclusion that the Vietnam War no longer met the "just war" criterion of "proportionality."

The 1983 Pastoral Letter was the first systematic moral evaluation of nuclear warfare and nuclear military policies from the perspective of the Catholic moral tradition.[84] Critics had been accusing the American bishops of concentrating inconsistently and one-sidedly on fighting abortion while neglecting the much greater threat to human life posed by the nuclear arms race. The bishops had also become aware that their one-sided support of the pro-life (anti-abortion) movement had been exploited politically by the New Right and the Reagan administration at a time when the nuclear policies of the administration were raising at least the apprehension if not the actual prospect of nuclear war.

In drafting their pastoral letter, the bishops proceeded inductively, discerning first "the signs of the times" and the new historical situation created by the possibility of nuclear human self-destruction. Then they brought to bear Catholic moral principles, such as the fundamental command to protect human life and the normative criteria of "just war," to come to the conclusion that no nuclear war could possibly meet such criteria as just cause, reasonable chance of "success," proportionality in the use of unjust means to achieve just ends, and discrimination in the use of violence.[85] It followed that no nuclear war could ever be morally justified.

The bishops stopped short of condemning the very possession of nuclear weapons as immoral, and, in the words of Bryan Hehir, a "centimeter of ambiguity" was left open considering the possibility that nuclear deterrence might be justified, but only as long as policymakers were pursuing arms reductions seriously and decisively. The very threat of nuclear retaliation against unarmed civilians was, however, immoral and to be condemned. The pastoral called for sharp arms reductions, for a "halt" (rather than a "freeze") to the production, testing, and deployment of new nuclear weapons, and for a rejection of "first use."[86]

The bishops did not derive their opposition to nuclear war from the absolute command "Thou shall not kill!" Against principled pacifism, the Catholic church has always maintained the position that killing other human beings may be justified "under certain conditions," self-defense being the most obvious of these conditions. Yet the "just war" theory was developed not in order to make war morally justifiable but, rather, to limit and restrict as much as possible the conditions under which killing would be morally permissible. Notwithstanding whether one evaluates the Catholic tradition in the actual application of its criteria as either rigorous or lax, it is evident that in this area the Catholic moral tradition allows for some flexibility in the application of its universal norms to particular circumstances and demands, precisely in order to be open to changing circumstances. The pastoral letter also stresses in unusual fashion the ultimate role of the individual conscience in making the final decision and, simultaneously, allows the right to dissent when the application of moral principle to contingent policies and circumstances demands prudential judgment.[87]

As a form of public moral discourse, the 1986 Pastoral Letter *Economic Justice for All* had similar characteristics. The main differences between the two letters derive from three factors: from the fact that there is a much more continuous and systematically developed tradition of modern Catholic social teaching from Leo XIII's *Rerum Novarum* (1891) to John Paul II's *Laborem Exercens* (1981), on which the American bishops relied in drafting the letter; from the fact that the American bishops have issued many more statements on the American economy since the 1919 *Program of Social Reconstruction* in the context of a more openly partisan, ongoing public debate on alternative economic policies and, therefore, critics could more easily try to discard the pastoral letter as a continuation of old Catholic support for New Deal policies;[88] and, finally, from the fact that modern economies and economic policies are much more complex structures, less susceptible to moral evaluation, and even less susceptible to moral regulation, than warfare or nuclear policies.

Economic Justice for All is the most detailed, systematic, and thorough application of Catholic social thought to a concrete, particular economy. The bishops are justified in calling their letter "a work of careful inquiry, wide consultation, and prayerful discernment."[89] Two aspects of the pastoral letter are particularly noteworthy. The first one is connected with the centrality that the principle of "the sacred dignity of the human person" has assumed in recent Catholic moral teaching, at least since John XXIII's encyclicals. Indeed, "the dignity of the human person" becomes the measure of all things. Accordingly, "every economic decision and institution" must be judged not only according to instrumental rational criteria but "in light of whether it protects or undermines the dignity of the human person." Every economic system has to be judged "by what it does *for* and *to* people and by how it permits all to *participate* in it."[90]

One of the consequences of using such a criterion is that it frees Catholic social thought from the ontological premises of natural law and from traditional conceptions of a natural social order. Catholic social thought can finally give up the old chimera of a Catholic "third way" between capitalism and socialism. There are no "Catholic" solutions to social problems. There are only more or less humane solutions. The moral task, therefore, is to humanize all social structures. This means that solutions cannot be mandated, much less imposed from the outside. They can only be proposed for public debate, for experimentation, and for adoption after a public consensus has been reached. According to the bishops: "There is certainly room for diversity of opinion in the Church and in the U.S. society on *how* to protect the human dignity and economic rights of all our brothers and sisters. In our view, however, there can be no legitimate disagreement on the basic moral objectives."[91]

It follows that generalized discourse can be the only appropriate procedure for reaching agreement on how best to protect those basic moral objectives. It is also obvious from the bishops' argumentation that they derive both the requirement for government intervention and the church's preferential option for the poor precisely from the need to universalize the equal access to discourse. Government has "the moral function" of "protecting human rights and securing basic justice for all members of the commonwealth."[92] This means that "those who are marginalized and whose rights are denied have privileged claims if society is to provide justice for *all*."[93] The church's "preferential option for the poor," in turn, "imposes a prophetic mandate to speak for those who have no one to speak for them, to be a defender of the defenseless, who in biblical terms are the poor."[94]

A second noteworthy aspect of the pastoral letter is the historicist consideration of the American economy not as a particular instance of an objective and universal natural social order but, rather, as a moment in the unfinished historical project of modernity. The bishops present their letter as a contribution to a public debate over what they call "a New American Experiment." They view the economic challenges of today in similar terms to the political challenges once confronting the founding fathers. "In order to create a new form of political democracy they were compelled to develop ways of thinking and political institutions that had never existed before."[95] Similarly, in order to complete what the bishops call "the unfinished business of the American experiment" and "to expand economic participation, broaden the sharing of economic power, and make economic decisions more accountable to the common good," it will be necessary to take steps as daring as those taken by the nations' founders when they created "structures of participation, mutual accountability, and widely distributed power to ensure the political rights and freedoms of all."[96] Ultimately, the relevance of the letter does not derive from the particular economic policies the bishops propose. Even if after public debate all the concrete proposals in the section "Selected Economic Policy Issues" were discarded for not being particularly useful, the relevance of the letter would still reside in the very proposal to extend public ethical discourse to the economic sphere.

The bishops speak on abortion. For almost two thousand years the Catholic church has morally condemned and consistently opposed the practice of abortion.[97] The church proudly considers this to be one of its greatest civilizational achievements against the allegedly "barbaric" Roman patriarchal practices of abortion and infanticide. This association of abortion and infanticide has fatefully determined the structure of Catholic moral reasoning on abortion. Vatican II reaffirmed the church's position when it declared that "abortion and infanticide are unspeakable crimes."[98] In 1967, right after the council, the American bishops made clear their opposition to the American Law Institute's Model Penal Code calling for the liberalization of abortion state laws. The bishops reiterated their opposition in a series of public statements beginning with *Human Life in Our Day* (1968).[99] The 1973 *Roe v. Wade* Supreme

Court decision only served to galvanize the bishops into renewed public statements and political action. The immediate reaction of the bishops was to refuse to "accept the court's judgment" and to advise people "not to follow its reasoning or conclusions."[100]

The most important public statements have been the 1974 testimony before the Senate Subcommittee on Constitutional Amendments, the 1976 testimony before the House Subcommittee on Civil and Constitutional Rights, the 1981 testimony in support of the Hatch Amendment, and the 1975 *Pastoral Plan for Pro-Life Activities*.[101] Most of the church's political activities have centered around various attempts to reverse *Roe v. Wade* through a constitutional amendment: the establishment of the National Committee for a Human Life Amendment as a lobby group, the launching and financing of the National Right to Life Committee, which later would become the independent right-to-life movement, and the bishops' intervention in electoral politics, particularly in the 1976, 1980, and 1984 presidential campaigns.

A comparison between the pastoral letters and the bishops' anti-abortion statements and activities reveals two radically different forms of moral discourse. The bishops' speech on abortion is inconsistent with their Pastoral Letters in three respects: internal *semantic* inconsistencies in the Catholic abortion speech, *performative* inconsistencies in their pragmatic application of moral principles, and *procedural* inconsistencies in the construction of the moral discourse. The attempt by the bishops to develop a consistently pro-life moral position, Cardinal Bernardin's "seamless garment," is indeed commendable.[102] But a closer look at the garment reveals that, far from offering a consistent ethic, the section on abortion is made up of a different fabric, the cloth has a different wearability, and, most important, it was made by different weavers using more hermetic techniques.

Semantic Inconsistencies

At first sight, the Catholic position on abortion appears airtight. At least in their testimonies, the bishops seem to imply that their moral reasoning has the irrefutable logical force of a deductive syllogism. Usually, the syllogism has the following form: human life is sacred; individuated human life begins at conception; therefore, abortion is the sacrilegious killing of an unborn person. The absolute, fundamentalist way with which the church defends the conclusion can only raise suspicion considering the ambiguities and uncertainties built into the two premises.

Catholic arguments tend to use the terms "human life" and "human person" interchangeably, thus begging the real question. Is "sacred dignity" an inviolable attribute of biological human life or of the human person? Given the otherworldly ascetic devaluation of life that one finds in traditional Catholic moral doctrines and in traditional Catholic practices, "moderns" cannot but welcome the zeal with which the Catholic church has recently assumed the defense of human rights throughout the world, worldly life being after all the most basic right and one of the fundamental values of modernity. But a church which every day celebrates not the life but the death of so many martyrs cannot possibly sacralize biological life itself. It is personhood, humanization, or, in traditional theological language, "ensoulment" that imparts sacredness to life, not the other way around.

To rely on modern biological science to answer the theological (or sociological) question of "animation," neglecting in the process the theological insights of the church's own tradition may make for good testimony before a congressional committee or may serve the purpose of political mobilization, but it does not necessarily produce better theology.[103] To try to hide or declare irrelevant the theological disagreements on this issue within the Catholic tradition, or, worse, to try to silence contemporary Catholic theologians who raise these issues, may make for clear and unambiguous official Catholic teaching but it may also undermine the public credibility of the church's teaching.

There is no doubt whatsoever that biological human life begins at conception. But to affirm categorically, without allowing any doubt or dissenting opinion, that the fetus is a person from the moment of conception disregards the fundamental ontological problem created by the fact that, at the very least, it is highly questionable to talk in absolute terms of human individuation as long as the possibility of twinning and recombination exists. An even more serious problem emerges from the fact that perhaps up to half of all fertilized eggs may be lost before implantation in the womb. As Karl Rahner and other Catholic theologians have implied, to claim categorically that the wasted eggs are human persons who deserve the same protection from God, "the Lord of life," as any other person presents serious theological difficulties. Only the most fatalistic conception of God as an arbitrary despot could humanly justify the ways of such a god.

The raising of these issues should not be read as semantic sophistry. Even if one accepts the view that none of these arguments undermines the basic Catholic moral principle that abortion is morally wrong, nonetheless they call into question the absolute, fundamentalist inflexibility of the Catholic claims by introducing at least one "centimeter of ambiguity" into Catholic moral discourse. A comparison with "just war" theory immediately shows the different criteria used in the two moral spheres. The direct killing of other human beings in war may be justified under certain conditions. But the direct killing of the unborn may never be justified, even when the life of the mother is endangered. There can be a "just war," but there could never possibly be a "just abortion."[104] Like the moral theory of "just war," the purpose of a moral theory of "just abortion" should not necessarily be to make the justification of abortion easy but, rather, to set morally consistent criteria that would delimit the conditions under which an otherwise regrettable and, if possible, avoidable action might nonetheless be permissible.

In the case of war, the Catholic moral tradition eschews both fundamentalist pacifism and amoral realpolitik. When it comes to abortion, however, the church's refusal to consider the parameters under which abortion may be morally justified leaves the field of moral discourse open to the extreme fundamentalist positions confronting each other on the abortion front: the pro-life position where every abortion is murder and the pro-choice position where the unlimited right to abortion is part of women's possessive right to their bodies or is simply a matter of individual free choice.[105] By contrast, public opinion polls consistently show that most people can accept the moral ambiguities inherent in the often distressing choice of abortion. Most people believe that abortion amounts to the regrettable killing of unborn life, but nonetheless they also believe that "under certain conditions" killing may be justified and is not the moral equivalent of murder.[106] The acceptance of this moral ambiguity has to be the point of departure for discourse ethics on abortion.

Performative Inconsistencies

One may distinguish four different levels in the bishops' speeches: the moral doctrinal teachings, the normative prescriptions to individual consciences, the public policy recommendations, and the calls to political mobilization. At each of these levels there are clear discrepancies between the speech on abortion and the speeches on war and the economy. At the level of moral theory, as already indicated, the pastoral letters admit different levels of authoritative validity claims in the bishops' teachings. From the universally valid principle of the sacred dignity of the human person, with which there can be no legitimate disagreement, to the particular norms concerning military and economic practices, there are complex intermediate reasoning steps and concrete circumstances to be taken into account that do not allow for absolute certainty in the normative conclusions. Concerning these conclusions, therefore, there is room for legitimate disagreement.[107]

When it comes to the teaching on abortion, however, the church leaves no room for legitimate disagreement. The church has censored and prohibited from teaching in Catholic universities theologians who, while accepting the official teachings, have shown some of the ambiguity and uncertainty on this issue that one finds in traditional Catholic moral theology.[108] Similarly, the church has severely reprimanded and demanded a recantation from priests and nuns who have expressed publicly their disagreement with some aspects of the official teachings on abortion.[109]

The same discrepancy can be found in the different prescriptive obligations with which the church presents its norms to the individual conscience.[110] In the case of the pastoral letters, a realm of contingent prudential judgment is left open where the individual conscience, guided by the Catholic normative tradition, has to assume ultimate moral responsibility for the personal decision.[111] When it comes to abortion, however, the church has drawn a very clear line. A canonical threat of automatic excommunication hangs over any Catholic procuring or helping to procure an abortion.[112]

At the level of public policy, the concrete policy recommendations in the pastoral letters are meant precisely as that, as recommendations which the bishops offer to the American public for deliberation and debate. In the case of abortion, by contrast, the church seeks to translate immediately its normative recommendations into law. One day after the Roe v. Wade Supreme Court decision, the NCCB ad hoc committee on pro-life activities replied that "every legal possibility . . . be explored to challenge the opinion of the United States Supreme Court decision which withdraws all legal safeguards for the right to life of the unborn child."[113] According to Bishop James McHugh, then staff director of the committee, this meant in practice organizing a campaign in favor of a constitutional amendment making abortion a legal crime.[114] By November of that year, the pro-life committee published a Resolution wishing "to make it clear beyond a doubt to our fellow citizens that we consider the passage of a prolife constitutional amendment a priority of the highest order."[115] Indeed, by their commitment of significant financial, institutional, and mobilizational resources to this goal, the bishops showed that this was no empty moral talk.

It is this resolute institutional commitment of the American Catholic church to the criminalization of abortion which has raised fundamental issues about the place and role of religion in the public sphere and reopened old concerns about the threat Romanism and Catholic power pose to modern freedoms and republican institutions.[116] Although some technical constitutional issues of the separation of church and state are also involved, particularly in terms of the tax-exempt status of religious organizations that commit their institutional resources to partisan political causes, I believe that the more fundamental issue is that of the differentiation of legality and morality in modern pluralistic civil societies. Indeed, against the charges of Romanist threats to American freedoms, the bishops could easily reply that they are acting in the typical American moral crusade fashion first established by Evangelical Protestantism in the nineteenth century. Against the charges of church establishment the bishops have always replied that they respect fully the constitutional separation of church and state and that their opposition to abortion takes place fully within democratic and constitutional channels. Against the charges that they are trying to impose "Catholic" morality, the bishops' usual reply is that abortion is not a "Catholic" issue, that what is at stake is the universal human issue of the violation of the most basic right to life of unborn "children."

From the bishops' statements it is obvious that their "fundamentalist" opposition to abortion does not derive solely, not even primarily, from traditionalist Catholic dogma. In their public interventions, they rarely make references to traditional Catholic doctrine and they no longer tend to base their reasoning on traditional natural law theory. Their fundamentalism seems to derive rather from the absolute certainty with which moderns tend to hold certain ideas as self-evident truths and certain claims as inalienable human rights. In addition, they buttress their reasoning with what they claim to be overwhelming empirical scientific evidence from modern biology and modern medicine that individuated life begins at conception. Finally, they defend their activism in terms of the prophetic mandate which the church has recently assumed as the defender of the weak, the defenseless, and the speechless. To the critics they untiredly reply with the same rhetorical question: Who could be more innocent, weak, defenseless, and speechless than the unborn "child"?

Given this combination of deeply felt convictions, which are shared unanimously by the American bishops, it is unlikely that the bishops will soon change their teachings or stop their public moral condemnations of the practice of abortion. But there is some evidence that the public debate which they themselves to a large extent initiated has forced them to rethink their ideas about how best to translate their moral theories into legal practice in the public-policy realm.[117]

The blunders of some bishops in the 1984 electoral campaign and the forceful reply of Mario Cuomo in his September speech at the University of Notre Dame probably marks a turning point in the public intervention of the bishops on the abortion issue.[118] Governor Cuomo showed that he could not be intimidated in the way that Archbishops John O'Connor and Bernard Law and Bishop James Timlin tried to intimidate vice-presidential candidate Geraldine Ferraro and other Catholic public officials for trying to separate "illogically" (B. Law) or "irrationally" (J. O'Connor) their private Catholic morality and their public support for the constitutional protection of the privacy of a woman's right to abortion. Governor Cuomo began his speech, "Religious Belief and Public Morality: A Catholic Governor's Perspective," by readily accepting the church's official teachings on abortion and by stating publicly that he (and his wife) felt dutybound in conscience to follow personally these teachings. Yet he argued publicly and compellingly his disagreement with the stated public policy goal of the American bishops to pass a constitutional amendment prohibiting abortion as well as with their support for restrictive legislation limiting public funding for abortion.

Instead of answering in customary liberal fashion that publicly elected officials are sworn to uphold the Constitution in public, Mario Cuomo offered compelling theoretical arguments for the need to differentiate morality and legality in modern pluralistic civil societies. In addition, he argued pragmatically that if the bishops truly wanted to see the number of abortions in the country decrease, they should accompany him in looking for other, more viable policy proposals which could accomplish this practical goal better than an ill-conceived constitutional amendment banning abortion, which would be nonenforceable and could only bring about the disastrous experience of Prohibition all over again. Since the speech, no bishop has said again that he does not understand how Catholic public officials can in good conscience fail to support a constitutional amendment banning abortion or how they can vote to fund abortion, or how Catholics can vote for such public officials.

Governor Cuomo's speech probably accomplished more than the attempts of liberal bishops to convince their conservative colleagues of the need to expand their all-consuming pro-life stand against abortion into an all-inclusive pro-life "seamless garment." At issue was not only the need to develop a more consistent ethic but, rather, the need to rethink more systematically the proper relation between religious doctrines, individual conscience, private and public morality, legality, and politics. Mary Hanna has observed that "the fascinating thing about the Catholic bishops' participation in the 1988 elections was how little of it there was."[119]

It is at the level of public mobilization that the discrepancies in the bishops' position have been most evident. Certainly, the bishops expected that Catholics would take the norms and the policy proposals stated in the pastoral letters seriously and would try to work toward their implementation. For instance, many Catholic citizens, bishops included, became involved in the peace movement, in strikes, or in initiatives related to economic policy issues. But the bishops, as bishops, did not try to mobilize Catholic citizens or voters in support of these initiatives, nor did they commit substantial financial or institutional church resources to such mobilization.

In the case of abortion, by contrast, the bishops played a crucial role in the launching of the right-to-life movement, which for a long time, even after its separation from the hierarchy, remained a predominantly "Catholic" movement.[120] The National Committee for a Human Life Amendment (NCHLA) probably became the most important lobbying group working for the passage of anti-abortion amendments. Moreover, beginning with the 1976 presidential campaign, by their screening of political candidates and elected public officials in terms of their positions on abortion, the bishops played a crucial role in making abortion a crucial "political" issue.

During the 1984 presidential campaign, in particular, some conservative bishops entered the electoral fray shamelessly. Openly contradicting the stated opposition of the National Conference of Catholic Bishops to "single-issue voting," Archbishop Bernard Law of Boston made public a statement signed by eighteen New England bishops citing abortion as "the critical issue in this campaign."[121] In their attempts to sway Catholic voters, the bishops had forgotten not only Bishop John England's "plain distinction" but the bishops' own official teachings from Vatican II:

It is of supreme importance, especially in a pluralistic society, to work out a proper vision of the relationship between the political community and the church, and to distinguish clearly between the activities of Christians, acting individually or collectively in their own name as citizens guided by the dictates of a Christian conscience and their activity along with their pastors in the name of the church.[122]

The fact that Cardinal O'Connor quotes this very paragraph in his 1986 reflection "From Theory to Practice in the Public-Policy Realm" indicates that the bishops may have learned an important public lesson. Yet he still seems puzzled by the fact that American bishops are expected to refrain from endorsing or criticizing particular candidates, learning to "separate issues from the persons who espouse them," while Cardinal Sin and the Philippine bishops are lauded for their opposition to President Marcos and Bishop Tutu is praised for his attacks on Mr. Botha and the system of apartheid. He asks, "Is there some uniqueness in the American system which, unlike the Philippine or South African experience, makes it possible to divorce policy from person in the practical order?"[123] The answer should be evident to anybody who understands the difference between modern, pluralistic democratic societies and authoritarian regimes or "racial democracies." The same Catholic bishops who were so effective in supporting the mobilization of civil society against authoritarian regimes in Spain, Poland, and Brazil have generally refrained from intervening in electoral politics once a democratic political society has come into place.[124]

Procedural Inconsistencies

Of all the inconsistencies in the bishops' public moral discourse, perhaps the most serious are the procedural ones, namely, the blatant discrepancies in the way in which the bishops construct their moral discourse in the pastoral letters and their moral discourse on abortion. In the pastoral letters they begin inductively, discerning "the signs of the times" and inviting all those concerned to participate in the open public construction of the moral discourse. The discourse went through several drafts, and the final text was approved using normal democratic procedures for reaching a consensus.

By contrast, when they construct their moral discourse on abortion, the bishops refuse to acknowledge one of the most evident and significant "signs of the times," the universal-historical movement of the liberation of women from patriarchy and all its consequences. The refusal to see the significance of this historical change in "the economy of salvation" can only be attributed to the patriarchal prejudice, to what feminist theologians call the "sin of sexism," that is inherent in the Catholic moral tradition and in the institutional structures of the church.[125]

One may find the church's response to the "social question" in the nineteenth century woefully inadequate, but the church recognized that the question existed and tried to offer its own solutions, thinking that the socialist response to the social question was inherently wrong. When it comes to the women's question, by contrast, the church still has to recognize that the question exists either in society or in the church. Apparently, there is a modern feminist heresy, but there is no modern women's question, at least not one that would require the revision of traditional Catholic moral teachings. To their credit, the American bishops have been ready to begin to face the issue in a new pastoral letter. But the tortuous progress of the letter so far, liberals and conservatives now agreeing that perhaps it would be better to remain silent rather than to commit some fundamental "error," indicates that Rome is not yet ready to come to grips with the question.[126] Most American bishops realize that the question is not going to go away. If they capitulate once again to Rome's pressure, however, trying to avoid a new "Americanist heresy," American Catholicism may again lose a golden historical opportunity to lead not only the universal church but also American society on this issue.[127]

In contrast to the process of consultation used in writing the pastoral letters, binding normative decisions on abortion are handed down from above without giving all those concerned any chance or recourse to a hearing, explanation, justification, or claim. Indeed, the most striking aspect of the episcopal moral discourse on abortion is not only that women are never consulted before the bishops hand down their moral commandments but that women—that is, pregnant women—do not even appear in the discourse as moral agents over whose lives the bishops moralize and decide. Women are deprived of moral agency. They become simply the bearers of a natural life process to which they have been destined by nature and with which they have no right to interfere.

Indeed, the church's assertion that in its opposition to abortion it is only defending the rights and the human dignity of the unborn person becomes more difficult to accept, the more the church refuses to recognize that those rights may be in conflict with the rights and the human dignity of pregnant women. The moral scenario in the church's abortion play is written in such a way that no right or claim could ever have precedence over or overrule the right to life of the unborn. Ultimately, it is a question of whether the church is willing to recognize the rights of women to become free moral agents and whether the human dignity of women is reconcilable with the notion that women and their consciences should be coerced into carrying unwanted pregnancies.

Two relevant points from the Catholic moral tradition could be brought into play in the ethical discourse of abortion. The bishops could argue, first, that the absolute privatization of individual morality dissolves the intersubjective nature of all morality into arbitrary decisionist freedom and, second, that possessive individualist property rights can never be absolute. But these points can never be properly heard as long as the church refuses to accept the fact that issues of women's freedom or women's control over their bodies have any relevance at all in discussing the "crime" of abortion. The result is "the clash of absolutes," the irreconcilable conflict of the claims of the two fundamental values of modernity, life and freedom, failing to recognize each other.[128]

Reactions, Consequences, and Public Relevance of the Bishops'
Public Speeches

By a strict rational-strategic criterion of success in achieving clearly stated goals, one would have to admit that the bishops' public speeches have not been very effective. If the aim of the pastoral letter on the economy was to change American economic policies, one may surmise that its effects were nil. American nuclear policies were altered in accordance with the aims of the pastoral letter in a way which even the bishops could not possibly have imagined. But it is safe to guess that the changes did not happen mainly or primarily because of the pastoral letter. Indeed, one could point to the amoral cosmic irony implied by the fact that it was the very realistic threat of uncontrolled escalation in the arms race posed by the policies of the Reagan administration that may have precipitated the collapse of the Soviet system and the end of MAD (Mutual Assured Destruction) nuclear deterrence policies. But it is in the case of abortion, where the bishops stated a clearly defined goal, the passage of a pro-life constitutional amendment, and where they acted most strategically, that it is obvious that the bishops' speeches did not have their intended effects. Today, the passage of such an amendment is as far away as ever and it has become obvious that the bishops do not even control "the Catholic vote." Even if one could still speak meaningfully of a Catholic vote, opinion surveys show that Catholic voters have increasingly moved away from their bishops precisely on the issue of abortion.

Yet it would be inappropriate, indeed fallacious, to attempt to measure the public relevance of the bishops' public speeches by using the criteria of rational-strategic action.[129] A look at some of the public reactions to the bishops' speeches may offer a more appropriate indirect indication of their public relevance. Measured by the sheer volume of public debate which they originated, the bishops had a resounding success. Moreover, when the bishops spoke, Wall Street, the Pentagon, Congress, and the White House not only listened but felt compelled to respond. But a look at the nature of some of the responses may serve to measure the public relevance of the speeches better than the sheer volume of response or the influential status of the respondents.

One of the immediate effects of the bishops' speeches was to challenge successfully liberal and secularist claims that religion ought to be restricted to an allegedly private religious sphere. Against liberal claims that religion should not "meddle in politics" and against the claims of theories of secularization that religion should "focus on its primary function" and concentrate on "finding answers to religious questions uncontaminated by secondary considerations stemming from the economy, the polity, the family, or science,"[130] the bishops established what J. Bryan Hehir has called "the right and competence of the church" to intervene in public affairs.[131]

Most important, however, the bishops did not secure this right and competence only for themselves as bishops. Instead, they defended against the technocratic claims of self-appointed experts the right and competence of all citizens to participate in the public debate of all issues which affect their lives. Indeed, the bishops stated repeatedly that they did not enter the public debate as "experts" in nuclear or economic policies. But by doing so, they questioned the attempts of the "experts" to protect these policies from public debate.[132] By establishing the right to bring Catholic normative traditions to bear upon deliberations of the rightness and justness of defense and economic policies, the bishops challenged the claims of the differentiated political and economic spheres that they should be evaluated solely in terms of intrinsic, functionally rational criteria without regard to extraneous moral considerations. Similarly, the bishops also challenged liberal claims that morality should be left to the individual moral conscience.

While acknowledging the right and competence of the bishops to speak publicly, critics have faulted the content of their speeches on various counts: for being too "partisan," for being too general without specific policy recommendations, for being "all talk no action," for being not radical and prophetic enough. The very contradictory nature of these criticisms may indicate not so much that the bishops may have been unclear in their aims as, rather, that their message was a complex one that defied easy characterization. Indeed, most critics may have missed what was perhaps the publicly most relevant aspect of the bishops' speeches, namely, the legitimation of discourse ethics itself in the political and economic spheres.

The accusation of political partisanship turns spurious the moment one considers that liberal critics accused the bishops of pro-Reaganism for their abortion stand, while conservative critics accused them of "ecclesiastical Mondaleism" in their pastoral letters. One may come to the conclusion either that the bishops were inconsistent and ineffective in terms of electoral party alliances or, more plausibly, that their normative position cuts across party lines. There is substantive evidence that the religious-political conflicts in American life do not fall along denominational lines but, rather, cut across denominations, creating what has been called "unlikely alliances."[133] One could easily draw three conclusions from the available empirical evidence. First, there no longer exists a Catholic vote, since Catholics tend to be distributed in a proportionate manner across the entire American political-ideological spectrum.[134] Therefore, the bishops can hardly be said to represent any particular political constituency or be its spokespersons. Second, Catholic religious leaders, like American Protestant and Jewish religious leaders, can be "dichotomized into *theologically* liberal and conservative camps."[135] Finally, and most important, Catholic religious leaders are more uniformly "conservative" on issues of sexual and family morality and more uniformly "progressive" on economic, political, and international issues than the American population, than the Catholic laity, and than other religious leaders. Since one finds a similar conservative uniformity on issues of sexual morality and a similar progressive uniformity on issues of economic, political, and international morality among Catholic religious leaders throughout the world, it would not be farfetched to conclude that the source of the American bishops' speeches is to be found in global Catholic doctrinal positions rather than in American electoral party preferences.[136]

While neoconservative critics, who did not like some of the bishops' concrete policy recommendations, tended to criticize the bishops for their partisanship or for their false prophetic pretensions, progressive Catholics by contrast tended to fault the bishops for their caution and failure to declare more explicitly their partisanship for specific policy recommendations, for their reticence to mobilize institutional resources in support of these recommendations, and for not being prophetic enough, having failed to present radical alternatives to the capitalist system.[137] By comparison with the determined commitment of the bishops to specific policies on abortion, the pastoral letters could indeed be viewed as vague, empty moralizing. But the bishops' failure to be more specific, to be more radical, and to call to action can be seen as virtues rather than defects. The internal Catholic critique, like the neoconservative one, tends to miss what may have been the most novel and relevant aspect of the bishops' pastoral letters. The fact that the bishops' rather meager policy recommendations could be classified as moderately center-left in the American ideological spectrum is not particularly relevant. One could even argue that the concrete policy recommendations were not central to the letters. It was the very reticence of the bishops to present authoritative Catholic solutions to contemporary societal problems that was most significant. What the bishops did was to present the Catholic normative tradition as the basis for public debate. They did not claim to know the answers, a claim which de facto would tend to preclude any public debate, leaving room only for partisan mobilization. In the pastoral letters the bishops only claimed to possess valid normative principles which should serve to inform the public debate, a debate in which all affected should participate and to which all should have equal access.

Ultimately, the most relevant aspect of the bishops' public speeches was the very fact of the bishops having entered what Richard J. Neuhaus has called "the naked public square,"[138] not in order to establish their church as the church in the square and not in order to mobilize its "divisions" against religious and secular enemies but, rather, in order to participate in public debate. One does not need to accept Neuhaus's neoconservative argument that without religion the public square will be "naked" and democracy will therefore suffer. But one could propose the more defensible thesis that normative traditions constitute the very condition of possibility for ethical discourse and that, fictional "ideal speech situations" and "original positions" notwithstanding, without normative traditions neither rational public debate nor discourse ethics is likely to take place. It seems self-evident that religious normative traditions should have the same rights as any other normative tradition to enter the public sphere as long as they play by the rules of open public debate. Indeed, it is when other nonreligious normative traditions have failed, abandoned the public sphere, or abdicated their public role that religious normative traditions are likely to step in to fill the public vacuum. One after another, all the modern public institutions which at first tended to exercise some of the public functions traditionally performed by religious institutions abandoned their public normative roles: academic philosophy, the specialized social sciences, the universities, the press, politicians, intellectuals.[139] Under such circumstances one cannot but welcome the return of religion to the naked public square.

This return, however, has brought into public view two probably unintended effects of the bishops' interventions. The first is that the bishops today have much less power of political mobilization than old Protestants and liberals feared that they would. At times the bishops sound much like prophets clamoring in the desert. The second is that the bishops cannot enter the public sphere without necessarily exposing Catholic normative traditions and ecclesiastical institutional structures to public scrutiny.

The failure to mobilize effectively the Catholic faithful and Catholic politicians behind a pro-life constitutional amendment only made publicly evident what had already become obvious in the sphere of private morality, namely, that the Catholic hierarchy does not control the consciences of American Catholics. The general rejection by lay Catholics of the church's teachings on sexual morality, particularly of those proclaimed in Paul VI's encyclical *Humanae Vitae* (1968), made clear not only that Catholics were ready to disobey church commandments, something which as sinners Catholics have always done, but that they were consciously dissenting from church doctrines, in good conscience, without thinking that they were acting immorally and without believing that they were unfaithful to the Catholic church.

Implicitly at least, by their ecclesiastical disobedience in combination with their expressed unwillingness to leave the church, indeed through their refusal to consider that by disobeying the church hierarchy they are breaking communion with the church, Catholics are saying that they have internalized the teachings of the Vatican II in a way the council fathers may not have anticipated when they proclaimed the doctrine of freedom of conscience and when they defined the church as the people of God. Implicitly at least, Catholics are saying that they are the people of God, that the church also belongs to them, not only to the hierarchy, that, irrespective of what the hierarchy says, they will not feel excommunicated from their church, that they also have a right to participate in the interpretation of the meaning of the Catholic normative tradition for contemporary circumstances, and that ultimately they individually have the moral obligation to apply in conscience Catholic normative principles to their own personal situation. What Andrew Greeley has called "do it yourself" or "selective Catholicism" is another way of saying that American Catholics have reached the level of modern reflexive religion or the stage of postconventional morality.[140]

If the hierarchy no longer controls the consciences of the faithful in the private sphere, much less do they control the consciences and the activities of Catholics in the public sphere. It is well understood that in a modern, pluralistic, democratic civil society the church can no longer legislate public morality and therefore has to abandon the model of church establishment. But beyond that, the church will also have to abandon the very model of Catholic political mobilization or Catholic Action in the public sphere. Given the pluralistic internal structure of "the people of God," every political mobilization in one particular direction can only call forth the countermobilization of dissenting Catholics in the opposite direction.

In their comprehensive survey of the beliefs, practices, and values of American Catholics, George Gallup, Jr., and Jim Castelli point to what they see as "a real contradiction": "On one hand, a majority of lay Catholics agree with positions taken by the bishops on issues such as arms control, Central America, abortion, education, and economic policy; on the other hand, there is a strong resistance to the Church's being involved in the political arena."[141] But there is no contradiction here. Lay Catholics are simply making a distinction between involvement in the public sphere of civil society and involvement in the public sphere of political society. Survey data suggest that Catholics for the most part want their bishops to speak up on public issues. In other words, they want Catholicism to be a public religion. Yet, as Gallup and Castelli point out, "American Catholics of all political persuasions do not want their bishops to appear even remotely to be telling them how to vote."[142] Nor would they apparently support a Catholic party, Catholic Action, or a Catholic political movement. Catholics respect the distinction drawn by Vatican II between their activities "in their own name as citizens guided by the dictates of a Christian conscience and their activity along with their pastors in the name of the church."[143]

The liberal wall of separation served historically not only to protect state and society from religious establishment and the political and economic spheres from extraneous normative concerns, but also to protect the private religious sphere from public intervention and from public scrutiny. If the bishops through their public intervention have now asserted their "right and competence" to intervene in public affairs, at least implicitly they also have come to recognize the public's right to judge their pronouncements in accordance with the universalistic criteria of open, rational debate which, at least ideally, govern the public sphere. Once they have come to accept these criteria in their public interventions, any attempt to draw a new wall of separation between the church as a public institution and the church as a private ecclesiastical institution will become increasingly difficult. Inevitably, criteria from the public sphere will spill over into the ecclesiastical sphere and one can expect that the people of God will demand participation in the continuous historical process of interpretation of the church's normative teachings, that women will demand equal access to the universal priesthood of the people of God, that eventually the ecclesiastical institution will have to learn to respect the human dignity of all its members, and that the church will have to stop inquisitorial proceedings against its own theologians and peremptory demands of public recantation from its dissidents.[144] Ultimately, a church which claims to be a public, universal church will have to accept "faithful dissent" within its walls in the same way that modern democratic societies have to accept the principle of "civil disobedience." Only by retreating again to a private sectarian refuge and abandoning its claims to be a public religion in the modern world can the church escape the unintended consequences of having entered the modern public sphere.

III

Conclusion

8   The Deprivatization of Modern Religion

The pre-text and point of departure of this study was the empirical proposition that we are witnessing the *deprivatization* of religion in the modern world. The impulse behind the study was the realization that the dominant sociological theories of religion in the modern world and the dominant liberal or civic republican models of analysis of the private/public distinction were of little help when trying to come to terms theoretically, analytically, and practically with this new, or at least newly appreciated, fact. Thus, there was a need to rethink systematically the relationship of religion and modernity, and the possible roles religions may play in the public sphere of modern societies. This study has been an attempt in this direction.

What are the conditions of possibility for modern public religions? This is the fundamental question that was addressed systematically in the first theoretical part through a critical reconstruction of the paradigm of secularization and through an analysis of various modes of conceptualizing the private/public distinction and their possible articulation with the religious sphere. A series of related general theoretical-analytical propositions are developed that are subsequently substantiated in the case studies.

The paradigm of secularization has been the main theoretical and analytical framework through which the social sciences have viewed the relationship of religion and modernity. A central thesis and main theoretical premise of this work has been that what usually passes for a single theory of secularization is actually made up of three very different, uneven and unintegrated propositions: secularization as differentiation of the secular spheres from religious institutions and norms, secularization as decline of religious beliefs and practices, and secularization as marginalization of religion to a privatized sphere. If the premise is correct, it should follow from the analytical distinction that the fruitless secularization debate can end only when sociologists of religion begin to examine and test the validity of each of the three propositions independently of each other.

It is simply fallacious to argue, for instance, that the permanence or increase in religious beliefs and practices, and the continuous emergence of new religions and the revival of old ones in the United States or anywhere else, serves as empirical confirmation that the theory of secularization is a myth. It only confirms the need to refine the theory by distinguishing between the general historical structural trend of secular differentiation and the different ways in which different religions in different places respond to and are affected by the modern structural trend of differentiation. Similarly, it is incorrect to claim that the role religion has recently played in political conflicts throughout the world serves to invalidate empirically the theory of secularization. But no less incongruous is the position of those defenders of the theory of secularization who use the thesis of privatization to accuse religion of trespassing illegitimately on the public sphere or of crossing systemic boundaries by assuming nonreligious roles.[1]

Properly speaking, this work is not a comprehensive or systematic study of the theory of secularization or is there any attempt to test or validate conclusively each of the three different propositions of the paradigm. The study's main aim was to develop an appropriate theoretical-analytical framework for the comparative historical study of public religions in the modern world. Nonetheless, the study offers some general claims or hypotheses about each of the three subtheses of the theory of secularization that later find at least partial substantiation in the comparative historical studies.

Concerning the first thesis, that of secularization as differentiation, it is a central claim of this study that this remains the valid core of the theory of secularization. The differentiation and emancipation of the secular spheres from religious institutions and norms remains a general modern structural trend. Indeed, this differentiation serves precisely as one of the primary distinguishing characteristics of modern structures. Each of the two major modern societal systems, the state and the economy, as well as other major cultural and institutional spheres of society—science, education, law, art—develops its own institutional autonomy, as well as its intrinsic functional dynamics. Religion itself is constrained not only to accept the modern principle of structural differentiation of the secular spheres but also to follow the same dynamic and to develop an autonomous differentiated sphere of its own.

This study is also not the place to explicate, illustrate, or substantiate this process of differentiation in each of the spheres. It has only attempted to analyze some aspects of the process of differentiation of the religious and the political sphere, first theoretically in the first part, by exploring the dynamics of differentiation of the religious and political communities, and then in the case studies by analyzing different patterns of separation of church and state. It is a central claim of this study, again first elaborated theoretically and later substantiated in the comparative historical studies, that established churches are incompatible with modern differentiated states and that the fusion of the religious and political community is incompatible with the modern principle of citizenship.

This claim, however, is not new. It is as old as the Enlightenment critique of religion in all its variants (American, French, or German), and it became a central tenet of modern liberalism. It was also central to the theological writings of the young Hegel and to the criticism of religion of the Young Hegelians.[2] Through them it entered into Weber's church-sect typology. When a religion becomes disestablished, when it loses its compulsory institutional character, it becomes a voluntary religious association, either a sect or a "free church." Once freedom of religion is established, moreover, from the perspective of the now secular state all religions, churches, and sects turn into denominations. This process—and this is another of the central claims of this study—is also a modern structural trend that has the same kind of "providential" force which Tocqueville attributed to democratization, or, one could add, which Marx attributed to proletarianization and Weber to bureaucratization. These are all modern, in the long run irresistible, structural trends.[3]

It stands to reason that churches may prefer to resist this trend, sects may prefer to withdraw into separate fundamentalist isolation, and states may still find it useful to master established religions for the sake of integration of their political communities. In my view, the study offers adequate empirical evidence in support of the claim that the long, protracted, and, in some places like Spain, tragically disastrous resistance of the Catholic church to the modern structural trend of differentiation of church and state, and of the religious and political communities, has come to an end. The Catholic church's declaration of religious freedom at Vatican II and the subsequent acceptance of the constitutional separation of church and state in newly established democratic regimes throughout the Catholic world offer indirect and direct confirmation of the "providential" character of this modern structural trend, at least for the time being and for the area under study here, that is, Western Christendom and its colonial outposts.

But the decline of religious beliefs and practices is manifestly not a modern structural trend, although it is very clearly a dominant historical trend in many modern Western, particularly European, societies. It is this second connotation of the modern process of secularization that is most questionable as a theoretical and as a general empirical proposition, and that has led many sociologists of religion to question uncritically and unjustifiably the entire theory of secularization. Although the present study does not attempt to validate or elaborate them systematically, it presents a series of general propositions it claims can offer a better explanation of the differential rates of secularization between, say, Western Europe and America, or Spain and Poland, than traditional sociological explanations in terms of the correlation between decreasing rates of religious beliefs and practices and increasing rates of industrialization, urbanization, education, and the like.

Some of the related propositions presented in the study are that the thesis of religious decline has its origins in the Enlightenment critique of religion; that this critique was not so much a theoretical statement or an empirical proposition as a practical political program; that this practical political program was most effective wherever churches had attained caesaropapist establishment and were resisting the process of differentiation and emancipation of the cognitive-scientific, political-practical, or aesthetic-expressive secular spheres from religious and ecclesiastical tutelage; that in such cases the Enlightenment critique of religion was usually adopted by social movements and political parties, becoming in the process a self-fulfilling prophecy; that once in power those movements and parties tended to translate the theory into applied state policies, in extreme cases enforcing and administering through violent coercion the process of secularization from above.

In very simple terms it could be said that the more religions resist the process of modern differentiation, that is, secularization in the first sense, the more they will tend in the long run to suffer religious decline, that is, secularization in the second sense. Since strictly speaking this is a study of public religions, it says very little about the types and nature of modern private religions, about the character and modes of self-reproduction of the modern differentiated religious sphere. But tentatively one could offer the related proposition that those religions, by contrast, which early on accept and embrace the modern principle of differentiation will also tend to accept the modern denominational principle of voluntarism and will be in a better position both to survive the modern process of differentiation and to adopt some form of evangelical revivalism as a successful method of religious self-reproduction in a free religious market. This, at least, seems to be the effective lesson of American religious "exceptionalism."

The lesson of Polish exceptionalism, by contrast—Poland being like the United States a highly industrialized, urbanized, and educated society with uncommonly high rates of religious practice and belief—seems to be that it is not resistance to modern differentiation per se which weakens religious institutions but, rather, resistance from a position of political or social establishment. When the resistance comes from a disestablished hierocratic institution opposing a process of differentiation that is being carried out by a state power which lacks societal legitimacy, then the resistance to secularization may be associated with societal resistance to illegitimate state power and such a resistance may actually strengthen hierocratic religious institutions.[4]

Finally, with respect to the third subthesis of the secularization paradigm, it is the major purpose and thrust of this study to show both theoretically and empirically that privatization is not a modern structural trend. In other words, this study has tried to show that there can be and that there are public religions in the modern world which do not need to endanger either modern individual freedoms or modern differentiated structures. It is true that, like religious decline, privatization is also a dominant historical trend in many societies, usually in the same ones which experience religious decline, both processes being interrelated. But privatization is not a modern structural trend but, rather, a historical option. To be sure, it seems to be a modern "preferred option," but it is an option nonetheless.

Privatization is preferred internally from within religion as a result of modern processes of religious rationalization. This preference is evinced by general pietistic trends, by processes of religious individuation, and by the reflexive nature of modern religion. Privatization is determined externally by structural trends of differentiation which tend to constrain religion into a differentiated, circumscribed, marginalized, and largely "invisible" religious sphere. But equally important, privatization is mandated ideologically by liberal categories of thought which permeate not only political ideologies and constitutional theories but the entire structure of modern Western thought.

For that reason, sociological theories and liberal political analysis have found it difficult to conceptualize properly and to comprehend that new phenomenon which I call the deprivatization of modern religion. The explanations one usually finds of the public character of many religions in the modern world are of two kinds. There are, on the one hand, utilitarian secularist explanations which reduce the phenomenon either to an instrumental mobilization of available religious resources for nonreligious purposes or to an instrumental adaptation of religious institutions to the new secular environment. There are, on the other hand, secular-humanist explanations which tend to interpret religious mobilization either as fundamentalist antimodern reactions of hierocratic institutions unwilling to give up their privileges or as the reactionary mobilization of traditionalist groups resisting modernization. Undoubtedly, many contemporary forms of religious mobilization may have such a character, but the deprivatization of modern religion cannot be reduced to any of those significations. Indeed, such explanations prefer to ignore the intrinsically religious character of the phenomenon and the normative challenge it presents to residual rationalist, secularist understandings of modernity. As will be shown shortly, a third type of explanation, the "return of the sacred," though more adequate in trying to come to terms with the specific and permanent nature of religion as a social phenomenon, also fails to capture the particularly historical, noncyclical character of the new phenomenon.

The partly theoretical, partly typological discussion of private and public religions in chapter 2 has been an attempt to develop a new analytical framework with which to tackle the historical dynamics of privatization and deprivatization of religion from a new perspective. The analysis proceeds in four steps. First, from the perspective of a broad historical sociology of religion it examines the built-in tensions between private and public religions by counterposing the Durkheimian functionalist perspective of social integration and the Weberian phenomenological perspective of salvational meaning at three different levels of analysis—the interactive, the organizational, and the societal levels. The analysis tries to show that religion cannot be reduced to any of the two poles. Religion always transcends any privatistic, autistic reality, serving to integrate the individual into an intersubjective, public, and communal "world." Simultaneously, however, religion always transcends any particular community cult, serving to free the individual from any particular "world" and to integrate that same individual into a transsocial, cosmic reality. Goffman's private/public distinction serves to illustrate the same tension, now from the perspective of modern religion, between the "invisible" religion of the self and associational denominationalism.

Next, the liberal and the civic-republican private/public distinctions are counterposed to one another in order to show how each of them alone is unable to categorize the new phenomenon of deprivatization of religion: the liberal perspective because it insists on the need to confine religion to a private sphere, fearing that public religions must necessarily threaten individual freedoms and secular differentiated structures; the civic-republican perspective because, while correctly stressing the relevance of public religions for intersubjective normative structures ("the common good"), for civic virtue, and political participation, like the liberal perspective, it also conceives of public or civil religions in premodern terms as coextensive with the political or societal community.

The next step is the introduction of a Habermasian discursive model of the public sphere and of recent theories of civil society which have incorporated reflexively the experience of recent transitions to democracy in Southern Europe, Eastern Europe, and Latin America and which operate with a tripartite analytical division of the polity into state, political society, and civil society.[5] This move allows both the construction of a typology of public religions based on this tripartite division and the conceptualization of a modern form of public religion characterized by the public intervention of religion in the undifferentiated public sphere of civil society. The result is a conception of modern public religion which is compatible with liberal freedoms and with modern structural and cultural differentiation.

Finally, the analysis incorporates Seyla Benhabib's synthesis of a radical proceduralist discursive model of the public sphere with a feminist critique of the privatization of gender and the feminine sphere.[6] Such a move allows us to view the deprivatization of religion in analogical terms as an agonic resistance to attempts to confine religion and morality to a private sphere ("home") and as a normative critique of the amoral public sphere of "work"—economic and state institutions. As in the case of feminism, this dual normative critique leads to a dual challenge of established boundaries. The deprivatization of religion has a double signification here in that it simultaneously introduces publicity, that is, intersubjective norms into the private sphere (analogous to the feminist dictum "the personal is political"), and morality into the public sphere of state and economy (the principle of the "common good" as a normative criterion).

Before indicating how this analytical framework for the study of public religions is used in the case studies, a few methodological comments are in order. As already mentioned, the case studies tell five different stories of the transformation of public religions on the roads to modernity. It is true that the comparative studies use the analytical framework developed in the first theoretical part, serve to illustrate the typology of public religions developed in chapter 2, and, in my view, serve to substantiate the main theoretical propositions concerning secularization and deprivatization. Nevertheless, this is not the sole or primary purpose of the comparative studies. On the one hand, the theoretical-analytical framework, since it examines the general conditions of possibility for modern public religions, is broader and more general than each and all the particular case studies. These particular case studies cannot and are not meant to prove any general theory. On the other hand, however, each of the case studies transcends the theoretical-analytical framework. In other words, the stories were not framed for theoretical-analytical purposes. I have tried to respect as much as possible the complexity and diversity of the different historical realities, avoiding the temptation to impose any homogenizing interpretive scheme upon them.[7]

I do not view history or social reality as a source of data for theory building, as a field laboratory for theory testing, or as a means to the advancement of scientific sociology. I view sociology, rather, as a source of theoretical concepts and analytical tools for the comparative historical interpretation of social reality and for the collective self-understanding of the present. The aim of sociology is to understand ourselves—that is, the historical actors and the practical contexts of individual and collective action—better. Consequently, the case studies were not constructed in such a way that they would best confirm any theory or illustrate any typology. They were meant to illuminate different contexts of action for actors and observers alike. The ability to throw new light upon a known reality I consider the ultimate test of the relevance of this or any sociological study. Typologies can be constructed from various points of view. This study has constructed a particular typology of public religions using the tripartite division of the modern democratic polity into state, political society, and civil society. Since to each of these levels there corresponds a different form of public sphere, there can be in principle public religions at the state level, public religions active in political society, and public religions which participate in the public sphere of civil society. As already indicated, the purpose of this particular typology is to facilitate the analysis of those forms of public religion which are compatible with modern individual freedoms and with modern differentiated structures. Other purposes would have required the construction of other typologies and the choice of other case studies.

Some of the varieties of public religion illuminated by this typology and illustrated by the case studies are as follows:

a) At the state level: established state churches, of which the Spanish Catholic church may serve as the paradigmatic example, and national churches in search of a state, of which the Polish church may serve as an equally illustrative paradigm.

b) At the political society level: on the one hand, one may consider the whole range of religious movements resisting disestablishment and the differentiation of the secular spheres (e.g., the mobilization of Spanish Catholicism against the liberal revolution and against the First and Second Spanish Republics; and the Protestant crusades to Christianize the American Constitution or common law) or the mobilizations and countermobilizations of religious groups and confessional parties against other religions or against secularist movements and parties (e.g., Catholic Action in Spain, Poland, and Brazil in the 1930s; the Catholic Electoral League (LEC) in Brazil or the Confederation of Autonomous Parties of the Right (CEDA) during the Second Spanish Republic; Christian Democratic parties; American Protestant nativist parties and movements; the electoral mobilization of Catholic immigrants; and the electoral mobilization of Protestant fundamentalism against "secular humanism"); on the other hand, one could mention religious groups mobilized in defense of religious freedom (Catholic mobilization in Communist Poland); religious institutions demanding the rule of law and the legal protection of human and civil rights, or protecting the mobilization of civil society and defending the institutionalization of democratic regimes (Catholic churches in Spain, Poland, and Brazil).

c) At the civil society level: one may distinguish between hegemonic civil religions (e.g., Evangelical Protestantism in nineteenth-century America) and the public intervention of religious groups, either agonically (e.g., the anti-abortion movement) or discursively (e.g., the Catholic bishops' Pastoral Letters) in the undifferentiated public sphere of civil society.

It has been maintained throughout this study that ultimately only public religions at the level of civil society are consistent with modern universalistic principles and with modern differentiated structures. Strictly speaking, established state religions are "public" only in one of three senses: (a) in the premodern medieval sense of "representative publicness," the public representational role of the Polish Primate as *Interrex* or the role of the British monarch as head of the caesaropapist Church of England being cases in point; (b) in the early modern etatist sense of being an administrative appendage of the absolutist caesaropapist state and thus partaking of the "public authority" of state institutions—here one could distinguish confessional states proper such as authoritarian Catholic regimes and the established churches of nonconfessional democratic states such as the Scandinavian Lutheran churches; and (c) in the sense of mobilizational religions taking over the modern state and its legal framework and shaping it in a theocratic-totalitarian direction, the fusion of clerical Catholic and fascist elements in the early mobilizational phase of the Franco regime being a stunted prototype, the Shi'ite hierocratic revolutionary regime in Iran being a more fully developed type.[8]

The first two forms of "publicness," the "publicness of representation" and the "publicness of administrative state authority," do not constitute a modern public sphere in the modern sense of a discursive or agonic space in principle open to all citizens and all issues.[9] The mentioned examples of the caesaropapist British monarch and the established Scandinavian churches are rather residual anachronisms which are compatible with the separate institution of a modern democratic public sphere. Mobilizational state religions, by contrast, are forms of deprivatization of modern religion which create a totalitarian participatory publicness that tends to destroy the very boundaries between the private and public spheres by infringing upon private rights (freedom of conscience being the most sacred of private rights) and destroying public liberties (freedom of speech being the constitutive principle of a modern public sphere).

Practically all the examples of mobilized public religion at the political society level mentioned above are transitional types. In the first group belong all types of public religion mobilized either to resist secularization or to counteract secularist movements and parties. This study contends that the age of secular-religious cleavages, of struggles over the historical process of modern secularization, has basically come to an end in the historical area of Western Christendom. As the Catholic church has finally accepted the legitimacy of the modern structural trend of secularization, that is, has accepted voluntarily disestablishment, and a mutual rapprochement between religious and secular humanism has taken place, the raison d'être of this type of mobilized political religion tends to disappear. As churches transfer the defense of their particularistic privilege (*libertas ecclesiae*) to the human person and accept the principle of religious freedom as a universal human right, they are for the first time in a position to enter the public sphere anew, this time to defend the institutionalization of modern universal rights, the creation of a modern public sphere, and the establishment of democratic regimes. This is what I call the transformation of the church from a state-oriented to a society-oriented institution. Churches cease being or aspiring to be state compulsory institutions and become free religious institutions of civil society. Insofar as the churches and their secular allies are successful in their struggles against authoritarian states, this type of mobilized political religion also loses its raison d'être—unless the churches resist full secularization and a new cycle of religious-secular cleavages, and mobilizations and countermobilizations begins. Of the case studies analyzed in this book, today such a scenario seems plausible, although unlikely, only in Poland.

The last cases of religion "going public" or taking a public stand for the sake of defending the very right to a modern public sphere already constitute examples of what I term the deprivatization of modern religion. As used throughout this study, the term deprivatization has three different connotations, one polemical, the other two descriptive. The term is used first of all polemically against those versions of the theory of secularization and those liberal political theories that prescribe the privatization of religion as a modern structural trend necessary to safeguard modern liberties and differentiated structures. This study has shown that such an indiscriminate position against all forms of public religion is unfounded, that there are some forms of deprivatization of religion which may be justifiable and even desirable from a modern normative perspective.

I admit to a certain uneasiness in coining and using such a unrefined neologism as deprivatization. But the barbarism may be justified as long as the term maintains its polemical value, that is, as long as it is not widely recognized that religions in the modern world are free to enter or not to enter the public sphere, to maintain more privatistic or more communal and public identities. Privatization and deprivatization are, therefore, historical options for religions in the modern world. Some religions will be induced by tradition, principle, and historical circumstances to remain basically private religions of individual salvation. Certain cultural traditions, religious doctrinal principles, and historical circumstances, by contrast, will induce other religions to enter, at least occasionally, the public sphere.

Besides its polemical connotation, however, the term has been used in this study to describe two different kinds of move or relocation of religion. The active role of the Catholic church in processes of democratization in Spain, Poland, and Brazil marks the passage from a nonmodern etatist (Spain), representational (Poland), or corporatist (Brazil) form of publicity to the modern public sphere of civil society. In these cases the descriptive connotation is somewhat misleading since we are not dealing so much with a move from the private to the public sphere as with a change in the type of publicity. The descriptive connotation of the term deprivatization is properly speaking only appropriate for cases such as the public mobilization of Protestant fundamentalism or the public interventions of the American Catholic bishops, both of which represent a move by religion from the private to the public sphere.

Nonetheless, despite the possible misunderstandings that may result from using the same term somewhat inaccurately for such different connotations, I think that it is appropriate and valid to maintain the term in order to call attention to the fact that these three diverse connotations of the term deprivatization may also be viewed as interrelated aspects of the historically new phenomenon analyzed in this study. Namely, it is my contention that the rejection by certain religious traditions of the privatized role to which they were being relegated by secularist modernization theories and by liberal political theories, that the role of the Catholic church in processes of democratization, and that the public interventions of religion in the public sphere of modern civil societies can no longer be viewed simply as antimodern religious critiques of modernity. They represent, rather, new types of immanent normative critiques of specific forms of institutionalization of modernity which presuppose precisely the acceptance of the validity of the fundamental values and principles of modernity, that is, individual freedoms and differentiated structures. In other words, they are immanent critiques of particular forms of modernity from a modern religious point of view.

As already mentioned, deprivatization in the sense of relocation of religion from a premodern form of publicness to the public sphere of civil society is a transitional phase which is conditioned by the very success of the move. Paradoxically, once the move has succeeded with the consolidation of a democratic regime, there is built-in pressure toward the privatization of religion. As the analysis of the Brazilian transition has indicated, this pressure toward the privatization of religion comes from four different sources:

a) There is a general trend toward the demobilization and privatization of civil society once "the hour of civil society" and its mobilized resistance against the authoritarian state passes and political society and its forms of representation and mediation by professional political elites become institutionalized.

b) Also noticeable are new Vatican directives and efforts to tame and control the public interventions of national Catholic churches and "progressive" Catholic groups, to restrain and regain control of the process of *aggiornamento* from above, and to remind pastoral agents of their primarily "pastoral" professional tasks and duties. Naturally, this is a particularly Roman Catholic conjunctural pressure, associated with the so-called project of "restoration" of Pope John Paul II and Cardinal Ratzinger. Undoubtedly, the internal hegemonic struggles between the Catholic left and the Catholic right are relevant in understanding this pressure.[10] But it is shortsighted to view the Vatican directives solely in this ideological light. They are better understood if viewed from the perspective of what John A. Coleman has called the institutional dynamics of *raison d'église,* that is, by the "organizational imperatives and predicaments" confronting a universal church which has finally accepted the structure of the modern world.[11] Surely, given the transnational, hierarchic, bureaucratic, and centralized character of the Catholic church, the Vatican attempt to regain administrative and doctrinal centralized control can easily be understood. But the Catholic church has to face two additional organizational imperatives which are connected with modern structural conditions and which also press toward privatization.

c) Under conditions of modern religious freedom the Catholic church is likely to face competition either from other religions or from secular worldviews. In order to face this competition successfully the Catholic church, while still counting on a large reservoir of traditional cultural allegiance among large sectors of the faithful, will have to learn from the American experience, concentrate on its pastoral tasks, and develop some form of voluntary, denominational, revivalist expression to reproduce itself successfully as a private religion of individual salvation. The Spanish example shows that in some places it may be too late to learn the American lesson, as Spanish Catholicism has joined general Western European secularizing trends, that is, has undergone a sharp decline of religious beliefs and practices.

d) Given modern structural conditions, if the Catholic church wants to maintain its universalist claims as a church, it will have to learn to live with social and cultural pluralism both outside and specially inside the church. This means that to maintain its viability as a private religion it will have to cater to the various pastoral needs of increasingly diverse Catholic groups, while to maintain its effectiveness as a public religion its public interventions will have to be and appear nonpartisan and nondenominational; that is, they will have to be framed in a universalistic language. This by no means precludes a "preferential option for the poor" or a continuation of the traditional Catholic opposition to abortion. On the contrary, it is the moral obligation to protect human life and to demand universal access to discourse, justice, and welfare that requires that the Universal Church take such a position or such an option. But most important, whichever position or option it takes, the church will have to justify it through open, public, rational discourse in the public sphere of civil society. Moreover, as the lesson of American Catholicism indicates, the church will have to learn to let all the faithful participate in the constant elaboration and reformulation of its normative teachings and allow for different practical judgments as to how to interpret those normative teachings in concrete circumstances.

As already indicated, privatization and deprivatization are historical options for modern religions. It has not been the intention of this study to counter the general, teleological theory of privatization with a general, teleological theory of deprivatization. To claim that we are witnessing a historical process of deprivatization of modern religion does not mean to imply that this is a new, general, historical trend. Indeed, it would be foolish to attempt to predict how general and how permanent this historical trend will turn out to be. The inclusion of the study of Spanish Catholicism, not intended originally, was meant to check any teleological impulse from author or reader to conceive deprivatization as a general historical reversal of processes of secularization. The Spanish lesson seems to be that, in some places, traditional theories of secularization in its triple connotation of structural differentiation, religious decline, and privatization of religion are still empirically valid. The advantage of the comparative historical analytical framework for the study of secularization developed here derives precisely from the fact that it is dynamic and flexible enough to be able to account for very different patterns of secularization and to be open to the varieties of ways in which different religions in different settings respond to modern structural trends of differentiation.

The claim that deprivatization is a historical option precludes the possibility of predicting the way in which any particular religion is going to respond. But on the basis of some evidence from the case studies and on some general theoretical assumptions, one could at least infer some of the conditioning factors that may be conducive to the intervention of religion in the modern public sphere.

The first condition is almost tautological. Only those religions which either by doctrine or by cultural tradition have a public, communal identity will want to assume public roles and resist the pressure to become solely or even primarily private "invisible" religions of individual salvation. Particularly, those religions which, after abandoning their identities as compulsory institutions, maintain their identities as churches—in the dual Durkheimian-Hegelian sense of ethical community and in the Weberian sense of having universalist salvational claims—will tend more likely than not also to claim the right and duty to assume public roles. This tendency will be the more pronounced the more such religions have a historical tradition of assuming prominent public roles.

The Spanish case shows, however, that neither doctrine nor historical tradition are per se sufficient for a religion to be able to maintain an effective public presence in modern civil societies, unless it is also able to maintain a dynamic and vital profile as a private religion of salvation. It is unlikely that a religion weakened by the process of secularization, which has suffered serious decline, will be able to withstand the pressures of privatization. This is the reason why cyclical theories of the return of the sacred or cyclical theories of religious revivals are ultimately flawed.

The two best-known variants, Daniel Bell's prediction of the return of the sacred and Rodney Stark and William Bainbridge's general theory of secularization, revival, and cult formation, despite significant differences are both predicated on the assumption that functional need—in Bell's case the universal and permanent anthropological need for meaning, in Stark and Bainbridge's case the need for supernatural compensation—is the mother of religious invention.[12] If the assumption were correct, the sacred should have returned and religious revivals or the birth of new religions should have occurred there, where secularization had gone the furthest and the absence of religion created the greatest need. Accordingly, we should have witnessed religious revivals in highly secularized societies such as Sweden, England, France, Uruguay, and Russia.

Yet the public resurgence of religion took place in places such as Poland, the United States, Brazil, Nicaragua, and Iran, all places which can hardly be characterized as secularized wastelands. What we witnessed in the 1980s was not the birth of new religions or the return of the sacred where religious traditions had dried up but, rather, the revitalization and reformation of old living traditions and the assumption of public roles by precisely those religious traditions which both theories of secularization and cyclical theories of religious revival had assumed were becoming ever more privatized and irrelevant in the modern world.

There is a third conditioning factor which both facilitates and induces religions to assume public roles, namely, the contemporary global context of action. Under conditions of globalization religions will tend to assume public roles whenever their identity as universal transsocial religions is reinforced by their actual situation as transnational religious regimes. In the case of Catholicism, the interrelated dynamics of globalization and public involvement of the various national churches in their particular societies has been obvious since the 1960s. Vatican II, the first truly global council, made the Roman church aware of its global reach and induced it to think globally. Simultaneously, however, the innerworldly turn of the Vatican *aggiornamento* led each national church to greater secular involvement in its particular society and to translate the universal Catholic message both literally and figuratively into the vernacular.

Two interrelated, only apparently contradictory, processes became noticeable throughout the Catholic world. There was, on the one hand, a strengthening of the process of centralization of the Roman Papacy, a long secular process which in its modern form has its origins in the Vatican's defensive response to the French Revolution and to the subsequent liberal revolutions spreading throughout Europe and Latin America. Vatican II produced not only administrative and doctrinal centralization but also the homogenization and globalization of Catholic culture, at least among the elites, throughout the Catholic world. On the other hand, Vatican II and the subsequent institutionalization of national bishops' conferences also reinforced a parallel process of decentralization and "nationalization" of Catholic churches, that is, of centralization at the national level, which in most places was begun by Catholic Action.

It was this combination of globalization, nationalization, secular involvement, and voluntary disestablishment that led to the change of orientation from state to society and permitted the church to play a key role in processes of democratization. The national churches stopped viewing themselves as integrative community cults of the national state and adopted a new transnational, global identity which permitted them to confront prophetically both the national state and the given social order. The study of American Catholicism indicated a similar transformation of identity from an affirmative, integrative American civil religion to a new type of critical, globally oriented public Catholicism. It is the new tension between a global orientation to human civil society and public involvement in the public sphere of a particular civil society that best explains the new dynamics of deprivatization.

Even in the case of Protestant fundamentalism one can observe a similar dynamic combination of globalization, nationalization, and secular involvement. Fundamentalist global thinking had a dual source in the global reach of evangelical missionary efforts and in premillennial apocalyptic visions of Armageddon, both of which awakened a keen interest among fundamentalists in American foreign policy and world politics, now viewed from the biblical perspective of the history of salvation. Underneath their sectarian rejection of modern America, fundamentalists had kept latent their intense Americanism and their faith in America's millennial destiny. Thus, once it came, the call to national revival, to turn America around and to become involved in a new Christian crusade, was eagerly heard. The direction taken by deprivatization in this particular case was a return from sectarian exile back to reestablishment as the hegemonic American civil religion.

Roland Robertson has argued convincingly that ongoing processes of globalization in the dual sense of the emergence of global humankind and the emergence of a global system of societies entail the relativization of the personal identity of the self in reference to humankind as a whole, the relativization of membership in any particular national society by reference to global humanity, and the relativization of particular national societies from the perspective of the world system of societies.[13]

Not surprisingly, global and transnational religions are well situated when it comes to responding to the challenges or taking advantage of the opportunities presented by processes of globalization. Perhaps the most significant new global development of the last twenty years has been the crisis of absolutist principles of state sovereignty and *raison d'état* and the emergence of global dynamics of democratization. Among some of the related developments are the collapse of the system of socialist states, the global defeat of national security doctrines, the crisis of the established principle of noninterference in the internal affairs of nation-states, and the crisis of state-led models of economic development and societal modernization. New dynamics of civil society formation both intrasocietally and globally have played no small part in those developments, while churches and religious movements have played a crucial role both in the revitalization of particular civil societies and in the emergence of a global civil society. It is not surprising that the crisis of territorial state sovereignty and the expansion of a global civil society offer special opportunities to a transnational religious regime like the Catholic church which had always found it difficult to reconcile its identity as a catholic-universal church with the reality of the modern system of territorial sovereign states.[14] Paradoxically, the old gods and the old religions, which according to Durkheim were on their deathbed, have been revitalized by becoming the carriers of the process of sacralization of humanity that Durkheim himself had announced.[15]

Only in a very broad sense is it appropriate to attribute the return of the old gods to the crisis of their old enemies, Enlightenment rationalism and secular modernity. It is at this level of analysis, however, namely, in terms of a crisis of Enlightenment rationalism and of the idea of progress, indeed as a crisis of secularity itself, that one may look for an explanation of the worldwide character of the contemporary religious revival across all civilizations.[16] When secular ideologies appear to have failed or lost much of their force, religion returns to the public arena as a mobilizing or integrating normative force. But it is not religion in the abstract which is returning, nor is it returning everywhere. At most, the crisis of secularity can serve as a common conditioning factor that allows certain religious traditions, which have not yet been weakened excessively by processes of secularization, to respond in certain ways.

Moreover, the case studies presented here indicate that what seems to precipitate the religious response are different types of state intervention and administrative colonization of the lifeworld and the private sphere. Such a response could be interpreted, therefore, as a defensive reaction along lines similar to those used by Habermas to analyze the "new social movements."[17] The mobilization of Protestant fundamentalism was clearly a response to state rulings coming from the Supreme Court, the Internal Revenue Service, and Congress. Even in the Catholic cases, where the internal reformation of the Catholic tradition associated with Vatican II was crucial, the role of state penetration as a precipitating factor in the transformations of Polish, Latin-American, and U.S. Catholicism was equally important.

In Poland, Catholic resistance and church-state conflicts were part of the struggle for the right to a private and social sphere free from totalitarian state intervention. But the transformation of Polish Catholicism marks the passage from a struggle centered around the corporatist interests of the church as an institution to a struggle first for human and national rights and then, after the founding of KOR and the emergence of Solidarity, for the rights of civil society to autonomy and self-determination.

In Latin America, the development of liberation theology was at first primarily a response to processes of capitalist expansion and colonization of the traditional lifeworld. But the radicalization of the church as an institution and its confrontation with the state throughout Latin America were a reaction to the institutionalization of the national security state and its violent penetration of the lifeworld—to the indiscriminate violation of human rights, the widespread and systematic use of torture, and the rapid increase in the number of "desaparecidos," victims of a new form of state terror.

Even in the United States, it was the 1973 Supreme Court decision legalizing abortion by subsuming it under a woman's right to privacy that galvanized the American Catholic church into the political arena, beginning the process that led the bishops to expand the principle of the moral protection of human life and of the sacred dignity of the human person to the two main subsystems, capitalist markets and sovereign states.

Looking particularly at those forms of religious intervention in the public sphere which have emerged in an advanced modern society like the United States, one could say that the deprivatization of modern religion has assumed three main forms. There is, first, the religious mobilization in defense of the traditional lifeworld against various forms of state or market penetration. The mobilization of Protestant fundamentalism and, to a certain extent, the Catholic mobilization against abortion can be seen as examples of this first form of deprivatization.

The argument presented here has been that even in those cases in which religious mobilization could be explained simply as a traditionalist response to modern processes of universalization, which are promoted or protected by state juridical interventions and which disrupt, for instance, the traditional patriarchal family or established patterns of racial or gender discrimination, the deprivatization of religion may have an important public function. By entering the public sphere and forcing the public discussion or contestation of certain issues, religions force modern societies to reflect publicly and collectively upon their normative structures. Naturally, one should not minimize the dangers a traditionalist backlash or a fundamentalist project of restoration may pose to modern normative structures. But in the very process of entering the modern public sphere, religions and normative traditions are also forced to confront and possibly come to terms with modern normative structures. Such a public encounter may permit the reflexive rationalization of the lifeworld and may open the way for the institutionalization of processes of practical rationalization.

A second form of deprivatization is manifested in those cases in which religions enter the public sphere of modern societies to question and contest the claims of the two major societal systems, states and markets, to function according to their own intrinsic functionalist norms without regard to extrinsic traditional moral norms. By questioning the morality of national security doctrines and the inhuman premises of nuclear defense policies, based on MAD scenarios, ready to sacrifice immeasurable numbers of human beings for the sake of state sovereignty and superpower supremacy, religions remind both states and their citizens of the human need to subordinate the logic of state formation to "the common good." Similarly, by questioning the inhuman claims of capitalist markets to function in accordance with impersonal and amoral self-regulating mechanisms, religions may remind individuals and societies of the need to check and regulate those impersonal market mechanisms to ensure that they are accountable for the human, social, and ecological damage they may cost and that they may become more responsible to human needs. Moreover, transnational religions are in a particularly advantageous position to remind all individuals and all societies that under modern conditions of globalization "the common good" can increasingly be defined only in global, universal, human terms and that, consequently, the public sphere of modern civil societies cannot have national or state boundaries.

There is moreover a third form of deprivatization of religion connected with the obstinate insistence of traditional religions on maintaining the very principle of a "common good" against individualist modern liberal theories which would reduce the common good to the aggregated sum of individual choices. As long as they respect the ultimate right and duty of the individual conscience to make moral decisions, by bringing into the public sphere issues which liberal theories have decreed to be private affairs, religions remind individuals and modern societies that morality can only exist as an intersubjective normative structure and that individual choices only attain a "moral" dimension when they are guided or informed by intersubjective, interpersonal norms. Reduced to the private sphere of the individual self, morality must necessarily dissolve into arbitrary decisionism. By bringing publicity into the private moral sphere and by bringing into the public sphere issues of private morality, religions force modern societies to confront the task of reconstructing reflexively and collectively their own normative foundations. By doing so, they aid in the process of practical rationalization of the traditional lifeworld and of their own normative traditions.

If the thesis presented so far is correct, the recent transformations of religion analyzed in this study are qualitatively different from what is usually understood as "the return of the sacred." The deprivatization of religion cannot be understood either as an antimodern or as a postmodern phenomenon. None of the religious phenomena presented here can be viewed meaningfully as instances of the kind of modern privatized religiosity which, in my view, is the true harbinger of the postmodern condition. All are grounded in that foundational tradition which Richard Niebuhr called radical monotheism.[18] All still publicly uphold universalistic normative and truth claims. The critique of Enlightenment rationalism and of the teleological grand narratives of progress and secular redemption—a critique usually associated with postmodern discourse—may have legitimated and facilitated, at least indirectly, the rehabilitation of those religious traditions which had usually been the target of rationalist critique. Nevertheless, it would be difficult to find either direct links or elective affinities between postmodernity and the public resurgence of religion.[19] As already indicated, it would seem more appropriate to view the public interventions of religion analyzed here as immanent critiques of particular forms of institutionalization of modernity from a modern normative perspective.

If correct, and beyond the relevance it may have for the sociology of religion, such an argument should have further implications for two general areas of sociology. In the first place, it may have relevance for theories of social integration by suggesting a specifically modern type of social integration through the undifferentiated public sphere of civil society. Such a model of modern social integration would present an alternative to the customary ways of conceiving social integration either through administrative state coordination or through self-regulating market mechanisms, through aggregated individual exchanges or through self-regulating systemic differentiation. According to this model, modern social integration emerges in and through the discursive and agonic participation of individuals, groups, social movements, and institutions in a public yet undifferentiated sphere of civil society where the collective construction and reconstruction, contestation, and affirmation of common normative structures—"the common good"—takes place. Unlike functionalist theories of normative societal integration, however, such a theory does not conceptualize modern civil societies as a homogeneous societal community sharing common norms and values but, rather, as a space and a process of public social interaction through which common norms and solidarities may be constructed and reconstructed. In other words, common norms cannot be presupposed as the premise and foundation of a modern social order but, rather, as the potential and always fragile outcome of a process of communicative interaction. Through such a process of communicative interaction in the public sphere of modern civil societies, normative traditions can be reflexively reconstructed—

that is, rationalized—and the differentiated subsystems of modern societies can be made responsible to a publicly defined "common good." By going "public," religions as well as other normative traditions can, therefore, contribute to the vitality of such a public sphere.

It should be obvious that this conception is very close to the theory of modern societies developed by Jürgen Habermas and to theories of civil society which build upon his theory.[20] Indeed, the main purpose of this study has been not so much to revise old theories of secularization as to examine the roles which religions and religious movements could still play in furthering processes of practical rationalization. In his reconstruction of Weber's Protestant ethic thesis Habermas has postulated the counterfactual hypothesis that, had the radical communitarian wing of the Reformation been the one to gain hegemony instead of the ascetic wing, perhaps instrumental rationalization would not have expanded so one-sidedly at the expense of practical rationalization.[21] Yet one of the conclusions one could derive from the case studies presented here is that, in the same way in which the deprivatization of religion raises questions for functionalist theories of secularization, what could be called the practical-rational potential of those religious movements also raises similar questions for Habermas's secularist theory of modernity.

The relevant issue here is not whether Habermas himself should or should not be interested in religious movements or in the role religion could possibly play in the reconstitution of the public sphere. The problem is whether Habermas's rigid theory of modern differentiation leaves any room open for such an interest. If religion is only the unity of culture before its modern differentiation into the cognitive, the moral-practical, and the aesthetic-expressive spheres, then religion is only an anachronism or a residue without much relevance or future. Religion may have a relevant past, as shown by Habermas's own counterfactual hypothesis concerning the radical ethical visions of brotherhood, which were, however, excluded historically by the institutionalized selectivity of capitalist modernity. Religion may even have a present in Habermas's theory in protecting defensively what little is left of traditional lifeworlds from state administrative penetration and from capitalist colonization. But religion has no future. In Habermas's model, conventional religion ought to be superseded by postconventional secular morality.

In addition to the obvious cognitive question concerning the empirical adequacy of such a theory in accounting for ongoing historical processes, there are two issues of practical relevance for those interested in advancing what Habermas calls "the unfinished project of modernity." The first issue has to do with the old problem of theory and practice. If, as Marx put it, "it is not enough that thought should strive to realize itself; reality must itself strive towards thought," could it be the case here that "the philosophical head" is not attentive enough to its own "heart," to what could become "its material weapon"?[22] Put in more Weberian terms, there is a need to identify the historical carriers of processes of moral-practical rationalization. Following Habermas's critique of Weber's nearly exclusive emphasis upon processes of instrumental rationalization, one could say that Weber's greatest contribution—the discovery of the crucial historical relevance of the economic ethics of the world religions for differential processes of instrumental rationalization—may have predisposed him to neglect the importance of the political ethics of the world religions for processes of moral-practical rationalization. What Weber said about "economic ethics," however, ought to be applicable also to "political ethics":

This term does not bring into focus the ethical theories of theological compendia; for however important such compendia may be under certain circumstances, they merely serve as tools of knowledge. The term "economic ethic" points to the practical impulses for action which are founded in the psychological and pragmatic contexts of religions.[23]

One should, therefore, distinguish between cognitive, intellectual contributions to moral-practical discourse and the historical institutionalization of moral-practical principles and norms. If Peter Brown was correct in pointing out that, while early Christianity may have made almost no innovation in moral matters, nonetheless it played a crucial historical role by "democratizing" the philosophers' upper-class culture and by putting into practice "what pagan and Jewish moralists had already begun to preach,"[24] then one may offer the conjecture, partially supported by the case studies presented in this work, that today as always religious organizations and religious movements continue to play similar historical roles. In three of the five cases studied here, religious movements and organizations played direct, immediate roles in processes of democratization. In the other two cases, religion played some role in enlivening the public sphere of civil society either directly, by raising publicly normative issues concerning the systemic functioning of the administrative state and the capitalist economy, or indirectly, by reacting to processes of administrative or juridical penetration of the lifeworld and, thereby, opening up for public debate normative issues concerning the very structure of the modern lifeworld.

In principle, there is neither need nor reason to privilege religion as the sole or main, direct or indirect carrier of processes of moral-practical rationalization. In the modern world, other secular movements and organizations have been, are, and will likely continue to be at least as important carriers as religion. Therefore, it is not necessarily the case that without religion the public square must be "naked."[25] But the actual continuous presence of religion in most moral-practical struggles of the modern world, frequently on both sides of every issue, tends to indicate that there is also no reason, other than secularist or rationalist prejudice and the conviction that there can be no such a thing as a "modern," that is, postconventional religion, why in principle a theory of moral-practical rationalization should systematically neglect religion.

This points precisely to a second practical issue, namely, to the danger of elitist, rationalist bias. Although some recent trends in the self-conceptualization of science and the self-understanding of professional scientific identities tend to put into question any rigid separation even at this level, nonetheless one could argue that at least when it comes to the cognitive sphere, one still needs to maintain a clear and rigid separation between science and religion.[26] For instance, there may be room for "belief" in creation or for symbolic, even mythical, language concerning the cosmos. But there can be no such thing as "creation science." But when it comes to the moral-practical and the subjective-expressive spheres, one may wonder whether such a rigid, clear-cut differentiation is possible, necessary, or helpful. One may justifiably question whether a theory which so clearly privileges intellectual rational discourse and a tradition of thought which so clearly privileges the aesthetic realm may not be oblivious to the fact that for ordinary people in most societies throughout the world religion and religious traditions continue to be an accessible and legitimate vehicle for moral-practical reflection and for innersubjective expression. In any case, before discarding contemporary religious movements as either anachronistic or purely defensive reactions, one would need to prove that ultimately there is incompatibility between religion and modern structures of consciousness.

I would agree, of course, that only a religion which has incorporated as its own the central aspects of the Enlightenment critique of religion is in a position today to play a positive role in furthering processes of practical rationalization. Only a religious tradition which reformulates its relationship to modernity by incorporating reflexively the three dimensions of the Enlightenment critique of religion—the cognitive critique of traditional religious worldviews, the moral-practical critique of religious ideologies of legitimation, and the subjective-expressive critique of religious asceticism and alienation—while upholding publicly the sacred values of modernity, that is, human life and freedom, may contribute to the revitalization of the modern public sphere. But the very resurgence or reassertion of religious traditions may be viewed as a sign of the failure of the Enlightenment to redeem its own promises in each of these spheres. Religious traditions are now confronting the differentiated secular spheres, challenging them to face their own obscurantist, ideological, and inauthentic claims. In many of these confrontations, it is religion which, as often as not, appears to be on the side of human enlightenment.

Western modernity has lost some of its haughty self-assurance and is beginning to manifest some doubts about its arrogant attitude toward the other, precisely at a time when the attempt to transcend itself from within through socialism has apparently failed. Meanwhile the two dynamos of modernity, the capitalist market and the administrative state, continue their self-propelled march toward a world system, wrecking and challenging every premodern tradition and life form that stands in their way. Some of these traditions accommodate and accept the private niche reserved for them in the cultural marketplace, where they may even thrive in the modern or postmodern pantheon.

Others, particularly non-Western traditions, emboldened by modernity's self-doubts, are able to reaffirm their own identity against the modern West. If Weber was correct when he argued that ascetic Protestantism played some role in helping to shape the particular historical form which the institutionalization of modern differentiation and the privatization of religion assumed in the West, theories of secularization and modernization should be open to the possibility that other religions may also play some role in institutionalizing their own particular patterns of secularization.

Finally, there are those traditions which have maintained an uneasy relationship with modernity, partly accommodating, partly recognizing some of modernity's values as their own but refusing to accept the claims of the market and the state that moral norms ought not to interfere with their systemic logic of self-reproduction through the media of money and power. Through their ongoing critical encounter with modernity, those traditions may be in a position to further both the processes of practical rationalization and the unfinished project of modernity.

Western modernity is at a crossroads. If it does not enter into a creative dialogue with the other, with those traditions which are challenging its identity, modernity will most likely triumph. But it may end up being devoured by the inflexible, inhuman logic of its own creations. It would be profoundly ironic if, after all the beatings it has received from modernity, religion could somehow unintentionally help modernity save itself.

Notes

Part One

1. By contrast, in the English translation, the term and the people behind it were flattened into the secular "the wretched of the earth." See Said Arjomand, *The Turban for the Crown: The Islamic Revolution in Iran* (New York: Oxford University Press, 1988), pp. 93–94.

2. Gustavo Gutiérrez, *Power of the Poor in History* (Maryknoll, N.Y.: Orbis, 1983).

3. Vaclav Havel, *Power of the Powerless* (New York: Sharpe, 1990).

4. Cf. Michael Walzer, *Exodus and Revolution* (New York: Basic Books, 1985), and Ernst Bloch, *Man on His Own* (New York: Herder and Herder, 1970).

5. From among the immense literature on the "new" religious movements, see David Bromley and Philip E. Hammond, eds., *The Future of New Religious Movements* (Macon, Ga.: Mercer University Press, 1987); Eileen Barker, ed., *New Religious Movements* (New York: Mellen, 1982); Charles Glock and Robert Bellah, eds., *The New Religious Consciousness* (Berkeley: University of California Press, 1976); Rodney Stark, ed., *Religious Movements: Genesis, Exodus, Numbers* (New York: Rose of Sharon Press, 1984); Steven Tipton, *Getting Saved from the Sixties* (Berkeley: University of California Press, 1982); Bryan Wilson, ed., *The Social Impact of New Religious Movements* (New York: Rose of Sharon Press, 1981); Robert Wuthnow, *The Consciousness Reformation* (Berkeley: University of California Press, 1976).

6. Mary Douglas, "The Effects of Modernization on Religious Change," in Mary Douglas and Steven M. Tipton, eds., *Religion and America. Spirituality in a Secular Age*, p. 25 (Boston: Beacon Press, 1982).

7. One could add that Catholicism is the largest and one of the most understudied religions. The sociology of Catholicism is still underdeveloped.

8. Whether this new trend will turn out to be a permanent or rather a merely transitory phenomenon is, of course, the kind of question to which only very tentative and speculative answers might be given.

Chapter One

1. On the ongoing "secularization debate," compare, on the one hand, Rodney Stark and William Sims Bainbridge, *The Future of Religion* (Berkeley: Uni-

versity of California Press, 1985); Theodore Caplow et al., *All Faithful People* (Minneapolis: University of Minnesota Press, 1983); Andrew Greeley, *Religious Change in America* (Cambridge, Mass.: Harvard University Press, 1989); and Jeffrey K. Hadden, "Desacralizing Secularization Theory," in Jeffrey K. Hadden and Anson Shupe, eds., *Secularization and Fundamentalism Reconsidered* (New York: Paragon House, 1989), with, on the other hand, Bryan Wilson, "The Secularization Debate," *Encounter* 45 (1975); "The Return of the Sacred," *Journal for the Scientific Study of Religion* 18 (1979); "Secularization: The Inherited Model," in Phillip E. Hammond, ed., *The Sacred in a Secular Age* (Berkeley: University of California Press, 1985); Karel Dobbelaere, *Secularization: A Multi-Dimensional Concept* (Beverly Hills, Calif.: Sage Publications, 1981); and "The Secularization of Society? Some Methodological Suggestions," in Hadden and Shupe, *Secularization and Fundamentalism*.

2. For an analysis of the various positions in the first secularization debate, see my earlier essay, "The Politics of the Religious Revival," *Telos* 59 (Spring 1984). Readers will readily recognize that this was my first provisional sketch of all the issues that are developed more systematically and, I hope, more satisfactorily in the present work. My position remains basically the same. But many issues, particularly the analytical distinctions I am introducing in this chapter and the new discussion of private and public religions, were not as clear to me then.

3. Distinctions are, of course, never merely analytical. They are always attempts to perceive, grasp, order, and organize reality itself in a particular way. For a distinctly subtle and differentiating account, see Eviatar Zerubavel, *The Fine Line: Making Distinctions in Every Day Life* (New York: Free Press, 1991).

4. On the concept of secularization, cf. Hermann Lübbe, *Säkularisierung-Geschichte eines ideenpolitischen Begriffs* (Freiburg: Alber, 1965); Hans Blumenberg, *The Legitimacy of the Modern Age* (Cambridge, Mass: MIT Press, 1983); David Martin, "Secularization: The Range of Meaning," in *The Religious and the Secular* (New York: Schocken Books, 1969); Peter Berger, *The Sacred Canopy* (Garden City, N.Y: Doubleday, 1969). Talcott Parsons, who in his peculiar usage of the term "secularization" follows Weber, acknowledged "being deliberately paradoxical in attributing to the concept secularization what has often been held to be its opposite, namely not the loss of commitment to religious values and the like, but the institutionalization of such values, and other components of religious orientation in evolving cultural and social systems." *Action Theory and the Human Condition* (New York: Free Press, 1978), p. 241, n. 11.

5. It is not surprising, therefore, that David Martin in the 1960s called for the elimination of the concept altogether. Fortunately for sociology, he did not follow his own advice, and a decade later he published a study which still remains the best comparative-historical analysis of different patterns of secularization throughout Europe and the United States. Cf. David Martin, "Towards Eliminating the Concept of Secularization," in *Religious and Secular*, and *A General Theory of Secularization* (New York: Harper & Row, 1978).

6. It would not be necessary to make these conceptual clarifications were it not for the fact that sociologists of religion have reduced the meaning of the

concept to such an extent that they are convinced they have proven that secularization is a *myth,* once they are able to show that, at least in the United States, none of the so-called "indicators" of secularization—such as number of churches per capita, church membership, attendance at church services, and monetary contributions to religious causes—evince any long-term declining trend. This is the only reason it has become necessary to retrace historical ground which some may find a commonplace. I want to insist, however, that only those who either do not know or have already forgotten the many layers of historical debris accumulated in the concept, and those who think that the developments depicted here are irrelevant superstructural events, can afford to ignore the concept of secularization. The rest, particularly those interested in the "genealogy" and "archeology" of modernity and postmodernity, may still find hidden behind the semantic debris a clue to "the order of things."

7. The fact that today we are witnessing the reappropriation by ecclesiastical institutions of some of these functions, after the state or other secular institutions abandoned them, may be viewed as a further indication that the boundaries between the religious and the secular spheres, as well as those between the public and private spheres, are shifting.

8. The following reconstruction does not claim to be either historically accurate or sufficiently complex. It is only meant as a point of departure for historically grounding theories of secularization that would otherwise appear to be too abstract. Some of the works on which I have relied for historical information or which have influenced my thinking on these issues are Ernst Troeltsch, *The Social Teaching of the Christian Churches* (New York: Macmillan, 1931); Mari-Dominique Chenu, *Nature, Man and Society in the Twelfth Century* (Chicago: University of Chicago Press, 1968); Richard Southern, *Western Society and the Church in the Middle Ages* (Harmondsworth: Penguin Books, 1970); Max Weber, "Political and Hierocratic Domination," in *Economy and Society,* vol. 2 (Berkeley: University of California Press, 1978); Fritz Kern, *Kingship and Law in the Middle Ages,* 2 vols. (Oxford: Blackwell, 1968); E. H. Kantorowicz, *The King's Two Bodies: A Study in Medieval Political Theology* (Princeton: Princeton University Press, 1957); Werner Stark, *The Sociology of Religion: A Study of Christendom.,* vol. 1, *Established Religion,* and vol. 3, *The Universal Church* (New York: Fordham University Press, 1966–67); Gerd Tellenbach, *Church, State and Christian Society at the Time of the Investitures* (New York: Harper & Row, 1970); Brian Tierney, *The Crisis of Church and State, 1050–1300* (Englewood Cliffs, N.J.: Prentice-Hall, 1973); J. A. F. Thompson, *Popes and Princes, 1417–1517* (Boston: Allen & Unwin, 1980); Geoffrey Barraclough, *The Medieval Papacy* (New York: Norton, 1979); Benjamin Nelson, *On the Roads to Modernity* (Totowa, N.J.: Rowman & Littlefield, 1981).

9. See one of the classic studies of religious sectarian movements, Norman Cohn, *The Pursuit of the Millennium* (New York: Oxford University Press, 1970).

10. For a volume which reviews the present state of scholarship on some of these issues, see Philippe Ariès and Georges Duby, eds., *A History of Private Life,* vol. 2, *From Feudal Europe to the Renaissance* (Cambridge, Mass.: Harvard

University Press, 1987). On the now very popular field of "popular religion," cf. James Obelkevich, *Religion and the People, 800–1700* (Chapel Hill: University of North Carolina Press, 1979); François Isambert, *Le sens du sacré—Fête et religion populaire* (Paris: Les éditions du minuit, 1982); Carlo Ginzburg, *The Cheese and the Worms: The Cosmos of a Sixteenth-Century Miller* (New York: Penguin, 1980); and *The Night Battles: Witchcraft and Agrarian Cults in the Sixteenth and Seventeenth Centuries* (New York: Penguin, 1984); William Christian, Jr., *Apparitions in Late Medieval and Renaissance Spain* (Princeton: Princeton University Press, 1981), and *Local Religion in Sixteenth-Century Spain* (Princeton: Princeton University Press, 1981).

11. On belief and unbelief in early modern Europe, cf. Lucien Febvre, *The Problem of Unbelief in the Sixteenth Century* (Cambridge, Mass.: Harvard University Press, 1982); and Keith Thomas, *Religion and the Decline of Magic* (New York: Scribner, 1971).

12. For a very useful compilation of most of the key texts of the early social sciences on religion, see Norman Birnbaum and Gertrud Lenzer, eds., *Sociology and Religion: A Book of Readings* (Englewood Cliffs, N.J.: Prentice-Hall, 1969).

13. Talcott Parsons, "The Theoretical Development of the Sociology of Religion," in *Essays in Sociological Theory* (New York: Free Press, 1954).

14. That secularization, for Durkheim, is both origin and telos of the universal process of differentiation is repeatedly stated throughout his writings. Durkheim sees religion as the fountainhead of society, "the concentrated expression of the whole collective life" from which "nearly all the great social institutions have been born." Except for economic activities, which would apparently be the profane realm par excellence, "religion has given birth to all that is essential in society." Emile Durkheim, *The Elementary Forms of the Religious Life* (New York: Free Press, 1965), p. 466. Sociology, as the science of morality, has as its task the establishing of the rational foundations of modern secular societies. The study of religion for Durkheim has precisely the function of uncovering the authentic social essence of religion, i.e., the essence of society, in order to separate it from its religious symbols and reproduce it in a secular and rational form, without mythological intermediaries. For one of the clearest among his many "secularist manifestos," see Emile Durkheim, "Introduction: Secular Morality," in *Moral Education* (New York: Free Press, 1973).

15. While acknowledging that it also has empirical points of reference, Luckmann has even argued that the theory of secularization "is primarily a mythological account of the emergence of the modern world." Thomas Luckmann, "Theories of Religion and Social Change," *Annual Review of the Social Sciences of Religion* 1 (1977).

16. Durkheim, *Elementary Forms*, p. 475. The most comprehensive analysis of Durkheim's theory of religion is W. S. F. Pickering's *Durkheim's Sociology of Religion* (London: Routledge & Kegan Paul, 1984).

17. Max Weber, "Science as a Vocation" and "Religious Rejections of the World and Their Directions," in H. H. Gerth and C. W. Mills, eds., *From Max Weber* (New York: Oxford University Press, 1946). The best and most comprehensive study of Weber's sociology of religion is Wolfgang Schluchter's

Rationalism, Religion and Domination: A Weberian Perspective (Berkeley: University of California Press, 1989).

18. The best-known formulations of the theory of secularization in the 1960s are those of Bryan Wilson, *Religion in Secular Society* (London: C. A. Watts, 1966); Peter Berger, *The Sacred Canopy* (Garden City, N.J.: Doubleday, 1967); Thomas Luckmann, *Invisible Religion* (New York: Macmillan, 1967); Joachim Matthes, *Die Emigration der Kirche aus der Gesellschaft* (Hamburg: Furche, 1964); and Sabino S. Acquaviva, *L'eclissi del Sacro Nella Civiltà Industriale* (Milan: Edizioni di Communità, 1966). The first critiques came from David Martin, *The Religious and the Secular;* and Andrew Greeley, *Unsecular Man: The Persistence of Religion* (New York: Schocken 1972).

19. Modernization is an equally problematic and fallacious concept and theory, which others would also like to bury and which I would like to maintain for the same reasons I am defending the concept and the theory of secularization. See Immanuel Wallerstein, " Modernization: requiescat in pace," in *The Capitalist World Economy* (Cambridge: Cambridge University Press, 1979), and José Casanova, "Legitimacy and the Sociology of Modernization," in Arthur Vidich and Ronald Glassman, eds. *Conflict and Control* (Beverly Hills, Calif.: Sage, 1979).

20. Today when we introduce, anachronistically as it were, modern economic, political, or cultural categories into the study of medieval reality, those secular categories reveal that reality in the medieval saeculum was by no means structured solely in accordance with the official religious view. There was a lively knightly and courtly feudal culture with a "civilizing" dynamic of its own and a "burgher" culture in the free cities with a "bourgeois" dynamic of its own. We may even stretch the anachronism to the point of turning the system upside down to reveal that the official system of classification was nothing but the religious superstructure of the real economic base. Marx's great historical-methodological insight, developed in the Introduction to the *Grundrisse,* was to show that it was the present that was the key to the past, not the past that was the key to the present; that bourgeois modernity permitted us for the first time to see the past in a way in which it could never see itself. Karl Marx, *Grundrisse* (New York: Vintage, 1973), pp. 104–8.

21. Weber, "Religious Rejections," p. 336.

22. For a compelling analysis from such a perspective, see Charles Tilly, *Coercion, Capital and European States, A.D. 990–1990* (Cambridge, Mass: B. Blackwell, 1990).

23. Niklas Luhmann has offered the most systematic formulation of a functionalist theory of religion along these lines. See his *Religious Dogmatics and the Evolution of Societies* (New York: E. Mellen Press, 1984).

24. For the purposes of this discussion, it is not necessary to enter upon the issue of the possible historical continuities between modern processes of secularization and their historical antecedents in the Renaissance, the late Middle Ages, etc., nor upon the relationship of what is conceptualized here primarily as a historical process of secularization, to developmental processes of secularization from a universal-historical perspective.

25. The unity of Christendom, of course, had always been a fiction, at least since the schism between Byzantium and Rome. First the "Second Rome" (Byzantium) and then the Third Rome (Muscovy) claimed to be the true heirs and guardians of Christian "orthodoxy." Cf. Steven Runciman, *The Byzantine Theocracy* (Cambridge: Cambridge University Press, 1977), and *The Orthodox Churches and the Secular State* (Auckland: Auckland University Press, 1971); and Nicholas Zernov, *Moscow: The Third Rome* (New York: AMS Press, 1971).

26. This view is, or rather was, shared by most Catholic apologists, who in the past always blamed Protestantism for opening the gates to all the ills and heresies of modernity. It is also shared by all avowed secularists who find it hard to accept the notion that religion may have had any "positive" impact upon "progressive" developments. Most economic historians, especially the critics of "the Protestant ethic thesis," also fall within this category.

27. Although it comes in many variations, this is basically the Marxist view of Protestantism. See Frederick Engels, *The Peasant War in Germany* (New York: International, 1966).

28. This view is represented by a whole tradition of thought, mainly Protestant, going from Hegel's *Early Theological Writings* through the Weber-Troeltsch axis to Parsons's extreme interpretation of modern industrial society as the institutionalization of Christian principles. See Talcott Parsons, "Christianity and Modern Industrial Society," in Edward Tiryakian, ed., *Sociological Theory, Values and Sociocultural Change* (New York: Free Press, 1963). Modern secular theologies from Dietrich Bonhoeffer through Friedrich Gogarten to Harvey Cox's *The Secular City* and the "Death of God" theology also build upon this tradition. Ultimately, it is a secularized Christian view of history through the prism of such Christian doctrines as the incarnation, the unfinished creation, and the millennium. See Karl Loewith, *Meaning in History* (Chicago: University of Chicago Press, 1949).

29. Cf. J. N. Figgis, *The Divine Rights of Kings* (Cambridge: Cambridge University Press, 1914); Marc Bloch, *The Royal Touch: Sacred Monarchy and Scrofula in England and France* (London: Routledge & Kegan Paul, 1973); and W. Stark, *Socioloy*, vol. 1, *Established Religion*.

30. Cf. Martin, *General Secularization;* Mary Fullbrook, *Piety and Politics: Religion and the Rise of Absolutism in England, Württemberg, and Prussia* (New York: Cambridge University Press, 1983); Felix Gilbert, ed., *The Historical Essays of Otto Hintze* (New York: Oxford University Press, 1975); Lord Acton, *Essays on Church and State* (New York: Thomas Y. Crowell, 1968).

31. Marx and Engels, "Manifesto of the Communist Party," remains the unequaled, i.e., the "classic," paean to the revolutionizing force of bourgeois capitalism. For the most comprehensive and systematic analysis of the global nature of this process, see Immanuel Wallerstein, *The Modern World System*, 3 vols. (New York: Academic Press, 1974–89)

32. Among the classic statements on religion and capitalism, cf. Max Weber, *The Protestant Ethic and the Spirit of Capitalism* (New York: Scribner's Sons, 1958); Richard Tawney, *Religion and the Rise of Capitalism* (New York: Harcourt Brace, 1926); Werner Sombart, *The Jews and Modern Capitalism* (New

York: Collier, 1962), and *Der moderne Kapitalismus* (München: Duncker & Humblot, 1919); Benjamin Nelson, *The Idea of Usury* (Chicago: University of Chicago Press, 1969); Christopher Hill, *Society and Puritanism in Pre-Revolutionary England* (Harmondsworth: Penguin, 1964). For an analysis of contemporary secularization as the penetration of the logic of commodification into the religious sphere see Berger, *Sacred Canopy*.

33. Cf. Blumenberg, *Modern Age*, and B. Nelson, *Roads to Modernity*.

34. Frank Manuel, *The Changing of the Gods* (Hanover, N.H.: University Press of New England, 1983).

35. Robert Merton, *Science, Technology and Society in Seventeenth Century England* (New York: Harper & Row, 1970); and James R. Jacob and Margaret C. Jacob, "The Anglican Origins of Modern Science," *Isis* 71 (June 1980).

36. Cf. Margaret C. Jacob, *The Newtonians and the English Revolution* (Ithaca, N.Y.: Cornell University Press, 1976), and *The Radical Enlightenment: Pantheists, Freemasons and Republicans* (London: George Allen & Unwin, 1981).

37. Susan Budd, *Varieties of Unbelief: Atheists and Agnostics in English Society, 1850–1960* (New York: Holmes & Meier, 1977).

38. Cf. Leopoldo Zea, *Positivism in Mexico* (Austin: University of Texas Press, 1974); João Cruz Costa, *O positivismo na Republica: Notas sobre a historia do positivismo no Brasil* (São Paulo: Companhia Editora Nacional, 1956); Oscar Teran, *Positivismo y nación en la Argentina* (Buenos Aires: Punto sur, 1987).

39. Bohdan Bociurkiw and Jonn W. Strong, eds., *Religion and Atheism in the USSR and Eastern Europe* (London: Macmillan, 1975).

40. It is symptomatic that the first study which systematically examined three different—one would say strikingly different—historical patterns of secularization did not come from a sociologist but, rather, from a historian of American religion. In *The Modern Schism*, Martin Marty examined the European continental pattern "towards utter secularity," England's pattern "towards mere secularity," and America's pattern "towards controlled secularity." Martin Marty, *The Modern Schism: Three Paths to the Secular* (New York: Harper & Row, 1969).

41. For a still unsurpassed analysis of "Catholic" secularization, see Bernhard Groethuysen, *Die Enstehung der bürgerlichen Welt-und Lebensanschauung in Frankreich*. 2 vols. (Halle, 1927–30), or the abridged English translation, *The Bourgeois: Catholicism versus Capitalism in Eighteenth-Century France* (New York: Holt, Rinehart & Winston, 1968).

42. In the dearth of comparative-historical, sociological studies of secularization David Martin's *A General Theory of Secularization* is perhaps the single outstanding exception. By taking into account the first three factors (Protestantism, the state, and the Enlightenment) plus the nature of the religious market (monopoly, duopoly, pluralist, etc.) and some other more historically particular variables, he has been able to differentiate systematically eight basic patterns and several subpatterns of secularization.

43. The two best-known theories of "modern" religion are Thomas Luck-

mann's theory of "the invisible religion" and Robert Bellah's less systematically developed twofold theory of modern religion, his theory of "civil religion," the public form of modern religion, and his theory of "modern religion" proper, its private form, developed within his theory of "religious evolution." Cf. Luckmann, *Invisible Religion,* and Robert Bellah, "Civil Religion in America" and "Religious Evolution," in *Beyond Belief: Essays on Religion in a Post-Traditional World* (New York: Harper & Row, 1970).

44. Most attempts I have seen that try to develop quantitative analyses of global religious trends appear to be nearly worthless. One cannot but look suspiciously upon theories based on quantitative data such as the following: "Spain—Catholic—100% in 1900—97.6% in 1970—Rate of decline 1970–1980 -.0007." James T. Duke and Barry L. Johnson, "Religious Transformations and Social Conditions: A Macrosociological Analysis," in William Swatos, Jr., ed., *Religious Politics in Global and Comparative Perspective* (New York: Greenwood Press, 1989), p. 108. Anybody who knows Spanish history knows also that such ciphers mean very little. Looking at the same kind of quantitative evidence which the authors offer for all the countries in the world, my intuitive guess is that well over half of the presented data are equally meaningless.

45. Frank Whaling, ed., *Religion in Today's World: The Religious Situation of the World from 1945 to the Present Day* (Edinburgh: T & T Clark, 1987). This is an excellent collection of essays by specialists discussing the religious situation in their respective areas of expertise. The collection includes entries on all the major world religions plus additional entries on "primal religions," Japan, China, "cults and civil religion," "secular world-views" and "spirituality."

46. Andrew Walls, "Primal Religious Traditions in Today's World," in Whaling, *Religion Today.*

47. Cf. Tu Wei-Ming, "The Religious Situation in the People's Republic of China Today," in Whaling, *Religion Today;* and Sabrina P. Ramet, *Social Currents in Eastern Europe* (Durham, N.C.: Duke University Press, 1991), and Pedro Ramet, ed., *Religion and Nationalism in Soviet and East European Politics* (Durham, N.C.: Duke University Press, 1989).

48. The introduction of evidence from Japan would not be pertinent here since I am discussing the process of secularization in strictly historical terms as the disintegration of Western Christendom and the process of differentiation which eventually replaced it. The very application of the concept of secularization to non-Western religions may be problematic. However, even a superficial look at the state of religion in Japan might serve to put into question some of the most cherished assumptions of the Enlightenment about religion and its future. Like the United States, Japan seems to be one of the most secular societies on earth, while being at the same time extremely hospitable to all kinds of religions. Indeed, one of the most striking aspects of religion in Japan is the coexistence and paradoxical fusion of what seem to be archaic sacromagical forms of religion (Shinto in all its various forms, public and private), historical universalist religions (Buddhism in all its striking forms, public and private), various "new" religions and "cults," including Christianity, and the most secular, worldly, and scientific world-views. In fact, since World War II Japanese society has experi-

enced several "rush hours of the gods." Equally striking from a Western perspective is the fact that the same individuals may actually partake variously in most of these forms of religion while also appearing, to Western eyes, to be hedonist, materialist, agnostic, and secular. A picture with the appropriate "surrealist" caption "A Buddhist Requiem for Broken Telephones at the Zojo-ji Temple in Tokio" may serve as the perfect illustration of this paradox. It shows three Buddhist monks, attired with the proper sacred vestments and implements, celebrating a ritual upon a pile of broken telephones, in front of a large seated audience of properly dressed men who would fit well in the boardrooms of corporate Japan. See Ninian Smart, *The World's Religions* (Englewood Cliffs, N.J.: Prentice-Hall, 1989), p. 465. In terms of Japan's "public" religions, equally interesting is the fact that both Buddhism and Shinto have alternated as established state religions in the past. Cf. Brian Bocking, "The Japanese Religious Tradition in Today's World, " in Whaling, *Religion Today;* Winston Davis, *Dojo: Magic and Exorcism in Modern Japan* (Stanford: Stanford University Press, 1980); H. B. Earhart, *Religions of Japan: Many Traditions within One Sacred Way* (San Francisco: Harper & Row, 1984); D. C. Holton, *Modern Japan and Shinto Nationalism* (New York: Paragon Books, 1963); Robert N. Bellah, *Tokugawa Religion* (Boston: Beacon Press, 1957); Horace McFarland, *The Rush Hour of the Gods* (New York: Macmillan, 1967); Anson Shupe, "Accommodation in the Third Civilization: The Case of Japan's Soka Gakkai Movement," in Jeffrey Hadden and Anson Shupe, eds., *Prophetic Religions and Politics* (New York: Paragon House, 1986).

49. Karl Marx, "On the Jewish Question," in *Early Writings* (New York: Vintage, 1975), pp. 217ff.

50. See Jon Butler, *Awash in a Sea of Faith: Christianizing the American People* (Cambridge: Harvard University Press, 1990).

51. Theodore Caplow et al. have revisited Middletown and found that, against the Lynd's own projections and expectations, most indicators show that since 1924 religion in Middletown has tended to rise rather than decline. Theodore Caplow et al., *All Faithful People: Change and Continuity in Middletown's Religion* (Minneapolis: University of Minnesota Press, 1983). Andrew Greeley has also shown that by most indicators the dominant religious trend in America since the 1940s has been continuity and persistence. Andrew Greeley, *Religious Change in America* (Cambridge, Mass.: Harvard University Press, 1989).

52. Theodore Caplow, "Contrasting Trends in European and American Religion," *Sociological Analysis* 46, no. 2 (1985).

53. In his 1904 visit to the United States, Max Weber was also struck by "the still impressively strong church-mindedness." Max Weber, "The Protestant Sects and the Spirit of Capitalism," in *From Max Weber,* p. 303. Three pages later, however, Weber corrects his first impression, stating that "church-mindedness *per se,* although still rather important, was rapidly dying out" (p. 306). Weber's observation could be interpreted either as anecdotal perceptive confirmation of the declining, secularizing trend in American religion from the 1890s to the 1920s, a trend noticed also by other observers such as the Lynds in their study of Middletown, or, rather, as I am inclined to think, as nothing

more than a confirmation of Weber's own assumptions about the universal process of secularization in the modern world. "Closer scrutiny," Weber adds, "revealed the steady progress of the characteristic process of 'secularization,' to which in modern times all phenomena that originated in religious conceptions succumb" (p. 307).

54. Luckmann, *Invisible Religion*, pp. 36–37. I have to admit that in 1984 I myself was still fully "European" in this respect, and I found Weber's and Luckmann's explanations naturally and intuitively convincing. See "The Politics of the Religious Revival."

55. This point is convincingly made by Sidney Ahlstrom in his now classic *A Religious History of the American People* (New Haven: Yale University Press, 1972).

56. The classic interpretation of American denominationalism along these lines is Sidney E. Mead, *The Lively Experiment* (New York: Harper & Row, 1976). One could suggest a similar explanation for another of the famous and puzzling American "exceptionalisms," that is, for the fact that generally throughout Europe the working class became de-Christianized and embraced socialism while the American working class did not. Why would Italian peasants become de-Christianized and embrace socialism or anarchism once they moved to Turin or Buenos Aires but not when they moved to New York? State repression of the socialist movements cannot be the explanation. What was different was the fact that state repression in Europe always came with the benediction of a state church. Furthermore, in Europe, in places where no state church existed or where the church tended to side with the workers (Poland, Ireland, the Basque country, etc.), the working class did not become de-Christianized either and one finds Catholic along with socialist trade unions.

57. Cf. "The church cannot share the temporal power of the state without being the object of a portion of that animosity which the latter excites. . . . Unbelievers in Europe attack Christians more as political than religious enemies; they hate the faith as the opinion of a party much more than as a mistaken belief, and they reject the clergy less because they are representatives of God than because they are the friends of authority." Alexis de Tocqueville, *Democracy in America*, vol. 1 (New York: Vintage, 1990), pp. 310 and 314. For Marx, "Since the existence of religion is the existence of a defect, the source of this defect must be looked for in the *nature* of the state itself." Marx, "On the Jewish Question," p. 217.

58. Caplow, "Contrasting Trends." In my view, however, Caplow misinterprets contemporary reality when he argues that it is the still continuous presence of church establishments throughout Europe that explains the still continuing decline.

59. See Andrew Greeley, *Religions and Values: Three English-Speaking Nations* (Chicago: NORC, 1987).

60. The thesis that there are close connections between the thesis of the secularizing decline of religion and the Enlightenment critique of religion is also old. Tocqueville exposed those connections very succinctly but, as with so many other aspects of his work, the social sciences preferred to ignore this insight.

"The philosophers of the eighteenth century explained in a very simple manner the gradual decay of religious faith. Religious zeal, said they, must necessarily fail the more generally liberty is established and knowledge diffused. Unfortunately, the facts by no means accord with their theory." *Democracy in America,* p. 308.

61. "What is Enlightenment?" Kant's reply to the query remains the best definition: "Enlightenment is man's release from his self-incurred tutelage. Tutelage is man's inability to make use of his understanding without direction from another. Self-incurred is this tutelage when its cause lies not in lack of reason but in lack of resolution and courage to use it without direction from another. *Sapere aude!* 'Have courage to use your own reason!'—that is the motto of enlightenment." Immanuel Kant, *Foundations of the Metaphysics of Morals and What Is Enlightenment?* (New York: Liberal Arts Press, 1959), p. 85. On the Enlightenment as an intellectual movement and its critique of religion, cf. Frank Manuel, *Changing of the Gods,* and *The Prophets of Paris* (New York: Harper & Row, 1965); Peter Gay, *The Enlightenment, an Interpretation: The Rise of Modern Paganism* (New York: Alfred A. Knopf, 1967); Lucien Goldmann, *The Philosophy of the Enlightenment: The Christian Burgess and the Enlightenment* (Cambridge, Mass.: MIT Press, 1973); Jacob, *Radical Enlightenment;* Paul Hazard, *The European Mind, 1680–1715* (London: Hollis & Carter, 1953); Reinhart Koselleck, *Critique and Crisis: Enlightenment and the Pathogenesis of Modern Society* (Cambridge, Mass.: MIT Press, 1988); Karl Löwith, *From Hegel to Nietzsche: The Revolution in Nineteenth-Century Thought* (New York: Holt, Rinehart & Winston, 1964); Sidney Hook, *From Hegel to Marx* (New York: Reynal & Hitchcock, 1936); Owen Chadwick, *The Secularization of the European Mind in the Nineteenth Century* (Cambridge: Cambridge University Press, 1975); Henri de Lubac, S.J., *The Drama of Atheist Humanism* (New York: Sheed & Ward, 1950); Henry F. May, *The Enlightenment in America* (New York: Oxford University Press, 1976); Bernard Bailyn, *The Ideological Origins of the American Revolution* (Cambridge, Mass.: Harvard University Press, 1967).

62. The cultural shock and religious crisis which the Darwinian revolution caused in Calvinist countries, while producing only ripples in Catholic countries, show the extent to which the Newtonian synthesis of faith and reason, with its premise that there could be no contradiction between the deist god of the Newtonian universe and the God of the Holy Scriptures, between natural and revealed religion, had been successful in Calvinist culture areas. On Scottish commonsense realism, the Enlightenment, and American Protestantism, cf. May, *The Enlightenment in America,* and Theodore Dwight Bozeman, *Protestants in an Age of Science: The Baconian Ideal and Antebellum American Religious Thought* (Chapel Hill, N.C.: University of North Carolina Press, 1977).

63. Cf. Durkheim, *Elementary Forms,* and E. E. Evans-Pritchard, *Theories of Primitive Religion* (Oxford: Oxford University Press, 1965). Ironically, even Durkheim, who recognized that the cognitive truth claims of religious worldviews were not essential to religion and that religion could therefore survive its historical competition with modern scientific worldviews by divesting itself of

these cognitive claims, nonetheless was caught in the same positivist fallacy. He had to explain religion as a primitive form of sociology in order to buttress Durkheimian sociology's own scientistic claims to be the new science of morality, whose task it was to replace the old religions in establishing the rational secular moral foundations of modern societies.

64. Max Weber, "Science as a Vocation," in *From Max Weber*.

65. Jean Jacques Rousseau, *The Social Contract* (New York: Hafner Publishing Co., 1947), pp. 119–20 and the entire section "Of Civil Religion."

66. Edward Gibbon, *The Decline and Fall of the Roman Empire*, vol. 1 (New York: Modern Library, 1932), pp. 25–26.

67. Frank Manuel, *The Changing of the Gods*, p. 38 and passim.

68. Cf. Karl Marx, "A Contribution to the Critique of Hegel's Philosophy of Right: Introduction," in *Early Writings*, pp. 243–45, and *Capital*, vol. 1 (New York: International Publishers, 1967), pp. 79–80.

69. Schluchter, *Rationalism, Religion*, p. 251 and passim.

70. Cf. Löwith, *From Hegel to Nietzsche;* Hook, *From Hegel to Marx;* and Rudolf Siebert, *The Critical Theory of Religion, the Frankfurt School* (New York: Mouton, 1985).

71. Cf. Herbert Marcuse, "A Study on Authority," in *Studies in Critical Philosophy* (Boston: Beacon Press, 1973), and Erich Fromm, *Escape from Freedom* (New York: Holt, Rinehart & Winston, 1941).

72. Paradoxically, while demanding the right to unlimited freedom of expression in the "public sphere," Kant reproduces the Lutheran split when he distinguishes between the "private" use of reason which one may make "in a particular civil post or office which is entrusted to him," as a military officer or as a clergyman heading a congregation, and the "public use of one's reason . . . as a scholar before the reading public." In the "private" sphere of the "office" one must obey without argument. "As a priest he is not free, nor can he be free, because he carries out the orders of another. But as a scholar, whose writings speak to his public, the world, the clergyman in the public use of his reason enjoys an unlimited freedom to use his own reason and to speak in his own person." Kant, "What Is Enlightenment?" pp. 87–88.

73. Frederick Engels, *Ludwig Feuerbach and the Outcome of Classical German Philosophy* (New York: International, 1941), p. 18.

74. Ludwig Feuerbach, *The Essence of Christianity* (New York: Harper & Row, 1957), pp. xvi–xviii. Ernst Bloch with his paradoxical "atheism for the sake of Christianity and Christianity for the sake of atheism" systematically followed this insight and line of thought in his utopian theory of religion.

75. Karl Löwith, *From Hegel to Nietzsche*, pp. 332ff.

76. Feuerbach, *Essence of Christianity*, pp. 12–13.

77. Ibid., p. 26.

78. Marx, *Early Writings*, pp. 252–53.

79. Sigmund Freud, "Obsessive Actions and Religious Practices," *The Standard Edition of the Complete Psychological Works of Sigmund Freud* (London: Hogarth Press, 1959), vol. 9, pp. 117–27; *Civilization and Its Discontents* (New York: Norton, 1962); *The Future of an Illusion* (Garden City, N.Y.: Anchor

Books, 1964); and Philip Rieff, *Freud: The Mind of the Moralist* (Chicago: University of Chicago Press, 1979).

80. Friedrich Nietzsche, *On the Genealogy of Morals* (New York: Vintage, 1967).

81. Feuerbach, *Essence of Christianity*, p. xliv.; and Löwith, *From Hegel to Nietzsche*, pp. 235–388.

82. Schluchter, *Rationalism, Religion*, pp. 253–54.

83. Thomas Luckmann, *Invisible Religion* (New York: Macmillan, 1967). In the following presentation I have drawn freely, at times literally, upon my own earlier and more elaborate presentation of Luckmann's thesis in "The Politics of the Religious Revival," pp. 9–12. It is important to stress that the structure of Luckmann's thesis would remain basically the same even if one were to admit that he undoubtedly exaggerated the decline and marginality of traditional religious institutions and their replacement by new "invisible" religions.

84. Luckmann, "Politics of the Religious Revival," p. 86.

85. One could perhaps say that, for some of the reasons enunciated above, solution (a) is the typical and generalized solution for a majority of American religious "believers," while solution (c) is the typical and generalized solution for a majority of European "unbelievers."

86. Luckmann, "Politics of the Religious Revival," p. 116.

87. Niklas Luhmann, "Durkheim on Morality and the Division of Labor" and "The Differentiation of Society," in *The Differentiation of Society* (New York: Columbia University Press, 1982).

88. Schluchter, *Rationalism, Religion*, p. 254.

89. Ibid., p. 256.

90. It was this insight that led to a fundamental revision in the Frankfurt school's critical theory of religion. Cf. Max Horkheimer and Theodor W. Adorno, *Dialectic of Enlightenment* (New York: Herder, 1972); Max Horkheimer, *Critique of Instrumental Reason* (New York: Seabury Press, 1974); and Theodor W. Adorno, "Theses upon Art and Religion Today," *Kenyon Review* 7, no. 4 (Autumn, 1945).

Chapter Two

1. Mary Douglas, "Judgements on James Frazer," *Daedalus*, Fall, 1978, p. 161.

2. Cf. Thomas J. Curry, *The First Freedoms: Church and State in America to the Passage of the First Amendment* (New York: Oxford University Press, 1986); William Lee Miller, *The First Liberty: Religion and the American Republic* (New York: Alfred A. Knopf, 1985); Georg Jellinek, *The Declaration of the Rights of Man and of Citizen* (Westport, Conn.: Hyperion Press, 1979).

3. H. J. McCloskey, "Privacy and the Right to Privacy," *Philosophy* 55 (1980); Edward Shils, "Privacy: Its Constitutions and Vicissitudes," *Law and Contemporary Problems* 31 (1966); Barrington Moore, Jr., *Privacy: Studies in Social and Cultural History* (Armonk, N.Y.: M. E. Sharpe, 1984).

4. Cf. Thomas Robbins and Roland Robertson, eds., *Church-State Relations:*

Tensions and Transitions (New Brunswick, N.J.: Transaction Books, 1987); Jeffrey K. Hadden and Anson Shupe, eds., *Prophetic Religions and Politics* (New York: Paragon House, 1986); and A. James Reichley, *Religion in American Public Life* (Washington, D.C.: Brookings Institution, 1985).

5. Jeff Weintraub, "The Theory and Politics of the Public/Private Distinction," in Jeff Weintraub and Krisnan Kumar, eds., *The Public/Private Distinction* (Chicago: University of Chicago Press, forthcoming).

6. See Jean L. Cohen and Andrew Arato, *Civil Society and Political Theory* (Cambridge, Mass.: MIT Press, 1992). The conception of civil society and of the public sphere used throughout this work is akin and much indebted to Cohen and Arato's theory.

7. See, for instance, Joseph Bensman and Robert Lilienfeld, *Between Private and Public: The Lost Boundaries of the Self* (New York: Free Press, 1979).

8. Cf. Erving Goffman, *Relations in Public: Microstudies of the Public Order* (New York: Basic Books, 1971) p. ix; *The Presentation of Self in Everyday Life* (Garden City, N.Y.: Doubleday, 1959); *Behavior in Public Places* (New York: Free Press, 1963); *Interaction Ritual* (New York: Anchor Books, 1967).

9. For a reconstruction as well as various critiques of the liberal conception of public and private, see S. I. Benn and G. F. Gaus, eds., *Public and Private in Social Life* (New York; St. Martin's Press, 1983).

10. Weintraub, "Public/Private."

11. Cf. Hannah Arendt, *The Human Condition* (Chicago: University of Chicago Press, 1958), and *On Revolution* (New York: Viking, 1963); Jürgen Habermas, *Structural Transformation of the Public Sphere* (Cambridge, Mass.: MIT Press, 1989), and "The Public Sphere," *New German Critique* 1, no. 3 (Fall, 1974); Seyla Benhabib, "Models of Public Space: Hannah Arendt, the Liberal Tradition and Jürgen Habermas," in Craig Calhoun, ed., *Habermas and the Public Sphere* (Cambridge, Mass.: MIT Press, 1991).

12. Cf. Albert O. Hirschman, *Shifting Involvements: Private Interest and Public Action* (Princeton: Princeton University Press, 1982); Alasdair MacIntyre, *After Virtue* (Notre Dame, Ind.: University of Notre Dame Press, 1981); Robert N. Bellah et al. *Habits of the Heart: Individualism and Commitment in American Life* (Berkeley: University of California Press, 1985).

13. Cf. Jean Bethke Elshtain, *Public Man, Private Woman* (Princeton: Princeton University Press, 1981), and "Moral Woman and Immoral Man: A Consideration of the Public-Private Split and Its Political Ramifications," *Politics and Society* 4, no. 4 (1974); Carole Pateman, "Feminist Critiques of the Public/Private Dichotomy," in Benn and Gaus, eds., *Public and Private*, pp. 281–303; Seyla Benhabib and Drucilla Cornell, eds., *Feminism as Critique* (Minneapolis: University of Minnesota Press, 1987).

14. In differentiating between these three levels of analysis, I am following Niklas Luhmann. See his "Interaction, Organization and Society," in *The Differentiation of Society* (New York: Columbia University Press, 1982), pp. 69–89.

15. William James, *The Varieties of Religious Experience* (New York: Penguin, 1982), p. 31. Italics in original text.

16. W. Robertson Smith, *Lectures on the Religion of the Semites* (New York: Macmillan, 1927) p. 55.

17. James, *Varieties of Religious Experience,* pp. 28–31 and passim.

18. Max Weber, *Economy and Society,* 2 vols. (Berkeley: University of California Press, 1978), vol. 1, chap. 6; vol. 2, chaps. 14–15. Indeed, W. James's few comments on institutional religion suggest Weber's theory of "routinization of charisma." For James, "Churches, when once established, live at second-hand upon tradition; but the *founders* of every church owed their power originally to the fact of their direct personal communion with the divine" (p. 30).

19. Emile Durkheim, *The Elementary Forms of the Religious Life* (New York: Free Press, 1965), pp. 59–63.

20. Bronislaw Malinowski, *Magic, Science and Religion* (Garden City, N.Y.: Doubleday, 1954), p. 57 and passim.

21. On the "individualist" aspects of primitive religion, see also, E. E. Evans-Pritchard, *Theories of Primitive Religion* (Oxford: Oxford University Press, 1965), and Paul Radin, *Monotheism among Primitive Peoples* (New York: Bollingen Foundation, 1954).

22. Max Weber, "The Social Psychology of the World Religions," in *From Max Weber,* p. 272.

23. W. Robertson Smith, *Religion of the Semites,* pp. 29 and 55.

24. In his study of *The Ancient City* Fustel de Coulanges writes that, "if we wished to give an exact definition of a citizen, we should say that it was a man who had the religion of the city. The stranger, on the contrary, is one who has not access to the worship, one whom the gods of the city do not protect, and who has not even the right to invoke them. . . . No one could become a citizen at Athens if he was a citizen in another city; for it was a religious impossibility to be at the same time a member of two cities, as it also was to be a member of two families. One could not have two religions at the same time." Fustel de Coulanges, *The Ancient City* (Garden City, N.Y.: Doubleday, Anchor Books, n.d.), pp. 194 and 196.

25. See W. James, *Varieties of Religious Experience,* pp. 127–258.

26. Following Max Weber, Benjamin Nelson made fraternization into a central category of his theory of processes of universalization. See Benjamin Nelson, *The Idea of Usury: From Tribal Brotherhood to Universal Otherhood* (Princeton: Princeton University Press, 1949), and *On the Roads to Modernity* (Totowa, N.J.: Rowman & Littlefield, 1981).

27. In this form, which basically implied that the church had to adapt to an already existing political structure which exercised control over it, the Byzantine church survived in the Second Rome and was continued in Muscovy, the Third Rome.

28. The unique complexity of Western developments was stressed by Joseph Strayer in "The State and Religion, an Exploratory Comparison in Different Cultures: Greece and Rome, the West, Islam," *Comparative Studies in Society and History* 1 (1958): 38–43. See also Randall Collins, "Historical Perspectives on Religion and Regime: Some Sociological Comparisons of Buddhism and Christianity," in Hadden and Shupe, *Prophetic Religions,* pp. 254–71.

29. See Edward Mortimer, *Faith and Power: The Politics of Islam* (New York: Vintage, 1982); and Hamid Dabashi, "Symbiosis of Religious and Political Authorities in Islam," in Robbins and Robertson, *Church-State,* pp. 183–203.

30. For Islam such an acceptance of modern processes of secularization is made much more difficult by the paradigmatic power of the myth of origins. Because the expansion of Western colonialism, the dissolution of the Turkish Empire, and the emergence of Islamic nation-states have undermined all the traditional historical forms of institutionalization of the *umma* as a dual religious and political community, it has opened up the way for all kinds of religious-political experiments in the name of returning to the original *umma*. It is misleading, therefore, to view Islamic "fundamentalism," assuming that the term itself is appropriate, primarily as an antimodern traditionalist reaction. It may be more appropriate to view it in its various manifestations as experiments in Islamic "reformation" and "revolution." On the varieties of such experiments and the ideas behind them, cf. Mortimer, *Faith and Power;* Hamid Enayat, *Modern Islamic Political Thought* (Austin: University of Texas Press, 1982); and James Piscatori, *Islam in the World of Nation-States* (New York: Cambridge University Press, 1986).

31. Karl Jaspers, *The Origin and Goal of History* (London: Routledge & Kegan Paul, 1953); Max Weber, *The Sociology of Religion* (Boston: Beacon Press, 1963).

32. Peter Brown, "Late Antiquity," in Philippe Ariès and Georges Duby, eds., *A History of Private Life,* vol. 1, *From Pagan Rome to Byzantium* (Cambridge, Mass.: Belknap Press of Harvard University Press, 1987), pp. 251–60.

33. Besides Max Weber and Ernst Troeltsch, I have also closely followed here Louis Dumont's analysis in his *Essays on Individualism: Modern Ideology in Anthropological Perspective* (Chicago: University of Chicago Press, 1986).

34. Cf. Mary Fulbrook, *Piety and Politics: Religion and the Rise of Absolutism in England, Württemberg, and Prussia* (New York: Cambridge University Press, 1983); and William J. Callahan and David Higgs, eds., *Church and Society in Catholic Europe of the Eighteenth Century* (Cambridge: Cambridge University Press, 1979).

35. On internal variations within Protestantism, cf. H. Richard Niebuhr, *Christ and Culture* (New York: Harper & Row, 1951), and Thomas G. Sanders, *Protestant Concepts of Church and State* (New York: Holt, Rinehart & Winston, 1964).

36. Weber, who was the originator of the church-sect typology later developed by Troeltsch, insisted that "a fully developed church—advancing universalist claims—cannot concede freedom of conscience" and that "the formula of the separation of church and state is feasible only if either of the two powers has in fact abandoned its claim to control completely those areas of life that are in principle accessible to it." Max Weber, "Sect, Church and Democracy," *Economy and Society,* vol. 2, pp. 1205 and 1207. Further, "Max Weber on Church, Sect and Mysticism," in Benjamin Nelson, ed., *Sociological Analysis* 34, no. 2 (1973): 140–49.

37. Ernst Troeltsch, *The Social Teaching of the Christian Churches,* 2 vols. (Chicago: University of Chicago Press, 1960). In typical German idealist fashion, Troeltsch conceived "church," "sect," and "individual mysticism" as the three alternative, yet equally authentic, forms of institutionalization of the Christian

idea in the world. Indeed, his magistral reconstruction of the history of Christianity is built as the logical and systematic unfolding of these three forms through history. For that very reason, Troeltsch could not have anticipated the emergence of what H. Richard Niebuhr called "the evil of denominationalism," since the denomination is not a form of institutionalization of the Christian idea but, rather, a form of adaptation of all religious organizations to the institutional differentiated structure of modernity. H. Richard Niebuhr, *The Social Sources of Denominationalism* (New York: Henry Holt & Co., 1929), p. 24.

38. Max Weber, "Religious Rejections of the World and Their Directions," "Science as a Vocation," and "Politics as a Vocation," in H. H. Gerth and C. W. Mills, eds., *From Max Weber* (New York: Oxford University Press, 1958).

39. This is shown by the tradition of social system analysis from Talcott Parsons to Niklas Luhmann. See, particularly, Niklas Luhmann, *The Differentiation of Society.* For a different perspective, see Benjamin Nelson, "Eros, Logos, Nomos, Polis: Shifting Balances of the Structures of Existence," in *On the Roads to Modernity* (Totowa, N.J.: Lowman & Littlefield, 1981).

40. See Robert Bellah's analysis of "modern religion" in "Religious Evolution," in *Beyond Belief* (New York: Harper & Row, 1970), pp. 39–44.

41. Bellah et al., *Habits of the Heart,* p. 221.

42. Troeltsch, *Social Teachings,* p. 997.

43. Including "those beliefs [which] certainly occupy in the life of that individual 'a place parallel to that filled by . . . God' (cf. *Seeger* 1965) in traditional religious persons" (*Welsh* 1970). From N. J. Demerath III and Rhys H. Williams, "A Mythical Past and Uncertain Future," in Robbins and Robertson, *Church-State Relations,* p. 80.

44. For references and a more systematic development of these points, see chaps. 6 and 7.

45. Robert Wuthnow, *The Restructuring of American Religion* (Princeton: Princeton University Press, 1988), chap. 5 and passim.

46. On the differences and ideological conflicts between Old Lights and New Lights, see Alan Heimert, *Religion and the American Mind: From the Great Awakening to the Revolution* (Cambridge, Mass.: Harvard University Press, 1966).

47. Alexis de Tocqueville, *Democracy in America* (New York: Vintage, 1990), vol. 1, p. 305. Religion may still be an important political institution in America even if one of the main reasons given by Tocqueville, that "it directs the customs of the community, and, by regulating domestic life, it regulates the state" (p. 304), may no longer be as valid today.

48. Jellinek, *Declaration of the Rights of Man.*

49. The separation of the state from religion and its supremacy over ecclesiastical institutions had already been defended by Hobbes in *De Cive* and first instituted in Lutheran Prussia under the absolutist rule of a Calvinist house. See Otto Hintze, "Calvinism and Raison d'Etat in Early Seventeenth-Century Brandenburg," in Felix Gilbert, ed., *The Historical Essays of Otto Hintze* (New York: Oxford University Press, 1975). Offering his rationale for welcoming Roman Catholics as citizens of his state, Frederick II, the enlightened absolutist

ruler and Voltaire's disciple, wrote: "All religions are equal and good, if only those people who profess them are honest people; and if Turks and heathens came and wanted to populate the country, we would build them mosques and churches," and "Religions must all be tolerated; only the Attorney General should see to it that none of them injures any other, for here everyone must be saved in his own fashion." Quoted in Peter Gay, *The Enlightenment,* pp. 348–49.

50. Thomas Robbins, "Church-State Tension in the United States," in Robbins and Robertson, *Church-State Relations,* pp. 67–75.

51. For some of these positions and debates, cf. Leonard Levy, *The Establishment Clause: Religion and the First Amendment* (New York: Macmillan, 1986); A. Stokes and Leo Pfeffer, *Church and State in the United States* (Westport, Conn.: Greenwood Press, 1975); Leo Pfeffer, *God, Caesar and the Constitution* (Boston: Beacon Press, 1974); Robert Drinan, *Religion, the Courts and Public Policy* (New York: McGraw-Hill, 1963); Richard Neuhaus, *The Naked Public Square* (Grand Rapids, Mich.: W. B. Eerdmans, 1984); James Reichley, *Religion in American Public Life.*

52. My argument here is similar to the one cogently made by Jean Cohen in a different context. See Jean Cohen, "Discourse Ethics and Civil Society," *Philosophy and Social Criticism* 14, 3/4 (1988).

53. Cf. Robert Bellah, "Civil Religion in America," *Daedalus* 96, no. 1 (1967); *The Broken Covenant: Civil Religion in Time of Trial* (New York: Seabury Press, 1975); Robert Bellah and Phillip Hammond, *Varieties of Civil Religion* (New York: Harper & Row, 1980); R. E. Richey and Donald G. Jones, eds., *American Civil Religion* (New York: Harper & Row, 1974); and Michael W. Hughey, *Civil Religion and Moral Order* (Westport, Conn.: Greenwood Press, 1983).

54. Jean Jacques Rousseau, *The Social Contract* (New York: Hafner Publishing Co., 1947).

55. Rousseau's anticlerical comments may serve to illuminate the contemporary globalization of Catholic politics and the way in which this globalization undermines the modern system of nation-states and contributes to the formation of a global civil society. "Communion and excommunication are the social compact of the clergy, by means of which they will always be masters over peoples and kings. All priests who communicate together, though they dwell in the two extremities of the earth, are fellow citizens; an invention which may be truly termed a masterpiece of politics." Rousseau, *Social Contract,* pp. 118–20. On globalization, see Roland Robertson and JoAnn Chirico, "Humanity, Globalization and Worldwide Religious Resurgence: A Theoretical Explanation," *Sociological Analysis* 46, no. 3 (1985), and Roland Robertson and William Garrett, eds., *Religion and Global Order* (New York: Paragon House, 1991).

56. Rousseau, *Social Contract,* pp. 120–21.

57. Ibid., pp. 123–24.

58. See Benjamin I. Schwartz, "The Religion of Politics: Reflections on the Thought of Hannah Arendt," *Dissent* 17 (March–April, 1970).

59. Alfred Stepan, *Rethinking Military Politics* (Princeton: Princeton University Press, 1988), pp. 3–12.

60. See Cohen and Arato, *Civil Society and Social Theory;* and Benhabib, "Models of Public Space."

61. The best and most systematic comparative-historical analysis of the various patterns of political mobilization of Christian religion in the modern world can be found in David Martin's *A General Theory of Secularization* (New York: Harper & Row, 1978). See, further, Joseph N. Moody, ed., *Church and Society: Social and Political Thought and Movements, 1789–1950* (New York: Arts, Inc., 1953); M. P. Fogarty, *Christian Democracy in Western Europe, 1820–1953* (Notre Dame, Ind.: University of Notre Dame Press, 1957); Ellen Lovell Evans, *The German Center Party, 1870–1933: A Study in Political Catholicism* (Carbondale: Southern Illinois University Press, 1974); Gianfranco Poggi, *Catholic Action in Italy: The Sociology of a Sponsored Organization* ((Stanford: Stanford University Press, 1967); Jean-Guy Vaillancourt, *Papal Power: A Study of Vatican Control over Lay Catholic Elites* (Berkeley: University of California Press, 1980); Owen Chadwick, *The Pope and European Revolution* (Oxford: Clarendon Press, 1981); Stein Rokkan, *Citizens, Elections and Parties* (Oslo: Universitets forlaget, 1970), and "Towards a Generalized Concept of Verzuiling: A Preliminary Note," *Political Studies* 4 (1977); J. Billiet and K. Dobbelaere, "Vers une déinstitutionalisation du pilier chrétien?" in L. Voyé et al., *La Belgique et ses dieux: Églises, mouvements religieux et laïques* (Louvain-la-Neuve: Cabay, 1985); K. Dobbelaere and J. Billiet, "Les changements internes du pilier Catholique en Flandre: D'un Catholicisme d'église à une Chrétienté Socio-culturelle," *Recherches sociologiques* 2, no. 14 (1983).

62. This does not exclude, of course, the possibility that some parties which continue to be called Christian-Democratic may last for some time or even emerge anew in Eastern Europe. Nor does it exclude the likelihood that open Protestant-Catholic warfare in Northern Ireland will continue into the future.

63. Such a development contrasts sharply, for instance, with the model of the ancient city where *oikos,* i.e., the household, was the sphere of "work," the sphere where all forms of human "labor" took place. The categories of Hannah Arendt's philosophical anthropology, as developed in *The Human Condition,* are informed precisely by the particular historical formation of antiquity. Arendt chose, as it were, to live in the categories of the Greek mind rather than mirror unreflectively, as most modern philosophies and the social sciences do, modern categories derived from the separation of "home" and "work."

64. Peter Berger, *The Sacred Canopy* (Garden City, N.Y.: Anchor Books, 1969), p. 138.

65. Ann Douglas, *The Feminization of American Culture* (New York: Alfred A. Knopf, 1977). For a more nuanced and complex historical analysis, see Nancy Cott, *The Bonds of Womanhood: 'Woman's Sphere' in New England, 1780–1835* (New Haven: Yale University Press, 1977).

66. See n. 12 above. Further, Rosemary Radford Ruether, "The Cult of True Womanhood," *Commonweal,* 9 November 1973. Paradoxically revealing, moreover, is the fact that, as pointed out by feminist critics, the public male/ private female split also runs internally through most religious institutions. The ministry and the ecclesiastical offices are reserved predominantly, in some denominations still exclusively, for males while the laity and churchgoers tend to be dispropor-

tionately female. Actually, it is this most female of spheres which reveals as perhaps no other sphere the signs of patriarchal domination. Cf. Mary Daly, *The Church and the Second Sex* (Boston: Beacon Press, 1985); Rosemary R. Ruether, *Sexism and God-Talk: Toward a Feminist Theology* (Boston: Beacon Press, 1983).

67. Benhabib, "Models of Public Space," p. 82.

68. Ibid., p. 22.

69. Ibid., pp. 88–89.

70. Ibid.

Part Two

1. It is important to realize that each of these documents was contested by traditionalist bishops at the Council, that it took several drafts and serious committee work until the documents were ready for passage by a two-thirds majority vote, and that everybody was aware that the documents constituted a departure from traditional theological definitions, even though they could be legitimated as a return to older, more authentic ones. See Walter M. Abbott, ed., *The Documents of Vatican II* (New York: Guild, 1966).

2. In terms of its effects on the tradition of authoritative magisterial teaching, the church is only now beginning to come to terms with, or actually trying to avoid the unintended consequences of, the modern principle of freedom of conscience.

3. The Ratzinger restoration is trying to revise the meaning of these four documents by stressing, (a) against doctrinal relativism and moral subjectivism, the duty of the individual conscience to submit to revealed truth and to the objective moral order; (b) against a "populist" definition of the church, the church as "supernatural mystery," and against an immanentist social gospel, the transcendent, eschatological, and spiritual character of God's Kingdom; (c) against the participation of the laity in the universal priesthood and of the theologians in the magisterium of the church, the hierarchic structure of the episcopal office under the authority of the pope; and (d) against the collegial structure of the episcopate and the doctrinal function of synods and episcopal conferences, the canonical, doctrinal, and ministerial sovereign jurisdiction of each bishop in direct communion with the pope. See Peter Hebblethwaite, *Synod Extraordinary: The Inside Story of the Rome Synod, November–December 1985* (Garden City, N.Y.: Doubleday, 1986).

4. Guillermo O'Donnell, "Tensions in the Bureaucratic-Authoritarian State and the Question of Democracy," in David Collier, ed., *The New Authoritarianism in Latin America* (Princeton: Princeton University Press, 1979).

Chapter Three

1. Brief but insightful histories of Spain are Jaime Vicens Vives, *Approaches to the History of Spain* (Berkeley: University of California Press, 1970), and Pierre Vilar, *Spain, a Brief History* (Oxford: Pergamon Press, 1967). Standard

histories of the period are J. H. Elliott, *Imperial Spain, 1469–1716* (New York: St. Martin's Press, 1964); Antonio Domínguez Ortiz, *El Antiguo Régimen: Los Reyes Católicos y los Austrias* (Madrid: Alianza, 1973). Further: Stanley Payne, *Spanish Catholicism: An Historical Overview* (Madison: University of Wisconsin Press, 1984); Henry Kamen, *The Spanish Inquisition* (New York: New American Library, 1966); Américo Castro, *The Spaniards: An Introduction to Their History* (Princeton: Princeton University Press, 1971); Claudio Sánchez-Albornoz, *Spain: A Historical Enigma* (Madrid: Fundación Universitaria Española, 1975); José Casanova, "The Spanish State and Its Relations with Society," *State, Culture, and Society* 1 no. 2 (Winter 1985); Fernando de los Ríos, *Religión y Estado en la España del Siglo XVI* (New York: Instituto de las Españas, 1927).

2. Cf. Fernand Braudel, *The Mediterranean and the Mediterranean World in the Age of Philip II*, 2 vols. (New York: Harper & Row, 1973); Perry Anderson, *Lineages of the Absolutist State* (London: New Left Books, 1974); Immanuel Wallerstein, *The Modern World System* (New York: Academic Press, 1974); Charles Tilly, ed., *The Formation of National States in Western Europe* (Princeton: Princeton University Press, 1975); Juan J. Linz, "Early State-Building and Late Peripheral Nationalisms against the State," in S. N. Eisenstadt and S. Rokkan, eds., *Building States and Nations* (Beverly Hills: Sage, 1973).

3. Cf. C. R. Boxer, *The Church Militant and Iberian Expansion, 1440–1770* (Baltimore: Johns Hopkins University Press, 1978); Geoffrey Parker, *The Army of Flanders and the Spanish Road, 1567–1659* (Cambridge: Cambridge University Press, 1972); J. H. Elliott, *The Revolt of the Catalans: A Study in the Decline of Spain (1598–1640)* (Cambridge: Cambridge University Press, 1963), and "Self-Perception and Decline in Early Seventeenth-Century Spain," *Past and Present* 74 (February 1977); Vicente Palacio Atard, *Derrota, Agotamiento, Decadencia en la España del Siglo XVII* (Madrid: Rialp, 1949); José A. Maravall, *Poder, Honor y Élites en el Siglo XVII* (Madrid: Siglo XXI, 1980); H. R. Trevor-Roper, "The General Crisis of the Seventeenth Century," in *Religion, the Reformation and Social Change* (London: Macmillan, 1967).

4. Cf. Luis Sánchez Agesta, *España al Encuentro de Europa* (Madrid: B.A.C., 1971); Pedro Laín Entralgo, *España Como Problema* (Madrid: Aguilar, 1957); Bernhardt Schmidt, *El Problema Español de Quevedo a Manuel Azaña* (Madrid: Edicusa, 1976); José Antonio Maravall, *Antiguos y Modernos* (Madrid: Sociedad de Estudios y Publicaciones, 1966); Ernesto and Enrique García Camarero, *La Polémica de la Ciencia Española* (Madrid: Alianza Editorial, 1970).

5. Cf. Richard Herr, *The Eighteenth Century Revolution in Spain* (Princeton: Princeton University Press, 1958); José A. Ferrer Benimeli, *Masonería, Iglesia e Ilustración*, 4 vols. (Madrid: F.U.E., 1975–77); William J. Callahan, *Church, Politics and Society in Spain, 1750–1874* (Cambridge, Mass.: Harvard University Press, 1984).

6. Cf. Miguel Artola, *Antiguo Régimen y Revolución Liberal* (Barcelona: Ariel, 1978); José Fontana Lázaro, *La Quiebra de la Monarquía Absoluta* (Barcelona: Ariel, 1971); Richard Herr, *An Historical Essay on Modern Spain* (Berkeley: University of California Press, 1970); Raymond Carr, *Spain. 1808–1939* (Oxford: Oxford University Press, 1970); Ramón Menéndez-Pidal, *The Span-*

iards in Their History (London: Hollis and Carter, 1950); Javier Herrero, *Orígenes del Pensamiento Reaccionario Español* (Madrid: Edicusa, 1973); José Manuel Cuenca, *La Iglesia Española ante la Revolución Liberal* (Madrid: Rialp, 1971); Emilio La Parra López, *El Primer Liberalismo Español y la Iglesia: Las Cortes de Cádiz* (Alicante: Instituto de Estudios Juan Gil-Albert, 1985); José Pérez Vilariño, *Inquisición y Constitución en España* (Madrid: ZYX, 1973).

7. Cf. Stanley Payne, *Politics and the Military in Modern Spain* (Stanford: Stanford University Press, 1967); Antoni Jutglar, *Ideologías y Clases en la España Contemporánea* (Madrid: Edicusa, 1968).

8. Cf. Callahan, *Church, Politics and Society;* Gerald Brenan, *The Spanish Labyrinth* (Cambridge: Cambridge University Press, 1943); Martin Blinkhorn, *Carlism and Crisis in Spain, 1931–1939* (Cambridge: Cambridge University Press, 1975); José M. Sánchez, *Reform and Reaction: The Politico-Religious Background of the Spanish Civil War* (Chapel Hill, N.C.: University of North Carolina Press, 1962); Joan C. Ullman, *La Semana Trágica: Estudios Sobre las Causas Socio-Económicas del Anticlericalismo en España* (Barcelona: Ariel, 1972); Julio Caro Baroja, *Introducción a una Historia Contemporánea del Anticlericalismo Español* (Madrid: Istmo, 1980).

9. David Martin, *A General Theory of Secularization* (New York: Harper & Row, 1978), p. 6.

10. Edward Malefakis, *Agrarian Reform and Peasant Revolution in Spain* (New Haven: Yale University Press, 1970); Pascual Carrión, *Los Latifundios en España* (Madrid: Gráficas Reunidas, 1932); Gabriel Jackson, "The Origins of Spanish Anarchism," *Southwestern Social Science Quarterly*, September 1955; Manuel Revuelta González, *La Exclaustración, 1833–1840* (Madrid: La Editorial Católica, 1976).

11. Cf. Antonio Ramos Oliveira, *Politics, Economics and Men of Modern Spain* (London: Victor Gollancz, 1946), p. 426; Jaime Vicens-Vives, *Historia de España y America*, vol. 5 (Barcelona: Editorial Vicens Vives, 1961), pp. 140–41; Payne, *Spanish Catholicism*, pp. 71–87; and Juan Sáez Marín, *Datos Sobre la Iglesia Española Contemporánea, 1768–1868* (Madrid: Editora Nacional, 1975).

12. While "tolerating" other religions, article 11 of the 1876 Constitution proclaimed that "Roman Catholicism is the religion of the state" and that "the Nation assumes the duty to maintain the [Catholic] cult and its ministers."

13. Cf. Frances Lannon, *Privilege, Persecution, and Prophecy: The Catholic Church in Spain, 1875–1975* (Oxford: Clarendon Press, 1987); Payne, *Spanish Catholicism;* Manuel Tuñón de Lara, *La España del Siglo XIX*, 2 vols. (Barcelona: Laia, 1980); José L. López Aranguren, *Moral y Sociedad* (Madrid: Edicusa, 1974); Domingo Benavides Gómez, *El Fracaso Social del Catolicismo Español* (Barcelona: Nova Terra, 1973); and *Democracia y Cristianismo en la España de la Restauración, 1875–1931* (Madrid: Ed. Nacional, 1978).

14. Cf. Yvonne Turin, *L'éducation et l'école en Espagne de 1874 à 1902* (Paris: P.U.F., 1959); J. B. Trend, *The Origins of Modern Spain* (New York: Russel & Russel, 1965); Elena de la Souchere, *An Explanation of Spain* (New

York: Random House, 1964); and the cited works of Lannon, Linz, Ullman, Brenan, and Herr.

15. Cf. E. Allison Peers, *Spain, the Church and the Orders* (London: Eyre & Spottiswoode, 1939); Gabriel Jackson, *The Spanish Republic and the Civil War* (Princeton: Princeton University Press, 1965); Richard Gunther and Roger Blough, "Religious Conflict and Consensus in Spain: A Tale of Two Constitutions," *World Affairs* 143 (Spring 1981); Herbert R. Southworth, *El Mito de la Cruzada de Franco* (Paris: Ruedo Ibérico, 1963); A. Montero Moreno, *Historia de la Persecución Religiosa en España, 1936–1939* (Madrid: B.A.C., 1961); Burnett Bollotten, *The Spanish Revolution* (Chapel Hill: University of North Carolina Press, 1979); Hilari Raguer, *La Espada y la Cruz (La Iglesia, 1936–1939)* (Barcelona: Bruguera, 1977); Julián Casanova et al., *El Pasado Oculto: Fascismo y Violencia en Aragón (1936–1939)* (Madrid: Siglo XXI, 1992).

16. On *Nacional-Catolicismo,* cf. Guy Hermet, *Les Catholiques dans l'Espagne Franquiste,* 2 vols. (Paris: Presses de la Fondation nationale de sciences politiques, 1980); Rafael Abella, *Por el Imperio Hacia Dios* (Barcelona: Planeta, 1978); J. M. Laboa, *El Integrismo* (Madrid: Narcea, 1985); William Ebenstein, *Church and State in Franco Spain* (Princeton: Center for International Studies, 1960); Norman Cooper, *Catholicism and the Franco Regime* (Beverly Hills: Sage, 1975); Ramón Garriga, *El Cardenal Segura y el Nacional Catolicismo* (Barcelona: Planeta, 1977); Juan José Pérez Rico, *El Papel Político de la Iglesia Católica en la España de Franco* (Madrid: Tecnos, 1977). On the fascist character of the Franco regime, cf. Juan Linz, "Some Notes toward a Comparative Study of Fascism in Sociological Historical Perspective," in Walter Lacqueur, ed., *Fascism: A Reader's Guide* (London: Wildwood House, 1976); and Julián Casanova, "La Sombra del Franquismo: Ignorar la Historia y Huir del Pasado," in *El Pasado Oculto.*

17. Cf. Juan J. Linz, "An Authoritarian Regime: The Case of Spain," in E. Allardt and Yrjo Littunen, eds., *Cleavages, Ideologies and Party Systems* (Helsinki: Academic Bookstore, 1964); Hermet, *Les Catholiques,* vol. 1, *Les acteurs du jeu politique;* Rafael Gómez Pérez, *Política y Religión en el Régimen de Franco* (Barcelona: Dopesa, 1976); B. Oltra and A. de Miguel, "Bonapartismo y catolicismo: Una hipótesis sobre los orígenes ideológicos del franquismo," *Revista de Sociología* 8 (1978); José Casanova, *The Opus Dei Ethic and the Modernization of Spain* (forthcoming); Jesús Ynfante, *La Prodigiosa Aventura del Opus Dei* (Paris: Ruedo Ibérico, 1970); A. Sáez Alba, *La Asociación Católica Nacional de Propagandistas* (Paris: Ruedo Ibérico, 1974); Daniel Artigues, *El Opus Dei en España* (Paris: Ruedo Ibérico, 1971).

18. Cf. Francisco Franco Bahamonde, *Palabras del Caudillo, 1937–1943* (Madrid: Editora Nacional, 1943); *Discursos y Mensajes del Jefe del Estado, 1955–1959* (Madrid: Editora Nacional, 1960); *Pensamiento Político de Franco* (Madrid: Ed. del Movimiento, 1975); Joachim Boor (Franco), *Masonería* (Madrid, 1952); Luis Carrero Blanco, *Discursos y Escritos, 1943–1973* (Madrid: I.E.P., 1974); Juan de la Cosa (Carrero Blanco), *Spain and the World* (Madrid: Publicaciones Españolas, 1954), and *Las Modernas Torres de Babel* (Madrid: Ediciones Idea, 1956).

19. José Casanova, "Modernization and Democratization: Reflections on Spain's Transition to Democracy," *Social Research* 50, no. 4, (Winter 1983); Francisco Gil Delgado, *Conflicto Iglesia-Estado (1808–1975)* (Madrid: Sedmay, 1975).

20. On "the pattern of reactive organicism" and Spain, see David Martin, *A General Theory of Secularization* (New York: Harper & Row, 1978), pp. 244–78.

21. Aurelio Orensanz, *Religiosidad Popular Española (1940–1965)* (Madrid: Editora Nacional, 1974).

22. Cf. José L. L. Aranguren, *Catolicismo y Protestantismo Como Formas de Existencia* (Madrid: Revista de Occidente, 1952); *Catolicismo Día Tras Día* (Barcelona: Noguer, 1955); *Contralectura del Catolicismo* (Barcelona: Planeta, 1978); Pedro Laín Entralgo, *El Cristiano en el Mundo* (Madrid: Propaganda Popular Católica, 1961); Federico Sopeña, *En Defensa de una Generación* (Madrid: Taurus, 1970).

23. P. Llabres i Martorell, "Cursets de Cristiandat: Un moviment apostolic mallorqui pels quatre vents del mon," *Questions de Vida Cristiana* 75–76 (1975); José Casanova, "The First Secular Institute: The Opus Dei as a Religious Movement-Organization," *Annual Review of the Social Sciences of Religion* 6 (1982); and *The Opus Dei Ethic and the Modernization of Spain.*

24. See José Castaño Colomer, *La JOC en España (1946–1970)* (Salamanca: Sígueme, 1978); and Hermet, *Les Catholiques.*

25. José Casanova, "The Opus Dei Ethic, the Technocrats and the Modernization of Spain," *Social Science Information* 22, no. 1 (1983).

26. Xavier Tusell, *La Oposición Democrática al Franquismo* (Barcelona: Planeta, 1977); Gonzalo Fernández de la Mora, *El Crepúsculo de las Ideologías* (Buenos Aires: Ed. Andina, 1970); Laureano López Rodó, *Política y Desarrollo* (Madrid: Aguilar, 1970); "Prólogo," to W. W. Rostow, *Política y Etapas de Crecimiento* (Barcelona: Dopesa, 1972).

27. Javier Angulo Uribarri, *Documentos socio-políticos de obispos españoles (1968–1972)* (Madrid: Propaganda Popular Católica, 1972).

28. Alfonso C. Comín, *España, ¿País de Misión?* (Barcelona: Salvaterra, 1966); Rogelio Duocastella et al., *Análisis Sociológico del Catolicismo Español* (Barcelona: Nova Terra, 1967); Fundación Foessa, *Informe Sociológico Sobre la Situación Social de España* (Madrid: Euramérica, 1971).

29. Pierre Jobit, *L'église d'Espagne à l'heure du Concile* (Paris: Spes, 1965).

30. Javier Tusell, *Historia de la Democracia Cristiana en España*, 2 vols. (Madrid: Edicusa, 1974); Manuel Fernández Areal, *La Política Católica en España* (Barcelona: Dopesa, 1970), and *La Libertad de Prensa en España, 1938–1971* (Madrid: Edicusa, 1971); Rafael Gómez Pérez, *Conciencia Cristiana y Conflictos Políticos* (Barcelona: Dopesa, 1972).

31. Cf., for instance, *Ecclesia, Vida Nueva, Razón y Fe.*

32. The clash between the young urbanized priest and the traditional Catholicism of rural Spain is well captured in the ethnography of the Spanish village of the period. Cf. William Christian, Jr., *Person and God in a Spanish Village* (New York: Seminar Press, 1972); Joseph Aceves, *Social Change in a Spanish Village*

(Cambridge, Mass.: Schenkman, 1971); Richard Barrett, *Benabarre, the Modernization of a Spanish Village* (New York: Holt, Rinehart & Winston, 1974); C. Lisón-Tolosana, *Belmonte de los Caballeros* (Oxford: Oxford University Press, 1966).

33. Cf. Lannon, *Privilege,* pp. 89–115; Payne, *Catolicismo,* pp. 225ff.; Victor Pérez Díaz, *El Retorno de la Sociedad Civil* (Madrid: Instituto de Estudios Económicos, 1987) chap. 15; Enrique Miret Magdalena, *Los Nuevos Católicos* (Barcelona: Nova Terra, 1966).

34. José M. Martín Patino, "La iglesia en la sociedad española," in Juan J. Linz, ed., *España: Un Presente para el Futuro,* vol. 1, *La Sociedad* (Madrid: Instituto de Estudios Económicos, 1984); Ruiz Rico, *Papel de la Iglesia,* pp. 189 and 213.

35. José L. Martín Descalzo, *Tarancón, el Cardenal del Cambio* (Barcelona: Planeta, 1982).

36. Ruiz Rico, *Papel de la Iglesia,* p. 236.

37. Alfonso C. Comín, *Cristianos en el Partido, Comunistas en la Iglesia* (Barcelona: Laia, 1977).

38. José M. Maravall, *Dictatorship and Political Dissent: Workers and Students in Franco's Spain* (London, Tavistock, 1978).

39. Juan J. Linz, "Religion and Politics in Spain: From Conflict to Consensus above Cleavage," *Social Compass* 27, nos. 2–3 (1980); Rafael del Aguila y Ricardo Montero, *El Discurso Político de la Transición Española* (Madrid: C.I.S., 1984).

40. Antonio Hernández Gil, *El cambio político español y la constitución* (Barcelona: Planeta, 1982); Emilio Attard, *La constitución por dentro* (Barcelona: Planeta, 1983); Joaquín Ruiz Giménez, "El papel del consenso en la constitución del estado democrático," *Sistema* 38–39, (1980). Basque nationalists were the only significant political force which chose not to take part in the making of the new constitution.

41. Richard Gunther and Roger Blough, "Religious Conflict and Consensus in Spain: A Tale of Two Constitutions," *World Affairs* 143 (Spring 1981).

42. For a noteworthy attempt to rethink these issues theologically and systematically, see Olegario González de Cardenal, *España por Pensar: Ciudadanía Hispánica y Confesión Católica* (Salamanca: Ediciones Universidad de Salamanca, 1984). In the case of Spain, the main competition facing Catholicism as a denomination does not come from other religions but, rather, from secular worldviews, which for many Spaniards have come to replace traditional religious ones.

43. Centro de Investigaciones Sociológicas (C.I.S.), "Iglesia, religión y política," *Revista Española de Investigaciones Sociológicas,* no. 27 (July–September 1984).

44. J. J. Toharia, *Los Jóvenes y la Religión* (Madrid: Fundación Santa María, 1985).

45. Martín Patino, "La Iglesia en la sociedad," pp. 202ff.

46. Pérez Díaz, *El Retorno de la Sociedad,* p. 457.

47. Ibid., p. 459.

48. Ibid., p. 460.

49. *El País*, Edición Internacional, Madrid, 30 September 1991, pp. 16–17.

Chapter Four

1. For good historical surveys of Poland, see Norman Davies, *God's Playground: A History of Poland*, 2 vols. (New York: Columbia University Press, 1982), and *Heart of Europe: A Short History of Poland* (Oxford: Clarendon Press, 1984). On the church and Catholicism in Polish history, cf. Bogdan Szajkowski, *Next to God . . . Poland* (New York: St. Martin's Press, 1983); Adam Piekarski, *The Church in Poland* (Warsaw: Interpress, 1978); and Oscar Halecki, *Tysiąclecie Polski katolickiej* (London: Veritas, 1966). On the fusion of Polish national and Catholic identities, see Konstantin Symmons-Symonolewicz, *National Consciousness in Poland* (Meadville, Pa.: Maplewood Press, 1983).

2. On religious pluralism, toleration, and conflict in early modern Poland, cf. Oscar Halecki, *From Florence to Brest* (Rome: Sacrum Poloniae Millennium, 1958); Ambroise Jobert, *De Luther à Mohila: La Pologne dans la crise de la chrétienté, 1517–1648* (Paris: Institut d'Etudes Slaves, 1974); Stanislaw Kot, *Georges Niemirycz et la lutte contre l'intolerance au 17-e siècle* (The Hague: Mouton, 1960); Frank E. Sysyn, *Between Poland and the Ukraine: The Dilemma of Adam Kysil, 1600–1653* (Cambridge, Mass.: Harvard University Press, 1985); Harry Dembkowski, *The Union of Lublin, Polish Federalism* (Boulder, Colo.: East European Monographs, 1982); Feliks Gross, "Tolerance and Intolerance in Poland: The Two Political Traditions," *Polish Review* 20 (1975).

3. David Martin, *A General Theory of Secularization* (New York: Harper & Row, 1978).

4. Cf. Andrzej Walicki, *Philosophy and Romantic Nationalism: The Case of Poland* (Oxford: Clarendon Press, 1982); Adam Bromke, *Poland's Politics: Idealism vs. Realism* (Cambridge, Mass.: Harvard University Press, 1967); Piotr Wandycz, *The Land of Partitioned Poland, 1795–1918* (Seattle: University of Washington Press, 1974); and Czesław Strzeszewski et al., *Historia Katolicyzmu społecznego w Polsce, 1832–1939* (Warsaw: Ośrodek Dokumentacji Studiów Społecznych, 1981).

5. Józef Majka, "The Character of Polish Catholicism," *Social Compass* 15, nos. 3–4 (1968).

6. Cf. Maciej Pomian-Srzednicki, *Religious Change in Contemporary Poland: Secularization and Politics* (London: Routledge & Kegan Paul, 1982); Georges Castellan, *Dieu garde la Pologne! Histoire du Catholicisme polonais, 1795–1980* (Paris: Laffont, 1981); Olga Narkiewicz, *The Green Flag: Polish Populist Politics, 1867–1970* (London: Croom Helm, 1976).

7. While in 1931 Catholics composed 65 percent of Poland's population, by 1946 the number of Catholics had risen to 96.6 percent of the population within Poland.

8. Jan de Weydenthal, *The Communists of Poland* (Stanford: Hoover Institu-

tion, 1986); Teresa Torańska, *"Them": Stalin's Polish Puppets* (New York: Harper & Row, 1987).

9. Czesław Miłosz, *The Captive Mind* (New York: Random House, 1951).

10. Szajkowski, *Next to God;* Ronald Monticone, *The Catholic Church in Communist Poland, 1945–1985* (Boulder, Colo.: East European Monographs, 1986).

11. Bohdan Bociurkiw and John Strong, eds., *Religion and Atheism in the USSR and Eastern Europe* (London: Macmillan, 1975); Eric Weingartner, ed., *Church within Socialism: Church and State in East European Republics* (Rome: IDOC, 1976); Jakov Jukic, "La religion et les sécularismes dans les sociétés socialistes," *Social Compass* 28, no. 1 (1981).

12. Lucjan Blit, *The Eastern Pretender* (London: Hutchinson, 1965); Andrzej Micewski, *Katolische Gruppierungen in Polen, Pax und Znak, 1945–1976* (Munich: Kaiser, 1978); Dennis Dunn, *Detente and Papal-Communist Relations, 1962–1978* (Boulder, Colo.: Westview Press, 1979).

13. Andrzej Micewski, *Cardinal Wyszyński: A Biography* (New York: Harcourt Brace, 1984). This work is perhaps the best single source on church-state-society relations in Communist Poland. See also Peter Raina, *Stefan Cardinal Wyszyński, Prymas Polski,* 2 vols. (London: Poets' and Painters' Press, 1979).

14. For a typical example, see Antoni Nowicki, *Wykłady o krytyce religii w Polsce* (Warsaw: Książka i Wiedza, 1965).

15. Karol Borowski, "Religion and Politics in Post–World War II Poland," in J. K. Hadden and A. Shupe, eds., *Prophetic Religions and Politics* (New York: Paragon House, 1986), and "Secular and Religious Education in Poland," *Journal of Religious Education* 70, no. 1 (1975); Ewa Morawska, "Civil Religion versus State Power in Poland," in Th. Robbins and R. Robertson, eds., *Church-State Relations* (New Brunswick: Transaction Books, 1987); Władysław Piwowarski, "Polish Catholicism as an Expression of National Identity," in L. S. Graham and M. K. Ciechocińska, *The Polish Dilemma* (Boulder, Colo.: Westview Press, 1987); Józef Majka, "Historical and Cultural Conditions of Polish Catholicism," *The Christian in the World* 14 (1981).

16. Lucjan Blit, "The Insoluble Problem: Church and State in Poland," *Religion in Communist Lands* 1, no. 3 (1973); Wiesław Mysłek, "Państwo i Kościół," *Nowe Drogi* 5 (1979); Zenon Rudny, "Cesarzowi—co Cesarskie, Bogu—co Boskie," *Polityka,* 242 October 1983.

17. Pomian-Srzednicki, *Religious Change;* Vincent Chrypinski, "Political Changes under Gierek," *Canadian Slavonic Papers* 15 (1973).

18. T. M. Jaroszewski, *Laicyzacja* (Warsaw: Książka i Wiedza, 1966), and "Pratiques et conceptions religieuses en Pologne," *Recherches internationales à la lumière du Marxisme,* 1965; Edward Ciupak, *Katolicyzm ludowy w Polsce* (Warsaw: PWN [Państwowe Wydawnictwo Naukowe], 1973); Jan Jerschina, *Młodzież i procesy laicyzacji świadomości społecznej* (Warsaw: PWN, 1978); Hieronim Kubiak, *Religijność a środowisko społeczne* (Kraków: Ossolineum, 1972).

19. Pomian-Srzednicki, *Religious Change;* Michael D. Kennedy and Maurice

D. Simon, "Church and Nation in "Socialist Poland," in Peter Merkl and Ninian Smart, eds., *Religion and Politics in the Modern World* (New York: New York University Press, 1983); Władysław Piwowarski, *Religijność wiejska w warunkach urbanizacji* (Warsaw: Więź, 1976); Witold Zdaniewicz, *Kościół Katolicki w Polsce* (Poznan-Warsaw: Pallottinum, 1979).

20. Micewski, *Wyszyński*, pp. 342–43. Further, Stefan Wyszyński, *A Freedom Within: The Prison Notes* (New York, Harcourt Brace, 1983), and *Kościół w sluzbie Narodu* (Poznan: Pallottinum, 1981). As in any highly rhetorical statement, the fundamental question is not whether it is true but whether it works. No Spanish cardinal could have ever pronounced such a sermon, and if anyone did, it would have had the opposite ideological effects than those intended by the rhetoric. There is sufficient evidence that most Poles found this rhetoric more acceptable than the counterrhetoric of the Communist regime, these two being the two main competing public rhetorics or ideological claims in Poland in the 1960s. According to an observer as perceptive and unbiased as Adam Michnik, Wyszyński's "greatness consisted in his flawless decoding of the nature of communism and his brilliant strategy of resistance. In this the cardinal was remarkably modern. But this modernness of practice went together with an anachronistic rhetoric and doctrine. His was the anticommunism of a conservative." Adam Michnik, *The Church and the Left* (Chicago: University of Chicago Press, 1993), pp. xiii–xiv.

21. Karol Górski, "L'histoire de la spiritualité polonaise," in *Poland's Millennium of Catholicism* (Lublin, Scientific Society of the Catholic University of Lublin, 1969); Jerzy Braun, "A Thousand Years of Christianity in Poland," in *Poland in Christian Civilization* (London: Veritas Foundation, 1983); Stefan Czarnowski, "Kultura religijna wiejskiego ludu polskiego," *Dzieła*, vol. 1, (Warsaw, 1956), pp. 88–107; Thomas W. I. and F. Znaniecki, *The Polish Peasant in Europe and America* (New York: Dover, 1958); *Social Compass* 15, nos. 3–4 (1968) (special issue on Poland with essays by J. Majka, W. Zdaniewicz, W. Piwowarski, et al.).

22. Ruben Cesar Fernandez, "Images de la Passion: L'église Catholique au Brésil et en Pologne," *Esprit*, December 1987.

23. More than any other Catholic church in the world, and in remarkable contrast with the Brazilian Catholic church, the Polish Catholic church exhibits an ideal-typical pyramidal structure. It is hierarchically concentrated at the top, around the Primate, with a solid clerical middle structure—245 priests per bishop and 1,860 inhabitants per priest—and a massive lay base devoid of much autonomy. See, Fernandes, "Images de la Passion."

24. Władysław Piwowarski, "The Image of the Priest in the Eyes of Parishioners in Three Rural Parishes," *Social Compass* 15, nos. 3–4 (1968); Bohdan Cywiński, "Myśli o polskim duszpasterstwie," *Znak* 23, no. 204 (1971).

25. Cf. Monticone, *Catholic;* Szajkowski, *Next to God;* and Lawrence Biondi, *Poland's Church-State Relations* (Chicago: Loyola University Press, 1981).

26. S. Małkowski, "Kościół a totalitaryzm," *Spotkania* (London) 3 (1978); and Michnik, *The Church and the Left.*

27. Jakub Karpiński, *Countdown: The Polish Upheavals of 1956, 1968,*

1970, 1976, 1980 (New York: Karz-Cohl, 1982); Peter Raina, *Political Opposition in Poland, 1954–1977* (London: Poets' and Painters' Press, 1978).
28. Szajkowsky, *Next to God,* p. 32.
29. Jan Lipski, *KOR* (Berkeley: University of California Press, 1985); Alain Touraine et al., *Solidarity: Poland, 1980–1981* (Cambridge: Cambridge University Press, 1983); Neal Ascherson, *The Polish August* (New York: Viking Press, 1982); Timothy G. Ash, *The Polish Revolution* (New York: Scribners, 1983); Abraham Brumberg, ed., *Poland: Genesis of a Revolution* (New York: Random House, 1983); Jadwiga Staniszkis, *Poland's Self-Limiting Revolution* (Princeton: Princeton University Press, 1984); Andrew Arato, "Civil Society against the State: Poland, 1980–1981," *Telos,* Spring 1981.
30. Cf. *Listy Pasterskie Episkopatu Polski, 1945–1974* (Paris: Editions du Dialogue, 1975); Jesús Iribarren, *Documentos Colectivos del Episcopado Español, 1870–1974* (Madrid: Editorial Católica, 1974); *Estudos da CNBB* and *Documentos da CNBB,* both series published periodically by Edições Paulinas of São Paulo.
31. John Courtney Murray showed most convincingly that the adoption of the discourse of human rights by the popes in their encyclicals, incipiently in the 1950s by Pius XII and definitively by John XXIII, found theological justification as the transference of the traditional and zealously guarded principle of *libertas ecclesiae* to the individual human person. See John Courtney Murray, "The Problem of Religious Freedom," *Theological Studies* 25 (1964): 503–75. The adoption of the new discourse by the Polish episcopate was nonetheless remarkable, given Cardinal Wyszyński's deep and well-known distrust of Vatican II. According to Michnik, "Modernity and the language of human rights left a foul scent for him as if part of some devious Masonic plot." Michnik, *The Church and the Left,* p. xiv.
32. Cf. Brian Smith, "Churches and Human Rights in Latin America," *Journal of Interamerican Studies and World Affairs* 21 (February 1979); David Hollenbach, *Claims in Conflict: Retrieving and Renewing the Catholic Human Rights Tradition* (New York: Paulist Press, 1979); Hubert Lepargneur, *A Igreja e o Reconhecimiento dos Direitos Humanos na Historia* (São Paulo: Cortez e Moraes, 1977); Robert F. Drinan, *Cry of the Opressed: The History and Hope of the Human Rights Revolution* (San Francisco: Harper & Row, 1987); Penny Lernoux, *Cry of the People* (New York: Penguin, 1980).
33. At long last, this seminal text of modern Polish intellectual and political history is available in English. First published in exile in 1976, it appeared in a French edition in 1979 and was first published in Poland in 1981. The American edition, edited and translated by David Ost, includes an excellent introduction by Mr. Ost explaining the hermeneutic context and the effective and controversial history of the text, as well as a series of "Afterwords" written by Michnik from 1976 to 1987 either as replies to the critics or as reviews of new "troubles" in the fragile Polish dialogue between the church and the left. It is a remarkable fact that this crucial document of the Eastern European Marxian-Christian dialogue encountered difficulties finding a publisher in America, while dozens of intellectually and politically much less relevant texts of the Latin-American ver-

sion of the dialogue easily found both publishers and eager audiences. Even the rather harsh and unfriendly critique by Józef Tischner, the leading Polish Catholic theologian, who also played a prominent role as spiritual mentor of Solidarity, found its way into the American literary market (ironically with a friendly Foreword by Michnik) sooner than Michnik's original text. See Józef Tischner, *Marxism and Christianity: The Quarrel and the Dialogue in Poland* (Washington: Georgetown University Press, 1987); and *The Spirit of Solidarity* (New York: Harper & Row, 1984).

34. In one of his typical early critiques of Polish Catholicism, Kołakowski had characterized Catholicism as "traditional, obscurantist, fanatical and dim-witted, with a decidedly provincial character." Leszek Kołakowski, *Notatki o współczesnej kontrreformacji* (Warsaw: Książka i Wiedza, 1962), p. 53. The personal and intellectual development of Kołakowski is perhaps the paradigmatic and most influential example of the transformation of the Polish left from a typical secularist, anticlerical position (in the Stalinist years he viewed himself as "a personal enemy of God") to a new open understanding and respect for religion and Polish Catholicism. For examples of Kołakowski's revised views, see Leszek Kołakowski, "La revanche du sacré," *Contrepoint* 13 (1977), and *Religion* (New York: Oxford University Press, 1982).

35. Michnik, *The Church and the Left*, p. xi. See also Leszek Kołakowski and Jan Gross, "Church and Democracy in Poland: Two Views," *Dissent*, Summer, 1980.

36. Ferenc Fehér and Agnes Heller, *Eastern Left, Western Left* (Cambridge: Polity Press, 1987); Adam Podgórecki, *The Polish Burial of Marxist Ideology* (London: Poets' and Painters' Press, 1981); Jeffrey C. Goldfarb, *Beyond Glasnost: The Post-Totalitarian Mind* (Chicago: University of Chicago Press, 1989); Andrew Arato, "Social Theory, Civil Society, and the Transformation of Authoritarian Socialism," in Ferenc Fehér and Andrew Arato, eds., *Crisis and Reform in Eastern Europe* (New Brunswick, N.J.: Transaction Books, 1991).

37. Pedro Ramet, ed., *Religion and Nationalism in Soviet and East European Politics* (Durham, N.C.: Duke University Press, 1989).

38. Indeed, the three historical traditions of Catholic, nationalist, and working-class solidarity, which in most countries have remained separate, often in an antagonistic relationship, came together to constitute the uniqueness of Solidarity as a movement. I believe that this unique historical configuration offers a better explanation for the persistently egalitarian, though not necessarily democratic, character of the values and attitudes of the Polish people than the ideological success of a socialist regime which in every other respect was so unsuccessful ideologically. For the latter view, see Stefan Nowak, "Values and Attitudes of the Polish People," *Scientific American* 245, no. 1 (July 1981).

39. Micewski, *Pax und Znak*; Michnik, *The Church and the Left*; Anton Pospieszalski, "Lay Catholic Organizations in Poland," *Survey* 24, no. 4 (Autumn 1979); P. Jegliński and A. Tomsky, " 'Spotkania'—Journal of the Catholic Opposition in Poland," *Religion in Communist Lands* 7, no. 1 (1979); Andrzej Świecicki, "Les origines institutionelles de mouvement 'Znak,' " *Actes de la 12ième conférence de sociologie religieuse* (Lille: CSIR, 1973); Bohdan Cywiński,

Doswiadczenie Polskie (Paris: Spotkania, 1984), and *Rodowody Niepokornych* (Warsaw: Więź, 1971).

40. Cf. Mieczysław Malinski, *Pope John Paul II: The Life of Karol Wojtyła* (New York: Seabury, 1979); George Williams, *The Mind of John Paul II: Origins of His Thought and Action* (New York: Seabury Press, 1981); George Blazynski, *Pope John Paul II* (London: Weidenfeld-Nicholson, 1979).

41. Grażyna Sikorska, "The Light-Life Movement in Poland," *Religion in Communist Lands* 2, no. 1 (1983). Cardinal Wojtyła also became an early sponsor and protector of the Opus Dei within the Roman Catholic church. For a more critical view of Wojtyła's conservatism, his role at Vatican II, and his project of restoration, see Peter Hebblethwaite, *Synod Extraordinary: The Inside Story of the Rome Synod, November–December 1985* (Garden City, N.Y.: Doubleday, 1986). Michnik has offered an apt characterization: "Wojtyła was the hope of intellectuals. He shunned nationalist rhetoric yet remained deeply rooted in the national tradition. He opposed communism in the name of human rights, broadly understood, yet maintained strong reservations toward the Western model of a tolerant society in a secular and democratic state. . . . In Poland, we greeted him as a friend of freedom. Western Europe saw him as a conservative trying to stop the church's progressive work." Michnik, *The Church and the Left*, p. xiv.

42. John Paul II, *The Acting Person* (Boston: Reidel, 1979), and *Toward a Philosophy of Praxis* (New York: Crossroad, 1981); *Return to Poland: The Collected Speeches of John Paul II* (London: Collins, 1979); Pope John Paul II, *Brazil: Journey in the Light of the Eucharist* (Boston: Daughters of St. Paul, 1980).

43. Michnik has captured the tension between the particularistic and universalistic aspects of the pope's Christian message. He concludes his commentary on the 1979 visit of the pope to Poland with the words, "Let me just say that when I listened to John Paul II's homily in Cracow, I had a strange feeling. When the pope asked the faithful Catholics 'never to forsake Him,' he was also addressing me: a pagan." Adam Michnik, *Letters from Prison and Other Essays* (Berkeley: University of California Press, 1985), p. 168.

44. The 1937 collective Pastoral Letter of the Spanish episcopate officially supporting and offering legitimation for the 1936 military uprising against the constitutional republican government is one of those rare instances. See Isidro Gomá Tomás, *Pastorales de la Guerra de España* (Madrid: Rialp, 1955).

45. Adam Michnik, "What We Want to Do and What We Can Do," *Telos* 47 (Spring 1981), p. 72.

46. See Andrew Arato, "Civil Society vs. the State" and "The Theory of the Polish Democratic Opposition: Normative Assumptions and Strategic Ambiguities," *Working Papers of the Kellogg Institute* (Notre Dame, Ind.: University of Notre Dame, 1984); and Adam Michnik, "A New Evolutionism," in *Letters from Prison*.

47. In the words of a member of KOR: "We would probably have had isolated strikes and maybe won some concessions from the government. But a Polish Pope united the Poles in a way I personally never imagined possible." In

Steven Stewart, *The Poles* (New York: Macmillan, 1982), p. 155. See also Radio Free Europe Research, "The Pope in Poland," *Spectator*, 9 and 16 June 1979; Alexander Tomsky, "John Paul II in Poland," *Religion in Communist Lands* 7, no. 3 (Autumn 1979), and "Poland's Church on the Road to Gdańsk," *Religion in Communist Lands* 1–2, 1981; Jerzy Turowicz, "Pięć Lat Pontyfikatu," *Tygodnik Powszechny* 16 October 1983.

48. Thomas Bird, "The New Turn in Church-State Relations in Poland," *Journal of Church and State* 24 (1982); Vincent Chrypinsky, "Church and State in Poland after Solidarity," in J. L. Black and J. W. Strong, eds., *Sisyphus and Poland: Reflections on Martial Law* (Winnipeg: Ronald P. Frye, 1986); Hannah Diskin, "The Pope's Pilgrimage to Jaruzelski's Poland," in Black and Strong, *Sisyphus and Poland;* J. B. de Weydenthal, "The Church and the State of Emergency," *Radio Free Europe: Research* 49 (19 February 1982); Peter Raina, *Kościół w Polsce, 1981–1984* (London: Veritas, 1985).

49. For a critical analysis of the church's mediation syndrome in Pinochet's Chile, see Hugo Villela, "The Church and the Process of Democratization in Latin America," *Social Compass* 26, nos. 2–3 (1979).

50. For a critical but balanced analysis of the church's role through the 1980s, see Aleksander Smolar, "The Polish Opposition," in Fehér and Arato, *Crisis and Reform in Eastern Europe;* David Ost, *Solidarity and the Politics of Anti-Politics* (Philadelphia: Temple University Press, 1990), and "Poland Revisited: Normalization and Opposition," *Poland Watch* 7 (1985). On the ongoing debate concerning "realism" and "idealism" in Polish politics, see Adam Bromke, *The Meaning and Uses of Polish History* (Boulder, Colo.: East European Monographs, 1987); *Poland's Politics: Idealism vs. Realism* (Cambridge, Mass.: Harvard University Press, 1967); "Poland's Idealism and Realism in Retrospect," *Canadian Slavonic Papers* 31 (March 1979); and Michnik, *Letters from Prison.*

51. Cf. Andrzej Micewski, "Kościół ostrzegał 'Solidarność,' " *Polityka*, 14 November 1987; Daniel Passent, "Miedzy Kościołem a Solidarnością," *Polityka*, 19 March 1988; Zenon Rudny, "Cesarzowi—co Cesarskie, Bogu—co Boskie," *Polityka*, 24 October 1983.

52. Cf. Patrick Michel and G. Mink, *Mort d'un Frère: L'Affaire Popiełuszko* (Paris: Fayard, 1985); Grazyna Sikorska, *Jerzy Popiełuszko, a Martyr for the Truth* (Grand Rapids, Mich.: Eerdmans, 1985); John Moody, *The Priest and the Policeman* (New York: Summit Books, 1987); Paul Lewis, "Turbulent Priest: Popiełuszko Affair," *Politics* 5, no. 2 (October 1985).

53. Jerzy Popiełuszko, *Kazania patriotyczne* (Paris: Libella, 1984) and *The Price of Love: The Sermons of Fr. Jerzy Popiełuszko* (London: Inc. Catholic Truth Society, 1985).

54. In an interview with *Famiglia Cristiana* (27 November 1985) Cardinal Glemp said: "Those who manipulated Father Popiełuszko were not the Church's people. They made him the chaplain of the opposition groups to which he felt very attached. He was definitely a victim." Quoted in Smolar, "The Polish Opposition," p. 242.

55. See David Ost, "Introduction" to Michnik, *The Church and the Left.*

56. David Ost, "Introduction," p. 20.

57. Prymas Polski, Józef Glemp, "Uwagi o projekcie dokumentu Prymasow-skiej Rady Społecznej," in *Aneks*, no. 53 (1989, London). For a discussion of the traditional Catholic position and its abandonment at Vatican II see, chap. 7, nn. 56–60.

58. The bill did not pass the lower house of the Sejm.

59. On the concepts of tutelary power, reserved domains, and perverse insti-tutionalization, see J. Samuel Valenzuela, "Democratic Consolidation in Post-Transitional Settings: Notion, Process, and Facilitating Conditions," paper pre-sented at Conference on Democratization in Central Europe and Latin America, UCLA, 1 December 1990.

60. On the responsibility and role of intellectuals, see Adam Michnik, "Trou-bles," in *The Church and the Left*.

61. Smolar, "Polish Opposition."

62. This was the lesson of the Chilean experience, which forced the Catholic church to rethink its political strategy everywhere. Brian H. Smith, *The Church and Politics in Chile* (Princeton: Princeton University Press, 1982).

Chapter Five

1. C. R. Boxer, *The Church Militant and Iberian Expansion, 1440–1770* (Baltimore: Johns Hopkins University Press, 1978).

2. Robert Richard, "Comparison of Evangelization in Portuguese and Span-ish America," *The Americas* 14 (April 1958).

3. Cf. W. Eugene Shiels, S.J., *King and Church: The Rise and Fall of the Patronato Real* (Chicago: Loyola University Press, 1961); Lloyd M. Mecham, *Church and State in Latin America* (Chapel Hill: University of North Carolina Press, 1966).

4. Mecham, *Church and Society*, p. 36.

5. Cf. Thomas C. Bruneau, *The Political Transformation of the Brazilian Catholic Church* (Cambridge: Cambridge University Press, 1974); Márcio More-ira Alves, *A Igreja e a Política no Brasil* (São Paulo: Editora Brasiliense, 1979).

6. Cf. Eduardo Hoornaert, *A Formação do Catolicismo Brasileiro, 1550–1800* (Petrópolis: Vozes, 1974); Bradford E. Burns, *A History of Brazil* (New York: Columbia University Press, 1970); Rubem César Fernandes, *Os Caval-heiros do Bom Jesus* (São Paulo: Brasiliense, 1982); C. R. Boxer, "Faith and Empire: The Cross and the Crown in Portuguese Expansion, 15th–18th Centu-ries," *Terrae Incognitae*, 1976; Donald Warren, "Portuguese Roots of Brazilian Spiritism," *Luso-Brazilian Review* 5, no. 2 (December 1968).

7. Mary Crescentia Thornton, *The Church and Freemasonry in Brazil, 1872–1875: A Study in Regalism* (Washington, D.C.: Catholic University of America Press, 1984). On Brazilian positivism, see João Cruz Costa, *O positivismo na República: Notas sobre a historia do positivismo no Brasil* (São Paulo: Compan-hia Editora Nacional, 1956).

8. Bruneau, *Political Transformation*, pp. 11–31.

9. Ibid., p. 29.

268   Notes to Pages 117–118

10. Cf. Bruneau, *Political Transformation;* Moreira Alves, *Igreja e Política;* Júlio Maria, *O Catolicismo no Brasil* (Rio de Janeiro: Ed. Agir, 1950); Roger Bastide, "Religion and the Church in Brazil," in T. Lynn Smith and Alexander Marchant, eds., *Brazil, Portrait of Half a Continent* (New York: Dryden Press, 1951); Pedro Ribeiro de Oliveira, "The Romanization of Catholicism and Agrarian Capitalism in Brazil," *Social Compass* 26, 2/3 (1979); Riolando Azzi, "O Início da Restauração Católica no Brasil, 1920–1930," *Síntese* 10 and 11 (1977). On the "Neo-Christendom Church," see Scott Mainwaring, *The Catholic Church and Politics in Brazil, 1916–1985* (Stanford: Stanford University Press, 1986). On Catholic Action, see Gianfranco Poggi, *Catholic Action in Italy: The Sociology of a Sponsored Organization* (Stanford: Stanford University Press, 1967).

11. Bruneau, *Political Transformation,* p. 37.

12. Mainwaring, *Catholic Church,* pp. 25ff.; and Emanuel de Kadt, *Catholic Radicals in Brazil* (New York: Oxford University Press, 1970).

13. Paulo José Krischke, *A Igreja e as Crises Políticas no Brasil* (Petrópolis: Vozes, 1979).

14. Margaret Todaro Williams, "The Politicization of the Brazilian Catholic Church: The Catholic Electoral League," *Journal of Interamerican Studies and World Affairs* 16 (1974), and "Church and State in Vargas's Brazil: The Politics of Cooperation," *Journal of Church and State* 18 (Autumn 1976).

15. Mainwaring, *Catholic Church,* p. 33.

16. Hélgio Trindade, *Integralismo: O Fascismo Brasileiro na Decada de 30* (São Paulo: Difel, 1974); Charles Antoine, *O Integralismo Brasileiro* (Rio de Janeiro: Editora Civilização Brasileira, 1980).

17. In addition to the sources already mentioned, see Ralph Della Cava, "Catholicism and Society in Twentieth-Century Brazil," *Latin American Research Review* 11, no. 2 (1976); Thomas Skidmore, *Politics in Brazil, 1930–1964* (New York: Oxford University Press, 1967); Peter Flynn, *Brazil: A Political Analysis* (Boulder, Colo.: Westview Press, 1978); Charles Antoine, *Church and Power in Brazil* (Maryknoll, N.Y.: Orbis Books, 1973).

18. Using an institutional analysis, Thomas Bruneau has offered a complex and subtle version of this answer. Within a descriptively rich analysis which clearly transcends his own analytical framework, Bruneau reconstructs the political transformation of the Brazilian church in purely instrumental terms as an strategy of institutional adaptation to changes in the environment, aiming to maintain or maximize the church's influence in that environment. While Bruneau's institutional analysis is correct in stressing the importance of the initial perception of threats to the church's influence as a catalyst for change, the analytical framework is too narrow to encompass the complexity and the novelty of the transformation. In addition to the one offered by Bruneau, Scott Mainwaring and Ralph della Cava, from different angles, have also offered excellent historical reconstructions of the same transformation, making any attempt to tell the same story again superfluous. Cf. Bruneau, *Political Transformation;* Mainwaring, *Catholic Church;* and Ralph Della Cava, "The 'People's Church,' the Vatican and *Abertura,*" in Alfred Stepan, ed., *Democratizing Brazil* (New York: Oxford University Press, 1989).

19. The hegemonic struggles can of course be understood as reactive and adaptive responses to changes in the church's internal and external environments. It is the instrumentalist-strategic assumptions of Bruneau's institutional analysis which are most problematic. In a similar vein, see David Muchtler, "Adaptations of the Roman Catholic Church to Latin American Development: The Meaning of Internal Church Conflict," *Social Research* 36, no. 2 (Summer 1969).

20. Cf. Enrique Dussel, *A History of the Church in Latin America: Colonialism to Liberation (1492–1979)* (Grand Rapids, Mich.: Eerdmans, 1981); and *De Medellín a Puebla: Una Década de Sangre y Esperanza* (Mexico City: Edicol, 1979); Hugo Latorre Cabal, *The Revolution of the Latin American Church* (Norman: University of Oklahoma Press, 1978); Penny Lernoux, *Cry of the People* (New York: Penguin, 1982).

21. Cf. Daniel H. Levine, *Religion and Politics in Latin America: The Catholic Church in Venezuela and Colombia* (Princeton: Princeton University Press, 1981); Brian H. Smith, *The Church and Politics in Chile: Challenges to Modern Catholicism* (Princeton: Princeton University Press, 1982); Jeffrey Klaiber, S.J., *Religion and Revolution in Peru, 1824–1976* (Notre Dame, Ind.: University of Notre Dame Press, 1977).

22. De Kadt, *Catholic Radicals*.

23. CNBB, *Plano de Emergência para a Igreja do Brasil* (Rio de Janeiro: Livraria Dom Bosco, 1963), and *Plano de Pastoral de Conjunto* (Rio de Janeiro: Livraria Dom Bosco, 1966).

24. Cf. Roger Bastide, *The African Religions of Brazil* (Baltimore: John Hopkins University Press, 1978); Boaventura Kloppenburg, *O Espiritismo no Brasil* (Petrópolis: Editora Vozes, 1964); Diana Brown, "Religion as an Adaptive Institution: Umbanda in Brazil," and Chester Gabriel, "Spiritism in Manaus: The Cults and Catholicism," in Thomas Bruneau et al., eds., *The Catholic Church and Religions in Latin America* (Montreal: Center for Developing Area Studies, 1985).

25. Cf. De Kadt, *op. cit.*, and Luís Alberto Gomes de Souza, *A JUC: Os Estudantes Católicos a Política* (Rio de Janeiro: Editora Civilização Brasileira, 1984).

26. Antoine, *Church and Power in Brazil*, and *O Integralismo Brasileiro*.

27. Antoine, *Church and Power in Brazil*, p. 29 and passim.

28. Bruneau, *Political Transformation*, pp. 126ff.

29. Della Cava, "The 'People's Church'," p. 150.

30. Cf. Alfred Stepan, ed., *Authoritarian Brazil* (New Haven: Yale University Press, 1973); and Maria Helena Moreira Alves, *State and Opposition in Military Brazil* (Austin: University of Texas Press, 1985).

31. José Comblin, *The Church and the National Security State* (Maryknoll, N.Y.: Orbis, 1979).

32. Actually, it is emerging everywhere, throughout the world and in most religious traditions. Jeffrey K. Hadden and Anson Shupe, eds., *Prophetic Religions and Politics* (New York: Paragon House, 1986); Michael Dodson, "Prophetic Politics and Political Theory," *Polity* 12 (Spring 1980).

33. Max Weber, *Ancient Judaism* (New York: Free Press, 1952).

34. The literature on liberation theology is immense and still growing. For

some representative statements, cf. Gustavo Gutiérrez, *A Theology of Liberation: History, Politics and Salvation* (Maryknoll, N.Y.: Orbis, 1973); Leonardo and Clodovis Boff, *Introducing Liberation Theology* (Maryknoll, N.Y.: Orbis, 1986); Phillip Berryman, *Liberation Theology* (New York: Pantheon Books, 1987); Paul Sigmund, *Liberation Theology at the Crossroads: Democracy or Revolution* (New York: Oxford University Press, 1990); Otto Maduro, ed., *The Future of Liberation Theology. Essays in Honor of Gustavo Gutiérrez* (Maryknoll, N.Y.: Orbis, 1989); John R. Pottenger, *The Political Theory of Liberation Theology* (Albany: State University of New York Press, 1989); Michael Dodson, "Liberation Theology and Christian Radicalism in Contemporary Latin America," *Journal of Latin American Studies* 11 (May 1979).

35. Enrique Dussel, *El Episcopado Latinoamericano y la Liberación de los Pobres, 1504–1620* (Mexico City: Centro de Reflexión Teológica, 1979).

36. Euclides da Cunha, *Rebellion in the Backlands* (Chicago: University of Chicago Press, 1944); and Ralph Della Cava, "Brazilian Messianism and National Institutions: A Reappraisal of Canudos and Joaseiro," *Hispanic American Historical Review* 48 (August 1968).

37. Cf. Mecham, *Church and State;* Frederick Pike, ed., *The Conflict between Church and State in Latin America* (New York: Alfred A. Knopf, 1967); Edward Norman, *Christianity in the Southern Hemisphere* (Oxford: Clarendon Press, 1981); Kalman H. Silvert, ed., *Churches and States: The Religious Institutions and Modernization* (New York: American Universities Field Staff, 1967); Daniel H. Levine, ed., *Churches and Politics in Latin America* (Beverly Hills: Sage, 1980).

38. Cf. Edward J. Williams, *Latin American Christian Democratic Parties* (Knoxville: University of Tennessee Press, 1967); Robert Cross, *The Emergence of Liberal Catholicism in Latin America* (Cambridge, Mass.: Harvard University Press, 1958); John J. Kennedy, *Catholicism, Nationalism and Democracy in Argentina* (South Bend, Ind.: University of Notre Dame Press, 1958); Carlos Mugica, *Peronismo y Cristianismo* (Buenos Aires: Ed. Merlin, 1973); Michael Fleet, *The Rise and Fall of Chilean Christian Democracy* (Princeton: Princeton University Press, 1985); Sergio Torres, *El Quehacer de la Iglesia en Chile, 1925–1970* (Talca: Fundación Obispo Manuel Larrain, 1971).

39. David C. Bailey, *Viva Cristo Rey: The Cristero Rebellion and the Church-State Conflict in Mexico* (Austin: University of Texas Press, 1974); Robert E. Quirk, *The Mexican Revolution and the Catholic Church, 1910–1929* (Bloomington: Indiana University Press, 1973).

40. Cf. Alexander Wilde, "Creating Neo-Christendom in Colombia," in Donald L. Herman, ed., *Democracy in Latin America* (New York: Praeger, 1988); and Levine, *Religion and Politics in Latin America.*

41. Cf. William D'Antonio and Frederick Pike, eds., *Religion, Revolution and Reform: New Forces for Change in Latin America* (New York: Praeger, 1964); Henry Landsberger, ed., *The Church and Social Change in Latin America* (Notre Dame, Ind.: University of Notre Dame Press, 1970); François Houtart, "Religion et lutte des classes en Amérique Latine," *Social Compass* 26, 2/3 (1979); François Houtart and Emile Pin, *The Church and the Latin American Revolution* (New York: Sheed and Ward, 1965); David Mutchler, *The Church*

as a Political Factor in Latin America (New York: Praeger, 1971); Frederick C. Turner, *Catholicism and Political Development in Latin America* (Chapel Hill: University of North Carolina Press, 1971); CELAM, *The Church in the Present-Day Transformation of Latin America in the Light of the Council,* 2 vols. (Bogota: General Secretariat of CELAM, 1970).

42. Scott Mainwaring and Alexander Wilde, eds., *The Progressive Church in Latin America* (Notre Dame, Ind.: University Of Notre Dame Press, 1989) discuss the three places. On Peru, see Catalina Romero de Iguiñiz, *Church, State and Society in Contemporary Peru, 1958–1988,* Ph.D. dissertation, Graduate Faculty, New School for Social Research, 1989. On Central America, cf. Phillip Berryman, *The Religious Roots of Rebellion: Christians in Central American Revolutions* (Maryknoll, N.Y.: Orbis, 1984); Teófilo Cabestrero, *Revolutionaries for the Gospel: Testimonies of Fifteen Christians in the Nicaraguan Government* (Maryknoll, N.Y.: Orbis, 1986); Margaret Randall, *Christians in the Nicaraguan Revolution* (Seattle: Left Bank, 1984); Andrew Reding, ed., *Christianity and Revolution: Tomás Borges' Theology of Life* (Maryknoll, N.Y.: Orbis, 1987); Michael Dodson and Tommie Sue Montgomery, "The Churches in the Nicaraguan Revolution," in Thomas Walker, ed., *Nicaragua in Revolution* (New York: Praeger, 1982).

43. CERIS, "Investigación sobre el Clero," in Isaac Rogel, ed., *Documentos sobre la Realidad de la Iglesia en América Latina, 1968–1969,* Cuernavaca, CIDOC, *Sondeos,* no. 54, 1970; Ivan Illich, "The Vanishing Clergyman," *Critic* 25 (June–July 1967); Renato Poblete, S.J. *Crisis Sacerdotal* (Santiago: Editorial del Pacífico, 1965); Renato Poblete et al., *El Sacerdote Chileno: Estudio Sociológico* (Santiago: Centro Bellarmino, 1971); Ivan Vallier, "Religious Elites: Differentiations and Developments in Roman Catholicism," in Seymour M. Lipset and Aldo Solari, eds., *Elites in Latin America* (New York: Oxford University Press, 1967); *Social-Activist Priests: Chile,* LADOC Keyhole Series no. 5 (Washington, D.C.: United States Catholic Conference, 1974); *Social-Activist Priests: Colombia, Argentina,* LADOC Keyhole Series no. 6 (Washington, D.C.: United States Catholic Conference, 1974); Michael Dodson, "Priests and Peronism: Radical Clergy in Argentine Politics," *Latin American Perspectives* 1 (Fall 1974), and "The Christian Left in Latin American Politics," in Levine, *Churches and Politics.*

44. Cf. Roland Robertson, "Liberation Theology in Latin America: Sociological Problems of Interpretation and Explanation," in Hadden and Shupe, *Prophetic Religions;* Alan Neely, "Liberation Theology in Latin America: Antecedents and Autochtony," *Missiology: An International Review* 6, no. 3 (1978); John Eagleson, ed., *Christians and Socialism: Documentation of the Christians for Socialism Movement in Latin America* (Maryknoll, N.Y.: Orbis Books, 1975).

45. Cf. José Casanova, "Religion and Conflict in Latin America: Conversation with Otto Maduro," *Telos* 58 (Winter 1983); Otto Maduro, *Religion and Social Conflicts* (Maryknoll, N.Y.: Orbis Books, 1982); Daniel H. Levine, ed., *Religion and Political Conflict in Latin America* (Chapel Hill: University of North Carolina Press, 1986).

46. Gustavo Gutiérrez, *A Theology of Liberation* and *The Power of the Poor*

in History (Maryknoll, N.Y.: Orbis, 1983). It makes a world of a difference, of course, whether "intellectuals" interpret this eruption as a "transvaluation of slave morality" and as a "rebellion of the masses" or, rather, as a eschatological, liberating, and redemptive process.

47. Luíz Bresser Pereira, *Development and Crisis in Brazil, 1930–1983* (Boulder, Colo.: Westview Press, 1984).

48. Gilberto Freyre, *The Masters and the Slaves* (New York: Alfred A. Knopf, 1946).

49. Inocêncio Engelke carta pastoral, *Conosco, sem Nós ou contra Nós Se Fará a Reforma Rural* (Rio de Janeiro, 1950); CNBB, *Pastoral da Terra* (São Paulo: Edições Paulinas, 1976); Vanilda Paiva et al., *Igreja e Questão Agrária* (São Paulo: Edições Loyola, 1985).

50. See Mainwaring, *Catholic Church,* p. 54.

51. Mainwaring has offered an excellent reconstruction of this process of radicalization in *Catholic Church.*

52. De Kadt, *Catholic Radicals.*

53. Cf. Paulo Freire, *A Educação como Prática da Liberdade* (Rio de Janeiro: Paz e Terra, 1967) and *Pedagogy of the Opressed* (New York: Seabury Press, 1970); Hélder Câmara, *Revolution through Peace* (New York: Harper & Row, 1970); Jose de Broucker, *Dom Helder Camara* (Maryknoll, N.Y.: Orbis Books, 1970); Luís Gonzaga de Souza Lima, ed., *Evolução Política dos Católicos e da Igreja no Brasil* (Petrópolis: Editora Vozes, 1979).

54. Teófilo Cabestrero, *Diálogos en Mato Grosso con Pedro Casaldáliga* (Salamanca: Sígueme, 1978); and Shelton Davis, *Victims of the Miracle: Development and the Indians of Brazil* (New York: Cambridge University Press, 1977).

55. Peace and Justice Commission, *São Paulo: Growth and Poverty* (London: Bowerdan Press, 1978).

56. The income of the bottom 50 percent of the population decreased from 16.6 percent of the national income in 1960 to 15.1 percent in 1980, while the income of the top 10 percent of the population increased from 39.4 percent of the national income to 48 percent. In 1975, the Northeast, with 30 percent of the country's population, received only 10 percent of its income. The per capita income in the Northeast was less than one-third of Brazil's per capita income. By contrast, the per capita income of the wealthiest state, São Paulo, was almost seven times that of the poorest state, Piauí. See Thomas Skidmore, *The Politics of Military Rule in Brazil, 1964–1985* (New York: Oxford University Press, 1988), pp. 284ff.

57. "Y Juca-Pirama. The Indians: A People Doomed to Die," in Mainwaring, *Catholic Church,* p. 94.

58. Cf. Emilio Willems, *Followers of the New Faith* (Nashville, Tenn.: Vanderbilt University Press, 1967); Cândido P. Ferreira de Camargo, *Católicos, Protestantes, Espíritas* (Petrópolis: Editora Vozes, 1973), and references in n. 24 above.

59. Cf. Bruneau, *Political Transformation,* pp. 242–51; and Moreira Alves, *Igreja e Política,* pp.57–104.

60. Cf. Leonardo Boff, *Ecclesiogenesis: The Base Communities Reinvent the*

Church (Maryknoll, N.Y.: Orbis Books, 1986); Marcello de Azevedo, S.J., *Basic Ecclesial Communities in Brazil: The Challenge of a New Way of Being Church* (Washington, D.C.: Georgetown University Press, 1987); Alvaro Barreiro, *Basic Ecclesial Communities: The Evangelization of the Poor* (Maryknoll, N.Y.: Orbis Books, 1982); Frei Betto, *O Que É Comunidade Eclesial de Base* (São Paulo: Editora Brasiliense, 1981).

61. In this sense, it represents almost an inverse image of the pyramidal structure of the Polish church. See Fernandes, "Images de la Passion."

62. Cf. CNBB, *Comunidades Eclesiais de Base no Brasil* (São Paulo: Ediçoes Paulinas, 1979); CNBB, *Diretrizes Gerais da Açao Pastoral de Igreja no Brasil, 1983–1986* (São Paulo: Ediçoes Paulinas, 1984); Riolando Azzi, *O Episcopado do Brasil frente ao Catolicismo Popular* (Petrópolis: Vozes, 1972) and *O Catolicismo Popular no Brasil* (Petrópolis: Vozes, 1978); Carlos Mesters et al., *Uma Igreja Que Nasce do Povo* (Petrópolis: Vozes, 1975); Helena Salem et al., eds., *Brasil: A Igreja dos Oprimidos* (São Paulo: Brasil Debates, 1981). As Gustavo Gutiérrez himself has pointed out, however, it is often overlooked that the idea behind the "preferential option for the poor" was not an invention of Latin-American liberation theology. In his 11 September 1962 broadcast, one month before the Council, Pope John XXIII urged that the church be presented "in the under-developed countries as the Church of all, and especially of the poor." The Pastoral Constitution on the Church in the Modern World begins by stating that the church wants to share in the joys and hopes of human beings today, "especially those who are in any way poor or afflicted." See Peter Hebblethwaite, *Synod Extraordinary* (Garden City, N.Y.: Doubleday, 1986), pp. 11–12.

63. Guillermo O'Donnell, "Tensions in the Bureaucratic-Authoritarian State and the Question of Democracy," in David Collier, ed., *The New Authoritarianism in Latin America* (Princeton: Princeton University Press, 1979).

64. Cf. Scott Mainwaring, "Grassroots Popular Movements and the Struggle for Democracy: Nova Iguaçu"; Margaret E. Keck, "The New Unionism in the Brazilian Transition"; and Francisco Weffort, "Why Democracy?" in Alfred Stepan, ed., *Democratizing Brazil* (New York: Oxford University Press, 1989). Further: Francisco Weffort, *O Populismo na Política Brasileira* (Rio de Janeiro: Paz e Terra, 1978); Scott Mainwaring and Eduardo Viola, "New Social Movements, Political Culture, and Democracy: Brazil and Argentina in the 1980's," *Telos* 61 (Fall 1984); Paulo Jose Krischke "Populism and the Catholic Church: The Crisis of Democracy in Brazil," Ph.D. dissertation, York University, 1983.

65. Francisco Weffort, *Por que Democracia?* (São Paulo: Ed. Brasiliense, 1984).

66. Fernandes, "Images de la Passion," p. 18.

67. Quoted in Mainwaring, *Catholic Church*, p. 103.

68. Dom Paulo Evaristo Arns, *Em Defesa dos Direitos Humanos* (Rio de Janeiro: Ed. Brasília/Rio, 1978).

69. Paulo Krischke and Scott Mainwaring, eds., *A Igreja nas Bases em Tempo de Transição (1974–1985)* (Porto Alegre: L & PM, 1986); José Alvaro Moisés et al., *Alternativas Populares da Democracia* (Petrópolis: Vozes, 1982).

70. Penny Lernoux, *People of God: The Struggle for World Catholicism*

(New York: Penguin, 1989); and Ralph Della Cava, "Vatican Policy, 1978–90: An Updated Overview," *Social Research* 59, no. 1 (Spring 1992).

71. David Martin, *Tongues of Fire: The Explosion of Protestantism in Latin America* (Cambridge, Mass.: B. Blackwell, 1990).

72. The proportion of Catholics within Brazil's population has decreased steadily since mid-century and dramatically in the last decade. Catholics constituted 95 percent of Brazil's population in 1940, 93.5 percent in 1950, 93.1 percent in 1960, 91.8 percent in 1970, 89.9 in 1980, and 76.2 percent in 1990. A recent survey in three Brazilian cities (São Paulo, Rio de Janeiro, and Brasília) showed that religious affiliation among the middle classes was distributed in the following way: 72 percent Catholics, 6 percent Espíritas, 6 percent Protestants, 4 percent Pentecostals, 7 percent "other," and 5 percent "none." Surveys also indicate that only around one-third of Brazilian Catholics practice regularly, i.e., attend Sunday mass. Meanwhile, the number of inhabitants per priest has increased continuously from 7,114 inhabitants in 1970, to 9,379 in 1980, to 10,591 in 1990. See "A Decadência do Catolicismo no Brasil," *Veja*, 25 December 1991, pp. 32–38.

73. In March 1991, after several years of inquisitorial harassment from the Vatican, Leonardo Boff was forced to resign from the editorship of the influential journal *Vozes* and from all his theological teaching positions. In a bitter letter to the Superior General of the Franciscan Order, Boff admitted that "they have succeeded in killing the hope within me. It is worse than losing one's faith. I desist." In June 1992, Leonardo Boff announced his resignation from the Franciscan Order and from the priesthood. See "Boff dice que el Vaticano ha logrado matar su esperanza," *El País*, Edición Internacional, 30 September 1991, p. 17.; and "Leonardo Boff renuncia al sacerdocio 'para mantener la libertad,'" *El País*, Edición Internacional, 6 July 1992, p. 17.

74. See "Pope Challenges Brazil Leaders on Behalf of Poor," *New York Times*, 15 October 1991. Throughout the transition the church had supported the call for agrarian reform. But this call was silenced by the overrepresentation of the oligarchic interests of the Northeast in Brazilian political society and in the Constituent Assembly. The pope's statements might have reopened the public debate once again, but the reaction so far has been negligible. Indeed, the welcome the pope received in his second visit to Brazil was neither as massive nor as enthusiastic as the one he received in his first visit, in 1980. On the first visit, see A. L. Rocha and Luís Alberto Gomes de Souza, eds., *O Povo e o Papa* (Rio de Janeiro: Editora Civilização Brasileira, 1980).

75. John S. Coleman, S.J., "Raison d'église: Organizational Imperatives of the Church in the Political Order," in Jeffrey Hadden and Anson Shupe, eds., *Secularization and Fundamentalism Reconsidered* (New York: Paragon House, 1989).

Chapter Six

1. For the most comprehensive study of varieties of contemporary fundamentalist movements in all world religions, see Martin E. Marty and R. Scott

Appleby, eds., *Fundamentalisms Observed* (Chicago: University of Chicago Press, 1991).

2. Among the immense literature on this issue, cf. Sidney E. Ahlstrom, *A Religious History of the American People* (New Haven: Yale University Press, 1972); Sidney Mead, *The Lively Experiment: The Shaping of Christianity in America* (New York: Harper & Row, 1963); Winthrop S. Hudson, *The Great Tradition of the American Churches* (New York: Harper, 1953); Jon Butler, *Awash in a Sea of Faith: Christianizing the American People* (Cambridge, Mass.: Harvard University Press, 1990); Robert T. Handy, *A Christian America: Protestant Hopes and Historical Realities,* 2d ed. (New York: Oxford, 1984); Martin E. Marty, *The Righteous Empire: The Protestant Experience in America* (New York: Dial Press, 1970); and Charles I. Foster, *An Errand of Mercy: The Evangelical United Front, 1790–1837* (Chapel Hill: University of North Carolina Press, 1960).

3. On the disestablishment of religion, cf. Thomas J. Curry, *The First Freedoms: Church and State in America to the Passage of the First Amendment* (New York: Oxford University Press, 1986); William Lee Miller, *The First Liberty: Religion and the American Republic* (New York: Alfred A. Knopf, 1985); and Leonard Levy, *The Establishment Clause: Religion and the First Amendment* (New York: Macmillan, 1986). On the "Jeffersonian moment," see Henry F. May, "The Jeffersonian Moment," in *The Divided Heart: Essays on Protestantism and the Enlightenment in America* (New York: Oxford University Press, 1991), and *The Enlightenment in America* (New York: Oxford University Press, 1976). See also Bernard Bailyns, *The Ideological Origins of the American Revolution* (Cambridge, Mass: Harvard University Press, 1967). On the role of religion in the revolution, see Gordon Wood, *The Creation of the American Republic* (Chapel Hill: University of North Carolina Press, 1969); Alan Heimert, *Religion and the American Mind: From the Great Awakening to the Revolution* (Cambridge, Mass.: Harvard University Press, 1966); and Catherine Albanese, *Sons of the Fathers: The Civil Religion of the American Revolution* (Philadelphia: Temple University Press, 1976).

4. On the protracted struggle to approximate reality to constitutional principles, see Morton Borden, *Jews, Turks, and Infidels* (Chapel Hill: University of North Carolina Press, 1984). According to a 1983 Gallup poll, a majority of Americans (51 percent) were still not ready to vote for "a qualified atheist" for president. Interestingly, there is a wide gap between Protestants and Catholics on this issue. Protestants would vote against an atheist by 64–31 percent. Catholics would vote for an atheist by 54–38 percent. See George Gallup, Jr., and Jim Castelli, *The American Catholic People* (Garden City, N.Y.: Doubleday, 1987), p. 61.

5. See Ronald P. Formisano, "Federalists and Republicans," and Paul Kleppner, "Partisanship and Ethnoreligious Conflict," in Paul Kleppner, ed., *The Evolution of American Electoral Systems* (Westport, Conn.: Greenwood Press, 1981); Paul Lopatto, *Religion and the Presidential Election* (New York: Praeger, 1985); and A. James Reichley, *Religion in American Public Life* (Washington, D.C.: Brookings Institution, 1985).

6. Alexis de Tocqueville, *Democracy in America* (New York: Vintage, 1990), vol. 1, p. 305.

7. On the various phases of the Protestant nativist crusade, cf. Ray A. Billington, *The Protestant Crusade, 1800–1860: A Study of the Origins of American Nativism* (New York: Macmillan, 1938); William Gribbin, *The Churches Militant: The War of 1812 and American Religion* (New Haven: Yale University Press, 1973); Paul Goodman, *Towards a Christian Republic: Antimasonry and the Great Transition in New England, 1826–1836* (New York: Oxford University Press, 1988); John Higham, *Strangers in the Land: Patterns of American Nativism, 1860–1925*, 2d ed. (New Brunswick, N.J.: Rutgers University Press, 1988); and David Brion Davis, "Some Themes of Countersubversion: An Analysis of Anti-Masonic, Anti-Catholic, and Anti-Mormon Literature," *Mississipi Valley Historical Review* 47 (1960).

8. Cf. Nathan O. Hatch, *The Democratization of American Christianity* (New Haven: Yale University Press, 1989); and Joseph Forcinelli, *The Democratization of Religion in America* (Lewiston, N.Y.: Edwin Mellen Press, 1990).

9. Cf. Perry Miller, *The Life of the Mind in America: From the Revolution to the Civil War* (New York: Harcourt Brace, 1965); Daniel Walker Howe, *The Unitarian Conscience: Harvard Moral Philosophy, 1805–1861* (Cambridge, Mass.: Harvard University Press, 1970); Donald G.Tewksbury, *The Founding of American Colleges and Universities before the Civil War* (New York: Teachers' College, 1932); Donald H. Meyer, *The Instructed Conscience: The Shaping of the American National Ethic* (Philadelphia: University of Pennsylvania Press, 1972); Theodore Dwight Bozeman, *Protestants in an Age of Science: The Baconian Ideal and Antebellum American Religious Thought* (Chapel Hill: University of North Carolina Press, 1977); Herbert Hovencamp, *Science and Religion in America, 1800–1860* (Philadelphia: University of Pennsylvania Press, 1978); and Bruce Kuklick, *Churchmen and Philosophers: From Jonathan Edwards to John Dewey* (New Haven: Yale University Press, 1985).

10. Cf. William G. McLoughlin, *Revivals, Awakenings and Reform* (Chicago: University of Chicago Press, 1978); Whitney R. Cross, *The Burned-over District: The Social and Intellectual History of Enthusiastic Religion in Western New York, 1800–1850* (Ithaca, N.Y.: Cornell University Press, 1950); Timothy L. Smith, *Revivalism and Social Reform: American Protestantism on the Eve of the Civil War* (New York: Abingdon, 1957), and "Protestant Schooling and American Nationality, 1800–1850," *Journal of American History* 53 (1966–67): 679–95; Ernest R. Sandeen, ed., *The Bible and Social Reform* (Philadelphia: Fortress Press, 1982); David Tyack, "The Kingdom of God and the Common School," *Harvard Educational Review* 36 (1966): 447–69; William B. Kennedy, *The Shaping of Protestant Education: An Interpretation of the Sunday School; and the Development of Protestant Educational Strategy in the United States, 1789–1860*, Monographs in Christian Education, no. 4. (New York, 1966); Anne M. Boylan, *The Sunday School: The Formation of an American Institution, 1790–1880* (New Haven: Yale University Press, 1988); and David P. Nord, "The Evangelical Origins of Mass Media in America, 1815–1835," *Journalism Monographs* 88 (1984): 1–30.

11. I have not found any satisfactory monographic study of the secularization of American higher education. For a general overview of the rise of the modern university, see Christopher Jencks and David Riesman, *The Academic Revolution* (New York: Doubleday, 1969). For a compelling analysis of the process of internal secularization of the social sciences from Protestant thought, see Arthur J. Vidich and Stanford M. Lyman, *American Sociology: Worldly Rejections of Religion and Their Directions* (New Haven: Yale University Press, 1985).

12. Henry F. May, *Protestant Churches and Industrial America* (New York: Harper, 1949), and Aaron Ignatius Abell, *The Urban Impact on American Protestantism, 1865–1900* (Cambridge, Mass.: Harvard University Press, 1943).

13. See Walter Rauschenbusch, *Christianizing the Social Order* (New York: Macmillan, 1913); and Ronald C. White, Jr., and C. Howard Hopkins, *The Social Gospel: Religion and Reform in Changing America* (Philadelphia: Temple University Press, 1976).

14. On Catholicism, see the next chapter. See, further, Leonard Dinnerstein, Roger L. Nichols, and David M. Reimers, *Natives and Strangers: Ethnic Groups and the Building of America* (New York: Oxford University Press, 1979); and Laurence R. Moore, *Religious Outsiders and the Making of Americans* (New York: Oxford University Press, 1986).

15. Marty, *Righteous Empire*. On black religion, Evangelical Protantism, and the black churches, see Albert J. Raboteau, *Slave Religion: The "Invisible Institution" in the Ante-bellum South* (New York: Oxford University Press, 1978); Milton C. Sernett, *Black Religion and American Evangelicalism: White Protestants, Plantation Missions, and the Flowering of Negro Christianity, 1787–1865* (Metuchen, N.J.: Scarecrow Press, 1975); and Franklin Frazier, *The Negro Church in America*, and C. Eric Lincoln, *The Black Church since Frazier* (New York: Schocken, 1974).

16. See Eric C. Lincoln, *Race, Religion, and the Continuing American Dilemma* (New York: Hill & Wang, 1984); and Forrest G. Wood, *The Arrogance of Faith: Christianity and Race in America from the Colonial Era to the Twentieth Century* (New York: Alfred A. Knopf, 1990).

17. On southern evangelical Protestantism, see John B. Boles, *The Great Revival, 1787–1805: The Origins of the Southern Evangelical Mind.* (Lexington: University of Kentucky Press, 1972), and "Evangelical Protestantism in the Old South: From Religious Dissent to Cultural Dominance," in Charles R. Wilson, ed., *Religion in the South* (Jackson: University of Mississippi Press, 1985); Donald G. Mathews, *Religion in the Old South* (Chicago: University of Chicago Press, 1977); Charles Reagan Wilson, *Baptized in Blood: The Religion of the Lost Cause, 1865–1920* (Athens: University of Georgia Press, 1980); Kenneth K. Bailey, *Southern White Protestantism in the Twentieth Century* (New York: Harper & Row, 1964); and David E. Harrell, Jr., ed., *Varieties of Southern Evangelicalism* (Macon, Ga.: Mercer University Press, 1981). On "Bible Belt" religiosity, see Rodney Stark and William S. Bainbridge, *The Future of Religion: Secularization, Revival, and Cult Formation* (Berkeley: University of California Press, 1985).

18. Cf. Perry Miller, *Errand into the Wilderness* (Cambridge, Mass.: Harvard

University Press, 1956); Robert Bellah, *The Broken Covenant: American Civil Religion in Time of Trial* (New York: Seabury, 1975); William G. McLoughlin, *New England Dissent, 1630–1833: The Baptists and the Separation of Church and State,* 2 vols. (Cambridge, Mass.: Harvard University Press, 1971), and *Isaac Backus and the American Pietistic Tradition* (Boston: Little, Brown, 1970); George M. Marsden, *The Evangelical Mind and the New School Presbyterian Experience* (New Haven: Yale University Press, 1970); Mark A. Noll, *Princeton and the Republic, 1768–1822* (Princeton: Princeton University Press, 1989); Russell E. Richey, *Early American Methodism: A Reconsideration* (Bloomington: Indiana University Press, 1991); Charles Edwin Jones, *Perfectionist Persuasion: The Holiness Movement and American Methodism, 1867–1936* (Metuchen, N.J.: Scarecrow Press, 1974); and Winthrop S. Hudson, "The Methodist Age in America," *Methodist History* 12 (1974).

19. On slavery and religion, cf. Donald G. Matthews, *Slavery and Methodism: A Chapter in American Morality* (Princeton: Princeton University Press, 1965); C. C. Goen, *Broken Nation: Denominational Schisms and the Coming of the American Civil War* (Macon, Ga.: Mercer University Press, 1985); and John R. McKivigan, *The War against Proslavery Religion: Abolition and the Northern Churches, 1830–1865* (Ithaca, N.Y.: Cornell University Press, 1984).

20. See William G. McLoughlin, *Modern Revivalism: Charles Grandison Finney to Billy Graham* (New York: Ronald Press, 1959). On American religious and political millennialism, see James West Davidson, *The Logic of Millennial Thought: Eighteenth-Century New England* (New Haven: Yale University Press, 1977); Ruth Bloch, *Visionary Republic: Millennial Themes in American Thought, 1765–1800* (New York: Cambridge University Press, 1985); Ernest L. Tuveson, *Redeemer Nation: The Idea of America's Millennial Role* (Chicago: University of Chicago Press, 1968); Cushing Strout, *The New Heavens and New Earth: Political Religion in America* (New York: Harper & Row, 1974); Albert K. Weinberg, *Manifest Destiny: A Study of Nationalist Expansionism in American History,* (1935) reprint (Chicago: Quadrangle Books, 1963).

21. Quoted in McLoughlin, *Revivals, Awakenings, and Reform,* p. 139.

22. Ibid., p. 130. On the Adventists, see Ruth Alden Doan, *The Miller Heresy, Millennialism, and American Culture* (Philadelphia: Temple University Press, 1987);

23. Quoted in George M. Marsden, *Fundamentalism and American Culture: The Shaping of Twentieth-Century Evangelicalism, 1870–1925* (New York: Oxford University Press, 1980), pp. 36 and 38.

24. Marsden's *Fundamentalism and American Culture* is the best single study of the emergence and the first phase of the fundamentalist movement. For an excellent, concise but comprehensive historical summary of fundamentalism from the turn of the century to the present, see Nancy T. Ammerman, "North American Protestant Fundamentalism," in Martin E. Marty and R. Scott Appleby, eds., *Fundamentalisms Observed* (Chicago: University of Chicago Press, 1991). See also Ernest Sandeen, *The Roots of Fundamentalism: British and American Millenarianism, 1800–1930* (Chicago: University of Chicago Press, 1970); and Timothy P. Weber, *Living in the Shadow of the Second Com-*

ing: American Premillennialism, 1875–1925 (New York: Oxford University Press, 1979).

25. See T. Dwight Bozeman, *To Live Ancient Lives: The Primitivist Dimension in Puritanism* (Chapel Hill: University of North Carolina Press, 1988); Richard T. Hughes, ed., *The American Quest for the Primitive Church* (Urbana: University of Illinois Press, 1988); Richard Hughes and Leonard Allen, *Illusions of Innocence: Protestant Primitivism in America, 1630–1875* (Chicago: University of Chicago Press, 1988); and David E. Harrell, Jr., *A Social History of the Disciples of Christ* (Nashville: Disciples of Christ Historical Society, 1966).

26. Cf. Sandeen, *Roots of Fundamentalism,* and Weber, *Shadow of the Second Coming.* See also Nathan O. Hatch, "Millennialism and Popular Religion in the Early Republic," in Leonard I. Sweet, ed., *The Evangelical Tradition in America* (Macon, Ga.: Mercer University Press, 1984); and Timothy P. Weber, "Premillennialism and the Branches of Evangelicalism," in Donald W. Dayton and Robert K. Johnston, eds., *The Variety of American Evangelicalism* (Knoxville: University of Tennessee Press, 1991).

27. William R. Hutchison, *The Modernist Impulse in American Protestantism* (Cambridge, Mass.: Harvard University Press, 1976).

28. Marsden emphasizes this point, linking it to the Reformed origins of these denominations and their concern with doctrinal orthodoxy. See *Fundamentalism and American Culture,* p. 225 and passim. Norman F. Furniss's *The Fundamentalist Controversy* (New Haven: Yale University Press, 1954) offers the most comprehensive analysis of the intradenominational conflicts, including related controversies in the Episcopal, Methodist, Disciples of Christ, and southern denominations.

29. H. Richard Niebuhr, *Christ and Culture* (New York: Harper & Row, 1951).

30. Marsden, *Fundamentalism and American Culture,* p. 223.

31. Ibid., p. 186.

32. Quoted in Marsden, *Fundamentalism and American Culture,* p. 187. See Gresham J. Machen, *Christianity and Liberalism* (New York: Macmillan, 1923; reprint, Grand Rapids, Mich.: Eerdmans, 1979).

33. For an excellent collection of essays on the various branches of twentieth-century evangelicalism, see Dayton and Johnston, eds., *The Variety of American Evangelicalism.*

34. Wade Clark Roof and William McKinney, *American Mainline Religion: Its Changing Shape and Future* (New Brunswick, N.J.: Rutgers University Press, 1987).

35. Quoted in Marsden, *Fundamentalism and American Culture,* p. 3.

36. See Eldon G. Ernst, *Moment of Truth for Protestant America: Interchurch Campaign following World War I* (Missoula, Mont.: American Academy of Religion, 1974); and Henry F. May, *The End of American Innocence: A Study of the First Years of Our Own Time, 1912–1917* (New York: Alfred A. Knopf, 1959).

37. Robert T. Handy, "The American Religious Depression, 1925–1935," *Church History,* March 1960.

38. See Paul Tillich, *The Protestant Era* (Chicago: University of Chicago Press, 1948); and Robert Wuthnow, *The Restructuring of American Religion: Society and Faith since World War II* (Princeton: Princeton University Press, 1988).

39. Sacvan Bercovitch, *The Puritan Origins of the American Self* (New Haven: Yale University Press, 1975).

40. Marty, *Righteous Empire*, pp. 92–93. Further: John R. Bodo, *The Protestant Clergy and Public Issues, 1812–1848* (Princeton: Princeton University Press, 1954); Clyde Griffin, *Their Brothers' Keepers: Moral Stewardship in the United States, 1800–1865* (Westport, Conn.: Greenwood Press, 1983).

41. Joseph R. Gusfield, *Symbolic Crusade: Status Politics and the American Temperance Movement*, 2d ed. (Urbana: University of Illinois Press, 1986).

42. See Allan J. Lichtman, *Prejudice and the Old Politics: The Presidential Election of 1928* (Chapel Hill: University of North Carolina Press, 1979). Lichtman's analysis confirms the importance of the pan-Protestant coalition against rum and Romanism. On the "pietist-liturgical" cleavage, see Paul Kleppner, *The Cross of Culture: A Social Analysis of Midwestern Politics, 1850–1900* (New York: Free Press, 1970).

43. Cf. Will Herberg, *Protestant-Catholic-Jew* (Garden City, N.Y.: Doubleday, 1955); Robert Bellah, "Civil Religion in America," *Daedalus* 96 (1967); R. E. Richey and Donald G. Jones, eds., *American Civil Religion* (New York: Harper & Row, 1974); and Sidney E. Mead, *The Nation with the Soul of a Church* (New York: Harper & Row, 1975). It is often overlooked that for Herberg such a civil religion was a "particularly insidious kind of idolatry."

44. Daniel Bell, *The Cultural Contradictions of Capitalism* (New York: Basic Books, 1976).

45. Cf. Jeffrey K. Hadden, "Religious Broadcasting and the Mobilization of the New Christian Right," and Benton Johnson and Mark A. Shibley, "How New Is the New Christian Right? A Study of Three Presidential Elections," in Jeffrey K. Hadden and Anson Shupe, eds., *Secularization and Fundamentalism Reconsidered* (New York: Paragon House, 1989), p. 238; and Tina Rosenberg, "How the Media Made the Moral Majority," *Washington Monthly*, May 1982. The social-scientific literature on Protestant fundamentalism and the New Christian Right is both voluminous and full of contradictory claims. One of the earliest and still one of the best collections of essays is Robert C. Liebman and Robert Wuthnow, eds., *The New Christian Right: Mobilization and Legitimation* (Hawthorne, N.Y.: Aldine, 1983). The best and most comprehensive monographic study of the social movement is Steve Bruce, *The Rise and Fall of the New Christian Right: Conservative Protestant Politics in America, 1978–1988* (Oxford: Clarendon Press, 1988). The best sociological interpretation of conservative evangelical Protestantism from the perspective of the theory of modernization (i.e., secularization) is James D. Hunter, *American Evangelicalism: Conservative Religion and the Quandary of Modernity* (New Brunswick, N.J.: Rutgers University Press, 1983). Its main drawback is Hunter's failure to distinguish between conservative evangelicals and fundamentalists. An excellent collection of voices

from within evangelicalism and analytical, critical (mostly sympathetic), and political commentary is Richard John Neuhaus and Michael Cromartie, eds., *Piety and Politics: Evangelicals and Fundamentalists Confront the World* (Washington, D.C.: Ethics and Public Policy Center, 1987). Good collections of essays examining public opinion surveys and the electoral-political impact are David G. Bromley and Anson D. Shupe, eds., *New Christian Politics* (Macon, Ga.: Mercer University Press, 1984), and James L. Guth and John C. Green, eds., *The Bible and the Ballot Box: Religion and Politics in the 1988 Election* (Boulder, Colo.: Westview Press, 1991). Good collections of cultural-historical, interpretative essays are George M. Marsden, *Understanding Fundamentalism and Evangelicalism* (Grand Rapids, Mich.: Eerdmans, 1991), and Marsden, *Evangelicalism and Modern America* (Grand Rapids, Mich.: Eerdmans, 1984).

46. See Mayer N. Zald and John D. McCarthy, eds., *Social Movements in an Organizational Society: Collected Essays* (New Brunswick, N.J.: Transaction, 1987). Much of their theoretical and analytical model is based on empirical studies of religious movements, of religious organizations, and of the role of religion as infrastructure of various social movement organizations.

47. On the construction of a separate fundamentalist lifeworld from the 1930s to the 1970s, cf. Joel A. Carpenter, "Fundamentalist Institutions and the Rise of Evangelical Protestantism, 1929–1942," *Church History* 49 (1980); G. W. Dollar, *A History of Fundamentalism in America* (Greenville, S.C.: Bob Jones University Press, 1973); and Jerry Fallwell, ed., *The Fundamentalist Phenomenon: The Resurgence of Conservative Christianity* (Garden City, N.Y.: Doubleday, 1981). For an excellent ethnographic study of a fundamentalist community in the urban Northeast, see Nancy T. Ammerman, *Bible Believers: Fundamentalism in the Modern World* (New Brunswick, N.J.: Rutgers University Press, 1987). On fundamentalist political involvement, see Leo Ribuffo, *The Old Christian Right: The Protestant Far Right from the Great Depression to the Cold War* (Philadelphia: Temple University Press, 1983); W. L. Vinz, "The Politics of Protestant Fundamentalism in the 1950s and 1960s," *Journal of Church and State* 14, no. 2 (1972); Gary K. Clabaugh, *Thunder on the Right: The Protestant Fundamentalists* (Chicago: Nelson-Hall, 1974); and Erling Jorstad, *The Politics of Doomsday: Fundamentalists of the Far Right* (Nashville, Tenn.: Abingdon Press, 1970). On televangelism, see Jeffrey K. Hadden and Charles E, Swann, *Prime Time Preachers: The Rising Power of Televangelism* (Reading, Mass.: Addison-Wesley, 1981), and Jeffrey K. Hadden and Anson Shupe, *Televangelism: Power and Politics on God's Frontier* (New York: Henry Holt, 1988). On the growth of conservative Protestantism, see Dean Kelley, *Why Conservative Churches Are Growing* (New York: Harper & Row, 1972).

48. For the various stages of this old dream of a rightist conservative majority, see Kevin Phillips, *The Emerging Republican Majority* (Garden City, N.Y.: Anchor, 1969); Patrick Buchanan, *The New Majority: President Nixon at Mid-Passage* (Philadelphia: Girard Bank, 1973); William A. Rusher, *The Making of a New Majority Party* (New York: Sheed & Ward, 1975), and *The Rise of the Right* (New York: Morrow, 1984); and Richard Viguerie, *The New Right: We're*

Ready to Lead (Falls Church, Va.: Viguerie Co., 1980). See also Timothy A. Byrnes, *Catholic Bishops in American Politics* (Princeton: Princeton University Press, 1991).

49. In Alan Crawford, *Thunder on the Right: The "New Right" and the Politics of Resentment* (New York: Pantheon, 1980), p. 3.

50. This is true, of course, only of what William Gamson has called "the organizational tributary" to the mainstream known as "resource mobilization." See William A. Gamson, "Introduction," and John D. McCarthy and Mayer N. Zald, "Resource Mobilization and Social Movements: A Partial Theory," in Zald and McCarthy, *Social Movements*. For overviews of various competing contemporary perspectives, see the special issue "On Social Movements," *Social Research 52*, no. 4 (Winter 1985); Jean L. Cohen and Andrew Arato, "Social Movements and Civil Society," in *Civil Society and Political Theory* (Cambridge, Mass.: MIT Press, 1992); and Bert Klandermans and Sidney Tarrow, "Mobilization into Social Movements: Synthesizing European and American Approaches," *International Social Movement Research* 1 (1988). See also Roy Wallis and Steven Bruce, *Sociological Theory, Religion and Collective Action* (Belfast: The Queen's University of Belfast, 1986).

51. See Dinesh D'Souza, *Falwell before the Millennium: A Critical Biography* (Chicago: Regnery Gateway, 1984).

52. First paragraph quoted in Reichley, *Religion in American Public Life*, p. 316. Second paragraph quoted in Bruce, *The Rise and Fall of the New Christian Right*, p. 138.

53. Bob Jones III was soon propagating the view that "a close, analytical, biblical look at the Moral Majority . . . reveals a movement that holds more potential for hastening the church of Antichrist and building the ecumenical church than anything to come down the pike in a long time, including the charismatic movement." In Bruce, *The Rise and Fall of the New Christian Right*, p. 173.

54. Even in those hardly imaginable extreme cases in which organizers could claim to have "manufactured" the motives, the fact that they needed to manufacture motives proves that even they believe that people need motives to act, that without motives, authentic or inauthentic, social action does not make sense either to the actors or to the observers.

55. Jerry Falwell, ed., *The Fundamentalist Phenomenon*, was written by Ed Dobson and Ed Hindson, two professors at Falwell's Liberty Baptist College. It includes a final section, "Future-Word: An Agenda for the Eighties," written by Falwell.

56. Jerry Falwell, *Listen America!* (New York: Doubleday, 1980).

57. Naturally, social movements are always made up of pluralities of organizations and actors with different motives and rationales, different strategies and levels of involvement, different identities and goals, etc. In my analysis I assume that the Moral Majority formed the organizational core of the New Christian Right, that Jerry Falwell and his associates formed the core leadership of the Moral Majority, and that Jerry Falwell's *Listen America!* articulated the core set of beliefs, grievances, and goals of this leadership. Steven Bruce's methodologi-

cally eclectic and comprehensive study of the movement confirms, in my view, my main assumptions. One would expect that anybody interested in studying the emergence of any movement would read and take seriously the manifestos of their leaders. Curiously enough, in the voluminous literature on the Protestant fundamentalist movement, I have not found any systematic analysis or consideration of Falwell's *Listen America!*

58. Cf. Perry Miller, *Errand into the Wilderness;* and Sacvan Bercovitch, *The American Jeremiad* (Madison: University of Wisconsin Press, 1978).

59. Despite repeated attempts, it has been proven again and again by Wittgensteinian linguistics, hermeneutics, ethnomethodology, and other phenomenological perspectives that specialized scientific interpretations can never free themselves completely from their foundation in ordinary, commonsensical, taken-for-granted interpretations of reality. See Jürgen Habermas, *On the Logic of the Social Sciences* (Cambridge, Mass.: MIT Press, 1988).

60. See Mayer N. Zald and Bert Useem, "Movement and Countermovement Interaction: Mobilization, Tactics, and State Involvement," in Zald and McCarthy, *Social Movements.*

61. Only when discussing pornography and commercial television do they recognize the threats of commercialism, commodification of human beings, and crash materialism. See Falwell, *Listen America!* pp. 190, 200–203.

62. The notion that threats (and opportunities) posed to traditional structures and lifeworlds by centralized state and market penetration play a crucial role in the emergence of social movements is central to perspectives as diverse as those of Charles Tilly and Jürgen Habermas. See Charles Tilly, *From Mobilization to Revolution* (Reading, Mass.: Addison-Wesley, 1978), and Charles Tilly, Louise Tilly, and Richard Tilly, *The Rebellious Century: 1830–1930* (Cambridge, Mass.: Harvard University Press, 1975); and Jürgen Habermas, *The Theory of Communicative Action,* vol. 2 (Boston: Beacon Press, 1985), and "The New Obscurity: The Crisis of the Welfare State and the Exhaustion of Utopian Energies," in *The New Conservatism: Cultural Criticism and the Historians' Debate* (Cambridge, Mass.: MIT Press, 1989). For a critical comparison of the two perspectives, see Jean Cohen and Andrew Arato, "Social Movements and Civil Society."

63. Falwell, *The Fundamentalist Phenomenon,* p. 188.

64. Ibid., p. 206.

65. Ibid., p. 208.

66. See also Tim La Haye, *The Battle for the Mind: A Subtle Warfare* (Old Tappan, N.J.: Revell, 1980).

67. See Gary North, *Political Polytheism: The Myth of Pluralism* (Tyler, Tex.: Institute for Christian Economics, 1989). On the reconstructionists, see also Ammerman, "North American Protestant Fundamentalism," pp. 49–54.

68. Falwell, *The Fundamentalist Phenomenon,* pp. 188–89.

69. For two representative attempts, see Reichley, *Religion in American Public Life,* and Richard John Neuhaus, *The Naked Public Square: Religion and Democracy in America* (Grand Rapids, Mich.: Eerdmans, 1984).

70. Quoted in Marty, *Righteous Empire,* pp. 42–43. It would seem that the

allegedly secularist readings of the First Amendment on the part of the Supreme Court since the 1960s are more consistent with the original intent expressed in those texts than with neoconservative revisionist interpretations. For a good collection of essays touching upon these issues, see Thomas Robbins and Roland Robertson, eds., *Church-State Relations: Tensions and Transitions* (New Brunswick, N.J.: Transaction Books, 1987).

71. Falwell, *The Fundamentalist Phenomenon,* p. 188. The lingering, but now much more sophisticated, post-Kuhnian and postmodern, defense of creationism as an alternative scientific paradigm to evolutionism indicates that, if they could, they would also gladly reestablish the Protestant cultural hegemony over public education. Cf. George Marsden, "Why Creation Science?" in *Understanding Fundamentalism and Evangelicalism;* Dorothy Nelkin, *The Creation Controversy: Science or Scripture in the Schools* (New York: Norton, 1982); and Langdon Gilkey, *Creationism on Trial: Evolution and God at Little Rock* (Minneapolis: Winston Press, 1985).

72. To get a sense of the dizzyingly pluralistic American religious sphere, see Catherine Albanese, *America: Religion and Religions* (Belmont, Calif.: Wadsworth, 1992).

73. Nathan Glazer, "Fundamentalism: A Defensive Offensive," in Neuhaus and Cromartie, *Piety and Politics,* p. 251. Also in this volume, see Richard Neuhaus, "What the Fundamentalists Want"; George Will, "Who Put Morality in Politics?"; William Buckley, Jr., "Yale and the Moral Majority"; William J. Bennett, "Religious Belief and the Constitutional Order"; and Joseph Sobran, "Secular Humanism and the American Way."

74. Cf. Frances Fitzgerald, "A Disciplined, Charging Army," *New Yorker,* 18 May 1981; J. Milton Yinger and Stephen J. Cutler, "The Moral Majority Viewed Sociologically," in Bromley and Shupe, *New Christian Politics;* Anson Shupe and William Stacey, "The Moral Majority Constituency," in Liebman and Wuthnow, *The New Christian Right;* and Bruce, *The Rise and Fall of the New Christian Right.*

75. See Phillip E. Hammond, "Another Great Awakening?" in Liebman and Wuthnow, *The New Christian Right;* McLoughlin, *Revivals, Awakenings, and Reform;* and Robert N. Bellah and Phillip E. Hammond, *Varieties of Civil Religion* (San Francisco: Harper & Row, 1980).

76. Hammond, "Another Great Awakening?" p. 208.

77. See, for instance, the cited works of Nancy T. Ammerman, James D. Hunter, and George M. Marsden.

78. See Nancy T. Ammerman, *Baptist Battles: Social Change and Religious Conflict in the Southern Baptist Convention* (New Brunswick, N.J.: Rutgers University Press, 1990), and "Organizational Conflict in the Southern Baptist Convention," in Hadden and Shupe, *Secularization and Fundamentalism.*

79. See James D. Hunter, *American Evangelicalism,* and *Evangelicalism: The Coming Generation* (Chicago: University of Chicago Press, 1987).

80. For one of the classic studies of the religion of the disinherited, see Liston Pope, *Millhands and Preachers: A Study of Gastonia* (New Haven: Yale University Press, 1942).

81. See David O. Moberg, *The Great Reversal: Evangelicalism and Social Concern* (Philadelphia: Lippincott, 1972).

82. See Martin Marty, *Righteous Empire*, and "The Protestant Principle: Between Theocracy and Propheticism," in Neil Biggar, Jamie S. Scott, and William Schweiker, eds., *Cities of Gods: Faith, Politics and Pluralism in Judaism, Christianity, and Islam* (Westport, Conn.: Greenwood Press, 1986).

83. They also have plenty of resources. Three theology professors, David Wells, Mark Noll, and Cornelius Plantinga, Jr., were recently awarded a $400,000 grant for a four-year project to strengthen the Reformed perspective within evangelical theology. See Robert K. Johnston, "American Evangelicalism: An Extended Family," in Dayton and Johnston, *The Variety of American Evangelicalism*, p. 271. This excellent collection of essays gives a good idea of the rich internal denominational diversity within the evangelical tent. Marsden, ed., *Evangelicalism and Modern America*, also offers a good collection of essays, representative of the internal intellectual debates within the evangelical denomination. For the view that the evangelicals have won the intellectual-theological battle with liberal Protestantism, see Edwin Scott Gaustad, "*Did* the Fundamentalists Win?" in Mary Douglas and Steven Tipton, eds., *Religion and America: Spirituality in a Secular Age* (Boston: Beacon Press, 1982).

84. A good sample of various representative public evangelical positions can be found in Neuhaus and Cromartie, *Piety and Politics*.

85. Martin Marty, "Public Religion: The Republican Banquet," in *Religion and Republic: The American Circumstance* (Boston: Beacon Press, 1987).

86. Paul J. Weber, "Examining the Religious Lobbies," *This World* 1 (Winter/Spring 1982).

87. Richard John Neuhaus, *The Naked Public Square: Religion and Democracy in America* (Grand Rapids, Mich.: Eerdmans, 1984), pp. 36–37. One could add that Neuhaus's own belief that without religion the public sphere would be "naked" is also questionable. The argument tends to privilege religious normative traditions over other normative traditions. Moreover, his argument that the Judeo-Christian tradition should be the religion of the public square because an overwhelming majority of Americans hold Judeo-Christian beliefs privately, contradicts his own principle that private beliefs should be submitted to public examination before becoming public truths.

88. See Seyla Benhabib, "Models of Public Space: Hannah Arendt, the Liberal Tradition and Jürgen Habermas," in Craig Calhoun, ed., *Habermas and the Public Sphere* (Cambridge, Mass.: MIT Press, 1991).

89. See Peter Berger, "Secularization and the Problem of Plausibility," *The Sacred Canopy* (Garden City, N.Y.: Doubleday, 1967).

Chapter Seven

1. Unfortunately, people in the United States have appropriated, all too frequently with messianic and imperial overtones, the name of an entire continent, America, to designate the land and the inhabitants of one particular country of that continent. While the attitude behind this linguistic usage is deplorable, I am

uncertain about the desirability of changing the linguistic practice itself. Somewhat reluctantly, therefore, I will adhere to common practice and will use the term American Catholicism to refer to Catholicism in the United States of America.

2. Most discussions and uses of the church-sect typology fail to distinguish these four dimensions.

3. Fortunately, there are available two excellent and complementary histories of Catholicism in America, on which I have relied in the first historical section of this study: James Hennesey, S.J. *American Catholics: A History of the Roman Catholic Community in the United States* (New York: Oxford University Press, 1981); and Jay P. Dolan, *The American Catholic Experience: A History from Colonial Times to the Present* (Garden City, N.Y.: Doubleday, 1985). An earlier historical interpretive essay worth reading is Andrew M. Greeley, *The Catholic Experience: An Interpretation of the History of American Catholicism* (Garden City, N.Y.: Doubleday, 1969).

4. These figures should be viewed as bare estimates. Every text I know offers different figures. The ones presented here are a composite of data taken from the sources mentioned above and from Robert Wuthnow, *The Restructuring of American Religion* (Princeton: Princeton University Press, 1988), p. 18.

5. George Gallup, Jr., and Jim Castelli, *The American Catholic People: Their Beliefs, Practices and Values* (Garden City, N.Y.: Doubleday, 1987), pp. 2–3. Other longitudinal surveys offer divergent data. See Andrew M. Greeley, *Religious Change in America* (Cambridge, Mass.: Harvard University Press, 1989).

6. Perry Miller, *The Life of the Mind in America from the Revolution to the Civil War* (New York: Harcourt Brace & World, 1965).

7. Ray Allen Billington, *The Protestant Crusade, 1800–1860: A Study of the Origins of American Nativism* (New York: Macmillan, 1938), p. 70 and passim.

8. In Hennesey, *American Catholics,* p. 119.

9. Hennesey, *American Catholics,* pp. 124–26.

10. William G. McLoughlin, *Revivals, Awakenings, and Reform* (Chicago: University of Chicago Press, 1978), pp. 140–78.

11. Dolan, *American Catholic Experience,* p. 161.

12. Cf. George M. Marsden, *Fundamentalism and American Culture: The Shaping of Twentieth-Century Evangelicalism, 1870–1925* (New York: Oxford University Press, 1980), and Willam R. Hutchison, *The Modernist Impulse in American Protestantism* (Cambridge, Mass.: Harvard University Press, 1976).

13. Joseph R. Gusfield, *Symbolic Crusade: Status Politics and the American Temperance Movement,* 2d ed. (Urbana, Ill.: University of Illinois Press, 1986); and Allan J. Lichtman, *Prejudice and the Old Politics: The Presidential Election of 1928* (Chapel Hill: University of North Carolina Press, 1979).

14. See Wuthnow, *Restructuring of American Religion.*

15. Andrew Greeley is never tired of exposing the "ugly little secret" of anti-Catholic prejudices among liberal educated upper-class groups. See Andrew Greeley, *The Catholic Myth: The Behavior and Beliefs of American Catholics* (New York: Charles Scribner's Sons, 1990); *The American Catholic: A Social Portrait* (New York: Basic Books, 1977); and *American Catholics since the*

Council (New York: Thomas More Press, 1985). All evidence to the contrary, 40 percent of liberal college-educated Protestants from the Northeast (vs. 30 percent of the general Protestant population and 20 percent of Jews) still agree that "Catholics are afraid to think for themselves" and "Catholics tend to think the way their bishops and priests want them to think." For a classic exponent of liberal anti-Catholic prejudices, see Paul Blanshard, *American Freedom and Catholic Power* (Boston: Beacon Press, 1958).

16. Will Herberg, *Protestant-Catholic-Jew* (Garden City, N.Y.: Doubleday, 1960).

17. Dolan, *American Catholic Experience*, p. 80.

18. In Hennesey, *American Catholics*, p. 68.

19. David O'Brien has offered the most systematic characterization of both styles of Catholicism. See David O'Brien, *Public Catholicism* (New York: Macmillan, 1989).

20. O'Brien, *Public Catholicism*, p. 5. See Bernhard Groethuysen, *The Bourgeois* (New York: Holt, Rinehart & Winston, 1968).

21. In Greeley, *The Catholic Experience*, p. 94. Bishop England was taking issue with statements made by President John Quincy Adams.

22. In O'Brien, *Public Catholicism*, p. 30.

23. In Hennesey, *American Catholics*, p. 124.

24. Greeley, *The Catholic Experience*, p. 107.

25. Cf. Robert D.Cross, *The Emergence of Liberal Catholicism in America* (Cambridge, Mass.: Harvard University Press, 1958); Thomas T. McAvoy, *The Americanist Heresy in Roman Catholicism, 1895–1900* (Notre Dame, Ind.: University of Notre Dame Press, 1963); Gerald P. Fogarty, *The Vatican and the American Hierarchy from 1870 to 1965* (Wilmington, Del.: Michael Glazier, 1985); and Bernard M. Reardon, *Roman Catholic Modernism* (Stanford: Stanford University Press, 1970).

26. William M. Halsey, *The Survival of American Innocence: Catholicism in an Era of Disillusionment, 1920–1940* (Notre Dame, Ind.: University of Notre Dame Press, 1980). On devotional Catholicism and the neighborhood parish, see Dolan, *American Catholic Experience*. On the Middle Ages and Thomism, see Philip Gleason, *Keeping the Faith: American Catholicism Past and Present* (Notre Dame, Ind: University of Notre Dame Press, 1987).

27. The debate was started by John Tracy Ellis's "American Catholics and the Intellectual Life," *Thought* 30 (1955).

28. See Greeley, *The Catholic Experience*, p. 283, for the relevant sections of the speech.

29. See, Jay P. Dolan, *The Immigrant Church* (Baltimore: Johns Hopkins University Press, 1970), and *American Catholic Experience*, chaps. 5–12, pp. 127–346.

30. Dolan, *American Catholic Experience*, p. 301.

31. There were, for instance, 1,515,818 Catholics worshiping in Italian-speaking parishes, 1,425,193 in Polish parishes, 1,026,066 in French parishes, and 552,244 in Spanish-speaking parishes. Dolan, *American Catholic Experience*, pp. 134–35.

32. Schisms, to be sure, occurred throughout the nineteenth century and into this century, particularly those of dissident parishes which fought with their bishops over ownership and governance. But eventually, most of them—with the significant exception of the Polish National Catholic church and the large number of Uniate Ruthenian-Ukrainians who joined the Russian Orthodox church—rejoined the Catholic church. For a further elaboration, see my "Roman and Catholic and American," p. 89 and passim.

33. Will Herberg's *Protestant-Catholic-Jew* remains the classic statement. But it is important to keep in mind a few qualifications. First, the immigration experience is still very recent. More than half of the Catholic population are still first- or second-generation Americans. Second, "the ethnics" have turned out to be much more unmeltable than the assimilation theories of the 1960s assumed. Finally, the immigrant experience is by no means over. Since World War II, the American Catholic church has continued receiving large influxes of Portuguese, Filipinos, Vietnamese, Haitians, and, above all, Hispanics. There are today more than 10 million Hispanic Catholics, which constitute roughly 16 percent of American Catholics. The Hispanics are facing the same problems every other Catholic immigrant group encountered before them. But the American Catholic church has become to such a large extent a white-European middle-class institution that it is finding it very difficult to meet the spiritual and social needs of the Hispanics. Cf. Harold J. Abramson, *Ethnic Diversity in Catholic America* (New York: Wiley, 1973); Gallup and Castelli, *Catholic People*, pp. 139–48; Greeley, *The American Catholic;* and Antonio M. Stevens-Arroyo, ed., *Prophets Denied Honor: An Anthology on the Hispanic Church in the United States* (Maryknoll, N.Y.: Orbis, 1980).

34. See Sidney E. Mead, "Denominationalism: The Shape of Protestantism in America," in *The Lively Experiment* (New York: Harper & Row, 1976), pp. 103–33.

35. Jay P. Dolan, *Catholic Revivalism* (Notre Dame, Ind.: University of Notre Dame Press, 1978).

36. David O'Brien, *American Catholics and Social Reform: The New Deal Years* (New York: Oxford University Press, 1968).

37. Cf. Charles Meconis, *With Clumsy Grace: The American Catholic Left, 1961–1975* (New York: Seabury, 1979); Mel Piehl, *Breaking Bread: The Catholic Worker and the Origin of Catholic Radicalism in America* (Philadelphia: Temple University Press, 1982).

38. Following a Parsonsian framework, Joseph Varacalli has shown how conceptions of "particularity" and "universality" were upgraded. Joseph A. Varacalli, *Toward the Establishment of Liberal Catholicism in America* (New York: University Press of America, 1983).

39. All the Protestant denominations broke ties with their mother church in Europe and made some concession to republican principles when establishing their system of church governance. See Sydney E. Ahlstrom, *A Religious History of the American People* (New Haven: Yale University Press, 1972).

40. To this day the control by the Vatican of the process of the selection of bishops remains, in the United States as elsewhere, a key factor in shaping the

direction of church policies. See Thomas Reese, "The Selection of Bishops," *America* 151 (25 August 1984).

41. See Patrick W. Carey, *People, Priests, and Prelates: Eclesiastical Democracy and the Tensions of Trusteeism* (Notre Dame, Ind.: University of Notre Dame Press, 1987).

42. Ibid., p. 15.

43. Bishop John England of Charleston offered in the 1820s an alternative system of church governance more in affinity with the American circumstance. But his fellow American bishops made sure that "this constitution or *democratic* method of ruling the Church (not) be approved by the Holy See." See Greeley, *The Catholic Experience*, p. 85 and passim.

44. John England was again the only bishop who saw the need to establish some national synodic structure. But here also his episcopal colleagues resisted all his plans and suggestions. See Greeley, *The Catholic Experience*, pp. 89–93.

45. See Timothy A. Byrnes, *Catholic Bishops in American Politics* (Princeton: Princeton University Press, 1991).

46. Dolan, *American Catholic Experience*, p. 190.

47. There had been, of course, the earlier involvement of some bishops in the labor movement, particularly in support of the Knights of Labor. See Henry J. Browne, *The Catholic Church and the Knights of Labor* (Washington, D.C.: Catholic University Press, 1949); and James Roohan, *American Catholics and the Social Question, 1865–1900* (New York: Arno Press, 1976).

48. Cf. Aaron I. Abell, *American Catholicism and Social Action: A Search for Social Justice* (Garden City, N.Y.: Doubleday, 1960); and Francis L. Broderick, *Right Reverend New Dealer: John A. Ryan* (New York: Macmillan, 1963).

49. In Hennesy, *American Catholics*, p. 252.

50. O'Brien, *Catholics and Social Reform*, pp. 150–81; and Alan Brinkley, *Voices of Protest: Huey Long, Father Coughlin, and the Great Depression* (New York: Alfred A. Knopf, 1982).

51. Alexis de Tocqueville, *Democracy in America* (New York: Vintage, 1990), vol. 1, pp. 301–2.

52. At the time those debates were taking place, Tocqueville had already argued that "the Catholic religion has erroneously been regarded as the natural enemy of democracy. Among the various sects of Christians, Catholicism seems to me, on the contrary, to be one of the most favorable to equality of condition among men." Tocqueville, *Democracy in America*, vol. 1, p. 300.

53. See Dorothy Dohen, *Nationalism and American Catholicism* (New York: Sheed & Ward, 1967), p. 95. Bishop Hughes was also unafraid of challenging the Evangelicals to a missionizing duel on their home territory, while mocking the conspiratorial fears of Protestant nativists.

54. Ibid., p. 111. Ireland was prone to composing the most mellifluous odes and outright idolatrous hymns to the American republic.

55. In Byrnes, *Catholic Bishops*, p. 19.

56. For the most lucid exposition and the best internal critique of the traditional Catholic position, see John Courtney Murray, "The Problem of Religious Freedom," *Theological Studies* 25 (1964): 503–75.

57. That "error has no rights" was still the line taken by Cardinal Ottaviani and the conservative bishops who were trying to block the declaration on religious freedom at Vatican II. See John Courtney Murray, "The Issue of Church and State at Vatican II," *Theological Studies* 27 (December 1966): 580–606.

58. Often the Americanists tied the mission of the republic to the mission of the church. "The Church triumphing in America," Ireland said, "Catholic truth will travel on the wings of American influence, and encircle the universe." In Dohen, *Nationalism*, p. 109.

59. John Courtney Murray, S.J., *We Hold These Truths: Catholic Reflections on the American Proposition* (New York: Sheed & Ward, 1960).

60. Vincent A. Yzermans, ed., *American Participation in the Second Vatican Council* (New York: Sheed & Ward, 1967).

61. Cf. Donald F. Crosby, S.J., *God, Church and Flag: Senator Joseph R. McCarthy and the Catholic Church, 1950–57* (Chapel Hill: University of North Carolina Press, 1978); Fogarty, *The Vatican;* and Dohen, *Nationalism.*

62. Cf. John Cooney, *The American Pope: The Life and Times of Francis Cardinal Spellman* (New York: Times Books, 1984), and Lawrence Fuchs, *John F. Kennedy and American Catholicism* (New York: Meredith, 1967).

63. Jim Castelli's *The Bishops and the Bomb: Waging Peace in a Nuclear Age* (Garden City, N.J.: Doubleday, 1983) presents the text of the pastoral letter as well as a helpful reconstruction of the process leading up to the various drafts and the publication of the final text. Phillip J. Murnion, ed., *Catholics and Nuclear War: A Commentary on "The Challenge of Peace"* (New York: Crossroad, 1983), offers one of the best collections of interpretive and evaluative essays on the pastoral letter. Thomas M. Gannon, S.J., ed., *The Catholic Challenge to the American Economy* (New York: Macmillan, 1987), does the same for the pastoral letter on the U.S. economy and also includes the complete final text. John A. Coleman, ed., *One Hundred Years of Catholic Social Thought* (Maryknoll, N.Y.: Orbis, 1991), offers an excellent collection of essays interpreting Catholic social thought on the family, work, and peace. On abortion, cf. Hans Lotstra, *Abortion: The Catholic Debate in America* (New York: Irvington Publishers, 1985), and Patricia Beattie Jung and Thomas A. Shannon, eds., *Abortion and Catholicism: The American Debate* (New York: Crossroad, 1988). Timothy A. Byrnes's *Catholic Bishops in American Politics* (Princeton: Princeton University Press, 1991) offers the best reconstruction of the American political context within which the three events took place.

64. My primary interest is not in the normative content of the texts but in their public nature as public events in the public sphere. Thus, the argument that the two pastoral letters and the public intervention of the bishops on the issue of abortion constitute two formally different types of public Catholicism is based primarily on the different modes of publicity involved.

65. John Tracy Ellis, the dean of American Catholic historians, wrote: "The American Catholics have known no comparable experience to what broke over them about 1966, nor, indeed, has there been anything of a like character within universal Catholicism since the French Revolution shook the Church to its foundations." John Tracy Ellis, Foreword, in Hennesey, *American Catholics,* p. xi.

66. Byrnes, *Catholic Bishops,* pp. 3–4 and passim.

67. Varacalli, *Establishment of Liberal Catholicism.*

68. When American bishops talk of the council, they usually do so in terms of a personal experience, "before" and "after," akin to conversion. See Archbishop John Quinn's testimony in Castelli, *Bishops and the Bomb,* p. 35.

69. For two different classical analyses of these transformations, see Daniel Bell, *The Coming of Post-Industrial Society* (New York: Basic Books, 1973); and Joseph Bensman and Arthur Vidich, *The New American Society* (Chicago: Quadrangle Books, 1971).

70. Even less applicable to the Catholic context is the thesis, used to explain the growth of conservative Protestant churches, that the political activism of a liberal clergy was alienating the more conservative laity. Opinion surveys show conclusively that, in general, ordinary Catholics welcomed the reforms from above and that once the original shock and the accompanying crisis were over, they have consistently expected and desired faster and further reforms. A storm will gather in the Catholic church only if those expectations are frustrated. Cf. Jeffrey Hadden, *The Gathering Storm in the Churches* (New York: Doubleday, 1969); James Hitchkock, *The Decline and Fall of Radical Catholicism* (New York: Doubleday, 1972); and Garry Wills, *Bare Ruined Choirs* (New York: Doubleday, 1972). Evidence from public opinion surveys can be found in Gallup and Castelli, *American Catholic People,* and Greeley, *American Catholics since the Council.*

71. Varacalli, *Establishment of Liberal Catholicism,* p. 171.

72. Ibid., p. 1 and passim.

73. Not surprisingly, the thesis comes from a liberal theologian turned conservative bishop-cardinal. See *The Ratzinger Report* (San Francisco: Ignatius Press, 1985).

74. Cf. Peter Hebblethwaite, *Synod Extraordinary: The Inside Story of the Rome Synod, November–December 1985* (Garden City, N.Y.: Doubleday, 1986); Penny Lernoux, *People of God: The Struggle for World Catholicism* (New York: Penguin, 1989); Ralph Della Cava, "Vatican Policy, 1978–90: An Updated Overview," *Social Research* 59, no. 1 (Spring 1992); and James Hitchcock, *Catholicism and Modernity: Confrontation or Capitulation?* (New York: Seabury, 1979); William D. Dinges and James Hitchcock, "Roman Catholic Traditionalism and Activist Conservatism in the United States," in Martin E. Marty and R. Scott Appleby, eds., *Fundamentalisms Observed* (Chicago: University of Chicago Press, 1991); George A. Kelly, *The Battle for the American Church* (New York: Doubleday, 1979), and *Keeping the Faith Catholic with John Paul II* (New York: Doubleday, 1990).

75. See Karl Rahner, "Dream of the Church," *Tablet* 180 (1981): 52–55.

76. The letters went through several drafts, which elicited public debate and reactions from those concerned even before the publication of the final text. In their public deliberations, the drafting committees and the episcopal conference also heard the testimony of numerous "experts," of representatives from the administration, of interest groups, of social movement activists, of other religious groups, and of dissenting Catholics. The bishops also consulted with Rome and with other episcopal bodies.

77. Strictly speaking, discourse ethics have a counterfactual character. See

Jürgen Habermas, "Discourse Ethics: Notes on a Program of Philosophical Justification," and other essays in Seyla Benhabib and Fred Dallmayr, eds., *The Communicative Ethics Controversy* (Cambridge, Mass.: MIT Press, 1990); and Jean L. Cohen and Andrew Arato, "Discourse Ethics and Civil Society," in *Civil Society and Political Theory* (Cambridge, Mass.: MIT Press, 1992).

78. In Hebblethwaite, *Synod Extraordinary*, p. 59.

79. During the Mexican-American and Spanish-American wars, American bishops had proudly called attention not just to the willingness of Catholics to die for their country but to their readiness to kill foreign fellow Catholics as proof of their American patriotism and as evidence that the charges that Catholicism was un-American and a danger to the republic because of its Roman transnational character were false. See Dohen, *Nationalism and American Catholicism*.

80. Mary Hanna has noted that "World War I produced only one American Catholic conscientious objector," while the two hundred Catholic conscientious objectors of World War II were nearly all followers of the Catholic Worker movement. Not surprisingly, she adds that "throughout American history the Catholic Church and its bishops were probably the biggest hawks in our skies." Mary Hanna, *Catholics and American Politics* (Cambridge, Mass.: Harvard University Press, 1979), pp. 40–42.

81. See George Q. Flynn, *Roosevelt and Romanism: Catholics and American Diplomacy, 1937–1945* (Westport, Conn.: Greenwood, 1976); Crosby, *God, Church and Flag;* and Seymour Martin Lipset, "Three Decades of the Radical Right: Coughlinites, McCarthyites, and Birchers," in Daniel Bell, ed., *The Radical Right* (Garden City, N.Y.: Doubleday, 1964).

82. See Patricia McNeal, *The American Catholic Peace Movement, 1928–1972* (New York: Arno Press, 1978); and Piehl, *Breaking Bread.*

83. Cf. Gallup and Castelli, *American Catholic People,* pp. 77–84; Greeley, *American Catholics since the Council;* William A. Au, *The Cross, the Flag, and the Bomb: American Catholics Debate War and Peace, 1960–1983* (Westport, Conn.: Greenwood, 1985); Meconis, *The American Catholic Left;* and "The Bishops and Vietnam," *Commonweal,* 15 April 1966.

84. John XXIII's *Pacem in Terris* (1963) had called for a ban on nuclear weapons and an end to the arms race, and had raised the possibility that atomic weapons had made the criteria of "just war" theory inapplicable. The Pastoral Constitution *Gaudium et Spes* (1965) had declared that "any act of war aimed indiscriminately at the destruction of entire cities or of extensive areas along with their populations is a crime against God and man himself," de facto condemning retroactively Allied bombing strategies and the use of atomic weapons in Hiroshima and Nagasaki. In his talk at the Peace Memorial Park in February 1981 in Hiroshima, John Paul II had reiterated the threat that nuclear warfare posed to the entire planet and the moral obligation to confront this threat. See Castelli, *Bishops and the Bomb,* p. 26.

85. For a good collection of essays on the Catholic "just war" theory, see Thomas A. Shannon, ed., *War or Peace? The Search for New Answers* (Maryknoll, N.Y.: Orbis, 1980).

86. It is necessary to stress that the letter was not a pacifist statement. What followed from the bishops' opposition to nuclear deterrence policies was not unilateral disarmament, as some critics argued demagogically. Given the serious Soviet threat, which most bishops took for granted, what followed was the obligation to rely on economically more costly and politically more risky conventional warfare defense policies. This was precisely the issue which irked the German Episcopate, and probably Cardinal Ratzinger, at a time when a strong pacifist movement was shaking the political order throughout Europe.

87. According to Jim Castelli, this emphasis was "largely due to the insistence of Rome." Castelli, *Bishops and the Bomb*, p. 180. One may guess that Roman insistence came either out of deep respect for the sacred dignity of the human conscience, a theme one finds frequently in John Paul II's statements, or, most likely, out of geopolitical concern to prevent the American bishops from issuing an outright condemnation of Western nuclear deterrence policies. Ironically, at Vatican II, it was thanks to the concerted efforts of the American bishops that the council stopped short of condemning the same Western nuclear deterrence policies.

88. See David M. Byers, ed., *Justice in the Marketplace: Collected Statements of the Vatican and the United States Catholic Bishops on Economic Policy, 1891–1984* (Washington, D.C.: USCC, 1985).

89. "Economic Justice for All: A Pastoral Message," no. 3, in Gannon, *Catholic Challenge*.

90. Ibid., no. 13.

91. Ibid., no. 84.

92. Ibid., no. 122.

93. Ibid., no. 87.

94. Ibid., no. 52.

95. Ibid., no. 95.

96. Ibid., nos. 296 and 297.

97. See John T. Noonan, Jr., "Abortion and the Catholic Church: A Summary History," *Natural Law Forum* 13 (1968): 85–131; John T. Noonan, Jr., ed., *The Morality of Abortion: Legal and Historical Perspectives* (Cambridge, Mass.: Harvard University Press, 1970); and John Connery, *Abortion: The Development of the Roman Catholic Perspective* (Chicago: Loyola University Press, 1977).

98. Abbott, *Documents of Vatican II*, p. 256.

99. It was followed by *Statement on Abortion* (1969), *Statement on Abortion* and *Declaration on Abortion* (1970), and *Population and the American Future: A Response* (1972). See Nolan, *Pastoral Letters*, vol. 3.

100. In Byrnes, *Catholic Bishops*, p. 57.

101. See USCC, *Documentation on the Right to Life and Abortion*, vol. 1 (Washington, D.C.: United States Catholic Conference, 1974); USCC, *Documentation on Abortion and the Right to Life*, vol. 2 (Washington, D.C.: United States Catholic Conference, 1976); Archbishop John R. Roach and Cardinal Terence Cooke, "Testimony in Support of the Hatch Amendment," *Origins* 11 (19 November 1981); and Nolan, *Pastoral Letters*, vol. 4.

102. See Cardinal Joseph Bernardin, "The Consistent Ethic: What Sort of Framework?" and commentaries by Margaret O'Brien Steinfels, John R. Connery, and Christine E. Gudorf, in Jung and Shannon, eds., *Abortion and Catholicism*.

103. See Archbishop John R. Roach and Cardinal Terence Cooke, "Testimony in Support of the Hatch Amendment."

104. The fact that the church allows "indirect" abortion in cases of ectopic pregnancy, for example, far from pointing to some moral flexibility only shows the inhumanity of a formal-legalistic type of moral reasoning which permits the indirect killing of the fetus by removing the mother's organ and making her infertile, but forbids the direct killing of that same fetus in order to save the mother and the organ. Indeed, considering the consistent zeal with which the church has always placed the life of the fetus before the life of the mother, it is incumbent upon the church to show that those feminist theologians who attribute the church's zeal to misogyny are wrong. See Uta Ranke-Heinemann, *Eunuchs for the Kingdom of Heaven: Women, Sexuality, and the Catholic Church* (New York: Penguin, 1991).

105. Cf. Marian Faux, *Crusaders: Voices from the Abortion Front* (New York: Carol Publishing Group, 1990); Kristin Luker, *Abortion and the Politics of Motherhood* (Berkeley: University of California Press, 1984); Joni Lovenduski and Joyce Outshoorn, *The New Politics of Abortion* (Beverly Hills: Sage, 1986); Rosalind Pollack Petchesky, *Abortion and Woman's Choice: The State, Sexuality and Reproductive Freedom* (New York: Longman, 1984); and Celeste Michelle Condit, *Decoding Abortion Rhetoric* (Urbana: University of Illinois Press, 1990).

106. See Roger Rosenblatt, *Life Itself: Abortion in the American Mind* (New York: Random House, 1992).

107. Prominent lay Catholics, for instance, could express publicly without fear of being reprimanded their disagreement with the church's teachings, at times even denying the church competence on these matters. For an attempt to undercut the "authority" of the bishops' pastoral letter on the U.S. economy before it was even published, see William Simon and Michael Novak, *Toward the Future: Catholic Social Thought and the U.S.. Economy* (New York: Lay Commission on Catholic Social Teaching and the U.S. Economy, 1984).

108. On the Charles Curran "affair," see Charles Curran, *Faithful Dissent* (Kansas City, Mo.: Sheed & Ward, 1986). Among Curran's works, see "Abortion: Its Moral Apects" and "Civil Law and Christian Morality: Abortion and the Churches," in Edward Batchelor, Jr., ed., *Abortion: The Moral Issues* (New York: Pilgrim Press, 1982); *Issues in Sexual and Medical Ethics* (Notre Dame, Ind.: University of Notre Dame Press, 1978); *Toward an American Catholic Moral Theology* (Notre Dame, Ind.: University of Notre Dame Press, 1987); and *Tensions in Moral Theology* (Notre Dame, Ind.: University of Notre Dame Press, 1988).

109. See Rosemary Radford Reuther, "Catholics and Abortion: Authority vs. Dissent," in Jung and Shannon, *Abortion and Catholicism*.

110. See Charles Curran, "Official Catholic Social Teaching and Conscience" and "Official Catholic Social and Sexual Teachings: A Methodological Comparison," in *Tensions in Moral Theology*.

111. Commenting on this unprecedented emphasis on the role of individual conscience, Jim Castelli writes: "If people may legitimately disagree over whether or not it is moral to start a nuclear war and still remain Catholics in good standing, the mind boggles at the implications for less cosmic issues like contraception, sterilization, abortion, divorce." Castelli, *Bishops and the Bomb*, p. 180.

112. In fact, women have been excommunicated for serving in public welfare agencies which help to procure abortions.

113. USCC, *Documentation on the Right to Life*, p. 60.

114. See Byrnes, *Catholic Bishops*, p. 57.

115. Ibid.

116. See Lawrence Lader, *Politics, Power, and the Church: The Catholic Crisis and Its Challenge to American Pluralism* (New York: Macmillan, 1987).

117. See Cardinal John O'Connor, "From Theory to Practice in the Public-Policy Realm," in Jung and Shannon, *Abortion and Catholicism*. Originally published in *Origins* 16 (19 June 1986). This is a very important statement by perhaps the most aggressively anti-abortion activist of all American bishops, who in a very thoughtful and even lucid manner raises very important questions about the proper way of moving from "anguished concern" over basic moral "wrongs" and injustices at home and abroad to "effective action," without pretending to know the answers. He even admits that "as one who has blundered more frequently than most in attempting the transition from concern to action, I have demonstrated rather dramatically that I don't know the answer" (p. 241). For an illuminating biographical study of Cardinal O'Connor, see Nat Hentoff, *John Cardinal O'Connor: At the Storm Center of a Changing American Catholic Church* (New York: Scribner's Sons, 1987).

118. See Mario Cuomo, "Religious Belief and Public Policy: A Catholic Governor's Perspective," in Jung and Shannon, *Abortion and Catholicism*. On the 1984 presidential campaign, see Richard P. McBrien, *Caesar's Coin: Religion and Politics in America* (New York: Macmillan, 1987).

119. Mary T. Hanna, "Divided, Distracted, and Disengaged: Catholic Leaders and the 1988 Presidential Campaign," in James L. Guth and John C. Green, eds., *The Bible and the Ballot Box: Religion and Politics in the 1988 Election* (Boulder, Colo.: Westview Press, 1991), p. 42.

120. See Connie Paige, *The Right to Lifers: Who They Are, How They Operate, Where They Get Their Money* (New York: Summit Books, 1983).

121. As a rationale for the urgent need to single out the evil of abortion, the bishops stated that "while nuclear holocaust is a future possibility, the holocaust of abortion is a present reality." In McBrien, *Caesar's Coin*, p. 145.

122. "Pastoral Constitution on the Church in the Modern World," no. 76, in Abbott, *Documents*.

123. O'Connor, "From Theory to Practice," p. 244.

124. Chap. 4 shows that the Polish case is still ambiguous and open.

125. Cf. Mary Daly, *The Church and the Second Sex* (Boston: Beacon Press, 1985); and Ranke-Heinemann, *Eunuchs for the Kingdom*.

126. See Ari L. Goldman, "Little Hope Seen for Letter on Women," *New York Times*, 19 June 1992; and Peter Steinfels, "Bishops May Avoid Stand on Women," *New York Times*, 17 November 1992.

127. "Poll Finds Backing of Female Priests," *New York Times*, 19 June 1992. Public opinion surveys show that American Catholics support women's rights both in the church and in society. For a decade Catholics have indicated greater support than Protestants, and much greater support than Evangelicals, for the Equal Rights Amendment and for electing women as president, governor, mayor, or member of Congress. They also are more likely than Protestants to believe that women still face discrimination in employment.

128. See Laurence H. Tribe, *Abortion: The Clash of Absolutes* (New York: Norton, 1990).

129. See Jürgen Habermas, *The Theory of Communicative Action*, 2 vols. (Boston: Beacon Press, 1981–87).

130. Karel Dobbelaere, "The Secularization of Society? Some Methodological Suggestions," in Jeffrey K. Hadden and Anson Shupe, eds., *Secularization and Fundamentalism Reconsidered* (New York: Paragon House, 1989), pp. 39–40.

131. J. Bryan Hehir, "The Right and Competence of the Church in the American Case," in Coleman, *Hundred Years of Catholic Social Thought*, pp. 55–71.

132. It is most telling that the accusations of "economic illiteracy," "ineptitude," "off-the-wall utopianism," "flight from complexity," "conventional wisdom," "lumpen clichés," and the like, usually came not from professional economists but from neoconservative critics whose claims to economic expertise would be even more spurious than those the bishops could have possibly set forth. See Peter Steinfels, "The Bishops and Their Critics," *Dissent*, Spring 1985, pp. 176–82.

133. See James Davidson Hunter and John Steadman Rice, "Unlikely Alliances: The Changing Contours of American Religious Faith," in Alan Wolfe, ed., *America at Century's End* (Berkeley: University of California Press, 1991); and Wuthnow, *The Restructuring of American Religion*.

134. One could say, at most, that Catholics tend to be generally more liberal than Protestants and slightly more liberal than the American population at large. Cf. Gallup and Castelli, *American Catholic People*, and Greeley, *American Catholics since the Council*.

135. See the results of the 1987 *Religion and Power Survey* in Hunter and Rice, "Unlikely Alliances."

136. A few survey results should suffice as illustration. Catholic religious leaders, in line with their general Catholic political affiliation, show a much stronger identification with the Democratic party than Protestant or Jewish religious leaders. The Democratic party identification was 46 percent among conservative and 77 percent among progressive Catholic religious leaders. Among Protestant leaders the Democratic party identification was 25 percent and 53 percent, respectively. Among Jewish religious leaders the Democratic party identification was 38 percent and 57 percent, respectively. The partisan gap between conservative and progressive religious leaders is evidently larger among Catholics (31 points) than among Protestants (28 points) and among Jews (19 points). On other issues one finds similar splits between conservative and progressive religious leaders. On support for the Equal Rights Amendments, for instance, the

results were 42 percent and 78 percent among Catholics, 31 percent and 80 percent among Protestants, and 54 percent and 88 percent among Jews.

But on issues like abortion, sexual morality, economic equality, and international world order, Catholic religious leaders diverge uniformly from other religious leaders and from their own Catholic laity. The opposition to abortion was 100 percent among conservative and 93 percent among progressive Catholic leaders, 93 percent and 41 percent among Protestants, and 40 percent and 8 percent among Jews. Similarly, the proportion of those who considered premarital sex morally wrong was 97 percent and 82 percent among Catholic leaders, 97 percent and 59 percent among Protestants, and 72 percent and 31 percent among Jews. Lay Catholics by contrast clearly disagree with their bishops on those issues. According to a May 1992 Gallup poll, 13 percent of Catholics said that abortion could never be a moral choice, while 41 percent said it was morally acceptable in rare circumstances and another 41 percent said it was morally acceptable in many or all circumstances. Indeed, according to Gallup polls, Catholic support for *Roe v. Wade* increased from 32 percent in 1974 to 40 percent in 1986, while Catholic opposition decreased from 61 percent to 48 percent. Among Protestants, by contrast, support for *Roe v. Wade* decreased from 48 percent to 42 percent, while opposition increased from 41 percent to 50 percent during the same period. Lay Catholics manifest an even more pronounced disagreement with their religious leaders on all issues of sexual and family morality. They tend to be more liberal than Protestants and the population at large.

The proportion of religious leaders who agreed that "government should work to reduce the income gap between rich and poor" was 90 percent among conservative and 92 percent among progressive Catholics, a 2-point gap. Among Protestants the proportion was 43 percent and 76 percent, respectively, a 33-point gap. Among Jews the proportion was 59 percent and 78 percent, a 19-point gap.

The proportion of religious leaders who supported a "freeze" in the construction and deployment of nuclear weapons by both superpowers was 95–98 percent among Catholics, 77–95 percent among Protestants, and 72–90 percent among Jews. The proportion of support for a unilateral "freeze" by the United States alone was 35–70 percent among Catholics, 16–52 percent among Protestants, and 10–29 percent among Jews. Lay Catholics also tend to be more dovish than Protestants and the general population, but by no means as markedly and uniformly as their religious leaders.

The proportion of religious leaders who thought that as a nation America tends to treat people in the Third World unfairly was 50–87 percent among Catholics, 27–71 percent among Protestants, and 19–39 percent among Jews. The proportion of support for sanctions against South Africa was 83–90 percent among Catholics, 52–87 percent among Protestants, and 47–78 percent among Jews. In favor of a Palestinian homeland in Israel, the proportion was 87–85 percent among Catholics, 42–82 percent among Protestants, and 3–20 percent among Jews. Among the general population it was on Central American issues that the divergence between Catholic and Protestant and general public opinion was most marked. It would not be difficult to trace this divergence back to transnational Catholic links. For these and other survey results, see Hunter and Rice, "Unlikely Alliances," pp. 232–39; and Gallup and Castelli, *American Catholic People,* pp. 70–76, 80–87, 91–102. For the May 1992 Gallup poll, see *New York Times,* 19 June 1992.

137. Cf. Philip Berryman, *Our Unfinished Business: The U.S. Catholic Bishops' Letters on Peace and the Economy* (New York: Pantheon, 1989); and George E. McCarthy and Royal W. Rhodes, *Eclipse of Justice: Ethics, Economics, and the Lost Tradition of American Catholicism* (Maryknoll, N.Y.: Orbis, 1991).

138. John Richard Neuhaus, *The Naked Public Square: Religion and Democracy in America* (Grand Rapids, Mich.: Eerdmans, 1984).

139. Cf. Jürgen Habermas, *The Structural Transformation of the Public Sphere* (Cambridge, Mass.: MIT Press, 1989); Alisdair McIntyre, *After Virtue: A Study in Moral Theory* (South Bend, Ind: University of Notre Dame Press, 1981); Alan Wolfe, *Whose Keeper? Social Science and Moral Obligation* (Berkeley: University of California Press, 1989); Russell Jacoby, *The Last Intellectuals: American Culture in the Age of Academe* (New York: Basic Books, 1987).

140. Andrew Greeley has pointed out that close to 80 percent of regular church attenders reject the official birth control teaching and that more than one-third of those who reject the church's teaching on premarital sex receive Holy Communion as often as they attend church. See Greeley, *American Catholics since the Council,* pp. 64–71. On the new Catholicism, see further, Eugene Kennedy, *Re-Imagining American Catholicism* (New York: Vintage, 1985) and *Tomorrow's Catholics. Yesterday's Church. The Two Cultures of American Catholicism* (New York: Harper & Row, 1988).

141. Gallup and Castelli, *American Catholic People,* p. 184.

142. Ibid.

143. "Pastoral Constitution on the Church in the Modern World," no. 76, in Abbott, *Documents.*

144. Cf. Bishop Raymond A. Lucker, "Justice in the Church: The Church as Example," in Coleman, *Hundred Years;* and Hans Küng and Leonard Swidler, *The Church in Anguish* (San Francisco: Harper & Row, 1986).

Chapter Eight

1. For representative statements of these positions, see n. 1 of chap. 1.

2. See G. W. F. Hegel, *Early Theological Writings* (Chicago: University of Chicago Press, 1948); and Sidney Hook, *From Hegel to Marx* (New York: Reynal & Hitchcock, 1936).

3. It was of course the thrust of Tocqueville's comparative historical analysis of democratization in France and the United States that these structural trends can assume very different patterns and forms and that the different legacies of the ancien régime notwithstanding, historical actors could do something to influence the different direction of those patterns.

4. This would also seem to be the lesson of the Iranian revolution. Thus, it is simply shortsighted to view—as does Karel Dobbelaere from the perspective

of a Luhmannian functionalist theory of secularization—the resistance of the Polish Catholic church to the Communist regime or the resistance of the Shi'ite Ulama to the shah's regime simply or even primarily as a fundamentalist hierocratic reaction against evolutionary processes of modernization. Fundamentalist hierocratic reactions could not have been that instrumental in toppling both regimes, nor can such an interpretation explain the alliances of the religious and the secular leftist oppositions to both regimes. That today the religious and the secular components of the two alliances occupy very different positions in both postrevolutionary regimes only shows that one is dealing here with different types of public religion. See Karel Dobbelaere, "The Secularization of Society? Some Methodological Suggestions," In Jeffrey K. Hadden and Anson Shupe, eds., *Secularization and Fundamentalism Reconsidered* (New York: Paragon House, 1989).

5. Here I have followed particularly Jean L. Cohen and Andrew Arato, *Civil Society and Political Theory* (Cambridge, Mass.: MIT Press, 1992); and Alfred Stepan, *Rethinking Military Politics* (Princeton: Princeton University Press, 1988).

6. Seyla Benhabib, "Models of Public Space: Hannah Arendt, the Liberal Tradition and Jürgen Habermas," in Craig Calhoun, ed., *Habermas and the Public Sphere* (Cambridge, Mass.: MIT Press, 1991).

7. One of the aims of the comparative historical studies has been precisely to show that there are many different forms of Catholicism.

8. On modern Shi'ite hierocracy, see Said A. Arjomand, "Shi'ite Jurisprudence and Constitution-Making in the Islamic Republic of Iran," in Martin E. Marty and R. Scott Appleby, eds., *Fundamentalisms and the State: Remaking Polities, Economies, and Militance* (Chicago: University of Chicago Press, 1993), and "Millennial Beliefs, Hierocratic Authority and Revolution in Shi'ite Iran," in Arjomand, ed., *The Political Dimensions of Religion* (Albany, N.Y.: SUNY Press, 1993). The traditional Islamic *umma* also had its own internal restricted public sphere. It is the transposition of the *umma* onto a modern mobilizational state that gives it its theocratic-totalitarian direction. On the tradition of Islamic public criticism and efforts to modernize it in Saudi Arabia, see Talal Asad, *Genealogies of Religion* (Baltimore: Johns Hopkins University Press, 1993), chap. 6.

9. See Jürgen Habermas, *The Structural Transformation of the Public Sphere* (Cambridge, Mass.: MIT Press, 1989).

10. Ralph Della Cava, "Vatican Policy, 1978–90: An Updated Overview," *Social Research* 59, no. 1 (Spring 1992).

11. John S. Coleman, S.J., "*Raison d'église:* Organizational Imperatives of the Church in the Political Order," in Jeffrey Hadden and Anson Shupe, eds., *Secularization and Fundamentalism Reconsidered* (New York: Paragon House, 1989).

12. Daniel Bell, "The Return of the Sacred? The Argument on the Future of Religion," *British Journal of Sociology* 28, no. 4 (1997); and Rodney Stark and William S. Bainbridge, *The Future of Religion: Secularization, Revival, and Cult Formation* (Berkeley: University of California Press, 1985).

13. Roland Robertson and JoAnn Chirico, "Humanity, Globalization, and Worldwide Religious Resurgence: A Theoretical Explanation," *Sociological Analysis* 46, no. 3 (1985).

14. All significant differences notwithstanding, the situation of Islam is similar in this respect.

15. Cf. Émile Durkheim, *The Elementary Forms of the Religious Life* (New York: Free Press, 1965), p. 475, and "Individualism and the Intellectuals," in *Emile Durkheim: On Morality and Society*, Robert N. Bellah, ed. (Chicago: University of Chicago Press, 1973).

16. Cf. Gabriel Almond, Marvin Chodorow, and Roy Harvey Pearce, eds., *Progress and Its Discontents* (Berkeley: University of California Press, 1982); Robert Bellah, "New Religious Consciousness and the Crisis of Modernity," in Charles Glock and Robert Bellah, eds., *The New Religious Consciousness* (Berkeley: University of California Press, 1976); and Peter Berger, "From the Crisis of Religion to the Crisis of Secularity," in Mary Douglas and Steven Tipton, eds., *Religion and America: Spirituality in a Secular Age* (Boston: Beacon Press, 1983).

17. See Jürgen Habermas, "New Social Movements," and Axel Honneth et al., "The Dialectics of Rationalization: An Interview with Jürgen Habermas," *Telos* 49 (Fall 1981). See also chap. 6, n. 62.

18. H. Richard Niebuhr, *Radical Monotheism and Western Culture* (New York: Harper & Row, 1970).

19. For such an attempt, see Harvey Cox, *Religion in the Secular City: Toward a Postmodern Theology* (New York: Simon & Schuster, 1984).

20. Cf. Jürgen Habermas, *The Theory of Communicative Action*, 2 vols. (Boston: Beacon Press, 1984–87); and Cohen and Arato, *Civil Society and Political Theory*.

21. Habermas, *The Theory of Communicative Action*, vol. 1, *Reason and the Rationalization of Society*, pp. 143–271.

22. Karl Marx, "A Contribution to the Critique of Hegel's Philosophy of Right: Introduction," in *Early Writings* (New York: Vintage, 1975), pp. 252 and 257.

23. Max Weber, "The Social Psychology of the World Religions," in *From Max Weber* (New York: Oxford University Press, 1958), p. 267.

24. Peter Brown, "Late Antiquity," in Philippe Ariès and Georges Duby, eds., *A History of Private Life*, vol. 1, *From Pagan Rome to Byzantium* (Cambridge, Mass.: Harvard University Press, 1987), p. 260.

25. This is the thesis of John Richard Neuhaus's *The Naked Public Square: Religion and Democracy in America* (Grand Rapids, Mich.: Eerdmans, 1984).

26. Robert Wuthnow has offered the intriguing hypothesis that the reason for the widespread irreligion one finds among social scientists may derive from the social science discipline's own insecurity and from their related need to maintain a clear and rigid separation between the two cognitive fields. According to Wuthnow, the more precarious the cognitive status of any scientific discipline, the greater the professional need to maintain an irreligious attitude. Robert Wuthnow, "Science and the Sacred," in Phillip E. Hammond, ed., *The Sacred in a Secular Age* (Berkeley: University of California Press, 1985), pp. 187–203.

It is interesting to observe that the calls for a new synthesis between science and religion tend to come today more frequently from natural scientists and laymen, "awed" by new scientific discoveries that continue to reveal the ever greater "mystery" of the universe, than from theologians. The latter's reluctance to link once again cognitive religious structures to science should not be surprising given negative past experiences, as well as the increasingly shorter durability and ever more precarious character of modern scientific paradigms. For some recent religious inspirations coming from postmodern science, cf. Stephen Toulmin, *The Return to Cosmology: Postmodern Science and the Theology of Nature* (Berkeley: University of California Press, 1982); Huston Smith, *Beyond the Post-Modern Mind* (New York: Crossroad, 1982); John M. Templeton and Robert L. Herrmann, *The God Who Would Be Known: Revelations of the Divine in Contemporary Science* (San Francisco: Harper & Row, 1989).

Index

abortion
  the Catholic church's opposition to: in
    Poland, 111–13; in Spain, 90; in the
    United States, 58, 184, 185, 192,
    193, 197
  Catholic teachings on, 192–95, 197
  the politics of, 185, 189, 192, 193; the
    Catholic church's intervention in,
    192, 193, 196–99; the pro-choice po-
    sition, 195; the pro-life position, 185,
    193, 195, 198; and the right-to-life
    movement, 193, 199
  See also American Catholic bishops,
    public speech of
absolutism
  absence of, in Poland, 92
  and alliance of throne and altar, 29,
    31
  in Spain, 75–77
  See also caesaropapism
Adventists, 140
aggiornamento
  Catholic: ideological struggles over,
    186–87, 222; as innerworldly turn,
    62, 186; in Latin America, 119, 124,
    125; in Poland, 102–3; in Spain, 83,
    84, 102; in the United States, 181,
    183–85
  Evangelical, 74, 164
  See also Vatican Council
American Catholic bishops
  and Americanist controversy, 181–83
  and episcopal power, 178–80
  and the immigrant church, 172–73
  intervention in electoral politics, 184,
    197–99
  public speech of: on abortion, 184,
    192–201; impact of and reactions to,

201–7; levels of normativity and validity claims of, 188, 190, 195; on
  nuclear policies, 184, 189–90; performative, procedural, and semantic
  inconsistencies in, 193–200; two different types of, 187, 193, 195; on
  United States economy, 184, 190–92.
  See also National Conference of Catholic Bishops; pastoral letters, of American bishops
American Catholic church
  patriotism of, 168, 183, 189, 292n.79
  role of, in assimilation of Catholic immigrants, 172–73
  tensions within, 175–81
  See also American Catholic bishops;
    American Catholicism; American
    Catholics; Americanism
American Catholicism
  and American civil religion, 53, 167,
    178, 182–83
  anticommunism of, 183, 186, 189
  conservative, 174, 178, 183, 185, 186
  as denomination, 8, 74, 171–75
  four factors shaping, 167–68
  immigrant phase of, 171–72
  liberal, 174, 178, 183, 185, 186
  as member of Roman Catholic church,
    181–82
  as minority sect, 168–71
  as national church, 175–81, 288n.33
  new public style of, 175, 180
  republican phase of, 171–72
  See also American Catholic bishops;
    American Catholics
American Catholics
  as an ethnic group, 167, 173, 175, 176
  mobility of, 174, 177, 186

303